Time Enough to Cry

The Children of the Greatest Generation

Carlton Randolph Crane

TIME ENOUGH TO CRY:
The Children of the Greatest Generation

ISBN (Paperback): 978-1-964494-73-9
ISBN (Hardback): 978-1-964494-75-3
ISBN (Ebook): 978-1-964494-74-6

Printed in the United States of America.

PROMINENT
BOOKS
EDGE

5830 E 2nd St, Ste 7000 #9983
Casper, WY 82609
USA

CONTENTS

PART THREE

The Fall of 1962
The Tragedies

PART FOUR

The Summer of 1967
The Young Adults

PART FIVE

The Spring of 1968
Vietnam

PART SIX
The Autumn of 1970
The Weddings

PART SEVEN
The Summer of 1987
The Reunion

I dedicate this book to my grandchildren and great-grandchildren:

Colton Randolph Crane
Grayson Avery Crane
Staley Anne Crane
Jordyn Ivy Crane
Harper Ryan Nelson
Cole Randolph Crane
Brooke Lynn Fouts

So that they will know that I, like the characters in this book, am a child of the Greatest Generation, and their values have been passed on and still live inside all of us who bear the title Children of the Greatest Generation.

—*Carlton Randolph Crane*

FORWARD

This book is a work of Historical Fiction, which means that many of the events in this book are based on actual historical events. This is especially true in the parts of the book that deal with the Vietnam War. The battles described in those parts of the book actually happened. Specifically, I'm talking about the battle for "Hamburger Hill" and the battle for "Khe Sanh". These two battles were bloody, costly, and hard fought. I did my best to remain truthful to these battles. I kept the descriptions of these battles as true to the actual battle as I could. Of course, my characters are fiction and all of their actions are fiction. So, I created fictitious actions for my characters inside the framework of the actual battles. I didn't use any name of any person who was actually in either of those two battles; that is not intentionally. If a name should appear of someone who was actually in either of those two battles, it's purely accidental.

All of the cities and towns mentioned during the Vietnam War chapters are real and still exist today. Those being: Hue, Phu Bai, and Da Nang. Some of the fire bases used by the American Forces are also true; such as Camp Eagle. However, other places described in the book such as Cobra Umbrella One are fiction.

Nearly everything said in the above paragraph can also be applied to the U.S. Army Nurse Corps. China Beach and the 95th EVAC Hospital were real places. The MASH units in the book, specifically the 1066th MASH, are fiction but are modeled after real Vietnam MASH and

MUSH units. However, as with the battles described above, the nurses are fiction and all of their actions are fiction. Any names that match any nurses who served in Vietnam are purely accidental.

I, myself, am a Vietnam Veteran and, as such, I would never, never do anything to insult or cast any dishonor on the men and women who served so valiantly during Vietnam. My story is of three young men who meet three young women in that theater of war called South Vietnam. All six of these young people are the Children of the Greatest Generation, and this is their story.

ACKNOWLEDGEMENTS

There is one member of my immediate family that must be acknowledged for what he did to help me complete this book, and that would be my grandson, Colton Crane.

It was he who so much wanted me to write a sequel to my first book, "So Much to Give: A Story of America's Greatest Generation". It was his love for the first book that encouraged me to write this second book. He wanted to know what happen to the children of the greatest generation. Thus, I undertook the writing of this book, "Time Enough to Cry: The Children of the Greatest Generation".

Without Colton, I'm sure that I would've never started, much less finished, this book.

GLOSSARY OF TERMS

This glossary of terms is here to be of help to the general reader who doesn't understand military terminology. Since the later part of this book takes place in South Vietnam, during the Vietnam War, and specifically takes place during 1968 to 1970, it may be necessary for some readers to refer to this glossary of terms to get a better understanding of what is being said or described.

TERM   DESCRIPTION

DMZ   Demilitarize Zone. In the case of this
                        book, it is the zone marking the boundary
                        between North and South Vietnam.
                        By definition, no military personnel were
                        allowed in this buffer zone. However, the
                        North Vietnamese used it freely while the
                        American Forces were not allowed.

TDY   Temporary Duty assignment. This is
                        used to send personnel on a temporary
                        assignment but allowing them to stay
                        assigned to the current post.

MIA	Missing In Action. A term used to describe personnel who are unaccounted for after a battle or action.
PDQ	Pretty Damn Quick.
R&R	Designating Rest and Relaxation. Military personnel in a combat zone are given a set number of days per tour for Rest and Relaxation or R&R.
MOS	Military Occupational Specialty. This is a number that is assigned to specific jobs in the military.
Five-by-Five	This is a radio reply telling the person on the over end how they are being received. Five-by-Five is very good. The first number will always be one through five and indicates the signal strength. The second number is also one through five and indicates the clarity of the person speaking. So, Five-by-Five means the signal strength is the strongest and the voice clarity is the best.
The Ho Chi Minh Trail	This was a trail that ran along the border of South Vietnam from North Vietnam through Laos and Cambodia (See Map 2). The trail was used by the North Vietnamese freely to move supplies and reinforcements into South Vietnam.

Again, American Forces were not allowed to enter Laos and Cambodia so the North Vietnamese used this trail as a sanctuary.

Military Time

The military uses a twenty-four hour clock. So that midnight is 0000 hours or 2400 hours, 1 AM is 0100 hours, 2 AM is 0200 hours and so on. Noon is 1200 hours and 1 PM is 1300 hours and so on. Therefore after noon, one must add twelve hours to the time. As an example: 3 PM is 1500 hours and 8 PM is 2000 hours.

Slick

This term is military slang for a troop carrying helicopter.

Medivac

This term is short for Medical Evacuation. Medivac was applied to helicopters that evacuated wounded soldiers to medical facilities or to fixed winged aircraft that flew wounded personnel to other hospitals out of country; such as Japan.

Assault Choppers

This term is used for heavily armed helicopters used for assault missions against the enemy.

Dust Off

This term was used by the helicopter pilots, medivac and assault, to describe the method of setting on the ground with their engine running and their rotor blades turning. This was done so they could take off immediately if need be, or Dust Off, which referred to the dust kicked up by the rotor blades.

Push — The term used by nurses to describe a large number of incoming wounded.

One-oh-first — Military slang for the 101st Airborne Division.

Seabees — Construction Battalion (CB). Using the initials CB, the Construction Battalion is called the Seabees. They are a part of the United States Navy.

Klick — Meaning one kilometer. Five kilometers would be five klicks. A kilometer is equal to .62 miles. Therefore five klicks would equal to 3.1 miles.

Short Timer — Generally someone that has less than 30 days to go before they leave South Vietnam, or, for that matter, any duty station.

M60 — A heavy sixty caliber machine gun used by the US Military in several environments including ground combat and in assault helicopters,

M16 — The standard issued rifle for US Military personal during the Vietnam War.

OR	Operating Room.
CO	Commanding Officer.
XO	Executive Officer. The second in command to the CO.
HQ	Headquarters.
RPG	Rocket Propelled Grenade. A very effective hand held grenade launcher.
LZ	Landing Zone. An area designated for the landing of aircraft, mostly helicopters, to deliver troops and supplies or to medivac wounded troops.
Autorotation	A means of landing a helicopter without engine power. It uses the upward flow of air through the rotor blades to provide enough lift to allow the helicopter to land safely.
VC	Viet Cong. These were guerrilla fighters from South Vietnam that fought with the North Vietnamese.
Charlie	Another term for the Viet Cong. It comes from the phonetic sign for the Viet Cong; Victor (for V) and Charlie (for C). Instead of saying the entire Victor Charlie it was shorten to just Charlie.

'Nam   Military slang for Vietnam.

Alpha   The phonetic term for the letter 'A'. An example would be saying "Alpha Company" instead of 'A' Company.

Bravo   The phonetic term for the letter 'B'.

Charlie   As mention above is the phonetic term for the letter 'C'.

Delta   The phonetic term for the letter 'D'.

PAVN   Meaning the People's Army of Vietnam, which was the official name of the North Vietnamese Army. It was pronounced by the military as PAV-IN.

ARVN   Meaning the Army of the Republic of Vietnam, which was the official name of the South Vietnamese Army. It was pronounced by the military as ARE-VIN.

ANZAC   Australian and New Zealand Army Corps. Pronounced in military slang as And Zack.

The Following are officer ranks and their military slang in the army and marines. These ranks are all worn on the left and right shoulders of the uniform or can also be worn on the collar:

Gold Bar   Indicating the rank of 2nd lieutenant.

Silver Bar   Indicating the rank of 1st lieutenant.

Rail Road Tracks   Two silver bars that look like 'Rail Road Tracks' indicating the rank of captain.

Gold Oak Leaf   A gold oak leaf indicating the rank of major.

Silver Oak Leaf   A silver oak leaf indicating the rank of lieutenant coronal.

Chicken or Bird Coronal   A silver eagle indicating the rank of a full coronal.

MAPS

To assist in the ability of the general reader to locate and identify the places that are discussed in the Vietnam War parts of the book, there are three maps included here. The maps are named Map 1, Map 2, and Map 3. It is suggested by the author that these maps be used freely as they're a great help in finding locations and establishing distances. There are notes with the maps to help the reader understand where certain actions and story lines take place.

MAP 1

Northern Provinces of South Vietnam 1968 to 1970

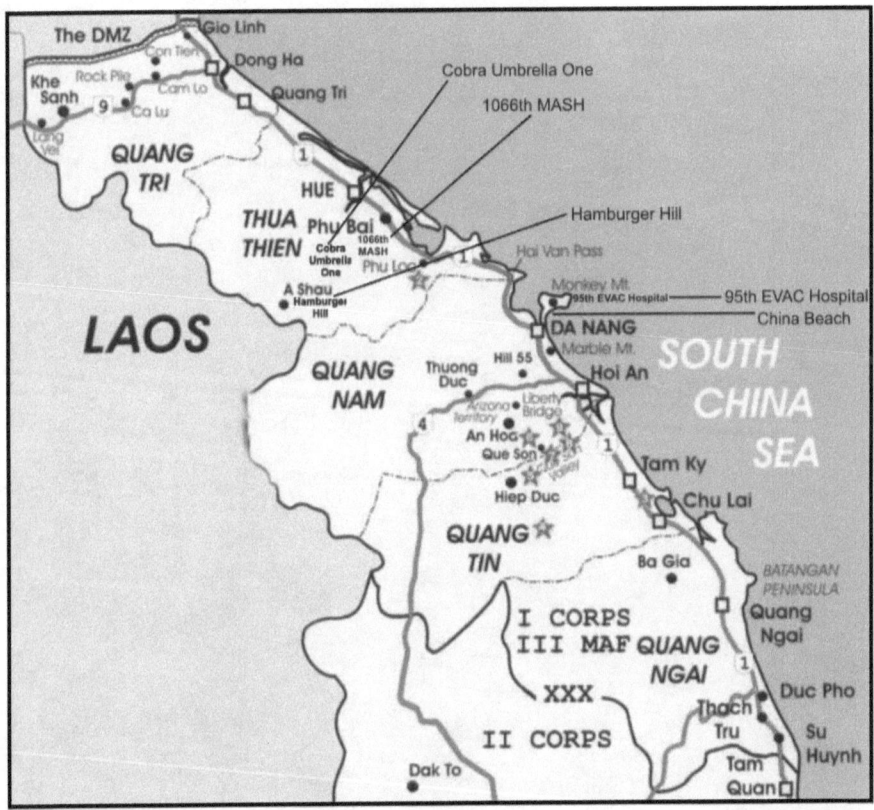

Note: That the Cobra Umbrella One base and the 1066th MASH are fictional, but other than that the map is a true representation of the Northern Provinces of South Vietnam during 1968 through 1970.

MAP 2

Complete Map of South Vietnam 1968

Note: The heavy route is the Ho Chi Minh Trail. It shows the route down through Laos and Cambodia along the border of South Vietnam and the entry points used by the North Vietnamese.

MAP 3

The Regions and Provinces of South Vietnam 1968 and 1970

Note: During sections of this book that take place in South Vietnam, nearly all the action and storylines take place in the three most Northern Provinces: Quang Tri, Thua Thien, and Quang Nam.

PART ONE

The Summer of 1955
The Children

CHAPTER ONE

Kellie Jean Anderson

It was a beautiful sunny and mild day in St. Paul, Minnesota as ten year old Kellie Jean Anderson stood in the street looking down at Old Denver. Old Denver, her dog since before she could remember had just been hit by a car. There was no doubt in her young mind that he was dead. Kellie was short and thin for her age. Her hair was jet black and was always tied into a pony tail that hung down past the middle of her back. She had a beautiful face with a small turned up nose. Her mouth was dainty and thin lipped. Her eyes were a blue that changed shades depending on her mood. She was always dressed like the tomboy she was. She wore old faded jeans with the legs rolled up to just below her knees. She wore one of her father's old white dress shirts with the tail hanging almost to her knees. On her feet, she had a pair of high top black sneakers.

"Hey little girl is that your dog?" The question was being asked by an elderly man who approached her. He was obviously shaken and upset by what had just happen. He walked towards her with unsure steps. "Is that your dog?" He asked again, as he knelt down beside her and placed his hand on her shoulder. The smell of alcohol washed over her as the old man spoke. Slowly, Kellie turned her gaze from the dog to the man. Her sky blue eyes were hard as steel as she stared at him.

"Yes, he was my dog," she said with hate dripping on each word. "And you just killed him."

"I'm sorry," the elderly man stammered. "It was an accident. He just ran out into the street and I didn't see 'im in time. You understand don't you?" Kellie's eyes continued to burn into the man without pity. "Don't you?" He asked again weakly.

"I understand you're drunk!" She shouted. "Take your hand off me and get away from me." The drunken man got to his feet and backed away from her. He looked confused and worried. He staggered backward looking around in all directions.

"I didn't mean to hit your dog," he stammered again. "I'll get you a new dog." He brightened as the idea came to him. "Yes, that's it. I'll buy you a new dog." He was still smiling when Kellie turned and started walking towards him. The smile left his face when he saw her eyes. He started backing up again, as she walked toward him.

"I don't want a new dog," she said slowly, as she walked. "I want to hurt you. I want to run over you like you did Denver."

The old man was stunned by her words. He turned and started running back to his car. He stumbled and fell as he tried to run ahead and look back at her at the same time. He got to his feet and finished the distance to his car. Jumping into the car, he gave one last look at her before he put the car in gear and drove off. She was still walking toward him when the tires squealed and he disappeared from sight.

"I'll remember you," Kellie said to herself, as she watched his car disappear. "I'll always remember you and your car. And someday, I'll hurt you." Kellie turned around and walked back towards Old Denver's body. As she approached, she saw her father running towards her.

"Kel," he yelled. "Kel, what's happened?" The words were hardly out of his mouth when he noticed the dog. "Oh no," he moaned. He knelt down beside the dead dog and bowed his head. "Jesus, Denver. I told you not to go into the street. You old dumb dog. I told you not to go into the street."

"It wasn't Denver's fault," Kellie said simply. "And Denver wasn't dumb. An old drunk hit him."

The sound of Kellie's voice made Doctor Jacob Anderson remember his daughter. "I'm sorry, Kel," he said softly. "I didn't mean Denver was really dumb. I just mean I tried to teach him to stay out of the street, but I guess I failed."

"It doesn't matter what you taught him, Dad," Kellie persisted. "It wasn't Denver's fault. It was a drunk that hit him. It was his fault."

"Well, I guess it doesn't matter now. Come on sweetheart I'll carry you home then I'll come back and take care of Denver." Dr. Anderson reached down and picked his daughter up into his arms. Carrying her, he started walking to their house about a block down the street. Kellie put her arms around her father's neck and rested her head on his shoulder. She watched behind them, as Denver's body faded from sight. "We'll go home and you can have a good cry. That always helps. Just have a good cry to let the hurt out." He patted her on her back as he walked.

But he couldn't see Kellie's face as he walked and talked. There were no tears in her eyes. She strained to see Denver as they got farther and farther away.

"It wasn't Denver's fault," she said again to her father. "There'll be time enough to cry later. Right now, we should find that old drunk."

"Okay, we'll work it out," Dr. Anderson said, as he patted her on the back and walked along. "Let's give it the old thumbs up sign." He held his fist up in the air extending his thumb. Without saying anything, Kellie slowly lifted her small fist and gave the thumbs up sign behind her father's back.

CHAPTER TWO

Veronica Leigh Mann

It was a blazing hot and dusty day in Sweetwater, Texas as ten year old Veronica Leigh Mann watched two young boys torment a scorpion. They each had a short stick and, surrounding the insect, they continued to push it into a crazed nest of red ants. As the scorpion would fight its way free of the madding attack, the boys would laugh and, using their sticks, push it back into the nest.

She watched for a short while, then turned away from the boys and their ugly game and started walking down the hard packed sand road. Veronica was tall and thin with a narrow face that was spotted with small freckles. Her long stringy and unkempt blonde hair hung down passed her shoulders and, much of the time, down in her face. Veronica's main claim to beauty was her bright green eyes. However, they were set in an average looking face and usually hidden by her unkempt hair. She wore a simple blue cotton dress that came down to just below her knees and hung loosely on her skinny frame. Somehow, her bare feet resisted the boiling heat from the sandy road.

Veronica's appearance was mostly due to her economic status and not to any failure on her part. For instance, she tried to keep her hair groomed neatly. But her family rarely could afford the shampoo necessary to make her hair shine, and her mother usually didn't have the time to keep it brushed out. Veronica tried to keep it brushed, but she was unable to consistently keep it neat. However, when the shampoo was available and when her mother did take the time to brush her hair out, it was beautiful. At those times, she would sit for hours in front of the mirror in her parent's bedroom looking at her image, touching the softness of her hair, and dreaming of being a beautiful woman of the world.

Her mother, Jane, was a beautiful woman, or, at least, she had been. Life in the roughneck camps of the West Texas oil fields was hard on a woman. It tended to drain her of her beauty and make her old before her time. Such was the case for Jane Mann. A woman of a mere thirty-two years, her skin had become hard and crusty, her Irish red hair had lost much of its fiery luster, and her face was continually draw into a worried look causing facial lines that had become permanent. It wasn't that Veronica's father didn't try: he did. But, limited by his eighth grade education, George Mann took what work he could. Fortunately, George Mann was a big strong man and there was always a need for strong backs in the oil fields. He was of German descent and it was from him that Veronica had gotten her blond hair.

However, despite all of the financial problems, Veronica was a happy child. At her early tender age, she really didn't realize that she was poor because most of the kids she went to school with were in the exact same situation as she. In addition, the oil rich families in Sweetwater were recently wealthy and, as yet, not far removed the economical status of the Mann family. As a result, they had not yet established the snobbish air about them that would come in later years. Because of these factors, Veronica was treated as an equal in school by both poor and rich. She was invited to parties at some of the wealthiest houses in Sweetwater. In fact, her best friend, Jodie Connors, lived in one of the largest houses on Main Street in downtown Sweetwater. It was to Jodie's house that Veronica was headed when she stopped to watch the boys and their ugly game. Last week at school, Jodie had invited Veronica to her birthday party, which was today. As she continued her walk to Jodie's house, Veronica suddenly stopped. She looked down at her dress and then down at her bare feet. This was no way to go to someone's birthday party she thought. What had she been thinking when she left home? Quickly, she turned around and started walking back the other direction at a faster pace. She would change into her best Sunday dress and shoes. Maybe her mom could even brush her hair out. At first, as she hurried toward home, Jodie's birthday party filled her thoughts. But as the minutes passed and she walked along, her mind, as it had a habit of doing, began to wander. Daydreams replaced her conscious mind and she walked along blind to her surroundings; daydreams of being a beautiful woman and traveling the world. A smile crossed her face as she walked and the daydreams became real to her.

CHAPTER THREE

Kyle Gene Collie

A thick drizzle of fog and rain hung over Coalville, Texas as thirteen year old Kyle Gene Collie struggled underneath a barbed-wire fence. He was tall for his age and looked lanky on his skinny frame. His jeans and shirt were soaked from the wet ground and, to make matters worst, his shirt tail was caught on one of the barbs. The more he struggled the more entangled his shirt became. Finally, he relaxed on the ground and reached behind him and gave the shirt a quick short pull. He heard the cloth rip as it pulled free.

"Shit," he cried out and slammed his small fist into the ground. "Mom's goin' to give me hell about this."

Pulling free of the barbed-wire, Kyle pushed himself to his feet and started running across the open field. The grass in the field was tall and wet. Combined with early morning dew, the drizzling rain soaked through his P.F. Flyer sneakers. His short but thick blonde hair was now plastered to his forehead and, at times, got into his deep blue eyes blocking his vision. As he ran across the field, he slipped several times and fell to his knees. Upon slipping once again, he stopped to catch his breath. As he panted, he thought that maybe he should have done this later in the day. He strained his eyes in the early morning dark to look at his small wrist watch. The hands and numbers on the watch dial glowed back at him showing 5:30 in the morning. He was running a little behind schedule. Jumping to his feet, he again started running across the field.

As he approached the small irrigation ditch on the far side of the field, he could see that Bennie was already waiting for him. Bennie sat crouched down by the waters edge just below the edge of the ditch. When Kyle reached the edge of the ditch, he jumped down to where Bennie was crouched.

"You're late," Bennie whispered. "I've been here nearly ten minutes."

"I had some trouble at the fence," Kyle said, pointing to his shirt. "I got tangled up and tore my shirt. Mom's goin' to give me shit over this."

"Why'd we have to do this so early in the morning anyway?" Bennie asked, still whispering.

"Will you stop whisperin'?" Kyle shot back. "There's no one near here to hear us. And I had to do it this early so my folks don't know about it. I've got to be back for my chores before the sun's full up."

"Okay. Okay", Bennie said. "Do you have the plan?"

Kyle looked at Bennie for a long minute. Bennie was the same age as Kyle, but a little shorter and huskier. He had short cut black hair that looked like a skull cap. Although they were the same age and general appearance, there was one major difference between Bennie and Kyle. Bennie was black. He was the son of William J. Washington, who was the field manager for Kyles's father's real estate holdings in and around Coalville. Bennie and Kyle had been secret friends for the last three years. Kyle carefully kept his meetings with Bennie secret from his parents. From past experiences, Kyle knew that Bennie's father would not approve of his friendship with a white boy; much less the son of his boss. Kyle was relatively sure that his parents would have no problem with the friendship, but he respected Bennie's wish to keep things secret. Bill Washington had worked for the Collie family for nearly six years. He had been hired by Kyle's father, Daryl Collie, to help his wife, Sue Ann, manage their real estate investments while he went off to fight in the Korean War. Upon returning from the war, Kyle's father kept Bill Washington on because he had done such a good job and it freed the Collie's up to come and go as they pleased.

But even with the good relationship between employer and employee, Bill Washington had fixed ideas about the boss's family and his own. Colored should stay with colored, and whites should stay with whites. It was that simple for Bill Washington.

Despite the racial and family problems, Kyle and Bennie had become fast friends. They shared the same powerful interest in flying. They would hide for hours and talk about the newest military airplanes. They shared books, papers, comics, and magazines; anything that talked about airplanes and flying. Because Bennie went to the colored school on the south side of town, they didn't see each other except when they made time for their secret meetings. The time they had together was limited but exciting.

"Well," Kyle started. "The plan is to get to where we've got the glider hidden and take an inventory of what we still need. I brought a pencil and pad so we can write it all down."

"Okay," Bennie said, jumping to his feet. "Let's get goin' and get it done so I can get back to my own chores before Dad finds I'm gone."

With that, Kyle got to his feet and both boys took off at a run.

CHAPTER FOUR

Jordan Orland Costillo

The day in Marfa, Texas was stiflingly hot and dry as eleven year old Jordan Orland Costillo walked from his home toward the center of town. Jordan was short and stocky with a head full of curly black hair. His eyes were a light hazel color and were set wide apart on a full oval face. Now, he carried a small letter sized package that was wrapped in plain brown paper and tied with white cotton string. His job today was to deliver a piece of special jewelry work that his mother had done for one of her best clients. The client lived in an expensive house near the Marfa business district.

The Costillo house was about a mile from Marfa itself and it was another half mile to the client's house. Jordan's walk would take him through a rough part of town that he had to go through each day while walking to school. He didn't like having to go through this area with such a valuable piece of jewelry, but he didn't say anything to his mother. He never said anything to his mother about his problems walking to school; about the bigger boys picking on him and stealing his lunch money day in and day out. They would call him, "Wet Back" and "The Little Half Greaser". His mother would never have given him the job if she had any idea that her son could be robbed or hurt.

But Jordan wanted the job. He wanted to please his mother and he wanted to do something important for her. Jordan knew the piece of work he carried was very valuable and could not be replaced. His mother had worked on it for several months. It was for her client's daughter on her wedding day. If Jordan could complete this job for his mother, he would have the pride in himself that he so desperately wanted.

As he walked along, his mind thought about all of these things, until suddenly he was shaken out of his thoughts when he heard someone yell out.

"Hey! Grease Ball. What're you doin' around here today? There's no school today."

Jordan turned to his right to see three boys walking towards him from an adjacent alley. They were bigger than him; maybe a year ahead of him in school. He thought about making a run for it but he knew he would never make it, and anyway this just might be the right time for his plan. They weren't strangers; he had seen them many times before; almost every day on his way to and from school. Normally he avoided physical conflict by simply turning over his lunch money, or, if his mother made his lunch, giving it up. Sometimes they would order him to do things for them. Many times the things they ordered him to do were illegal; such as stealing things from the nearby stores. There were times when things got physical and they hurt him. When his happened, he had to take pains to be sure his mother didn't see the cuts or bruises. They were usually careful not to hurt his face so as not to invite investigation by other authorities.

What the three boys accosting him didn't know was that Jordan had been preparing for them over the last year or so. He had secretly been taking self-defense lessons from a friend that was the son of one of his mother's clients. Even his mother didn't know about the lessons. In reality, Jordan had been waiting for a job just like the one he was doing for his mother now. He had been waiting for a long time. It couldn't be on a school day; it had to be on the weekend so that no one else was involved.

Now, today was Saturday, he was carrying something very valuable, and everything was perfect. The day had finally arrived.

"I'm making a delivery for my mother," Jordan said softly.

"Well, Grease Ball, show us what ya got." The one who spoke was the leader and the biggest of the three.

"It's personal and it doesn't concern you," Jordan replied forcibly.

"Okay Grease Ball, you should know the drill by now. Hand it over." As the leader spoke, the others started to fan out to surround Jordan.

Jordan stepped back quickly to keep them all in front of him. Then, he moved farther back and stood in front of a brick wall that was the side of a General Store. With his back to the wall, Jordan slowly, keeping his eyes on the three attackers, took his package and leaned it against the brick wall. He then turned and squared himself before the three boys in a firm karate stance. The self-defense lessons were good but that didn't change Jordan's young age, size, or strength. He had to rely on how to use his head, his reflexes, and his speed; just as he had been taught. Also, in front of bullies, he must show no fear. He must make them think twice about what they are doing.

"We have a new drill," Jordan said with a smile. "You see, now, I don't hand it over. You have to come and take it."

The boys stopped immediately in their tracks. This was something new. This hadn't happened before. They had that crucial moment of being unsure.

Finally the leader spoke. "Now, Grease Ball, we don't want to have to mess you up. Be a good little Wet Back and hand over the goods." As he spoke, the others started moving again but now much slower.

Suddenly, and faster than any of the boys expected, Jordan spun out of his stance and unleashed a solid karate kick to the face of the boy on his far right. The kick was delivered and Jordan was back in his stance before the others could react. The boy who received the kick crumbled to the ground with a yell of pain. He rolled over and came up on his knees holding his nose as blood washed freely over his hands.

"My nose," he cried. "He's busted my nose."

The others were stunned and staring at the boy on his knees. This was just the time Jordan needed. Once again he spun out of his stance and landed a well place kick to the crotch of the boy on his far left. The boy doubled over in pain and before anyone could react, Jordan followed the kick through with a smashing elbow blow to the back of the boys head sending him to the ground yelling in pain. Then, as before, Jordan was back in his stance quickly.

The two smaller boys were now on the ground in pain and out of action. That just left the big leader. The leader looked around about him in confusion. He wasn't sure what to do next. He started to take a step forward but stopped when Jordan moved his stance a step closer to him. The other two boys had gotten to their feet by now but backed away instead of moving towards Jordan. A stand-off between Jordan and leader ensued. Time went by with neither of them moving. Finally, the leader stepped back.

"Come on you guys, we're gettin' outa here," he said loudly as he grabbed the other two boys and started pushing them away.

The three boys walked away down the street and around a corner. Jordan relaxed his stance and turned and picked up his package. But just as he was about to continue on his journey, the leader came back around the corner and stood firmly in Jordan's path. He just stood there for a minute.

Then he said with a smile, "Nice goin' Grease Ball." He waved briskly, turned, and walked back around the corner.

That afternoon when Jordan was back at home and in his room studying, his mother came to his door and peeked in.

"I got a call from Mr. Mailer a little while ago," she said. "He was very happy with the necklace I made for his daughter. What is more, he spoke very highly of your promptness and your good manners. I am very proud of you, son; very proud indeed."

"Thank you," Jordan replied. "I was happy to deliver the necklace for you. I'll be happy to help again anytime you need me."

Jordan continued with his karate lessons for many more years. His trips to school became uneventful from that time on. He would see the three boys from time to time but they never gave him any trouble again. In fact, the leader always gave him a smile when they passed. Jordan would find out that the leaders name was Gerald Kellen. It was a name that would come back into his life in later years.

CHAPTER FIVE

Kathleen Fiona O'Rourke

The "Hell's Kitchen" section of Manhattan in New York City was sultry and hot as ten year old Kathleen O'Rourke was being pulled along by her father. He held her by her small hand and hurried down 39th Street towards their rented tenant house. Because her father was a big husky Irishman with long legs, she had to run at times to keep up. Kathleen, or Kat as she was called, was a typical Irish girl. She had flaming red hair that hung down to just below her shoulders. Her face was structured beautifully with shiny light green eyes and a small dainty nose, which was sprinkled abundantly with an array of red freckles. The freckles stood out boldly on her pale white skin. She was tall for her age and her frame was somewhat thin but not skinny. Because of the uncomfortable weather, she was wearing a sleeveless yellow dress that hung loosely on her body and came down to her mid-calf. The dress had two large pockets, one over each thigh. On her feet she was wearing simple shoes known at the time as "flats".

As they approached the house where she had lived since she was born, her father tugged on her hand and started up the front steps that led almost directly to the front door. All the houses on the block looked just about the same. Actually the only way to tell them apart was by the house number or by any special way the tenants decorated their front porches; such as with flowers on the porch railings or with chairs and bench swings.

Robert O'Rourke pushed open the unlocked front door and entered the house briskly dragging Kathleen behind him. "Woman of the house," he yelled loudly. "Please come here and discipline your daughter." There was no immediate reply so he yelled again, "Woman of the house please come and discipline your daughter."

Finally, a woman with a head full of rumpled red hair looked around the door frame that led to the kitchen. She blinked her eyes as she looked at her husband standing in the middle of the living room holding her daughter's hand. Mary O'Rourke was an older version of her daughter. She had the same beauty as her daughter when she cared for herself, but the busy housework and the stifling heat kept her from making the effort. "What's this all about?" She asked, as she stepped into the door way.

"Your daughter needs some discipline," he repeated loudly.

"And for what, may I ask?" She asked tiredly.

"Well," he began, "I was called off my job at the docks to go down to Benny's Candy Store and get my daughter who was bein' held there with two of her friends by the beat cop."

Mary took a step forward and looked down at her daughter with a curious look. Then, she looked up at her husband and asked simply, "Why?"

Robert took a deep breath and let it out slowly. He released Kathleen's hand and put his hands on his hips. Then, in a softer tone, he said, "She was caught stealin' candy with the two other girls. Benny had been watchin' them carefully as they filled their pockets with several different types of candy. He stopped them as they were headed out the door. He then waved down the beat cop who took their names and who their parents were. Why he called me at my job instead of callin' here at home I don't know. I was instructed to come and get my daughter and there would be no charges or anythin' if the girls gave back the candy, which they all did."

"Why, Kat?" Her mother asked in a hurt voice. "We don't have much but we can surely afford to get you some candy. We've gotten candy there before. There was no need to steal it."

Kathleen's eyes began to fill with tears as she looked up at her mother. "Yes, Mom, we can afford to get me some candy now and again. But my friends can't."

Mary and Robert looked at each other for a long moment. Then Mary knelt down and looked her daughter straight in the eyes and asked, "You mean you stole the candy for the other girls?"

Kathleen looked at her mother with wet eyes. "They're my friends. I didn't want 'em to think I was uppity or better than them 'cause their dads are out of work and my dad has a good job with the Longshoremen. I didn't want to steal, but I didn't want to desert my friends more."

Mary slowly got to her feet but her eyes never left her daughters eyes. "Well," she said softly, "I admire your intentions, but the O'Rourke family doesn't steal. We'll not abide stealin' for any reason." Then, still looking her daughter in the eyes she said firmly, "You know what this means I guess."

"Yes, Ma'am, it means the switch."

Robert finally spoke up. His voice had taken on a different and softer tone. "Maybe this time we can just do with some extra Bible study each night. Do you think, Mary? Just some extra Bible study and a sound lecture from Father Conway."

Mary looked at her husband. "You came in here yellin' for discipline. Then discipline it'll be. I'll not abide a thief in my household."

Then turning to Kathleen she said in barely audible voice, "Kat, you know what to do. Go in the kitchen and get a knife, then go out back to the old willow tree and cut a good switch and clean it off good so it's clean. You know how; you've done it before."

"Yes, Ma'am," Kathleen replied as she ran passed her mother to the kitchen.

After Kathleen was gone, Robert whispered, "I don't think this is needed, Mary."

"You asked me to discipline my daughter. Tell me now if you're takin' that responsibility away from me. If so, say it to me out loud and that's the way it'll be between us from now on."

Robert lowered his head and said quietly, "No, I'll not take that responsibility away from you. It'll be as it's always been; you discipline Kat and I'll discipline Rob Junior."

Mary simply nodded her head and then turned and went back into the kitchen.

A short time later, after Robert had gone back to work, Kathleen came into the house carrying a three foot long thin green switch. She found her mother sitting in her rocking chair in the living room. She walked over and handed the switch to her mother.

Mary took the switch and looked at it then smiled at her daughter. "Well done Kat," she said, "very well done."

Kathleen didn't say anything she only turned and started for the stairs. She knew she would get her switching in her and her brother's bedroom. Her mother got up from her chair and followed her daughter. But as they reached the stairs Robert O'Rourke Junior was standing on the first step blocking their way.

Rob, as he was called, was Kathleen's older brother. He was two years older than her. His looks were not as Irish as the rest of the family. His hair was a light sandy brown and his eyes were a dark brown. He had a handsome face with a small nose and thin lips. He didn't move from his position on the stairs as Kathleen and his mother approached.

"What's this, Rob?" His mother asked.

"I want to take Kat's switchin' for her, Mom," he said firmly.

"You do," Mary said unemotionally.

"Yes, Ma'am, it's a rule we have in the family isn't it?"

"Yes, it is in certain situations," Mary said stepping back from the stairs. "But it's never been used and do you suppose this is one of those situations."

"Well, I'd like to use it now and I'd suppose it's one of those situations."

Kathleen went to Rob and threw her arms around his waist and hugged him burying her face in his chest since he was a head taller than her and was standing on the first stair step.

Mary studied her children for a long moment and then said, "Okay, Rob, but you'll tell your father about it when he gets home."

"Yes Ma'am," Robert said as he turned to go upstairs.

Mary had started for the stairs again when Kathleen quickly reached up and grabbed her brother's hand and stopped his assent. Robert turned back and looked at Kathleen in surprise.

Kathleen continued to hold Robert's hand and tears began to roll down her freckled face. Then she said with heavy emotion, "No, Rob, I'll take my own switchin'. But God in Heaven knows I love ya for bein' willin' to take it for me."

"Kat," Robert pleaded, "I really want to do it. Please let me. You're so soft, Kat, you're so soft."

"No," Kathleen said simply as she released Robert's hand. She turned and looked back to her mother and said, "I'll be in our room." She then hurried up the stairs to their bedroom and went in and sat down on her bed and waited.

Several minutes later, Mary watched as her daughter walked down the stairs to her brother, who was waiting for her in the living room. She watched as they joined hands and then walked out the front door. Mary leaned back against the bedroom door frame. She was still holding the switch with which she had given her daughter five hard strokes across her naked behind. She had a mixture of dampness in her eyes and soft smile on her face. Then she pushed herself away from the door frame and stood at the top of the stairs. In a loud voice and to an empty house she shouted, "I've got me a couple of really great kids. I mean a couple of really, really great kids." Then she took the switch in one hand and used the other hand to wipe away the dampness in her eyes. Smiling, she walked down the stairs slapping the switch against her side.

CHAPTER SIX

William Clyde Barnett

Ten year old William Barnett sat at the kitchen table in his family's farm house just outside of Coalville, Texas. He was sipping on a glass of iced tea. William was a nice looking boy and his Grandma Barnett said that with his sandy blonde hair, deep brown eyes, and lightly freckled face he was the spitting image of his dad, who had died a hero in World War II. William was tall and solidly built, as his chores on the farm kept him strong and fit.

It was late June and it amazed him, even at his early age, how his mother could drink hot tea in this summer heat. He knew she was from England and that the English loved their tea hot, but she had been here in Texas for over ten years now. In his mind, she should have adjusted by now.

His mother sat at the table with him sipping her hot tea. She had asked him to join her at the table for a nice long talk. She had asked him but he knew it wasn't a request. So, he sat quietly sipping his tea waiting for her to start the conversation.

After one last sip of her steaming tea, Anne Barnett looked at her son and said in a matter-of-fact tone, "I need to tell you about a couple of events that will be happening in fairly quick succession. Both of these events will affect you directly so I need to tell you about them in some detail. But before we got started could I ask you to please go and get your Grandma Sally and ask her to join us."

"Yes, Ma'am," William said as he jumped from his chair and scampered to his Grandma's bedroom.

By the time William and Sally Barnett got to the kitchen, Anne already had a tall glass of iced tea waiting for Sally. William returned to his chair and Sally took a seat across from Anne where her glass of tea was awaiting her. "What's going on?" Sally asked in a cheerful voice.

Anne looked across at Sally and smiled. "I'm just going to go over a couple of events that are going to happen starting in two weeks from today. Since both of you will be involved, I want to explain them in great detail." Anne stopped and looked from Sally to William and back. "So, is everyone ready?"

Sally looked at William and then back to Anne and said, "Sure, fire away."

"Yeah, Mom, fire away," William laughed.

Anne took a sip of her hot tea, smiled and then started, "The first event is that William and I will be leaving in two weeks to go to England." She stopped to let that sink in. Neither Sally nor William said anything. They only looked at each other briefly and then back to Anne with curious looks on their faces. "I want William to see the land where I was born and raised, I want him to meet his grandma on my side of the family, I want him to see where I met his father, and where we fell in love during a raging war. He won't be able to see his grandpa because my father died three years ago and it hurt me deeply not to be able to go to his funeral. But now, at least, William and I can visit his grave and say a prayer over him. And I want William to know what it means to everyone in my family that he bears my father's name as his middle name." Anne stopped talking again as she could feel tears welling in her eyes. She blinked her eyes and looked at Sally and William with a small, weak smile. Everyone was quiet for a long moment.

Finally, Sally spoke, "I think that's an outstandin' idea."

"Yeah, Mom, that's a great idea. I'd love to learn all those things and see my other grandma."

"Now, it's a long trip," Anne continued, "and during that time, I'll tell you all about your father. It will be much more than things you already know; especially about how he won the Congressional Medal of Honor."

"You mean the medal that hangs over his picture on the fireplace mantel?" William asked, although he already knew the answer.

"Yes, that's the one," Anne replied smiling through tears that were forming again. "And William," Anne continued in a very serious tone, "there is a lot more about that medal that you don't know and I'm going to tell you right here and now."

William sat up straight in his chair and leaned over the table and looked at his mother intently. "What more is that, Mom?" He asked in wonderment.

"That medal," Anne started with her voice quivering, "is the highest medal for bravery that our country can give someone. They only give it to someone that has performed a great, great act of heroism.

"Yeah, I know, Mom, you've told me before about Dad at the Battle of the Bulge."

Anne held up her hand to stop William. "It's more than that, William. You see when someone wins that medal our country is so proud of that person that they also pass on an award to his son or daughter."

"You mean I have an award that I don't know about?" William asked with growing curiosity.

"Yes, you do, and it's a very big and important award." Anne stopped and waited for William to ask more questions but he only stared at her quizzically. She felt a small level of frustration because she was worried that she wasn't explaining this whole thing in a manner that a ten year old boy could understand. Although William was a very smart child and made excellent grades in school, this could be, and probably was, going to be hard for him to grasp. "You see William," Anne continued, "because of your dad's medal you'll be allowed to attend West Point when you come of age, and if you have the academic grades to qualify. Do you understand what that means? Do you know what West Point is?"

William's facial expression didn't tell Anne anything and her frustration level grew.

"Yes, Ma'am, I know what West Point is. We've read about it in school. It's a military academy; a big and important military academy. Most all the big general's went there."

"That's right," Anne smiled. "It's the most important military academy in the United States."

William tilted his head. "And I'm goin' to get to go there?"

"Yes, you are. In fact, I've already talked to our State Senators about your appointment. I have been assured that your appointment will be accepted if you have the academic grades. And you will have the grades, young man, you will have the grades."

Finally, Williams face lit up with a large smile. "Yes, Ma'am, I'll have the grades. I promise on Dad's grave."

That statement coming from such young child took Anne's breath away. "I think that was a very nice and grown up thing to say, William. I'm very proud of you."

All this time, Sally hadn't said anything but her face showed concern. At first, Anne didn't notice it because of her concentration on William, but now she could see it. "Is there a problem, Sally?" Anne asked softly.

Sally was nervous and it showed but she slowly forced a question out. "Doesn't goin' to West Point mean that William will have to give a certain amount of years to the military after he graduates?"

"Yes, it does," Anne replied sharply. "But that's a discussion for another time. We have a long time before we have to discuss that." The look on Anne's face indicated that there would be no more said about that subject at this time.

Sally leaned back in her chair and took a sip of her tea and simply said, "Another time."

Anne took a deep breath and stood up. "Now, before the second event, does anyone need a break for more tea or to go to the loo?"

William laughed out loud, "Mom, why do you still call the toilet a loo?"

Anne laughed with him and said, "I guess for the same reason I like my hot tea."

After everyone had refreshed their tea and gone to the loo, they all gathered back at the kitchen table. It was quiet for a while as Sally and William watched Anne gather herself before she started laying out the second event. She seemed to be delaying the conversation about the second even, as she would alternately wring her hands together and then take a sip of her hot tea.

"Mom, are you goin' to tell us about the other event?" William asked, obviously getting tired of waiting.

"Yes. Yes, I am," she almost shouted. She put her tea cup down and started," You both may remember that last year I attended a reunion for 101st Airborne Division. I was there to represent your dad, William. While I was there, I met a retired Colonel named John Barnes. Mister Barnes and I became good friends. You might even say we became very, very good friends. In fact, he and I have been seeing each other socially for the past year. I have kept this private for reasons of my own. He lives in an apartment in North Dallas. So, if you've wondered about my many trips to Dallas lately, or if you've wondered about all the silly reasons I've given for those trips, well now you know. I'm sorry about keeping this a secret relationship but I wasn't sure how you two would receive it. But that's neither here nor there now." She paused and looked into the faces of her son and mother-in-law. They looked back at her in what could only be described as disbelief, but neither of them said a word. "With all of that said," she continued, "the fact is that John and I are going to be married as soon as William and I get back from England. He will be moving in here at the farm. That means that you, William, will have a step-father, and that you, Sally, will have a son-in-law of sorts. Now, that's it. Does anyone have anything they would like to say?"

There was a long silence as they all just stared at each other. Then, Sally said, "Well, it had to happen sooner or later. You're still a young and attractive woman, Anne. I think Bill would want you to marry and enjoy life as well as giving William the presence of a man in the house. But I would ask what your intentions are for William's name?"

Anne, who, had been very tense, relaxed and her face reflected the deep love she had for Sally. "I swear to you, Sally, and to you William, that my son's name will always and forever be William Clyde Barnett."

Sally nodded her head and smiled. "I thank you for that and I'm sure so does Bill."

With all the tension eased, William said, "Well, as you people from England always say 'Good on you, Mum'."

Anne chuckled and pointing at William said, "Nice try, William, but I think it's the Australians that say that."

They all had a good laugh and hugged each other.

That night after William and Sally and gone to bed Anne slipped on her robe and walked out to the small Barnett cemetery that was about fifty yards from the farm house. She didn't need a flashlight, as there was a bright full June moon. She walked over to Bill's grave and placed her hand on his tombstone. On the tombstone was carved the image of the Congressional Medal of Honor. As she traced her finger around the image, a small tear ran down her cheek and dropped onto her robe. "I'll always love you Billy Bob Barnett," she whispered. "I'll always and forever love you."

PART TWO

The Spring of 1960
The Young Hearts

CHAPTER SEVEN

Kellie and Mike

Fifteen year old Kellie Anderson looked back in frustration at her class partner, Mike Linsberg. "Come on, Mike," she yelled. "We're going to miss the rest of the class."

They had been out for the last two hours on a biology class field trip to find a specimen upon which to write a report. The specimen had to be some form of 'safe' insect. 'Safe', meaning it couldn't be a wasp or any other kind of pain inflecting insect. The biology teacher had given them strict instructions about what insects they were allow to pursue. He made it very clear he didn't want any irate parents because some careless student got stung or bitten. Each student was given a small jar in which to put their specimen, and then paired up with another student. At least one member of the pair was required to have a watch, because a two hour time limit was placed on the excursion. They were taken to a large wooded area several miles from school and turned loose to obtain their specimens.

Kellie had been paired with Mike and she knew exactly why. It was because she and Mike were the two least popular kids in class. After all of the other kids had picked their friends for partners, she and Mike were the only ones left. Kellie didn't really mind except that Mike was such a strange character. He never played sports with the other boys and was never involved in any of their rough games. Usually boys like Mike were very smart in class, because if they couldn't play sports or rough house, they at least made good grades in school. Such was not the case with Mike Linsberg. As far as Kellie knew, Mike couldn't do anything well.

As for herself, Kellie knew why she wasn't popular. It was simply because she was too smart and she didn't have time for anyone who wasn't on her level. The other kids in school were jealous of her straight 'A' report card and disliked the way she held herself above them. But the truth was that Kellie didn't care how the other kids felt about her. The only thing she cared about was becoming a doctor like her father. She wanted to make the best grades possible so she could get into a good college and then on to medical school. It would be a long hard road for a girl, but she knew exactly what she wanted and how she was going to get it.

"Why're you in such a hurry?" Mike asked, as he finally caught up with Kellie on the narrow path. "We still have over a half an hour to go."

Kellie stopped and turned to face him and said, "We've already got our specimens and I just want to make sure we don't get left behind."

There was a short silence as Kellie looked at Mike. He was a tall skinny fifteen year old with a narrow face and a large thin nose. His short curly dark brown hair clung to his head like a skull cap and he wore huge thick dark rimmed eye glasses that made his hazel eyes look larger than they really were.

"By the way," she finally continued. "What've you got in your jar?"

"A grasshopper," he answered simply, holding up his jar for her to see.

"A grasshopper," she repeated laughing.

"Yeah, what's wrong with a grasshopper?" The tone of his voice gave away his disappointment in her laughter.

"Nothing much," she replied smartly. "It's just that I'm sure over half of the class will have grasshoppers. It's not the kind of specimen that'll get you an 'A' on your report."

He looked back and forth from his jar to her smiling face several times. "Well," he exclaimed, "not everybody is as smart as you. Not everybody is going to make an 'A'." He looked down at the jar she held in her hand. "What've you got that's so much better?"

The smile on her face broadened and her blue eyes became bright. "This," she said holding the jar up in front of his face and tapping it with her index finger, "is a praying mantis."

He took the jar from her hand and moved it closer to his face. He adjusted his glasses and stared into the jar at the insect inside. The praying mantis seemed to stare back at him with a threatening glare. "Wow!" He breathed. "That thing sure looks mean."

"It is mean," she said as she reached up and took the jar away from him. "This is the terror of the insect world. It can eat almost any other insect." She stopped talking for a moment as they both stared at the insect in her jar. Then she continued with an air of confidence, "Now, this is the kind of specimen that'll get you an 'A' on your report."

He stepped back and looked at her silently for several moments. "We still have some time," he finally stated. "Would you help me find a better specimen?"

"What?" She asked surprised.

"Please," he said quickly. "You're one of the smartest kids in school, and believe me I could sure use an 'A' about now. Come on, give me a hand."

"Why should I do that?" She shouted.

"Well, why not?" He shouted back. "Why would it hurt you to do something nice for once?"

She looked surprised and the brightness began to leave her eyes. "Whata ya mean by that?" She demanded. "Are you trying to say I'm not a nice person?"

"Come on," he laughed loudly. "If you were a nice person you wouldn't be here with me. You know, and I know, why we're paired up on this trip. Nobody likes me because I'm not very smart, I'm different, I'm not handsome, and because I'm a Jew. You see, I know why nobody likes me. But you, why don't the kids like you? It's not because you're dumb; you're not. It's not because you're ugly, because you're actually very beautiful. So what is it, Kellie? Why don't the other kids like you? You've got all the tools to be one of the most popular kids in school, but, instead, you're in the same class with me. And, here we are together because no one else wanted to be with us."

Kellie was stunned by his outburst. It took her several minutes before she could find any words to say, and when she did finally think of something to say, she thought better of it. She set her jar on the ground and reached over and took his from his hands. Opening the top, she freed the grasshopper confined inside. By looking at him, she could tell he was uncomfortable and somewhat embarrassed by his outburst. He simply stood there looking at her but saying nothing. She handed him back his jar and turned and started walking into the wooded area. She had taken only a few steps when she turned and looked back at him. "Aren't you coming?" She asked in a matter-of-fact tone. "We don't have a lot of time to find you another specimen."

Nearly fifteen minutes later, Kellie and Mike were once again hurrying down the path to join their classmates at the designated meeting point. Mike had a huge smile on his narrow face, for in the jar he carried at his side was a cocoon that would shortly become a beautiful butterfly. The cocoon was still attached to the small tree twig that they had carefully broken away from the larger branch.

"Thanks again," he said as they hurried along. "I think even I can get a good grade using this for my report."

"Good," she said simply, without looking at him.

However, after a short distance, Kellie stopped and turned to face him. "What you said earlier about people not liking you because you're a Jew. Is that true? Are you a Jew?"

He looked at her in disbelief. "Good grief," he said with a small laugh. "My name is Linsberg. What do you think?"

She looked puzzled for a minute. "I didn't know you could tell what someone was by their name."

Mike laughed softly. "Kellie," he exclaimed. "You really do live in your own world." He paused for a second then said, "Now that I've gotten to know you, I think I'm going to like you."

"Well that's certainly a relief," Kellie said sarcastically. "I don't know how I would've gotten along without you liking me."

With that she started walking along the path again and he quickly followed after her. They had only walked for about a minute when Kellie stopped again. Her sudden action caused Mike to nearly run into her. She looked at him curiously. "The other thing you said back there," she said haltingly, "the thing about me being beautiful. Is that true? Am I beautiful?"

At first, Mike was embarrassed and didn't know exactly how to reply. But the look of innocence on her face and the sincerity in her eyes told him she really didn't know if she was beautiful or not. "Yeah," he finally answered softly. "You're very beautiful." He moved his eyes from her and looked down at the ground. "Guys like me," he continued, "can only dream of dating girls like you."

There was a short silence as she watched him standing there looking down at the ground. "That's a very nice thing for you to say," she said gently.

"Not really," he said shrugging his shoulders. "It's just the truth."

"Come on," she said signaling him with her hand. "We better get a move on."

When Kellie got home from school that evening, she went to her room and stood in front of her dressing mirror. She stared at herself closely. The reflection looking back at her had long black hair and bright blue eyes. Its skin was clear and soft. The facial features were finely sculptured and, even though she wore a pair of faded jeans for the field trip, the hour glass shape of her young body showed through. Maybe she was beautiful she thought. Maybe Mike was right.

Throughout high school, Mike and Kellie would never have a real date. But they would be the best of friends for the rest of their lives.

CHAPTER EIGHT

Veronica and the Tart Trio

Fifteen year old Veronica Mann bent over the jukebox in Little Eddie's Drug and Soda Shop examining the song selection. She could feel the eyes of the boys in the booth behind her fixed on her. Even at her early age, her body was as developed as most girls at twenty or twenty-one. Her long blond hair was well brushed and shined with beauty. The freckles that once dotted her face were now gone and she wore no make-up. Her bright green eyes had a moody look. Finally she dropped in a dime and selected three Elvis Presley songs; she really liked Elvis. She then quickly turned around and went back to the small booth she was sharing with two other girls.

"Is Elvis all you can play?" Jodie asked as she took a sip of her malt through a long straw. Jodie Connors was a small thin girl with big brown eyes that were covered by large rimmed glasses. Her light brown hair hung in disarray around her head as if she hadn't combed or brushed it in a week. From a physical standpoint, Jodie and Veronica had nothing in common.

"I like Elvis", Veronica said simply.

The other girl in the booth said nothing but continued to munch on the hamburger she held in her hands. Her name was Margie Mason. Though not as developed as Veronica and not as physically beautiful, she was a very attractive girl. Like Jodie she was thin, but she, however, was tall. Her flaming red hair clashed with hazel colored eyes that were set in a nicely structure face. Her nose was small and slightly turned up and her lips were small and dainty looking. She also had one other trait that set her apart from the other two girls; she was very, very smart. She had a straight 'A' report card, was on the Honor Roll, and would probably be the Valedictorian in her senior year. Margie, however, was not an aggressive girl, nor was she prone to taking advantage of her mental superiority. Therefore, Veronica felt it her duty to help guide Margie in directions needed to accomplish results that would best benefit the three friends, but mostly benefit Veronica.

The girls were at lunch period during school. As they did many times, they walked down to the drug store to have a quick lunch, talk, and watch the boys that came there. They usually got there in time to get a booth by the jukebox.

"Okay, so what's the plan for Friday night?" Veronica asked as she leaned forward and put her elbows on the table.

"Come on Ronnie, do we have to have a plan?" Jodie asked still sipping on her straw.

"Of course we have to have a plan," Veronica answered in frustration.

"But it just a party," Jodie continued. "Why can't we just go and have fun? Why does there have to be a plan?"

Veronica's face took on a tired look. "Marg, can I have a little help here?"

Margie didn't respond but took another bite of her almost gone hamburger.

Trying to keep her voice down so the surrounding booths couldn't hear, Veronica said in a harsh whisper, "Marg, you can jump in to the conversation anytime now."

Finally, Margie gently put the remains of her hamburger down, softly patted her lips with a napkin, and turned and looked at Jodie with a motherly smile. "It's very simple, Jo. A plan is required so that the three of us, The Tart Trio, can out maneuver the other girls at the party to get the boys we have identified as desirable."

Jodie took the straw from her mouth and pushed the remainder of the malt away. "And that's another thing," she said disgustedly, "how did we get that stupid name, 'The Tart Trio'? What's my mom goin' to say if she ever finds out I run around with a group that calls themselves, 'The Tart Trio'?"

"That's another issue," Veronica smiled, "right now we have a plan to put in place, which brings us back to you, Marg. Just how far along are you on the plan? Today's Wednesday and the party is Friday night. Let's not cut things too close."

Margie smiled and tilted her head to one side. "The fact is I have most all the plan in place. All I need is a list of the names of the boys that we know will be at the party and the ones we want to isolate. If you get me that list today, I can work on it tonight and we can go over it right here tomorrow at lunch."

A broad smile crossed Veronica's face. "Well, you have your fact and I have mine," she said softly, "my fact is that I already have that list ready. And more, I have it broken down under each of our names. I'll give it to you when we get back to class."

"You mean you've *assigned* boys to me!" Jodie almost shouted.

Veronica let out a sigh. Then, as if trying to stay calm, she looked at Jodie and said, "Jo, you need to trust me on this. You're goin' to come out ahead here. This is an area where I do well. Now if it were school work, I am sure Marg would be the one to help you out. But we're in my area here. But, I guess first we have to agree you need help in this area. Do we agree on that?"

No answer came immediately. There was just silence.

"Do we?" Veronica repeated.

Jodie's face expressed that she was fighting a battle inside herself. Finally, she put her hands palms down on the table and looked hard into Veronica's eyes. "Yes, we agree on that," she said with her voice shaking. "But could I ask a favor?"

"Ask away," Veronica replied curtly.

"Please don't embarrass me! I know I'm not really pretty like you and Marg and I want to have a boyfriend, as much and maybe more, than you two. But please don't make me do somethin' that will hurt me inside, please don't." When she finished, she lowered her head and stared down at her hands. She was almost crying.

Margie was taken aback. "Jo, I'd never hurt you; never. Anythin' in the plan you don't like we take it out. I swear we take it out." Then looking to Veronica she said, "Won't we Ronnie, won't we?"

Veronica reached over and took Jodie's hands and pulled them across the table and pressed them to her lips. Then she pulled Jodie's hands to her chest and said softly and gently, "I promise. I promise a hundred times over. I love you Jo. You're one of my best friends. We go back to our little girl days. You know the first party I ever went to was your birthday party. Remember?"

Jodie lifted her head and looked at Veronica and a small smile crossed her face. Her eyes were wet with tears. "I remember, Ronnie," she said choking. "I remember it like it was yesterday."

Veronica smiled back at her and said, "And there's somethin' else you need to remember, Jo, and that is that beauty is not just on our outside. It's also on our inside. You may not know it, kiddo, but you're the lucky one in this trio because you've got beauty on the inside and the outside. So, Jo, don't you ever in your life forget that."

"But you're beautiful on the inside too, Ronnie. Who else could put up with Jodie Connors for all these years?

Veronica kissed Jodie's hands once again then put them back on the table. She stood up and looked down at the other two girls. "Come on Trio, I guess we better head back to class."

"Wait," Margie said quickly. "You just can't leave without lettin' me in on this." She reached over quickly and put her hands on top of Jodie's. "I mean," She said tearfully, "I want to be beautiful on the inside too. Sometimes just because I'm smart and make good grades people think I don't have feelings. But I do have feelings. I meant what I said Jo. I would never hurt you. Please believe me. I never would."

"I know that," Jodie said. "I know that." She got to her feet and reached over and pulled Margie to her feet. "Your right Ronnie the Trio needs to get back to class. But what a lunch this has been, uh? I hope after high school we can still be friends and always be able to see each other. Even after we're all married with kids and grown old. Do you think that could happen?"

"Well, you never know," Margie laughed. "You just never know."

"That's a fact," Veronica said soberly, "you just never know."

The girls were headed out the door of the drug store when Veronica stopped them. "You girls go ahead I'll catch up. I forgot I need to get some notebook paper."

The two girls walked on and Veronica went back into the drug store. Once back inside, she went to the large drug store window and watched as her two friends walked away holding hands. She stood there until they were out of sight then she turned her back on the window and put her head in her hands and started crying.

CHAPTER NINE

Kyle and Bennie Go Their Separate Ways

Eighteen year Kyle Collie was meeting Bennie Washington for the last time. It was April of 1960 and, next month, Kyle would be graduating from high school and heading off to summer school at the University of Texas. He would be following in his father's footsteps. His father, a highly decorated naval fighter pilot from World War II and Korea, had already taught Kyle to fly. In fact, Kyle had been flying with his dad since he was eight years old. His father was also an alumnus of the University of Texas and had used his influence to get Kyle into the Air ROTC program. But to get in on the ground floor and be a full cadet he had to go through the entire summer program.

Kyle's father was Rear Admiral Daryl Collie, who not only flew for the United States Navy in World War II but had flown with the Royal Air Force American Eagle Squadron in 1941 before America had entered the war. His dad was one of only a dozen other flyers that had become Aces in the Eagle Squadron and in both the European and Pacific Theaters. All-in-all, Kyle had some awfully big shoes to fill and he was not overly excited about doing it. He loved flying and the thought of following his dad into the Navy and flying jets off a carrier did excite him. But he knew that being the son of Rear Admiral Daryl Collie was not going to be easy; either professionally or personally.

He was meeting Bennie at the state park just outside of his hometown of Coalville. The park commemorated the old coal mining days that had once made Coalville a boomtown. A few years back the town had petitioned the state to put up a monument to the people from Coalville who had served their country during World War II and Korea. Kyle's father's name was on the bronze monument along with his Uncle Dick and the name of every person that had served.

Kyle was sitting on a bench that was near the top of a place known as Lonesome Hill. It overlooked the beautiful pine trees below. His dad and uncle had told him some wild stories about their adventures on this hill years before the park was built. As he sat calmly taking in the view, Bennie walked up and sat down beside him.

"How're things goin', Kyle?" Bennie asked simply.

Kyle turned to look at Bennie and said, "Oh, about the same, and yourself?"

"I guess I can't complain too much."

There was a long silence and then Kyle said, "I hear you're goin' to Prairie View A&M."

"Yeah, I'm already registered for the fall semester."

"You don't sound too fired up about it."

Bennie ignored Kyle's comment and asked, "I hear you're off to UT for the summer semester. Why the big hurry?"

Kyle took a big breath. "It's Dad's idea. He wants me to be a full cadet by the fall semester."

"So, you'll be followin' in your dad's footsteps, uh?"

"Yeah, that's about it," Kyle said smiling. "But I don't really mind. You know flyin' is what I want to do anyway."

"Yeah, I know," Bennie laughed. "How many times did I push you off that barn roof in the stupid glider we made?"

Kyle laughed out loud and slapped Bennie on the back. "Man, how'd I avoid gettin' killed or crippled for life?"

Bennie was laughing as loud as Kyle. "Well, if I remember it correctly, you did get some pretty good cuts and bruises. I never did know how you hid those from your parents."

"Aw, they knew. Dad was gone a lot but Mom knew. She'd just patch me up and tell me not to do anythin' stupid."

"Well, stupid was what it was," Bennie chuckled. "Why you wanted to build that glider in the first place was weird to me because your dad was always takin' you up and teachin' you to fly. Hell, I guess you're as good a pilot as a lot of guys that have a license."

Kyle stopped laughing and looked hard a Bennie. "I know you want to fly too, Bennie. What're you goin' to do at Prairie View?"

Bennie stood up and walked a few steps away from the bench and turned back and looked at Kyle with a mournful look. "Well," he started, "I think my best plan is to get two years in at Prairie View and then transfer to a big school with a good ROTC program and one that'll allow coloreds. I guess that'll be somewhere up north. I have to research it."

Kyle lowered his head and spoke without looking up. "I wish you could go with me, Bennie. It's not fair that it has to be this way. It's not fair."

"I know it's not fair, but it will be someday. Things are changin' and I may miss out on it but my kids won't. I'm bettin' I'll be able to do for my kids what your dad is doin' for you."

Kyle stood up and walked over and grabbed Bennie by the shoulders. "I'm bettin' that same way, Bennie. And our kids will be able to play with each other without keepin' secrets. Anyway, I should've been a better friend to you and pushed you off that barn roof a few times."

Bennie placed his arms on Kyle's and the boys embraced. "No thank you, I never felt the need to go off that roof in that glider." Then turning serious he said, "But I can tell you that you couldn't have been a better friend. These last years buildin' model planes, reading books, and gettin' magazines, and even buildin' that stupid glider, have been some of the best times for me. We may be goin' our separate ways for now, but we'll see each other again. And there's nothin' in this world that'll wash away these great memories."

Then the boys pushed themselves apart and just stood there looking at each other for a time. Then Kyle said, "Good luck, Bennie, and God speed."

Bennie smiled and replied, "Good luck, Kyle, and God speed."

Bennie sat back down on the bench and turned his back to Kyle. Kyle turned and started walking back down the hill.

CHAPTER TEN

Rosa Tells Jordan the Truth

Fifteen year old Jordan Costillo sat calmly at the dining room table as his mother had instructed him. She had told him she wanted to speak with him about some matters of high importance. That was early in the morning before he had gone to school. She had told him to wait for her at the dining room table after school. He had now been waiting for almost ten minutes and he was getting restless.

All day at school he had tried to think what this could all be about. He knew there were things she had promised to tell him when he reached eighteen. Things about his father and others he should know about. He had always wondered about them, and also how they afforded to live in this large expensive house. For the first five years of his life they had lived in a small three room cabin outside the Marfa city limits. Then, suddenly, when he turned six years old they moved from the cabin to their current luxury home in the Marfa city limits. He didn't understand how they afforded their extravagant house. As far as he knew, their only income was his mother's making and selling of Mexican and Indian jewelry.

So, he concluded that these were the things she wanted to talk to him about. However, in a couple of months he would be sixteen; not eighteen. Why would she change her mind and discuss these things with him two years earlier than she originally planned? This led him to believe that it must be something else she wanted to speak to him about. Maybe it was to start planning for college, because he was in the process of working on an academic scholarship. But finally he simply leaned back in his chair and decided not to worry about it anymore but to wait for his mother.

His wait was only a few more minutes as his mother came walking into the dining room carrying two large portfolios. She put them on the table near Jordan and then sat down across from him on the other side of the table. So far she had said nothing. Finally she folded her hands together and spoke.

"Jordan," she said seriously, "I have some things of great importance to talk with you about. I'll need for you to listen to me carefully and then I'll allow you to ask questions. I'll answer them as truthfully and as accurately as I possibly can. Can you do this for me?"

"Of course, Mother," Jordan replied nodding his head.

Rosa lowered her head for a long moment and then looked back up at Jordan. "First, I must confess to you that the trips I've been taking to Midland haven't been for business as I told you." Jordan started to speak but Rosa held up her had to stop him. "We had a deal that you would ask questions later, okay?"

Jordan said nothing but only nodded.

Then Rosa continued, "The trips have been of a medical nature. Our old friend Dr. Martinez, who brought you into the world, found a serious medical condition that he felt special doctors in Midland could help me with better than his limited ability. So, I've been going up to Midland about every other week to have it checked out. They've found that I have a bad cancer, one that can't be cured."

Jordan couldn't contain himself, "What're you tellin' me, Mother?" He shouted jumping to his feet.

Rosa held up her hands and said in a demanding voice, "Sit down, Jordan, and listen. You must act like a man now." She then pointed to his chair indicating for him to sit down. Slowly, Jordan retook his seat but his eyes burned into his mother with intensity. "What all of this means," she continued, "well, it means that I'm dying. The doctors believe I may have as much as two years to live if I take the proper treatments."

There was a long silence as Jordan struggled with what to say. Then in a soft and shaking voice he asked, "What kind of cancer is it? Is everyone sure you can't be fixed?"

Rosa looked at him with great love in her eyes and said, "It's called Melanoma and it has already spread through my lymph node glands. There's nothing anyone can do except give me treatments to make me as comfortable as is possible."

"Are you goin' to Midland to stay in the hospital?"

"No, I'll stay here 'til the end. Doctor Martinez will help me with the treatments." Then she took a deep breath and reached over and took his hands into hers. "But when the end comes," she breathed softly, "you must be strong for both of us. Can you be my strong man?"

Jordan's eyes were wet but he didn't cry. "You know I will, Mother," he said firmly. "I'll be whatever you require because I love you, Mother. No son as ever had a mother like you; never in the history of time. Even Mary the Mother of Jesus couldn't be a better mother than you."

Rosa smiled at him. Her heart was breaking. "That's a very sweet thing for you to say to me," she said as the tears she had tried so hard to hold back slowly ran down her cheeks. Then, in a sharp change of emotion, she sat up straight in her chair and clapped her hands together and said in an all business like tone, "Now, there are things that I must tell you. Things that I'd planned to tell you when you graduated from High School. But now is the time."

She stood up and began walking back and forth along the length of the table. "First," she said pointing her finger into the air, "I must tell you somethings about Judy and Jimmy Orland, who you call Aunt Judy and

Uncle Jimmy." She paused for a moment and took a deep breath. Jordan continued to watch her closely but didn't speak. "They," she continued, "aren't your aunt and uncle. In fact, Judy Orland is actually your big sister." She stopped again to let that information sink in.

Jordan faced changed from an expression of close attention to an expression of total shock. He slowly rose from his chair continuing to watch his mother. "But she's so much older than me," he breathed. "How can all this be true?"

"Please sit back down, Jordan," Rosa said softly, waving her hand at him.

Jordan slowly sat back down and then stared at his mother waiting for her to explain.

"Yes that's true," she said nervously. "To be exact there's twenty-five years between you." Rosa began walking back and forth the length of the table again. She rubbed her hands together. As she walked she began talking again. "This summer," she began, "I'll be sending you to stay with Judy in Dallas." She saw Jordan was about to speak and quickly held up her hand to silence him. "You see, Judy and Jimmy have for a long time now been our benefactors. Over the years they've invested in the oil companies for us. Because of them, we have this nice house and, though you don't know it, we're quite wealthy. You'll inherit a lot of money and property when I'm gone." She paused shortly to gather her thoughts and then continued, "Judy will introduce you to some of your real relatives and explain the whole story about your father and me, and all the things that happened." After a short pause, she continued, "You see, Jordan, your father and I were never really married. That's why you carry my family name instead of his. But know this, Jordan, your father died fighting for his country and was awarded an Air Medal that one day will be yours."

There was a long silence as they both studied each other. Then, Jordan lowered his head and asked softly, "But you're my real mother aren't you?"

She quickly ran round the table to where he was sitting and grabbed him by the shoulders and pulled him up out of the chair. Pulling him to her tightly, she said in a shaking voice, "Oh, yes, Jordan. Yes, yes, yes, I'm your real mother. I am. I truly am."

As she squeezed him to her, he put his arms around her and they stood there for a long time just holding each other.

CHAPTER ELEVEN

Kathleen and Her Brother

It was late evening as fifteen year old Kathleen O'Rourke was finishing up the dinner dishes, as her brother walked up behind her. He reached over and tapped her on the shoulder gently. She spun around in surprise and, through some miracle, was able to hold on to the plate she had been in the process of drying. "God, Rob O'Rourke," she said holding tight to the plate, "you scared the livin' shit outa me. Don't be sneakin' up on me like that. If I'd broken one of Mom's cherished plates, you'd have hell to pay."

Rob held up his hands in mock surrender. "I'm sorry, I'm sorry," he said with a slight chuckle. Then pointing his figure at her, "And you better watch that language young lady or Mom'll have your hide."

Kathleen relaxed and smiled at him. Her smile was a thing of beauty. Her face still had some freckles but they were receding and her lips were full with a natural pink color as she was still not allow lipstick as yet. At fifteen, she was developing a nice figure to go with her short frame which stood only five foot three inches tall. Her hair was still a beautiful flaming Irish red. Her smile faded slightly as she spoke, "Mom says a lot worse than that. Anyway, Mom and Dad are off to Mickey's Bar. She can't hear me." After a short pause she asked, "Do you want somethin'?"

Rob turned from her and walked a short distance across the kitchen. He stuffed his hands into his pants pocket and kept his back to her. "Yeah, there is somethin', Kat," he said softly, "I need you to help me with somethin'." Then he quickly spun around to face her again and blurred out, "And it's somethin' kind of tough."

Kathleen carefully placed the plate she had been holding into the cabinet with the others. She turned to her brother and looked at him very hard and folded her arms across her chest. "What, may I ask, are you up to Robert O'Rourke?"

He lowered his head and said, "I need you to help me with Mom and Dad."

Her eyes widened. "How can I help you with Mom and Dad since you're already their favorite? What could I said that they would listen to me over you?"

"Okay, okay," he said holding up his hands in surrender, "maybe what I really meant was to have your support. You know, to kind of stand beside me."

She unfolded her arms and put her hands on her hips. "Before I commit to anythin' I guess I should know what you need my support with."

There was a long pause as he gathered his thoughts. Then, he began very slowly. "Well, you know that I'll graduate from high school this May and I'll turn eighteen in July." He stopped and looked at her as if waiting for her to ask a question.

"I know all that," she said irritably.

"And you probably know that Mom and Dad have been scrimping and saving for both of us to go to Saint Mary's Catholic Prep School in Boston. In fact, Father Conway has already gotten me accepted and he'll start workin' on you next year."

Kathleen dropped her hands from her hips and held them rigidly at her side and practically yelled at him, "When, for Christ sakes are you goin' to tell me somethin' I don't already know? Can you just get to the point? Please!"

He instantly shouted back at her, "I don't want to go to Saint Mary's. I want to join the marines."

She was stunned. All she could do was just stared at him. He didn't say anything he just stared back at her.

"Where in Christ's name did that come from?" She stammered.

He turned from her and took a few steps across the kitchen, then turned back to her and said, "I've been thinkin' about it for a long time really. I'm tired of school for now. I want to do somethin' else; some excitement and some travel. I can always go to school when my enlistment's up and I'll have the GI Bill to help." He seemed to be pleading with her to understand.

She didn't know what to say but she managed to exclaimed, "But where did the marines come from?"

He shrugged his shoulders and said simply, "I've been talkin' to a recruiter that has been visitin' with us seniors. I like what he has to say and I want to join up."

"But isn't that kind of dangerous?" She was trying to reason with him.

"Sis, there's nothin' goin' on right now. It's a perfect time. And anyway, my mind is made up. Right now I'll need them to sign for me but in July after I'm eighteen I won't. I just would like your moral support. I'd like for you to stand with me when I tell 'em."

Kathleen sighed and looked at Rob with frustration. "Okay, you know I'll stand with you for all the good it'll do. Mom and Dad are *NOT* goin' to like this; not one little bit."

There was a long silence when neither of them spoke. Then, Kathleen asked, "When do you want to do this?"

"The sooner the better," he said. "I'm thinkin' as soon as they get back from Mickey's."

"But Rob," she pleaded, "it's still over a month to your graduation. How do you think things are goin' to be in this house for that month?

It'll be terrible. Mom and Dad will continually be at you about not goin' to school. I mean, they may not even go to your graduation. Have you thought about all that?"

He looked at her thoughtfully. "No, honestly I haven't thought about everythin'. But I do know things will be hard. I guess it all depends on how they react."

"So, what's the hurry?" She challenged. "Why can't it wait?"

Rob leaned back against the kitchen counter, pushed his hands in his pocket and asked, "How old are you Kat?"

"You know I'm fifteen."

"How old am I?" He pressed.

"You're seventeen and almost eighteen."

He pushed off the counter stepped close to her and looked into her eyes intently. "Yes," he said forcibly, "you're fifteen and I'm almost eighteen and we still share the same bedroom. We've been sharing that room since you were born."

She looked at him almost reading his thoughts but she didn't speak.

"That's not natural, Kat," he continued. "We have another room but Mom wants to keep it as a guest room for who knows who. You and I both have used it when I had someone over or you did. I've asked to move into it but Mom just won't let go."

Final Kathleen exploded, "What, in heaven's name, does any of that have to do with any of this?"

"Just this," he yelled back, "part of us tellin' them about the marines is that I'm goin' to demand to move into the guest room. That way if they want to shut me out, then I'll have my own room to stay in away from everyone else."

"But what if Mom still says no?" She asked in a softer tone.

"In that case, I'll move out. I've already talked with Harry Collins and his family has said I can use their spare room."

"Move out," she cried. "You can't move out."

"I'll do what I have to, Kat." Then after a short pause, "Are you still with me?"

She hesitated for only a moment and then replied, "Okay," she replied, "let me finish up in here and I'll join you in the living room and we can wait for them in there."

"Fair enough," he said nodding his head, "and I'll repay you for this, Sis. Somewhere down the line, I'm goin' to repay you."

She had started back to the kitchen sink but stopped and turned back. He had already started for the living room but her voice stopped him and he turned to look at her. She was wearing that beautiful smile again. "Well, you know, you did volunteer to take a switchin' for me once upon a time."

"Yeah, I did, once upon a time. And by the way, if you'll keep wearin' that smile, Mom and Dad won't have chance." With that he hurried into the living room.

Kathleen was right, their parents didn't like what Robert Junior had to say the least little bit. Even her beautiful smile made no difference. The discussion raged on until after midnight and she stood right there with her brother the whole time.

In the end, it was agreed that the papers to allow Robert Junior to enlist in the marines would be signed, but on the condition that he finished high school and graduated. In addition, it was agreed that Robert Junior could move into the guest room until such time as he left for the marines. Their parents also agreed to attend his graduation.

Kathleen was silent for most of the conversation, or argument whichever fit best, until they came to the part about Robert Junior's school money. Her parents had decreed that Robert Junior's school money would be transferred to Kathleen's school account. Kathleen exploded with anger and absolutely refused to take any of her brother's money. After her outburst, nothing more was said about the money.

However, unknown to Kathleen, the money was transferred the week after her brother left for the marines.

CHAPTER TWELVE

William and His Step-Father

Fifteen year old William Barnett and his Grandma Sally were at his father's grave site placing flowers as they did at the start of each new month. As Sally arranged the flowers, she casually asked William a question without looking up, "William, how're you and your stepfather gettin' on?"

William was somewhat taken aback by the question. He walked over and knelt down on the other side of the grave facing her. He spoke softly, "Why do you ask, Grandma?"

She finished arranging the flowers but remained kneeling. "Well," she began in a reluctant tone, "the last five years have been really busy you know. You've been to England, your mom got married, and in a few months you're goin' to have either a little half-sister or a little half-brother."

"But, Grandma, that doesn't answer my question. Why do you ask about John and me?"

She tilted her head to one side and looked deeply at him. "It's just that grandmas can pick up on things that other people miss. There's nothin' I can't put my finger on but I get the feelin' that there's somethin' goin' on under the surface." She paused briefly and then continued, "Am I right?"

He stood up. Her eyes followed him but she remained kneeling. "Well, there might be a couple of minor issues."

"Such as," she pressed.

He lowered himself back down but instead of kneeling he sat down on the ground and crossed his legs in front of him. She did the same and adjusted her dress to cover her legs. "Wouldn't you be more comfortable in a chair on the front porch?" He asked seriously.

"I'm fine, William, but thank you for thinkin' of me. Anyway we can have some privacy here."

They both just sat there for long period of time just looking at each other. Finally, she said, "Well, are you goin' to tell me somethin' or not?"

"It's really not a big deal, Grandma."

"Then I guess it'll be okay to tell me."

He took a deep breath and let it out in a rush. "Okay, the main thing is my name. John and Mom have been havin' words about John adoptin' me and changin' my name to Barnes. I mean they haven't really argued about it, but John's been kind of pressurin' Mom about it. But Mom won't budge. So, he came to me about it to try and get me to tell Mom that I think it would be a good idea."

"Wait a minute, just you wait a minute," Sally said firmly holding up her hands. "Are you tellin' me that he's gone behind Anne's back to enlist you in his cause?"

"Kind of but not really,' he replied.

"What does that mean? How do you *kind of but not really*?"

"I told him no and that he shouldn't have asked me. He told me I was right and he apologized to me, and then he went to Mom and told her what he had done and apologized to her as well. At first Mom was real mad, but in the end they worked it out and he promised it was a dead issue."

Sally carefully unfolded her legs and gingerly pushed herself to her feet. William followed suit. His last words had calmed her down. "Well, I'm happy that's over with and that John and Anne or okay. But you said a couple of issues. What's the other one?" He didn't answer right away so she reached over and took his hand and give it a tug. "Come on let's walk and talk. Okay?"

"Sure Grandma."

As they walked back toward the house, she didn't pressure him to talk. After a short distance he said, "The other thing is he wants me to call him Dad. I call him John and he feels our relationship would be better if I called him Dad. You know, since he's taken over runnin' the feed store for Mom, we work together a lot. And he's really a great guy and he's really nice to me. I can tell you he's goin' to make a great dad for that new baby."

He stopped talking as if expecting Sally to say something, but she remained silent. He pulled her hand to stop them from walking. They had covered more than half way to the house. Then in deeply pleading voice he asked, "What should I do, Grandma? I'm all mixed up about this thing. I don't know what the right thing to do is."

"Have you talked to your mom about it?

"No, I don't want to bother her with it right now. She's havin' a baby and we just settled the issue about my adoption." He paused and took Sally's other hand and held them both tightly. "Grandma, my dad was your son. I know what his memory means to you; and to me as well. Please tell me what you think I should do. I know whatever you tell me will be right."

Sally looked up at her grandson. At fifteen, he was already a head taller than her. She pulled her eyes from his and glanced back at the grave they had just left. Her eyes became moist as she remembered so many little things about her son. And the boy standing before her looked so much like him in every way.

William saw the tears forming in his grandmother's eyes. "Oh no, don't cry Grandma. I don't want to make you cry. Please don't cry."

Sally reached up and patted him on his cheek. "Don't worry about it, William," she whispered. "I cry because I had a wonderful son in your dad and I have a wonderful grand-son in you. I have a wonderful daughter who has given me two wonderful grandchildren. Everything is wonderful, just wonderful. And because I had such a wonderful son, I know he would want you to treat your stepfather with all the respect he is due. Therefore, I think I can tell you with certainty that my son would prefer that you call your stepfather, Dad."

"Oh, Grandma," William shouted loudly, "you're the one that's wonderful. From this moment on my stepfather will be Dad and not John. And I already feel real good about it."

Sally reached up patted his cheek again. "Why don't you run to the house and tell your mom what you've decided."

"I'm on my way," he shouted as he turned and started for the house at a full sprint.

Sally watched him run and said out loud as if she were speaking to someone, "He runs just like his dad, he runs just like Billy Rob."

PART THREE

The Fall of 1962
The Tragedies

CHAPTER THIRTEEN

Kellie and Her Mom

Seventeen year old Kellie Jean Anderson stood in a soft falling rain looking down at her mother's freshly covered grave. It was late evening and darkness was settling over the small graveyard. The funeral had been over for hours and everyone was gone. Only Kellie remained; standing in the rain without an umbrella. Her long black hair was soaked with rain and stuck to her face and forehead. The simple black dress she wore clung wetly to her body. No tears came from her eyes. Only the dark blue of anger radiated from her eyes as the rain pelted her face. The flowers that surrounded the grave site drooped under the weight of the rain. A bright flash of lightning lit the sky and the low roll of thunder added to the gloom of the moment.

Kellie looked up as her father approached. He walked slowly with his hands pushed into the pockets of his long black trench coat. Rain dripped from the brim of his felt dress hat. The hat was pulled down low on his forehead hiding his eyes, but Kellie could see they were still red. His face was wet not only from the rain but from the tears that still flowed freely down his cheeks. When he reached the side of the grave opposite Kellie, he stopped and looked up at her.

"It's time to go home, Kel," he said softly. Kellie did not move but continued to stare at him with her dark blue eyes. "It's time to go," he repeated more firmly this time.

"She shouldn't have died," Kellie said coldly. "It was a simple appendectomy. People don't die from appendectomies in today's world. It just shouldn't happen. You're a doctor; you know it's true."

Kellie's outburst was punctuated by another flash of lightning streaking across the sky followed by a loud crack of thunder.

"Kel, things happen that none of us can control," he sighed. "Your mom had a reaction to the anesthetic. There was no way anyone could know, it wasn't anybody's fault!"

"Mom was only thirty-nine years old," Kellie persisted. "We'd just picked out my prom dress. Mom and I had a life time ahead of us. She shouldn't be dead!"

"Yes, Kel, I know she shouldn't be dead. Nobody knows it more than me. You think you and your mom had a life time a head of you? Well, I was expecting to grow old with Carol Anderson, that wonderful, wonderful woman." He stopped and tried to choke back his emotions as the tears started flowing again. "I know it's not fair for either of us, but that's the way it's happened."

"Jesus, Dad, doesn't it bother you that someone's negligence killed Mom? Someone is responsible and someone should be punished."

He removed his hands from his trench coat pockets and pushed his hat back on his head revealing red and swollen eyes. "I'll tell you what does bother me, Kel," he said in a broken voice. "It's the fact that you're more concerned with punishing someone than you are with the loss of your mother. You're so full of anger that you haven't shed a tear for her."

"Is that what you want me to do, Dad, cry?" Kellie shot back. "That's your answer to make everything okay is to cry! That's all you wanted me to do when Old Denver was killed, was cry. I wanted to get the guy that killed him, but you just wanted me to go have a good cry. Now, what do you want me to do, Dad? Go home and have a good cry? Is that what little girls are supposed to do? Go home and cry?"

He was somewhat taken aback by the level of her anger. He stepped back and looked at her long and hard. "Crying isn't just for little girls," he said quietly. "As a doctor, I can tell you that crying is for everyone. Sometimes it's the only thing that keeps one's sanity. There has to be some way to get the hurt out. Anger alone will eat away at your soul and keep happiness out of your life." He paused and there was a long silence between them. "You can cry for your mother, Kel, and still be angry."

"I'm not mad at you, Dad," she said in a much kinder voice, "it's just that I don't understand is all."

He walked around the grave to where Kellie was standing. He took her hand and gave a gentle pull. "Let's go home, Kel. Mom wouldn't want you standin' in the rain."

They turned together and started a slow walk out of the graveyard towards their car parked out on the road. It had gotten dark now and they made their way carefully. When they reached the road, Kellie stopped and turned to look back at the grave one last time. A bright flash of lightning lit the sky and bathed Kellie's face in light. There were still no tears in her eyes.

"Thumbs up," her father said in a shaking voice, as he held his fist out and gave her the sign.

"Yeah, sure Dad," she said softly, returning the sign to him, thumbs up."

CHAPTER FOURTEEN

Veronica and Michael Connors

Seventeen year old Veronica Mann stood near a large monument in the Sweetwater Cemetery. There was a large tree next to it that offered her a little shelter and together with the monument helped to hide her from view. She guessed she was about a hundred yards from where the funeral was taking place.

She hadn't been able to attend the funeral, although that had been her intention. She had gotten all dress up in her Sunday best and had started for the church. Before she had left the house, her father had offered to drive her, but she just wanted to be alone and told him simply that she wanted to walk. He had been nice about it because he knew how she was hurting inside. He had just said, "Take as long as you like, sweetheart, but please be home before dark."

She hadn't said anything but just nodded as she left the house. As the church had come into view and she saw all the cars and people, she had made a quick turn and had walked to the cemetery instead. There she had found the tree and monument and decided that it was a good place to wait and watch.

Now as the funeral was breaking up, she watched patiently as everyone slowly made their way to their cars and drove away. The funeral home crew was quick to start taking down the tent and picking up the chairs. Veronica watched as they finished their work by covering the open grave with the dirt piled to one side. The whole operation had taken over an hour. During that time, Veronica had made herself comfortable by sitting down and leaning back against the tree. Finally the funeral home crew was finished with all their work and piled into a nearby truck and drove away. She continued to sit there for at least another half an hour. It was evening by now and the sun was low in the west. Finally, she got to her feet and started towards the grave. She walked slowly as if almost afraid to reach the grave, but she did finally arrive.

She walked around to the foot of the grave and looked up at the newly piled dirt next to the large headstone. The headstone was made of beautiful pink marble. It was very expensive as befitting the family of the one who lay in the grave. Tears began to fill Veronica's eyes as she read the headstone.

HERE LIES JODIE MAY CONNERS
LOVING DAUGHTER OF MICHAEL AND
SUSAN CONNERS
SHE WAS A PRECIOUS CHILD
AND WOULD HAVE BEEN A WONDERFUL
WOMAN
GOD PLEASE TAKE HER INTO YOUR KINGDOM

BORN MAY 24, 1945 GONE TO GOD
OCTOBER 15, 1962

Veronica clasped her hands together and put them to her lips. The tears that were welling in her eyes now began to slowly run down her cheeks. As she pressed her clasped hands to her lips, a hundred thoughts began to run through her mind.

It had happened back in May of this year. Mr. Conners had gone out to oversee the installation and testing of a new drill bit that he hoped would improve and speed up the drilling process to reach the oil deep below the surface of his oil rich land. His daughter, Jodie, had begged to go along, since she had finished her exams at school and was at home all alone. Her brothers were still taking exams and her mother had gone shopping. As he usually did, Mr. Conners gave in and told her she could come along, but she was ordered to stay out of the way, as this was an important test and would take at least an hour.

That's how it all started. That was the prelude to the accident. No one actually saw the accident. Mr. Conners was busy working with the oil rig crew and there was no one else around as they were far out into what was known as, 'The Patch'.

When the testing was finished, Mr. Conners yelled for Jodie but she didn't answer. At first, he simply thought she had wondered off looking at rocks or just nosing around. But it didn't take him long to become alarmed as he got no answer to his constant calls for Jodie. He hurried back to the rig and enlisted the crew of six men to spread out and help him look for Jodie. It didn't take long for them to find her. She hadn't gone far from the car. One of the men found her lying behind a large stack of drilling pipe. The stack was over twenty feet high and twenty yards long. The pipes themselves were each forty feet long.

When they found her, she was lying at the bottom of the stack of pipes. Blood was running slowly from her nose, mouth, and ears; there was a large pool of blood around her head. Mr. Conners let out a loud and anguished scream as he scooped her up and put her in the car. He drove like a madman to the nearest hospital which was thirty miles away in Midland.

In the end, the County Sheriff surmised that Jodie had tried to climb to the top of the stack of pipes. One of the pipes must have rolled out from under her foot and she had fallen backward and cracked her skull on the pipes as she tumbled to the bottom of the stack.

Jodie didn't die right away. The doctors at Midland Memorial Hospital work fanatically to save her. It was said by all that they did an amazing job to keep her alive. All of this happened in May and Jodie would linger on until October 10th when she would finally breathe her last breath without ever regaining consciousness.

Mr. Conners blamed himself and couldn't be consoled. He had left his oil company in the hands of others as he spent nearly all of his waking hours at Jodie's bedside. And that's how it had happened.

Veronica felt someone touch her shoulder and it brought her out of her thoughts with a shock. She spun around quickly to see Mr. Conners standing there. He looked awful. He had lost a dangerous amount of weight and he was drawn and pale. His eyes were puffy and red obviously from crying during the funeral.

"Mr. Conners," Veronica stammered, "you scared me out of my wits."

"I'm sorry," he said softly. Then after a long pause he asked, "Why're you here by yourself, Ronnie?"

Veronica lowered her head and said in a soft voice that he could hardly hear, "I miss her so, Mr. Conners. I didn't even get to say goodbye. I just didn't think I could stand being at the funeral."

He stepped near her and patted her on the shoulder. "I know," he whispered. "We all feel the same way. It's all I could do to be there myself." Then, smiling a forced smile, he reached down put his finger under her chin and lifted her face up to look at him. "I guess there won't be a Tart Trio anymore, uh?"

Veronica's eyes widened. "You knew about that name?"

He forced a soft chuckle and said, "Sure we knew. Susan and I both knew."

"Oh, Mr. Conners can you ever forgive me?" She was starting to cry again. "It was completely my fault. That name was my idea. Jodie didn't like it. She really didn't."

He step closer and took her in his arms and hugged her tightly. "Sure she did," he said flatly. "She loved you and Marg like sisters. She would've done anything for you two."

Veronica pushed back from him and looked at him firmly. "I know she would, and she did. That's why this is so much the harder for me."

He looked at her quizzically and said, "I don't understand"?

She took a deep breath and fought back the tears. "You see, Mr. Conners, I was the boss of The Tart Trio and I got my way most of the time. I felt bad about it a lot but it didn't stop me. And standin' here, today, I know in my heart that Jodie was a lot better friend to me than I was to her, and knowin' that is just killin' me inside." She ran over and threw her arms around his waist and buried her head in his chest. "It's just killin' me," she repeated.

They stood there for a short time while Veronica cried into the suit jacket he was wearing. Slowly, he pushed her back from him to about arm's length. He looked at her long and hard. She looked back at him but neither of them spoke.

Finally, he took her by the hand and held it tightly. He looked up at the sky and saw the sun beginning to sink down to the horizon. The orange glow of the West Texas sunset was just starting to set the sky ablaze. He looked back down at her and gently tugged on her hand. "Come on," he said softly. "I'll drive you home. I'm pretty sure that your mom and dad don't want you out by yourself after dark."

"No, sir, they don't. And I would really appreciate the ride."

They continued to hold hands as he guided her to his car. They got into the car and drove away. As he drove, Michael Conners thought that maybe both of them had lifted a heavy burden from their shoulders.

CHAPTER FIFTEEN

Kyle, His Father and Bennie

It was October and twenty year old Kyle Collie was driving home from the University of Texas to spend the Columbus Day weekend with his family in Coalville. He had just started his third year at the university and was an official junior. It was also his third year in the Air ROTC program. Counting all the credits he accumulated in summer sessions, he already had enough credits to enter any branch of the service as an officer. But there was no question in his mind or his families that he would continue on and get his Bachelor of Science Degree before entering the military.

As he drove, he found it hard to keep his mind on driving. He found himself allowing his new car, which was given to him by his father, to wander all over the road. He knew he had to get his mind back on driving or he was going to have an accident. What was troubling Kyle was the news he would be giving to his dad when he got home. His father had always assumed that Kyle would follow in his footsteps and join the United States Navy and fly jets off a carrier deck. But over the last year, Kyle had become excited about flying helicopters instead of fixed winged aircraft. Without telling his father, he had been logging a lot of helicopter flying hours in training courses, as well as personal flying with ROTC friends of his at the university. What troubled Kyle was how his father was going to react to his change in careers, because this meant that Kyle would be joining the army to fly helicopters and not the navy or the air force. Although the navy and air force both had helicopters, they couldn't match the combat helicopters the army was starting to use.

As Kyle pulled into the driveway at home near noon, his sixteen year old sister, Lilly Jo was standing on the front porch watching him drive up. Lilly Jo was a work of art. She looked just like her mother, who at the age of forty-two still was a real beauty. Lilly was wearing a pretty sleeveless green dress that came to just below her knees. Her long blonde hair fell to her shoulders. From her beautifully structured face, bright green eyes match her dress. Kyle smiled to himself as he got out of his car and said softy under his breath, "She's goin' to be a real heartbreaker someday; if not already."

Lilly came running up to him and leaped on him throwing her arms around his neck. "It's my big brother come home from the university wars," she laughed.

Kyle gave her a hard hug and swung her around. They were both laughing when their parents came out onto the porch. "Well, Sue Ann, it looks like your son finally made it home," his father shouted while waving to him. Kyle waved back with a big smile on his face but quietly wondered why his dad was in his full dress uniform; admiral stars and all. Kyle ran to the porch and embraced both his parents. As he did so, he could sense that something was wrong despite all the laughing and smiles.

Once everyone was inside, quietness fell over the room. Kyle looked around uncomfortably and then went straight to the small bar that his father had built next to the large fireplace. He reached into the bar cabinet took out a nearly half full bottle of Jack Daniels Black Label. "Okay, Dad," he said joyfully, "how about joining me in a holiday drink."

As Kyle was setting up the glasses, his dad said softly, "Sorry Son, I can't be drinkin' at this time."

"At this time," Kyle repeated. "What's so special about *this time*? What would Grandpa Collie say if he knew you turned down a drink of Jack Daniels? Maybe we should just walk across the road to his place. I'll bet he'd be ready for a holiday drink."

"Son, please, this is really, really hard."

Kyle stopped acting and being sarcastic. "Okay, Dad, I guess it must be," he replied in a serious tone. "You in your dress uniform with all the trimmings, everyone so gloomy, and you turnin' down the traditional drink then I guess it must be very serious." After a long pause, Kyle said in a hard flat tone, "So, I guess you better just tell me, Dad."

Admiral Daryl 'Dee' Collie took a deep breath, looked at his son and said in almost a whisper, "It's Bennie, Kyle. He's been killed."

Kyle slowly placed the glasses he'd been holding back down on the bar. He gently put the bottle of whiskey down next to them. He turned back to face his father. "But, that can't be, Dad," he said in disbelief. "I just talked to Bennie last week. He called me long distance from Champaign, Illinois. He was excited beyond belief. He had just been accepted into the University of Illinois ROTC program. He went on and on about how they accepted his Associates Degree from Prairie View and how much hard work he had to do to catch up with the other guys. But he was totally dedicated to gettin' it done. I tell you he must've burned up five dollars in long distance expenses. So, you see he can't have been killed, I just talked to him." Then, lowing his head and in a fading voice he repeated, "I just talked to him."

Dee walked over to his son and put his hand on his shoulder. "It just happened this mornin', Kyle. Bill Washington came here in a panic. He was totally crushed and didn't know what to do. He had received the phone call about 10 AM. They told him what happened and that his son's body was being held at the Champaign, Illinois city morgue. They wanted instructions on what to do with the body. I told—." Kyle held up his hand to stop his father in mid-sentence.

"You said killed," Kyle blurred out. "How was he killed and who killed him?"

"Please stay calm while I tell you all I know," Dee said firmly. It sounded like an order and it was. Kyle lowered his hand and nodded his head. "As I was sayin', I told Bill I would help him in every way possible. We talked for about an hour and then I sent him home to give me time to organize some things. He's goin' to be back here at 3 PM." Dee stopped talking for a short moment to make sure his son was taking it all in. When he felt that Kyle was still under control he continued, "I got on the phone with the Naval Air Station near Dallas and made arrangements for a C-47 cargo plane to be made available to me with pilot and co-pilot. We're scheduled to leave Dallas at 5 PM and arrive in Champaign around 6:30 PM. The city morgue there has agreed to wait for us. Once there, we'll make arrangements to have Bennie taken to the plane."

Dee stopped again and took a deep breath before continuing, "All of this is why I'm in my dress uniform with stars and medals because I need all the clout I can get to overcome this bein' a personal mission. I could get into some hot water for this. But, then, I've been in hot water before." At this point, Dee shrugged his shoulders, turned away from his son and walked back and put his arm around Sue Ann.

Kyle walked over and took both his parents in his arms. "I'm sorry," he said softly. "I'm so, so sorry for the way I've acted. It's just so hard to take in."

"I know, Son," Sue Ann said patting him on the back. "We all loved Bennie and always thought how silly it was for you two to try and hide your friendship."

By now Lilly had join the group hug and they all just stood there holding each other for a long moment. Finally, Kyle pulled away and looked at his father very hard. "You said killed. Can you explain that?"

Dee removed his arm from around Sue Ann and stood straight and looked into his son's eyes. "Drunk driver," he said simply. "Bennie and two other ROTC cadets were drivin' from the university campus early this mornin' headin' for the airfield when a drunk driver from an all-night drinkin' spree ran a red light and hit their car broadside. Bennie and the driver were killed. The guy in the backseat was hurt but is in good condition at the hospital."

"Well," Kyle said coldly, "and what about the drunk driver?"

Dee looked down for a moment then back into his son's eyes and said, "He walked away without a scratch. The police have him in jail and are holdin' him on a charge of vehicular manslaughter."

"I guess all he'll get is some jail time and a fine," Kyle said sarcastically.

"Maybe, but probably some hard prison time," Dee replied.

"Well, if he's lucky," Kyle said with hate dripping from each word, "he won't get out of prison while I'm still alive. If he does, it might not be so healthy for him. Does anyone know his name?"

Dee shook his head no. "I don't," he said, "but I'm sure we can find out in Champaign."

Kyle stood there as if transfixed and everyone in the room just stared at him for a minute, and then he said, "Well, that's for another time." Then he quickly turned and kissed his mom on the forehead. He then grabbed Lilly and planted a big kiss on her cheek and gave her a breath-stopping hug. Then he turned to face his father. "Well, Dad, I guess you know I'm goin' with you and Bill to get Bennie?"

"Yeah, I thought you might."

"No objections, Admiral, sir?"

"Would it matter?" Dee asked smiling at him.

"No, sir, it wouldn't matter at all."

CHAPTER SIXTEEN

Jordan Says Goodbye to Rosa

Seventeen year old Jordan Costillo sat in a large easy chair in his living room. The room was large and, except for him, it was completely deserted. He was very apprehensive because Dr. Martinez was in the master bedroom attending his mother and trying to make her as comfortable as possible. The cancer had finally caught up to her and she was dying. The last two years had been unbelievably hard for Jordan. He had worked so hard to do all his mother had asked of him. The hardest was spending the last two summers with Judy and Jimmy Orland in Dallas. He hated leaving his mother alone but she had insisted that he spend the time with Judy to learn all about his heritage. She assured him that Dr. Martinez would be available to her when she needed him; in addition, she intended to spend several weeks at the hospital in Midland while he was gone for the summer. So, as always, he did as she asked.

It wasn't that Judy and Jimmy were hard on him, it was just the opposite; they were very kind and understanding. It was just he hated to be away from his mother when he knew she needed him. But the two summers he spent with them he learned about things he had wondered about all his young life. They took him to his father's grave; they told him the long story about how his father went from deserter in World War I to war hero in World War II. He was given his father's Air Metal to keep for himself. He learned that Judy was raised by his father until she was twelve years old and he learned how his father had come to find her as a baby. It was explained to him how his mother and father met and how they lived together but were never married. He was sworn to secrecy about how his father escaped from prison and the part Judy and Jimmy had played in it, and, more importantly, his mother's part in the whole matter.

They took him to meet all the people who had played a part in his father's life, including Ruth Jordan his father's wife, and Dick Jordan his father's son by Ruth. Dick Jordan was actually his brother by blood. Many, many people in Coalville, Texas touched his father's life, and, by extension, they were a part of his life as well. On these summer visits to Dallas, of all the people he met and got to know, Dick Jordan was by far his favorite. Not just because Dick was his blood brother, but because he had a natural attachment to Dick. He and Dick would talk for hours about Dick's experiences during World War II. It was these conversations that got Jordan to first start thinking about enlisting in the marines first and waiting to go to college second, but he had been very careful not to let anyone know about his possible plans.

As he sat there in the big easy chair thinking about all these things and wondering why the doctor was taking so long, the doorbell rang. Jordan struggled out of the deep easy chair and hurried to the door. He opened the door and to his surprise there stood Judy and Jimmy Orland. It took him a moment to get over his surprise and then he quickly said, "Come in you two. This is a surprise. What brings you here?"

Judy and Jimmy looked at each other strangely as they walked into the house and closed the door behind them. "Come on into the living room," Jordan said pointing to a large room, "the doctor is in with Mom and I'm waitin' for him to come out so I can go in and see her."

When they were all seated, Judy looked at Jordan with a worried look on her face. After struggling with herself she said, "Dr. Martinez called us, Jordan. Has he not spoken to you about your mom?"

Jordan eyed them closely. Then he said slowly, "He certainly didn't say anythin' about callin' you guys." After a long pause when no one spoke, Jordan continued, "Is there somethin' more I should know other than that the doctor is here on one of his regular visits with Mom."

Judy stood up and started to approach Jordan, who was now standing himself. She had only taken a few steps with the door to the master bedroom opened and Dr. Martinez came out. He face carried a grim look. He gently closed the door and turned toward the group in the living room. He walked past Judy and stop in front of Jordan. He took a deep breath and placed his hand on Jordan's shoulder. He had to reach up because Jordan, who would soon turn eighteen, stood a full head taller than the doctor.

Jordan turned his head and eyed the doctor's hand on his shoulder. He then looked over to Judy and then Jimmy. He turned his eyes back to the doctor and said, "Give it to me, Doc. What is it that everybody knows but me?"

Dr. Martinez removed his hand from Jordan's shoulder and looked down at the floor. "You need to go in and see your mom, Jordan," he said haltingly. "I think she may only have ten or so minutes to live. She wants to hold your hand as she passes."

Jordan stared at the doctor in disbelief. He knew his mother was dying but he didn't know how fast it had come upon them. The doctor reached over and shook him hard. "Go now, Jordan. Time is very short. Go now!"

As if snapping out of a trance, Jordan move away from the doctor and hurried to the door of the master bedroom. He stopped and gathered himself and then opened the door and went in, closing the door behind him.

It was only a short time later that Jordan emerged from the bedroom and walked slowly into the living room. Everyone stood up as he approached. His eyes were puffy and red, and he held his hands tightly together. He looked around at everyone and then started speaking without looking at anyone in particular. He said in a shaky voice, "She wants me to thank you doctor for all you did to help her through this terrible time, and she wants me to thank you Judy and Jimmy for all you did to make our life a happy one." He stopped and looked around at everyone while nodding his head to them. Then he gathered himself up and said loudly, "You know she never said a thing about herself. Her only regret was havin' to leave me so soon. As she passed, I was holdin' her hand and the last thing she did was to reach over and pat my hand. Then she was gone." He sank to his knees and dropped his hands to his side. "My Mom is gone," he repeated. "My Mom is gone."

The funeral was held at the Jordan family plot in Coalville. Judy had gotten permission from Ruth and Dick Jordan to bury her there. Ruth, Dick, and Dick's wife Cheryl were all so incredibly nice. Jordan was stunned by the way that everyone seemed to care deeply for his father and they didn't have any animosity towards Rosa in the least, and the feelings were for him as well. The attendance overwhelmed him. The entire Collie family was there as well as the entire Jordan family and the Orland family. Jimmy Orland had donated a beautiful headstone that read simply:

ROSA ELENA COSTILLO

LOVING MOTHER OF JORDAN COSTILLO

SHE WAS ONE OF GOD'S MOST
PRECIOUS CREATIONS

BORN FEBRUARY 10, 1924
TAKEN UNTO GOD NOVEMBER 16, 1962

After the funeral, most everyone gathered at the house of Dick and Cheryl Jordan. There were drinks and small talk for nearly an hour, then things began to breakup and people went on their way. Jordan was sitting quietly in a rocking chair on the front porch, when Jimmy came up to him and asked, "Jordan, could you and I have a short talk?"

Jordan immediately jumped to his feet. "Yes, sir," he replied. As he spoke, he tugged at the tie he still wore. He hated wearing the black suit and tie that Judy had gotten him. He thought his mother wouldn't recognize him.

"Hold on, Jordon," Jimmy laughed, "it's just some issues we need iron out. And why the 'sir' you use to call me Uncle Jimmy?"

"Well," Jordan started slowly, "that was when I looked on you and Judy as my aunt and uncle. Now, I guess you're more like a brother-in-law."

Jimmy thought about it for a minute and then said, "Yeah, I guess you're right. So, why don't we just settle on you callin' me Jimmy, okay?"

"Yes, sir, Jimmy it is," Jordan said smiling. Then after a short pause, "What kind of issues do we need to talk about?"

"It's all about you," Jimmy said as he signaled for Judy to join them.

Jordan took a deep breath and exhaled. "Yeah, I guess we need to figure out what to do with me."

"We already know what to do with you," Jimmy said simply, as Judy joined them.

"We do?" Jordan asked with a puzzled look.

"Look, why don't you sit back down and I'll grab a couple of those foldin' chairs for me and Judy." Before Jordan could say anything, Jimmy ran to the end of the porch and got two folding chair that had been used earlier for all the people who had come to the house. When he returned, he unfolded them and he and Judy seated themselves in front of Jordan, who had returned to the rocking chair.

Once they were all seated and comfortable, Jimmy started talking. "First, I need to tell you that you have a trust fund. It's a very large trust fund. In fact, it's just a little over a million dollars."

Jordan's eyes widened, "A million dollars?"

"Yes," Jimmy continued, "and I'm the executor of your trust. Your mother asked me to handle the trust for you until you reach twenty one. At that time, all the money in trust will be yours to do with as you see fit. Until that time, I'll give you a monthly income from the trust to support you."

"Did all that money come from the oil on the land you gave Mom?" Jordan asked in a soft voice.

"Yes, the largest amount of it came from the oil. Other money comes from land leases that your mom held and is part of the trust."

Jordan eyed Jimmy and Judy closely. "So, I'm rich?" He finally asked.

"You will be when you turn twenty-one. Until then, the income I will give each month from the trust will take care of you very comfortably and see you into college." Jimmy stopped talking and just stared at Jordan trying to read his expression. Jordan didn't say anything but just stared back at Jimmy. Then, Jimmy continued, "Now, for the second issue and that is how and where you will live until you get out of high school and go to college. Judy and I would love to have you stay with us in Dallas and finish high school there."

"We would really love that, Jordan," Judy inserted.

Jordan slowly stood up and looked down at them. "That's very kind of both of you, but I want to finish school in Marfa. That's were my friends are and that's where Mom's home is. I'll always keep Mom's home. I'll never sell it."

Judy lowered her head for a moment and then looked up at Jordan. "I understand," she said softly. "But we just can't leave you alone there by yourself. You'll need someone to stay with you until you graduate high school and go off to college."

"I'll be alright. I'm seventeen now and I'll be a senior next year. So, I've only got about a year and a half before I graduate."

Jimmy shook his head and stood up and looked hard at Jordan. "Your mom would never have stood for that and neither will Judy and I. You can have your way and stay in Marfa, but you will have an adult with you until you graduate. There can be no discussion on this issue."

"Who's goin' to be this adult?" Jordan asked somewhat forcibly.

Jimmy put his hand on Jordan's shoulder. "I suspected that you might want to stay in Marfa, so I made arrangements for someone just in case. She'll be there when you get back home."

"She," Jordan exclaimed. "Who's she?"

Judy flew Jordan back to Marfa in her little private racing plane. It was the same little plane she had used in the women's airplane racing circuit back in the 1930's. She loved the little plane and kept it in its original state as best she could over the years. It still had the same engine that had powered the plane back in her racing days. She had been meticulous in keeping it in top running condition. The only modification that she had made, and reluctantly, was that she had added a second cockpit behind the original cockpit to accommodate a passenger. In addition, she added a long canopy that covered both cockpits; the main cockpit in front and the added one in the back. With all these changes, of course, came modified controls so the person in back could take over and fly the plane and updated communication so the pilot in front could talk with the person in back and vice versa.

Jordan knew about Judy's days as a racer and her days, during World War II, flying with the WASP; the Women's Airforce Service Pilots. He had no fear of flying with her as he knew she was an excellent and experienced pilot. At times, Judy would turn control over to him and let him fly the powerful little plane. He loved it.

Upon arriving back in Marfa, Jordan found out who the mysterious *she* was. It was Rosa's mother; his grandmother. Jordan had never met his grandparents on his mother's side. It was always his understanding that Rosa's parents had disowned her when she decided to stay with his father instead of coming back to Mexico when her initial housekeeping job was complete. Her father had as much as called her a whore. As a result, he had never had any contact with his mother's family. In fact, he was in total shock when finding out who she was and why she was there.

Judy had taken Jordan aside and explained that her husband, Jimmy, had gone to Mexico and spent a lot of time talking with Rosa's parents about getting over the issue of disowning Rosa. Jimmy and Rosa's parents had been friends for many, many years via an oil deal Jimmy had worked out for them in the late 1930's. It was Jimmy who had initially brought Rosa to Texas to do the housekeeping and cooking for his father, while his father worked on learning all about being a flight engineer on a B-17 bomber.

No matter how much Jimmy talked, Rosa's father would not change his mind, but he did leave it up to Rosa's mother to do as she pleased. Rosa's mother, who was named Maria, was not concerned about what Rosa had done or how she did it; she only wanted to see and get to know her grandson. Now was her chance and she was not going to pass up the opportunity. She agreed to go to Marfa, Texas and stay with her grandson for the next year or so until he graduated high school and left home for college.

Although Rosa's father didn't like the idea of his wife being gone from home for so long and being in another county, he relented. Jimmy had offered to pay for Maria's time. This was not taken kindly. Rosa's father looked at Jimmy harshly and said in Spanish, "You are my friend, Jimmy Orland. And you will remain so until we meet again in God's Heaven. But, please, do not insult me. No matter how I feel it does not change the fact he is my grandson. I will take care of my wife's expenses and needs. That is my duty."

And that's the way it had all happened. Jimmy supplied Maria with a work visa and other documents she needed to stay in America as Jordan's guardian. At first, the relationship between Maria and Jordan was very strained, but over time things evolved. Jordan was fluent in Spanish but he insisted that Maria learn English if she were to stay here with him. This she did. As time went by, their relationship went from tolerance to understanding, and then to acceptance, and then to friendship. And, in the end, as Jordan left for, not college but the United States Marines, there was true family love.

CHAPTER SEVENTEEN

Kathleen's Father Has an Accident

Seventeen year old Kathleen O'Rourke paced impatiently up and down the corridor of the emergency room at the Roosevelt Hospital in Hell's Kitchen. She still wore her uniform from Saint Mary's Preparatory School. It consisted of a plain white short sleeved blouse which was tucked into a red and green plaid skirt that came to just below her knees. Her beautiful long red hair bellowed out from under a small billed cap that was red and green plaid matching her skirt. She worn long white stockings that rose to just above mid-calf and on her feet were flat black shoes that had a single thin strap that buckled on the side.

She was notified while in class about her father's accident. The school immediately supplied her transportation to the train station where she got a seat on a train from Boston to Grand Central Station in New York City. From Grand Central Station, she took a cab directly to the hospital bypassing her home. Now, she was alone in the waiting room. Her mother and Father Conway were in the room with her father. Her brother had not arrived yet. He did call the hospital to get a status on his dad and told them he was in route and to please notify his family. Strangely enough,

Rob Junior was already in route home when the accident happened. He had left the marine base at Parris Island, South Carolina on a seven day furlough the day before the accident. When he called last he was already at Grand Central Station. He had arrived there about an hour after Kathleen.

Kathleen was becoming very impatient. She had removed her cap and placed it atop her school satchel which lay in the seat next to her. Inside the satchel were some books and papers she had brought with her along with her purse. The purse was small and only contained her school ID card and some money she had picked up before leaving school.

It had been more than an hour since she had arrived and no one had come out to speak with her. She reached the decision to force herself on the desk nurse and demand to know what was going on with her father. She had just pushed herself up from her seat and started towards the desk nurse's positon, when she saw her brother come through the swinging emergency waiting room doors. Quickly she turned and ran to him.

"Thank God, a friendly face," she breathed, as she threw her arms around his waist and hugged him tightly.

He returned her hug and then lifted her face up and looked into her eyes. His faced showed fear and confusion. "What do you know?"

She pushed away from him and spread her arms out in frustration. "Not a hell of a lot," she blurred out, "all I know is what they told me at school. I've been here for over an hour by myself. Mom and Father Conway are in with Dad. No doctors have been out to see me or anythin'."

"Well, what'd they tell you at school?" He pressed.

"They just told me that Dad had been in a very serious accident and that I needed to get to Roosevelt Hospital as soon as I could. One of the nuns gave me a ride to the train station and here I am. What about you?"

"I was on my way home on the train when I was intercepted by a marine officer at the Washington D.C. station. He told me that my father had been involved in a serious accident and I needed to bypass goin' home and head directly to the hospital. And, like you, here I am."

They both stopped talking and took stock of each other.

"You look nice in that uniform," she said smiling. "I see you've gotten a couple of stripes on your sleeve since the last time we saw each other."

"Yeah, there's just no tellin' who they'll make a corporal these days," he laughed. "But look at you," he continued, "you look all grown up even in that schoolgirl uniform."

"Well," she said as she stepped back and spread her skirt out, "one more year of this thing and I'm done with Saint Mary's."

"And then what? He asked.

"Boston College," she replied simply.

"Wow," he said in admiration, "a girl from Hell's Kitchen goin' to Boston College." He shook his head smiling, "You have to give Mom and Dad credit; they did it right despite our efforts to mess it up."

They were smiling and making small talk when they saw their mother and Father Conway walking towards them with a doctor in-between them. The doctor had one arm around their mother and the other around Father Conway. Mary O'Rourke was crying profusely. The siblings looked at each other and then hurried to meet them. As they approached, Mary broke from the doctor and ran to her children throwing herself against them. She grabbed them but her legs had begun to melt away and she began to sink to her knees. Rob quickly caught her and half carried and half guided her to a seat. Mary couldn't speak through her sobbing. Father Conway sat down beside her and tried consoling her. As he did, he signaled for Rob and Kathleen to go and speak to the doctor.

Once they had the doctor a safe distance away from their mother, Rob quickly and in a demanding voice asked, "What's happenin', doctor? What's goin' on?"

The doctor seemed to hesitate looking for the right words to use.

Rob straightened up and took Kathleen by the hand. "Give it to us straight if you would, doctor. There's no need for tryin' to spare our feelin's."

"Okay," the doctor said, taking a deep breath. "My name is Doctor Mills. I've been treating your father since he was first brought into the ER.

You'll have to get the details of the accident from the police. I can only give you the results of the accident." The doctor paused briefly and then continued, "Your father's left side from just below his hip up to his lower rib cage was crushed by a very heavy cargo crate that fell from a loading crane. Although the crate shattered as it hit the cement dock, a large portion of it smashed into your father pinning him down. Unfortunately, he was pinned for nearly fifteen minutes before they could free him. By the time he got to our ER, he had massive internal bleeding and his left kidney was completely nonfunctional. His left lung had been punctured by several of his shattered ribs." The doctor stopped talking and looked from Rob to Kathleen and back again. He didn't know what else to say.

Rob gathered all his internal strength and asked, "So, you're tellin' us that our dad is dead?"

Dr. Mills straighten up and said in a much softer voice, "No, he hasn't died as I'm speaking to you. We're keeping him alive by artificial means at this time. But the internal bleeding is too massive and the damage to the kidney and lungs can't be repaired." The doctor paused again and then said with finality, "We expect your father to pass away within the hour."

Rob stepped back from the doctor; still holding Kathleen's hand. He turned and walked over to his mother pulling Kathleen along with him. Kathleen was stunned but she knew what was happening and she began to cry. By the time they reach their mother, Mary had gain control of herself thanks to the support of Father Conway. She remained seated but looked up at her children. "Although your dad is under heavy sedation, he's in control of his mental facilities. He knows he's dyin'. Before I left his room, he asked if his kids were here. I told him I wasn't sure. He said if you were here to please let him see you. I told him I would."

At this point, the doctor, who had followed Rob and Kathleen, interjected solemnly, "I recommend you go now. I'll take you to the room."

As Rob, Kathleen, and the doctor started up the corridor, Rob stopped and looked back at Father Conway. "Father, do you want to come?" He asked.

Father Conway shook his head. "No, I've already administered the last rites. I think he just wants to see you two now."

The walk down the corridor and through the ER door to their father's room only took a few minutes. As they entered the room, they saw several nurses working at various jobs and they saw their father. He was lying on his right side and there were tubes coming out of his arms and chest. There was a large tube in his mouth going down his throat. Upon entering the room, the doctor signaled for all the nurses to leave the room, which they promptly did. Dr. Mills guided Rob and Kathleen over to a position on the right side of the bed where their father could see them.

Their father's dull eyes came to life when he saw his children. He looked at Dr. Mills and tapped the tube in his mouth with his free right hand. The doctor understood what he wanted. Even though he knew it would hurry his death, the doctor gently pulled the tube from Robert O'Rourke Senior's mouth. That job done, he patted Rob and Kat on their shoulders and left the room.

Smiling, their father managed to speak with a gurgling in his voice. "Well, look at my two kids; and in their uniforms too. My, Junior, you look fine in your marine uniform. And Kathleen, that uniform can't hide the woman inside it."

Kathleen couldn't hold back her tears and Rob's eyes filled with moisture.

"Now, now, you two, we can't be cryin'. 'Cause I got somethin' important to say before I go with God. First, I'm awfully proud of both of you. You just can't imagine all the happiness you've brought me over these years." He had to stop for a second to get his breath, and then he continued, "Now, what I'd ask of you is to go out there into that world outside Hell's Kitchen and make me and your mom proud. 'Cause I'll be watchin'. God'll let me do that. Father Conway told me so." Then with the last of his strength he signaled for them to come closer. They both moved their faces to within inches of his lips. Then he spoke his last words that were so soft they could barely be understood. "Remember, Kathleen, when you were just ten years old and Rob wanted to take a switchin' for you, but you just wouldn't allow it. That was my girl. And you, Rob, standin' up for your sister the way you did. That was my boy. You see, you both have honor and love and you don't even know it." Then, his last breath escaped his mutilated body.

And so, Robert O'Rourke Senior died on October 16th, the Year of Our Lord 1962.

CHAPTER EIGHTEEN

William Leaves
the Farm

Seventeen year old William Barnett stood on the porch of the farm house leaning against one of the porch support post with his arms fold across his chest. He stared aimlessly out across the vast Barnett farm land. Today was not a happy day for William. For today, September 7th, is the day he is to leave for San Antonio and the Texas Military Institute. There, he is scheduled to enter the Senior Class of 1962.

This was all his mother's doing. Getting into the school was not easy but William is the son of a Congressional Medal of Honor winner. This had all been planned for years and was already paid for. His mother's reasoning was to make sure that William's grades met all the qualification for entrance to West Point. And what better way to do that than for William to spend his senior year at one of the most prestigious military schools in the country. And the Texas Military Institute was certainly that, and it was not far away in San Antonio, Texas.

William didn't like to argue with his mother. She would always win and she was nearly always right. However, he did remind her that he was a straight 'A' student and was in the National Honor Society, and that he really wanted to graduate with his friends at Coalville High School. He also mentioned to her that he had made All District as a wide receiver on the Coalville Mighty Miners High School football team and that the coach and the team were looking for, and needing him, to return for his senior year.

As he explained all this logic to his mother, she simply tilted her head to one side and smiled up at him, as he towered at least six inches above her short frame. Her long sandy blonde hair would fall down and hang beautifully in the air. Now, it had streaks of grey in it but that didn't take away from its beauty. Her light brown eyes would shine and seem to reflect her hair, and her gaze would look softly into his eyes. When she spoke it was very softly, "William, I think, and I'm sure if Bill were here he would too, that by passin' up graduation at Coalville for the prestige, honor, and discipline of a diploma from the Texas Military Institute, would certainly be worth the sacrifice, since, after all, you'll be goin' to West Point." After a short pause in her speaking but no pause in the soft gaze from those shining eyes, she asked, "Don't you think so?"

He was completely defeated. He shook his head from side to side and smiled back at her with a smile that reminded her so much of Billy Rob. "Mom, no wonder Dad loved you so much. Did he ever say 'no' to you?"

Knowing she had won, she said with a laugh, "Well, truthfully, he didn't get a chance to say 'no' because we almost always agreed on things."

At any rate and for whatever reason, he gave in without much of a fight. So, now here he stood on the porch waiting for his stepfather to bring the old Ford pickup around. His mom, grandma, and his Aunt Sue Ann were all on the porch with him to see him off. He stepped down from the porch and walked a short distance out onto the front yard. He unfolded his arms and stuffed his hands into his pockets. He took a long look at the farm as if it were going to be his last time to see it. He knew he would come home from TMI at Christmas and again during Spring Break. But somehow he felt uncomfortable about leaving the old farm that his family had had for many, many years. He also knew that after he graduated from TMI it would be a short summer and he would be off to West Point. Once there, how often he could get home was anybody's guess.

As he stood there looking around at the farm, he felt a soft touch on his shoulder. He turned around to see his mother standing there. He turned to face her but she didn't remove her hand from his shoulder. There were tears forming in those bright beautiful eyes. He started to speak but she held up her hand to stop him. She reached into the pocket of her house dress and pulled out a bundle of letters that were tied together tightly by a red ribbon. She handed them to William.

She choked back the tears as she spoke. "I want you to have these," she said. "These are letters between me and your dad. Some might call them love letters, but they're much more than that. They're a binding between two people. Over the next few months while you're at TMI and when you have time, I'd like for you to read them. They'll tell you a lot about your dad, but mostly they'll tell you a lot about the English girl who fell in love with a boy from Texas; so much in love that she would leave her home and family to come and live on a farm in deep East Texas. They'll help you to understand how I am and why I do the things that I do. I know making you go off to TMI is a hard thing for you. You may not know it, but it's a hard thing for me too. I guess your dad and I both had to do things we didn't want to do during that awful war. And I guess doing things you don't like, but are necessary, became part of our makeup. I learned that from your dad, and from living here in Texas." She stopped talking removed her hand from his shoulder and took a step back. She wiped the tears from her eyes and then continued in forceful voice, "Yes, I'm a girl from England and that will always be the case, but I'm as Texas as anybody in this state. You better believe that a mixture of English and Texan makes for an independent and hardheaded person. And you've got that same blood!" She held up her hand and shook her finger at him. "And don't you ever forget that, young man. Don't you ever, ever forget that!" Then, she threw her arms around his waist and buried her face in his chest.

He was holding his mom when his stepfather arrived with the pickup truck. He pulled the truck to a stop just outside the fence that surrounded the front yard. Getting out, he was smiling and waving. He was unaware of the emotional scene that had just taken place. William pushed his mom away and he picked up his bags from the porch. He walked slowly out to the pickup and pitched the bags into the back. Everyone watched him as he secured the bags and then walked back to where his mother remained standing. He reached down and took her hand and said, "What do you say, Mom, will you come with me while I say goodbye to Dad?"

She smiled at him through her tears and took his arm as they started the walked to the small Barnett grave yard.

"Hey," it was his Aunt Sue Ann yelling, "Can an aunt come along?"

"Yes and maybe an old grandma?" Sally asked.

William turned and looked back at the family he loved so deeply. "Of course you can come," he yelled signaling them to come on. Then, turning to look at his stepfather, he said firmly, "Everyone can come along. Come on Dad and join us."

John nodded his head and trotted up and took Anne's other arm.

PART FOUR

The Summer of 1967
The Young Adults

CHAPTER NINETEEN

Kellie Leaves Medical School

Twenty-two year old Kellie Anderson sat on a bench on the campus of The University of Minnesota Medical School in Minneapolis, Minnesota. It was early August and it was not hot but it was overly warm. She wore a pair of thigh-length blue shorts and a gold University of Minnesota t-shirt. On her feet was a pair of low-cut white tennis shoes without socks. Kellie had blossomed into a very beautiful woman. Her body had developed into a slim and shapely figure. Her hair remained a dark black and her blue eyes still varied from a light blue to a cloudy blue depending on her mood. Now her eyes were clouded over into their moody mode. She stared at the entrance to the large Medical School Administration Building. She had a difficult decision to make. A decision that she knew would not only affect her but also her father.

Two years ago, Kellie had graduated from the University of Minnesota in St. Paul with a Bachelor's Degree in Biology. She had graduated early because she had attended summer school for two semesters, and she had been at the top of her class. After that, she was accepted into medical school and, last year, she had finished her first year; again at the top of her class. Now it was August 1967 and she was here to register for the fall semester of her second year of medical school.

But over the summer things had changed for her. The war in Vietnam was raging and men and women were being killed and wounded. She felt a terrible need to go there and help; to help her country in the best capacity she could. She had seen the demonstrations against the war all over the country and even here on her own campus. She despised those demonstrations with a passion. Her father had served during the Korean War as a surgeon in a Mobil Army Surgical Hospital or MASH unit. He had come home from the war as a major in the army reserves. He still remained in that capacity today, except now he was a Lt. Colonel. She hoped that his military experiences would ease the pain for what she was about to do.

She reached over and picked up her school briefcase that was setting beside her on the bench. Reaching inside, she pulled out the Register Nurse Certification that she had obtained during July by passing the National Council Licensure Examination. Passing the exam had been easy for her with her background; a BS in Biology and one year of medical school.

She held it in her hand. She would stare at it and then look back to the entrance of the administration building. An internal struggled raged in her. She knew what she wanted to do and she knew how her father was going to take it. She wanted to enlist in the United States Army Nurse Corps. She had already discussed it with a recruiter at the main university campus. The plan was for her to enlist, and then go through the army basic training, then the Advanced Individual Training, or AIT as it was called, and then be commissioned as a 2nd lieutenant. At this point, she would be shipped to Vietnam at her specific request. It all seemed so simple until she would glance back at the entrance to the administration building.

She sat there on the bench for nearly an hour as the battle raged inside her. Then finally with a deep breath, she put the certificate back into her briefcase, picked up the briefcase and turned away from the administration building and started back home.

When she got back home, her father was in his study working on some medical reports. The door to his study was open. She thought about going straight to her room but decided to face the issue here and now. Putting her briefcase down just outside the door to her father's study, she knocked gently on the door frame.

He looked up and smiled and his eyes sparkled behind his reading glasses, "Come in, come on in here," he said happily. He leaned back in his office chair and asked, "Well, how did registration go?"

She entered the room slightly and then leaned back against the door frame. "It didn't," she said simply.

He looked surprised and removed his glasses. "What do you mean?" He asked.

"I mean," she said haltingly. "I didn't register."

His face took on a very worried look. "Can you explain or clarify that for me?"

She pushed herself away from the door frame and walked over and sat down in a chair across from his desk. In her mind, she decided there was no need to talk around the subject. So, she just looked him in the eyes and told the truth. "I've decided to forego medical school for a short while. Please keep in mind that I'm not quitting. I still intend to become a doctor. I'm just going to delay it for a couple of years."

To say he was surprised would be an understatement. He slowly stood up and looked down at her. "Is this a joke?"

"It's no joke, Dad. And please sit down and hear me out."

As he sat back down, he pitched his reading glasses on the desk. He settled back in his chair, folded his hands across his chest and said slowly, "Okay, I'm listening."

She kept her cloudy blue eyes fixed on his. "I've decided to join the Army Nurse Corps. I've already gotten my RN certification. I'll go through army basic training and AIT and then be commissioned a 2nd lieutenant. With my medical background, I'll have no trouble getting an assignment to Vietnam."

"Vietnam!" He exclaimed. "Why would you do that?"

"Well, Dad, I guess a better question would be why shouldn't I do that?"

"I'll tell you why you shouldn't," he shouted, as he leaned forward in his chair and unfolded his hands, "first, because you could get killed and second because you can serve humanity better as a doctor. And in addition to that, you've already put in *FIVE* years to become a doctor."

"Dad, before we take this any farther can I add something that I feel is very important to this discussion?"

He shrugged his shoulders and again leaned back in his chair. "Of course you can. We've always been upfront with each other."

She continued to look into his eyes, but her eyes soften and they changed back to their light blue mode.

"Oh, God," he murmured, "your eyes have changed. I probably don't have a chance now."

She only smiled at him and spoke to him in a soft and reasonable tone, "I know that Grandpa Anderson fought in World War II with the Big Red One, The US Army First Division. He landed with them at Omaha Beach. And I know you did your part in the Korean War with the one-oh-oh-seven MASH unit."

He held up his hand to stop her. "What does all that have to do with you?"

She spread her hands palms up in frustration, "It's simple; I want to do my part now."

He shook his head back and forth. "No, no, those were different wars. You've seen all these protesters. Grandpa and I came back to honors. You'll probably come back to a bunch of idiot bullshit. You need to think about that."

"I've seen the protesters and I've thought about it." Then she paused and then asked pointedly, "Is it because I'm a woman and I'm your daughter?"

He move uneasily in his chair but didn't reply.

"Because if it is, I'm proud to be a woman and I'm proud to be your daughter and a member of the Anderson family. But a lot of good women are already over there making a difference right now. And, yes, some have died. But, Dad, don't you see, all of them are somebody's daughter, or somebody's wife, or somebody's mother. If I don't become part of it, Dad, I'll never be able to hold my head up in this family again. I'll never be able to justify it to myself."

She was near tears, but she didn't cry. Then, she stood up and looked down at him. Her eyes were still the light blue. She straightened her shoulders and said, "But, if you tell me not to go, I won't go. Tomorrow I'll go back to the administration building and register for the fall semester."

He was silent for a long time but she didn't move; she continued to stand straight with squared shoulders. He leaned forward over his desk and stared at her intently. "Kel," he said in a surprised voice, "are those tears I see in your eyes?"

She stiffened, "*They most certainly are not*," she replied firmly, "my eyes are watering from emotional stress. It's a medical condition you should be aware of, doctor."

He smiled. "Yes, I'm aware of it."

"As I've told you many times before, there'll be time enough to cry later. Right now we need to resolve this issue. So, do I go and register tomorrow or not?"

He stood up and walked around his desk and took his daughter into his arms. "No, Kel, you don't need to register tomorrow. You do what you feel you have to do and you'll do it with my blessing."

Kellie Anderson would follow her plan and became a 2nd lieutenant in the Army Nurse Corps. After some special training and basic training at Fort Sam Houston in Texas, she was ready for deployment. But it would be March of 1968 before she was on a plane headed for Vietnam. By that time, and because of her medical background, she had already been promoted to 1st lieutenant.

CHAPTER TWENTY

Veronica Joins the Army Nurse Corps

Twenty-two year old Veronica Mann stood in the line of graduates at the graduation ceremonies at Texas Woman's University in Denton, Texas. She was dressed in her graduation cap and gown and wearing a huge smile. She was still extremely beautiful but the girlish look had gone and was replaced that of a woman. Her hair was still a shiny blonde and it hung loosely from under her cap. Overall, she looked like that same teenage girl from high school, except there was a maturity about her now.

The line was long as there were over two hundred students graduating, and they were lined up in alphabetical order, which met that Mann was more than half way back in line. It was early June and it was hot dressed in the cap and gown with her regular clothes on underneath. Even the air conditioning in the auditorium couldn't keep the graduates from sweating.

But Veronica didn't mind. Her big smile was mostly for her benefactor who sat with her parents in the front row of the audience watching the ceremonies. That benefactor of course was Michael Conners. After Jodie's death, he had kind-of adopted Veronica and Marge. He had them over for meals, took them on trips and, in short, used them to replace Jodie. At first, Veronica and Marge's parents were suspicious of the whole thing, but Michael Conners won them over by talking with each family and assuring them of his intentions. And those intentions were to help the two girls in any way he could. He was very wealthy and wanted to do these things in memory of his lost daughter. Both sets of parents, slowly but surely, allowed Michael Conners to become the benefactor of their girls. This lasted all through the rest of high school and then Michael Conners offer to pay the tuition and upkeep of both girls to any college they wished. Of course, the parents of both girls were very thankful but didn't want to be in debt to Michael Conners.

In Veronica's case it was the only way she could afford to go to college because her family simply didn't have the money even for a state school. So, after much discussion between Veronica's parents and Michael Conners, they finally relented for the sake of their daughter. In Marge's case, she had already gotten an academic scholarship to Abilene Christian College in Abilene, Texas. But still, Michael Conners insisted on helping her with her dorm fees and other needs. Marge's family also finally relented. Marge, because of her academic standing and moving ahead in her senior year, graduated high school before Veronica and didn't graduate with her original class.

Veronica had chosen Texas Woman's University for one reason and one reason only; because it had the best nursing school in the State of Texas and was one of the best in the entire country. After seeing how the nurses worked and took care of Jodie in her final days, she swore that, given the chance, she would become a Registered Nurse and be able to help people in need. The memory of Jodie was always with her, and so was the guilt.

Over the years in college, Marge and Veronica drifted apart. Being miles apart and concentrating on their school work took its toll on their once tight friendship. Always being the smart one, Marge made it through ACC with honors. Veronica had had great expectations for

Marge, but strangely enough those great expectations took an entirely different route than Veronica could have ever envisioned. For Marge, the once up standing member of the Tart Trio, met a nice Christian boy at ACC and fell deeply in love. She was married three months after she graduated from ACC. She moved to Houston with her husband who was getting in on the ground floor of the newly booming computer business. The last Veronica heard from Marge she was happily married, pregnant, and enjoying the life of a housewife.

Now, Veronica moved slowly along as each graduate accepted their degrees and said a few words and then moved on off the stage. It seemed an eternity, but at last Veronica was standing at the foot of the steps leading up to the stage. Then she finally heard, "Our next graduate is Veronica Mann who has earned a Bachelor of Science degree in Nursing. Please come forward Veronica."

Veronica, as gracefully as she could, walked up the steps and over to the College Dean who handed her the degree. Veronica accepted the degree with a slight nod of her head and then stepped to the microphone. She held the degree up and smiled down at her parents and Michael Conners and softly said into the microphone, "I accept this degree in the name of my friend forever, Jodie Conners." She then turned and hurried down the steps and off the stage. There her parents and Michael Conners awaited her. There were many smiles, hugs, and kisses as everyone congratulated her.

Finally, after things had calmed down and Veronica had removed her cap and gown, they all sat round a table in the campus lunchroom. Everyone was sipping iced tea and making small talk when Michael asked, "So, what're your plans now that you've got that degree? Maybe there's a job I can help you with?"

She smiled at Michael. She loved him almost as much as she loved her parents. He had been so good to her without asking for anything in return. "Michael," she said tenderly, "you've done so much for me and I can never repay you. But now it's time for me to move on and be my own person. I'm not a child or teenager anymore. I'm a grown woman and I've already made a decision on what I'm goin' to do."

She stopped talking and took a long sip of tea. Everyone at the table was waiting for her to continue but she didn't. Finally, her mother blurred out, "So, girl, out with it. What 're you planin'?"

"Well, actually, I've already done it. I've committed to enlist in the United States Army Nurse Corps upon receiving my degree in nursing, and I now have that degree. I want to go to Vietnam and help those boys over there." Then, looking directly at Michael, she continued, "I think it's what Jodie would do."

To her amazement, no one seemed surprised. Her mother and father both got up and reached over and hugged her warmly. Her mother was in tears but managed to say, "I know you'll do yourself proud, Baby."

"But if you forget to write home, I'll personally come over there and give you a good spankin'," her father chimed in.

The talking and laughter continued into the evening before it finally began to break up. As she and her parents headed for the lunchroom door, Michael lagged behind. Just as Veronica and her parents were walking out the door, Michael called out to Veronica. She stopped and turned back to face him.

"Remember The Tart Trio, Veronica," he said with emotion. "Always remember The Tart Trio, and you know, I think what you're doin' is exactly what Jodie would've done." With that he gave a short wave and turned and walked away in the opposite direction.

Veronica Mann did join the Army Nurse Corps that August. She would go through all the army training and special requirements. She worked hard and with extreme dedication. To her it had seemed like an eternity but in March of 1968 she was deployed to Vietnam as a 2nd lieutenant in the United States Army Nurse Corps.

CHAPTER TWENTY-ONE

Kyle, His Dad and Helicopters

Twenty-five year old 1ˢᵗ Lieutenant Kyle Collie paced nervously up and down the hallway just outside the office of Lt. Coronel James Billings the Commander of Camp Walters. Camp Walters was the main helicopter training base for the United States Army and it was where Kyle had been stuck for most of the last two years. He was angry and frustrated but he had to be careful and not take it out on the commander, especially since he didn't know why he'd been summoned to see the commander.

As he paced, his mind went over and over things. Maybe his father had been right and he should've joined the Navy and flew planes off a carrier deck. But he had been set on flying helicopters in combat. The Vietnam War was raging and he was still at Camp Walters doing different training jobs and being the Executive Officer of a training company. People came and went but he was still here. In fact, some of the new trainees called him "The Old Man."

He guessed it was too late to reflect back on what he should've or could've done. When he graduated from the University of Texas in June of 1964, things were going great. With his ROTC background and a Bachelor of Science Degree in Aeronautics, he had no trouble getting into the army as an officer with his pick of assignments. Naturally, his pick was to be a helicopter pilot. So, after the standard army officers training and other courses he was commissioned a 2nd lieutenant and sent off to Camp Walters to learn to fly helicopters. And did he ever learn to fly helicopters. He learned to fly almost every model of helicopter that the army had. He even got a shot a flying the new AH-1 Cobra attack gunship. But no matter what he did or how well he did it, they liked him as the XO of a training company. A year ago they had promoted him to 1st lieutenant, but that didn't ease his frustration. Being a 2nd lieutenant and flying combat missions was better than being a 1st lieutenant and being the XO of a training company at Camp Walters, Texas.

On one of his last leaves when he went home, he talked it all over with his dad. But there was nothing he could do. Back in 1964 after Kyle had graduated from UT, his dad had retired from the Navy and it had been total retirement; no staying in the reserves. So, he was Retired Admiral Daryl Collie now. As a result, his mom and dad took off to travel the world. His little sister, Lilly, had just graduated from Baylor University this last May. All of this was happening in his family and yet here he was still at Camp Walters.

As he was thinking about all these things and he was continuing his pacing, he heard a voice behind him ask, "Lieutenant, Collie?"

He spun around a little too quickly and had to regain his balance. He smiled in embarrassment at the Staff Sergeant standing before him with a quizzical look on his face. "Yes, Sergeant, I'm Lieutenant Collie."

"The Commander will see you now, Lieutenant, please follow me."

The sergeant opened the door to the commander's office then stepped back and held it open for Kyle. After Kyle had entered, the sergeant quickly left the room shutting the door behind him. Kyle quickly stepped before the commander's desk and came to stiff attention. "Lieutenant Collie reporting as ordered, Sir," he said crisply.

"Yes, fine, Lieutenant, please take a seat." Lt. Coronel Billings was a tall man in his middle fifties with a full head of salt and pepper hair. He looked physically fit and had a small dark mustache on what could be called a handsome face. He fumbled around his desk for several minutes and finally picked up a folder. He opened it up and laid it out before him on his desk. "Well, Lieutenant, your file tells me you've done an excellent job since you've been with us here at Camp Walters. Your fitness reports from your Company Commander have been exemplary."

"Thank you, Sir," Kyle replied.

The Commander flipped through a few more pages and then looked up at Kyle with a small smile on his face. "I also have here a request for transfer to a combat unit in Vietnam. In fact, Lieutenant, it seems I've been getting one of these request from you each and every month for the last year." He paused and then continued still wearing his small smile. "I thought I might call you in and resolve this continual request issue, Lieutenant."

Kyle move uneasily in his chair and simply replied, "Yes, Sir."

"Looking at your record, Lieutenant, you're in perfect position to take over a company of your own. And it seems obvious that you would do us a good job."

Kyle struggled to keep his expression neutral but his mind was saying to him, here it comes. There're goin' to promote me to a Company Commander and keep me her for who knows how long.

"However," Coronal Billings said standing up, "I also know that you're one hell of a helicopter pilot and are qualified on most every model we have on this base. It's for this reason that I've decided to grant your transfer request."

Kyle shot to his feet to stiff attention with an unbridled smile on his face. "Thank you, Sir. I think the Commander has made a wise decision."

Coronal Billings' smile turned very serious. "Stand at ease, Lieutenant," he said in a firm command tone, "and listen up."

Kyle's smile faded and he assumed the position of at ease.

"In truth," the Commander continued, "you've been picked to join a special unit in Vietnam. You'll be flying the Huey UH dash IC Heavy Scout gunship. You'll be stationed at a special field code named 'Cobra Umbrella One'. On this field will be UH dash IC Heavy Scout gunships, the new AH dash 1 Cobra attack gunships, and other variations of your UH dash 1C Heavy Scout. Your mission will be twofold. First, you'll support the transport choppers carrying troops and supplies into battles zones. This part of the mission will be handled mostly by the AH dash 1 Cobra's, but on large assaults the Heavy Scout's will be needed also. Now the second part of the mission will involve your Heavy Scout's almost exclusively. Five klicks from your field there's a MASH unit. That MASH unit is in a very vulnerable spot. Its job is to get wounded in, treated, and then transported to an EVAC base as fast as humanly possible. Of course, the wounded will be brought in and out by medivac choppers. Your job and the job of the other Heavy Scout's, will be to give high cover to the medivac choppers as they come in and go out. You're to stay above the MASH unit and keep the bad guys away from the MASH unit itself and the medivac choppers."

After a short pause, he came around his desk and stood within inches of Kyle's face. They were about the same height so they were nearly nose-to-nose. He then continued, "Most of the pilots for this special mission are coming from right here at Camp Walters. I feel a special responsibility for the success of this mission because you guys were trained here by me and my staff. *DO NOT* let me down, Lieutenant! And *DO NOT* look to be a glory guy or a hot head! *DO YOUR JOB! I DO NOT* want to get any report back here of one single medivac chopper being shot down, or that any member of that MASH unit has been killed or wounded. You guys are representing Camp Walters and I expect you to act like it! Is all of that clear, Lieutenant?"

Kyle didn't move but continued to stand nose-to-nose with the Commander. "Yes, Sir," he said with authority, "I understand and will comply."

The Commander nodded and then turned and walked back behind his desk. "Good," he said as if satisfied, "so, here's what's next. From here you'll go to the Command Center and pick up your orders. They've already been cut and are waiting for you. From there you'll pack your gear and go on a thirty day leave. Your orders will tell you where and when to report after your leave. I wish you luck. Now, are there any questions, Lieutenant?"

Kyle came back to attention and said, "No, Sir, there are no questions. But I would like to say thank you for your confidence in me and for assignin' me to this mission. It has been an honor servin' with you, Sir." Kyle saluted and when the Commander returned his saluted he turned sharply and started for the door.

"Lieutenant," the Commander shouted after him.

Kyle stopped and turned back and faced the Commander with a questioning look on his face.

"There's one last thing, Lieutenant," the Commander mused as he opened his desk drawer and brought out a small box. He handed it to Kyle and continued, "We can't very well put a lieutenant in command of a gunship."

Kyle took the small box from the Commander and opened it. In it was a set of captain's bars.

Kyle arrived home on leave to find that is parents were on a trip to Canada to avoid the Texas summer heat. His little sister Lilly was holding down the fort at home until they returned. Lilly was happy to see him but not so happy to hear about his deployment to Vietnam.

During his leave they spent a lot of time together talking, going to movies and eating out nearly every night. Kyle marveled at his 'little twenty-one year old sister'. She was the spitin' image of their mother except for her height. Lilly was nearly five feet ten inches tall and towered over her mother. She had shiny long blonde hair, light hazel-green eyes set in a beautifully structured face, and her body was slim and well-shaped. As he had always said, she was goin' to be a heartbreaker. Along with being beautiful, she had just graduated from Baylor University, her Grandma Collie's and Aunt Cheryl's alma mater, with a Bachelor of Arts Degree in Education. To top it all off, she had informed him that she already had accepted a teaching job in the small town of Sulphur Springs, Texas, which was only about a hundred miles north of Coalville. She would be teaching history at Austin Elementary School. But she had emphasized that elementary school was just going to be her training ground. She fully intended to keep going until she was a full professor back at Baylor. Kyle had no doubt she could do it.

The time he was able to spend with Lilly Jo was beyond precious to him. He had hoped that he would be able to see his parents before he left but it was not to be. They weren't due back until more than a week after he had to leave. As the time came and he was packing his bags, Lilly came into his room. She sat down on the bed as he stuffed things into his duffle bag. "You *are* goin' to be careful over there aren't you?" She asked as her hazel-green eyes began to water.

Kyle looked at her and his love for her nearly tore his heart out. Then he laughed and said, "You know me sister dear. I always take care of myself."

"I do know you, Kyle," she choked, "why do you think I'm askin'?"

He stopped packing and grabbed her by the shoulders and pulled her to him. They hugged each other for several long minutes until; finally, Kyle pushed them apart. "Now," he said sternly, "you must watch out for Mom and Dad. Sulphur Springs is only up the road a piece. Can you do that?"

She had stepped back and put her hands on her hips. "You know I will," she replied with tears now rolling down her cheeks.

"Next! And this is important," he said pointing his finger at her. "You watch yourself. You've turned into a beautiful woman and guys are goin' to be after you like bees after honey. You be sure you get a good one, Lilly Jo. And be sure Mom and Dad meet him. Don't be rebellious and make a stupid mistake. I'm goin' to be gone for at least two years so I'm goin' to have to count on your brains and good judgement. Now, you tell me here and now if I can do that? I need you to swear it to me."

She tilted her head to one side and her long hair hung down loosely. The tears rolled down her cheeks and dripped to the floor. Pulling herself together she stood up straight and said chokingly, "I swear it. You can count on me, Big Brother. No guy's goin' to get hold of me unless you say, 'Lilly Jo he's okay'."

"Or Mom and Dad," he corrected.

"No," she stated firmly, "not 'til my big brother says he's okay."

Three weeks later Captain Kyle Collie would be in Vietnam.

CHAPTER TWENTY-TWO

Jordan and the United States Marines

Twenty-two year old Sergeant Jordan Costillo looked out the window of the C-47 cargo plane in which he was riding. He could see the Dallas skyline as the plane banked sharply to align itself into a holding pattern. The pilot had informed them that their gate at Dallas Love Field was not ready and they would be circling for maybe ten or fifteen minutes. It was only his second trip home since joining the marines after graduating from high school in 1963. He had been a marine now for just over four years. He leaned back in his seat and thought back over the last four years and the things that had happened to bring him to this second trip home and to what he had to tell his family. He closed his eyes and his mind floated back into time as if he were in a time machine.

After graduating from high school, everyone had expected him to go to Texas A & M as his half-brother Dick Jordan had. But what no one

knew was that Jordan had been speaking with Dick via telephone off and on during his entire senior year. The reason for these conversations was the United States Marines. Jordan knew all about Dick's heroics during World War II with the First Marine Division on Guadalcanal, Peleliu, and Okinawa. Dick had won the Silver Star at Peleliu and the Navy Cross at Okinawa. He was also awarded the Purple Heart with two clusters. Although Dick was now retired, he still had a lot of pull in the Marine Corps as he had retired a brigadier general. And it was that pull that Jordan wanted to use.

The telephone conversations were not getting the results that Jordan had hoped for. So, during the Christmas break in his senior year, Jordan managed a trip to Coalville to visit with Dick and his sister-in-law Cheryl. He would have an open discussion with Dick face-to-face.

The discussion didn't start out as Jordan had hoped for. Dick was fully aware of what Jordan wanted to talk about and was not completely pleased with the topic.

"Look, Jordan," Dick said with a certain level of discuss, "why did you pick Christmas for this little get together?"

"Because I probably can't get away again until graduation," Jordan replied with an equal level of irritation. "This is goin' to be my last chance to talk you into helpin' me."

Dick looked at him in frustration. "I told you over the phone that I don't agree with your plan of goin' into the marines before college. My God, Jordan, you're a rich kid. You can go to any university you want; it doesn't have to be A & M."

"It's not a question of the university," Jordan almost shouted. "I just don't want to continue school at this point. I want to get my military obligation done first. Anyway they'll probably draft me."

"No," Dick interjected. "Not if you get a deferment. You get a deferment and make good grades and you'll be fine."

"What about my obligation, Big Brother?" Jordan asked in a much softer tone. "What about that?"

Dick turned to look at Cheryl, who had been sitting quietly listening to her husband and brother-in-law shout at each other. He obviously was looking for some support but she only shrugged her shoulders and said nothing at first. There was a long silence and the tension hung heavy in the room. Finally Cheryl stood up. "If you two gentlemen will allow me, I can put in my two cents worth."

"Go ahead and speak your piece," Dick said welcoming what he thought was going to be some support on his behalf.

"This is what I know," she began, "durin' the Second World War, my husband served in the marines. He served with honor and courage. But he served much more than he had to."

Dick started to speak but Cheryl held up her hand to stop him. "I have the floor," she said firmly. Dick stepped back and bowed slightly yielding to her. Then she continued, "There was nothin' on God's green earth that would keep him from his beloved First Marine Division. He was wounded twice and durin' his convalescence he was miserable because his division went to war without him. As soon as he could he rejoined the division. Not me, not our little twin babies, not his mother, not even the marines could stop him from goin'."

Cheryl paused and turned and looked directly at Jordan. "That, my dear brother-in-law was his *obligation* as he saw it." Then, turning to look into Dick's eyes, she said, "You two have the same father. A father who felt the *obligation* to fly a combat mission and get himself killed. The same blood runs in your veins. Dick, my beloved husband, there's nothin' you can say or do to change Jordan's mind. He's goin' to go with or without your help. Can't you see that? Can't you?" She was almost yelling now.

Dick pulled his eyes away from Cheryl's fixed stare and looked back to face Jordan. He let out a long slow breath. "Your obligation can be fulfilled after school," he said, and then quickly held up his hand to silence Jordan who was about to speak. "But havin' said that; tell me again what it is you'd like for me to do."

Jordan relaxed his body as he had been standing almost rigid. A small smile crossed his face. The smile wasn't a victory smile but a smile of relief. "First, I want to thank both of you for workin' with me on this and I can see why everyone has such a high opinion of you, Cheryl." Then taking a step closer to Dick, "What I want from you Big Brother is for you to use your influence to make sure after basic trainin' I get assigned to the First Division and I get assigned to a Marine Recon Battalion."

Dick looked surprised. "You mean you want to be in Recon?"

Jordan nodded and said, "Yes I do."

"You do realize that the Marine Reconnaissance Battalion is the toughest outfit in the Corps?"

Jordan again nodded his head. "Yes, I realize that."

Dick reached over and put his hands on Jordan's shoulders. "This is what I can do for you. I can see to it that you get assigned to the First Division and I can get you into the Recon trainin' program. But, this is what I can't do for you. I can't help you make it in Recon. The trainin' is tough, hard, and unforgivin'. You'll have to make Recon all on your own. Like any other elite group it's a brotherhood. You'll have to earn that brotherhood yourself; I will not intervene in anyway." Dick pause for a moment and shook Jordan's shoulders gently. "Is all of what I said understood and do you agree to all of it?"

Jordan reached up and put his hands on Dicks. "It is all understood and it's all fair. I couldn't ask for anythin' more."

"One last thing," Dick said dropping his hands from Jordan's shoulders and stepping back, "it's up to you to make this family of ours understand why I'm doin' this, and that it's still against my better judgment."

Jordan put on a huge grin showing his fine white teeth. "Not to worry Big Brother, I'll be sure that everyone knows this is all on me."

Dick turned to Cheryl and laughed, "This kid," he said pointing at Jordan, "is goin' to be the richest marine in the corps."

Jordan was brought back from his mental time travel by the sharp banking of the plane as it lined up to enter the landing pattern. After nearly four years in the marines, he was now under orders to report to the Oakland Terminal for deployment to Vietnam. After years of training, including basic training, Recon training, several different NCO schools, and even a language school, he was finally on his way to a theater of war. The language school had taught him Vietnamese. Since he already spoke Spanish fluently, picking up Vietnamese had been easy for him.

He was allowed a fifteen day leave to visit his family before deployment. His first stop was here in Dallas to meet with Judy and Jimmy. They had been very kind to help him when he had joined the marines. Since his grandmother had returned to Mexico, there was no one to watch the house and he didn't want to sell it. So, Jimmy had stepped in once again and made arrangements for a property management firm to oversee it and keep it in good repair. He owed Judy and Jimmy more than he could ever repay. From Dallas, he would rent a car and drive down to Coalville to visit everyone down there and let them know he was on his way to Vietnam. Judy and Jimmy already knew as he had called them right after he had gotten his orders.

In reality, the entire family group down in Coalville had been kind to him. They had been shocked when he bypassed college for the marines but they all had adjusted to it and now supported him. He was actually looking forward to seeing the entire clan in Coalville; the Collie family, the Jordan family, the Barnett family, and, of course, the Orland family. All the families were intertwined with each other and he felt so very, very lucky to be a part of it all.

CHAPTER TWENTY-THREE

Kathleen Graduates Boston College

When Father Kelvin Conway entered the office at the back of the church on the campus of Boston College, he was surprised to see twenty-two year old Kathleen O'Rourke sitting calmly in one of the office's nice leather chairs. She had her feet propped up on an elegant looking hassock and was sipping on a bottle of Coke. Although the graduation ceremonies had been over with for a couple of hours, she was still wearing her graduation cap and gown. As he removed his jacket, she smiled and pointed her bottle of Coke at him and said in a cheerful tone, "Hello Father, I was beginnin' to wonder if you were ever goin' to show up."

He hung his jacket up and smiled back at here. "And to what do I own this honor of havin' a newly Boston College graduate in my humble presence?"

She stopped smiling and un-propped her feet. Sitting up straight in the chair, she placed the half empty Coke bottle on a small table beside the chair. She took off her cap and put it in her lap. Then, in a serious tone, she spoke very softly, "I just couldn't leave without tellin' you I could've never done any of this without you."

Father Conway held up his hand and waved off her comment. Then he asked with a puzzled look on his face, "Before this goes any farther, how did you know I'd be here? This office is used by many visitin' clergy."

A small smile returned to her face. "I have my ways, Father, I have my ways. And, Father, don't wave off what I'm tryin' to say. It means a lot to me."

He took a seat behind the desk, folded his hands and looked across at her with a great deal of love. "You must understand, Kat, that it wasn't I who got the Bachelor of Science Degree in Nursing, it was you. You can wear that Registered Nurse's emblem with great pride. You worked hard for it and sacrificed a lot for it."

She lowered her head so their eyes wouldn't meet. "But I owe so much too so many. My mom and dad for putting their hard earned money aside for me, and then me gettin' Rob's college money when he went into the marines. And, of course, there's you Father. Without you workin' so hard to get me that grant from the church, I could've never made it."

Father Conway titled his head and tried to look down at her eyes but she kept her face toward the floor. "I seem to recall," he said rubbing his chin, "that you worked as a waitress three nights a week for just about three years."

She looked up at him and her eyes were damp. "Aren't you goin' to let me say thank you?"

"You've already said thank you by gettin' your degree."

"You know, Father, that sounds just like you." She wiped her eyes and the small smile slowly spread across her face again.

"Okay now, turnin' to a more important issue," he started, "now that you've got that fancy degree what're goin' to do with it?"

"I've already done it," she replied simply.

"Really," Father Conway exclaimed. "And what've you gone and done?"

"I've joined the United States Army Nurse Corps. Actually I haven't joined yet. I had to get my degree first, but I committed to them and they've been waitin' on me. I report for trainin' next week."

Father Conway stood up and went over to her. He put his hands on her shoulders and pulled her to her feet. Her cap fell to the floor. He then hugged her to him tightly. He held her for a long minute and then pushed her back but continued to hold on to her shoulders. "I'm so proud of you," he stammered. "With you in the army and your brother in the marines, the military better get ready because the Irish are a comin'. And speakin' of that brother of yours isn't his tour in Vietnam just about up? Shouldn't he be comin' home soon?"

Kathleen dropped her head and stepped back from him. "Yeah, he should've been home already," she said without looking up.

"So, where is he?"

Kathleen looked up at him and rocked back on her heels. "He extended for another tour," she said softly. "He got promoted to Staff Sergeant, got himself a top secret clearance, and now works for the Navy Security Group. He's into some kind of intelligence work and I'm worried sick about 'im."

Father Conway took a deep breath and said, "Well, I guess he knows what he's doin'. I guess you're still gettin' letters from 'im?"

"Not much anymore," she replied, "since he's been in this intelligence stuff things have gone dark. I hardly hear from him at all. Mom is worried but she tries to keep it from me."

"Do you think you'll end up in Vietnam?" He asked slowly.

"Well, that's my plan."

"So, you'll both be there at the same time I guess."

"I guess," she said simply."

Then she stood on her tip-toes and planted a big kiss on his face. She reached down and picked up her cap and slipped it under her arm. "I gotta get goin'. I got a million things to do before I leave." When she reached the door she stopped and turned back and looked at Father

Conway. He was watching her intently. Then she said in a sad voice, "You know I know don't you, Father?"

His gaze fell to the floor as he lowered his head. "I figured you did," he said without looking up. "Like you said, 'you've got your ways'."

With a voice breaking with emotion she said, "You know the old church in Hell's Kitchen just isn't goin' to be the same without you."

"Well, Kat, I'm a soldier in the Catholic army. The General has seen fit to promote me to a Bishop and I follow orders."

"You could've turned it down couldn't you?"

"Yes, I could've. But just like your brother is a good marine, and just like you're goin' to be a good soldier in the army, I have to do what's right for our order. You can see that can't you?"

She winked at him, "Yeah, I can see that. Where're they sendin' you?"

"I'll be goin' to Washington DC."

"You give 'em hell down there, Father. I'll bet they've never see a Bishop like you're goin' to be. I wish I could be there when you start stirrin' the pot. But you know, Bishop Kelvin Conway doesn't seem to have the same ring to it as Father Kelvin Conway."

With that she slowly walked out the door and closed it gently behind her.

Kathleen did report for training the next week, but she had to ask for a three week extension to help her mother. As thing were now, Mary O'Rourke would be completely alone in the house. Her husband had died, her son was in the marines, and now her daughter was leaving for the army. The house that had once seemed so small and cramped now seemed large and empty. Mary urged her daughter not to worry about her and to leave for the army straight-away. She insisted she had enough money from Robert's insurance and the small pension from the Longshoreman's Union. Plus, Rob was sending her a small allotment from the marines.

But it wasn't the money that worried Kathleen, it was the loneliness. She fretted about how her mother would handle the loneliness. Her mother assured Kathleen that she had many things to keep her busy and she had good neighbors and the local bar where the neighborhood gathered often. She admitted that she was going to miss Father Conway, but that she would continue to go to church and support the new Father, who had the good Irish name of William Muldoon. She also spoke of Jenny Kelly down the street that had a son in the Navy. The two of them had agreed to meet twice a week to work on scrapbooks for the children in the military.

Mary tried very hard to put Kathleen's mind at ease. But, in the end, Kathleen stayed with her mother and helped get things organized the entire three weeks of the extension. Finally though, in August, Kathleen did leave and start her training at Fort Sam Houston in Texas. It was a long process but not very hard for Kathleen. She had prepared herself mentally and physically for what she wanted to do. It was in early December of 1967 that Kathleen was commissioned a 2nd lieutenant in the United States Army Nurse Corps. Then, just after Christmas, she received her deployment orders. She would leave for Vietnam in March of 1968.

CHAPTER TWENTY-FOUR

William Graduates from West Point

Twenty-two year old 1ˢᵗ Lieutenant William Barnett stood at the gate of the Barnett Cemetery on the Barnett Farm. The farm still carried the Barnett name even though his mother had remarried and now carried the name Barnes. Actually, she insisted that her full name was Anne Marie Fairchild Barnett Barnes. In his absence to West Point, his mother had made changes to the cemetery. All the headstones were clean and stood straight. The old fence around the cemetery had been replaced with a new freshly painted white picket fence. The gate was about a foot taller than the rest of the fence and had a shiny black latch on it. All the graves had flower holders attached to the headstones and were all filled with a variety of beautiful flowers. The grass was neatly cut and a bright green.

William turned to face his mother who had walked with him to the grave yard. "You've done an amazin' job with this place," he said softly. "How do you manage to keep the grass so green?"

"I water the hell out of it," she replied smiling.

Then he said grimly, "And our little cemetery keeps gettin' bigger."

He turned back to the gate and lifted the latch and pushed the gate open. It swung open easily and quietly. It worked as well as the rest of the cemetery looked. He walked into the cemetery and went immediately to the newest grave. It was the grave of his grandmother, Sally Barnett. She had died in October of 1965 during his second year at the Point. He had gotten a short leave to come to her funeral but had to return immediately after the burial. The cemetery didn't look anything like it did now. His mother had seen to it that Grandma Sally had a beautiful headstone.

SALLY LOUISE BARNETT

**LOVING MOTHER OF BILLY ROB AND
SUE ANN BARNETT
LOVING GRANDMOTHER OF
WILLIAM CLYDE BARNETT**

**SHE SAW HORRIBLE TRAGEDY AND
STILL REMAINED
ONE OF GOD'S KINDEST CREATIONS**

**BORN MARCH 9, 1899
DIED OCTOBER 24, 1965**

Without looking back to his mother and continuing to stare at the headstone, he said, "She was really, really good to me and treated me with such kindness. I will always remember the long walks we took all over this farm, and she would tell me all about Dad; things he did and where he played as a boy." Then after a short pause, "I miss her so much, Mom." His mother said nothing but stood behind him with her arms fold across her chest and her head bowed. Slowly William turned and put his hand on his mother's shoulder and whispered softly, "It's really strange, Mom, but I don't think I ever knew Grandma's middle name was Louise." His eyes were now damp as he reached down and took his mother's hand. "Come on, Mom," he said in a broken voice, "let's go back to the house we got some things to talk about."

With that said, William and his mother walked out of the little cemetery, closed the gate, and walked hand and hand back to the house.

When William had arrived at home, he came in a taxi all the way from Dallas Love Field. He had hardly stepped on the porch when he was happily greeted by this mother. She embraced him and couldn't stop going on about how proud she was of him and how sorry she was that she couldn't get away to be at his graduation ceremony. While she way talking, he couldn't help but notice that the house was very quiet.

He let his mother wind down before he said anything. Finally he got an opening, "Mom, where's everybody?"

"Oh," she said stepping back from him. "Well, the boys, Jacky and Andrew, are at summer church camp up near Gilmore and John had to go over to Athens with a load of fertilizer. So, it's just me here to greet you." Then, she stepped back a little more and looked him over carefully. "What kind of uniform are you wearing?" She asked.

William looked down at himself and smiled and said, "These are my fatigues that I wore at the Point. They make good for travel."

"Ah, but I do see those lieutenant bars on your shoulders."

Before she could say anything else he quickly asked, "Mom, can we go see Grandma Sally? I mean before we do anythin' else."

A gentle smile crossed her face. "Of course we can." She walked over and took his arm. "Let's go right now."

When they got back from the cemetery, William flopped down in a nice leather easy chair. He leaned back in the chair and closed his eyes for a moment and then reopened them to see his mother standing in front of him. Her hands were behind her back and she had her head cocked to one side.

"What?" He asked.

"Would you like a cup of hot tea?" She teased.

He smiled, "You and your hot tea."

"Well, would you?"

He slapped his knee and said firmly, "No, but if you've got somethin' stronger I could be interested."

She quickly turned and went into the kitchen; returning shortly carrying a whiskey glass with a brownish liquid in it. Ice tingled against the glass as she handed it to him.

He took the glass from her and nodded his head in thanks. Without wasting any time he took a long gulp and then let out a sigh. "Boy that's good stuff. What is it?"

"That, my dear Son, is Jamison's Irish whiskey. Now if you don't mind I'll go fix myself one."

"Only if you take my glass and refill it. This time I'll sip it."

Smiling she walked over and took his glass, turn around and hurried off to the kitchen again. Soon she returned with two glasses. This time they were both filled to the top. She handed one to William and then walked over and took a seat on the couch and looked at him with quizzical look. "Okay, William, now tell me what you've been holding back from me. It can't be all that bad."

William took a sip of his whiskey and then tilted the glass towards his mother, "No, Mom," he said, "it's not really all that bad."

"So, shoot."

"Well as you know I finished in the top ten percent of my class. Thanks to you for makin' me go to that military school my senior year in high school. You may or may not know that all Point graduates are allowed to put in their request for the assignment they want to perform. However, these requests are not guaranteed; unless you're in the top ten percent of your class. In that case, they are guaranteed. Therefore, my request for assignment is guaranteed."

At this point, he stopped talking and took another sip of his whiskey. "Well, that's a good thing isn't it?" His mother asked matter-of-factly.

"Yes, it's a good thing," he replied, "and I've already put my request for assignment in and it's already been accepted."

His mother took a healthy sip of her drink and stood up. "Let me guess," she said putting her finger to her temple, "you requested the airborne, and probably specifically the 101st Division Screaming Eagles."

William relaxed and leaned back in the easy chair again. He finished off his drink and smiled at her. "I guess I should've known you wouldn't be surprised."

"No, I'm not surprised but I am a little worried. I read the papers and see the telly. I know the 101st is in the thick of the fight in Vietnam. So, with that thought in mind, is there anything that I don't know."

"Yes, Mom, there is, my leave here is goin' to be short. I have to report to Fort Benning, Georgia on June 30th to begin parachute trainin'. After that, I go to a couple of special schools for airborne officers. All of that should take about four months. Then, I'll go to Fort Campbell, Kentucky for trainin' in assault helicopters. To make a long story short, my orders said I should be in Vietnam by the middle of March 1968." He stopped and took a deep breath and then said, "That's what you don't know."

PART FIVE

The Spring of 1968 Vietnam

CHAPTER TWENTY-FIVE

The New Lieutenants Meet

1st Lieutenant Kellie Anderson stood in the staging room at Travis Air Force Base looking out the large plate glass window at the huge C-141 cargo plane. She was sure it was the largest airplane she had ever seen. The sun was sinking in the west so light from large steel structures bathed the plane in artificial light. Men hurried around the plane doing various functions including fueling the large plane.

She turned away from the window and looked around at the others in the staging area. There looked to be maybe sixty to seventy other people milling about just as she was. All of the people were in some form of uniform ranging from army to marines and navy. She noticed that they were nearly all officers except for a few enlisted personnel wearing sergeant stripes on their uniforms. Of the officers, she had seen no one of a rank higher than a captain, but she couldn't be sure of that conclusion. Nearly everyone in the staging area was male except for herself and two other women. The two women wore the same uniform as she did; that of the United States Army Nurse Corps. She thought about going over to the other nurses and starting a conversion, but thought better of it because everyone seemed nervous.

Nearly a half hour earlier, a young air force lieutenant had come into the staging area and informed them that they should be prepared to board the plane within the hour. She guessed that they would be getting the orders to board at any time now. No sooner had that thought entered her mind when the young lieutenant came into the staging area again.

"Your attention please," he yelled. Everyone stopped what they were doing and gave him their complete attention. "We're now prepared to start boarding the aircraft. Please listen for your name to be called. When it is, please proceed through the staging area, out to the tarmac, and board the aircraft. Be sure you have a copy of your orders to show the sergeant at the boarding point. And one last thing there is no assigned seating so take any seat you want. There should be plenty of seats as we're carrying less than half of our passenger capacity." He paused and looked around and then nodded his head. "Okay, then without farther ado we'll begin."

The lieutenant took out a pin from his shirt pocket and looked down at the clipboard he was holding. He then, methodically, began to call out names. As their name was call, they picked up small carry-on bags, as their larger duffel bags had been checked before entering the staging area, and did as they had been instructed.

As it turned out, Kellie's name was the first one to be called out and immediately after her the other two women were called out. As she walked across the tarmac, she thought maybe they were first because they were women, but she hoped that was not the case. She was carrying a small handbag that was slung over her shoulder and a copy of her orders in her right hand. As she approached the sergeant standing at the boarding point, she handed him her orders. He briefly looked them over and then stamped them with a red ink pad that read, 'Flight 661'. He returned her orders to her and she proceeded up the boarding steps and into the plane.

When inside, she was somewhat taken aback by what she saw. There were twenty rows of seats. An aisle about four feet wide divided the rows into three seats on each side of the aisle; much like a commercial airline. All of the seats were the same so there was no special seating for any high ranking personnel. But the main thing that struck her was that there were no windows. As a result it was dark inside the passenger cabin except for some lighting that came from the just above the seats and ran the entire length of the cabin on both sides.

At first, Kellie seemed lost and didn't know which seat to take. So, she just stood there blocking the path into the cabin. Finally, one of the other nurses just behind her gave her a shove. "Come on, Sweetie; let's grab some seats near the back. I think that's where they keep the food and stuff." She gently pushed Kellie down the aisle to the last row of seats. There they stopped and threw their bags onto a couple of seats. When Kellie turned to look at the nurse, she was waving frantically and yelling to the other nurse who was behind her but, like Kellie, was unsure were to sit. "Come on, Red," she yelled. "All of us girls can sit together. Hurry up!"

By the time everyone had gotten onto the plane, the three nurses had settled in together in the last row on the right side. Kellie had ended up in the middle seat. The nurse who had shoved her was seated next to the side of the plane. She had removed her service cap and beautiful blonde hair hung down to her shoulders. Even the drab army uniform she wore couldn't hide her outstandingly shaped body. Her dark green eyes displayed a mischievous nature. Kellie thought to herself, '*boy, where we're going, they're going to love you*'. The nurse seated next to the aisle had also removed her service cap reveling flaming red hair. She had a smaller frame than the blonde nurse so her uniform kept secret the form of her body, but she had a very pretty face with light green eyes that seemed to shine. Kellie was anxious to get to know the other nurses but just as they were about to start talking a loud voice boomed over them.

"Okay, people, give me your undivided attention if you please." Everyone looked up to the front of the cabin to see a tall man standing there. He wore the uniform the United States Air Force. On his collar, he wore the gold oak leafs of a major. It only took a minute for everyone to fall quiet and wait for the Major to continue. "My name is Major Kingsman. It will be my job, along with Captain Mallory who is up front right now, to get you fine people to Da Nang in the Republic of South Vietnam. I'm goin' to give you some information so listen up and pay attention. First, you may or may not have noticed that most of you are officers. The highest rank among you is a couple of captains, which makes me the highest rank on this flight. Please keep that in mind. There are a few enlisted men on this flight. These enlisted men have a very special MOS and they all have Top Secret clearances. So, don't be askin' them what they do. It could get you in trouble. Secondly, except for me, you can disregard rank on this flight. It's goin' to be a long and tiring flight and we don't need rank issues." He paused and looked around but no one said anything. They only continued to watch him intently. Then he continued, "Now for the flight itself. You're probably wondering why we are leaving at night. We leave at night so that we chase the sun west. If it all works right, the sun will catch us from behind and we will land in Da Nang in the daylight. We don't want to land in Da Nang at night. If we get behind schedule we'll spend some extra time at Guam where we'll stop to refuel and resupply your food and drinks, which brings me to how we're configured. This is a C-141 cargo plane. It wasn't originally designed for passengers. This C-141, however, has been reconfigured to have a passenger cabin, which is what you're sitting in now. If you'll look behind you, you'll see a bulkhead about forty feet behind the last row of seats. Behind that bulkhead is cargo. Attached to the bulkhead you'll find places for sandwiches, coffee, and cokes. Please, when you get anything be sure to re-secure things as they were. We don't want stuff flying around if we hit rough weather. On either side of the bulkhead are the latrines; one for ladies and one for gentlemen. Now, about seat belts, wear them all the time you're in your seat. If you're up and about and you hear me announce over the speaker system to take your seats and buckle up; do it immediately, and I do mean immediately. Lastly, we have three of the finest army nurses in the world riding with us today. You officer's and gentlemen will *NOT* offend them in anyway. You will watch you language around them and treat them with the dignity they deserve. If you don't, you'll answer to me." He stopped talking and slapped his hands together. "Do we have any questions?"

"Sir," a voice from somewhere in the cabin yelled out, "how long can we expect the flight to be?"

"Well, it can vary. Generally it's about twelve hours plus a little to Guam. Then our layover there will depend on how good we're doin' but most often it'll be a couple of hours, give or take. Then, we have to run a strange course to Vietnam to avoid flying over different countries airspace and to avoid weather at times. But on the average I'd say we should get you to Da Nang in twenty-five to thirty hours. Are there any more questions?"

No one spoke.

"Good, then let's crank this bird up and get goin'."

It was only after the plane had taken off and was at its cruising altitude did the three nurses begin to talk. Kellie noticed that some of the male officers had already gotten up from their seats and were congregated around the coffee dispenser. So, she decided to start things off. She leaned forward in her seat, clasped her hands together and said loudly, "My name is Kellie Anderson, I'm from St. Paul, Minnesota and my friends call me Kel." When no one spoke, she turned the blonde and shrugged her shoulders and tilted her head with a smile.

"Oh," the blonde said in moderate surprise, "my name is Veronica Mann, I'm from Sweetwater, Texas and my friends call me Ronnie."

Without being prompted, the redhead said, "My name is Kathleen O'Rourke, I'm from Hell's Kitchen, New York and my friends call me Kat."

They were all smiling when Veronica suddenly blurred out, "Lieutenant Anderson, please excuse me. I've only just noticed that you're the rankin' officer among us. Please allow me to take the middle seat." With that, she began to undo her seat belt.

Quickly, Kellie reached across to stop her. "Keep your seat, Ronnie. You heard what the Major said. There'll be no rank issues on this trip. Let's save that for when we get to Da Nang."

"As you say," Ronnie smiled as she settled back into her seat.

After that, nothing could keep the new lieutenants quiet. They all told their stories about their homes, life, and how they ended up in the Army Nurse Corps. Through the long trip to Guam and then on to Da Nang, they would become the best of friends.

The lieutenants all slowly began to wake up from a short sleep as the plane began its approach to Da Nang. They stirred around and tried to get themselves in some kind of order. They started putting things away and making sure they had all their papers in order. It was during all of this that Kathleen noticed that Kellie was smiling as she worked.

"What're you smilin' about? She asked with a puzzled look on her face.

"I had kind of a dream while I was sleeping," she said continuing to smile.

"What kind of a dream?" Veronica asked jumping into the conversation.

"Well," Kellie replied slowly, "it's actually more of an idea than a dream."

"Come on then," Kathleen laughed, "let's have it."

The smile left her face as she turned and looked hard at Veronica.

"Hey, why're you lookin' at me like that? What's goin' on?"

Kellie continued to look into Veronica's eyes and said, "It's just that the idea is all up to you."

Now Veronica was getting nervous. "Why should it be up to me? What kind of idea is this anyway?"

"Yeah," Kathleen chimed in, "let us in on it."

Kellie took a deep breath and said, "Okay, here it is. I want to start up The Tart Trio again with the three of us."

Everyone was quiet for several moments. Then, Kellie continued, "We probably will get different assignments and there's no telling where we'll all ended up. I thought it would be a good thing if we all kept in touch no matter where we end up. We can write or call or meet or something. I don't want to lose you two. And I liked Ronnie's story about The Tart Trio. I'd like to start it up again with the three of us." Then, she paused and took Veronica's hand, "But it's up to you Ronnie. I know what it all meant to you."

Veronica looked from Kellie to Kathleen and then back to Kellie again. She seemed to be fighting a battle inside herself. Veronica didn't say anything so Kellie pressed on, "It's your call, Ronnie, but if I understood Jodie and her father the way I think you were trying to tell their story, I think they'd be very pleased and I think that somewhere in God's Heaven, Jodie is smiling."

Still Veronica didn't say anything. She simply slumped back into her seat.

"Okay, Ronnie, me and Kat understand. But at least we can make a Pac that we'll be good friends and stay in touch as best we can and maybe have a reunion when we all get home. Here's my hand on it." Kellie held out her hand palm down.

"I like the sound of that, so I'm in." Kathleen said smiling as she put her hand on top of Kellie's. "A Pac it is."

Veronica sat up in her seat and turned to face them. Her eyes showed a slight dampness but a smile slowly cross her face. She reached over and placed her hand on top of Kathleen's and said in a voice that was almost a whisper, "The Tart Trio rides again."

CHAPTER TWENTY-SIX

The Nurses Get Their Assignments

It was a tired and rumbled trio of nurses that landed in Da Nang. The plane finally arrived at the Da Nang airport just before noon on March 20th 1968. Because of weather they had been delayed nearly three hours at Guam. Then, when they did get airborne again, they had to skirt violent weather just west of Guam. All-in-all the entire flight took over thirty hours; everyone getting off the plane was completely beaten down. They staggered more than walked.

The good news for the nurses was that there was someone there to meet them. A Staff Sergeant was waiting for them in the terminal. He was holding a sign that read, 'For the Army Nurses'. He appeared to be in his late twenties or early thirties. He was short but had a solid, if not stocky, frame. Sandy blonde hair barely showed from under his service cap and dark brown eyes sparkled from his face, which was clean shaven. He wore the stripes of a Staff Sergeant on the sleeves of his well starched and neat uniform. When he saw the three nurses enter the terminal, he hurried over to them. They saw him approaching holding his sign up so they stopped in their tracks and dropped their small bags to the floor.

He was wearing a huge smile and popped off a halfhearted salute, which they didn't bother to return. "Hello, Lieutenants and welcome to Vietnam. I'm Staff Sergeant Masterson and I'm here to assist you in any way I can. I'm also here to give you transportation to what soon will be the 95th EVAC Hospital, which we lovingly call 'Hell's Half Acre'." He looked at them still smiling but they just stared back at him blankly. "Don't you get it?" He asked still smiling. They continued to look at him blankly. Without ever losing his smile, he tried to explain, "Hell's Half Acre is what we call the area that will soon be the 95th EVAC."

Kellie put her weight on one foot and took a deep breath, "Sergeant Masterson, we are very pleased to see you and would really, really appreciate your help, but we are dead tired. You might even say we're exhausted. So, if you could just tell us how to get our bags and what we should do next, it would make us very happy."

"Oh, yes Ma'am," he replied quickly. His tone had become serious and the smile had left his face. "Your bags are being taken care of as we speak. I have a jeep just outside the terminal. It's big enough for all three of you and we can tie you bags on to the back. I'm thinking your bags will already be at the jeep when we get there. But, if you could, I'll need to see a copy of your orders"

The nurses tiredly dug through their small bags and produced their orders. The sergeant examined them and then handed them back. "Sorry 'bout that, but I'm required to verify exactly who I'm picking up and exactly where I'm supposed to take them."

"No problem, Sergeant," Kellie said putting her orders back in her bag.

"Let me take those bags and if you'll follow me we'll talk while we walk." He then took their bags, turned and signaled for them to follow, which they did. "We'll be driving down to what we call Red Beach, which is part of what we call China Beach. There, at the Acre, you'll meet with Major Morningstar. She'll take charge at that point and get you situated. I'm stationed near the Acre so I'll be available to help you with your acclimation."

Kellie wanted to ask some questions but decided to wait until they got to the jeep, which only took a few minutes. Just as Sergeant Masterson had predicted, their bags were already secured to the back of the jeep.

Sergeant Masterson opened the door on the passenger side of the jeep and signaled for them to get in. Kellie started to get in but backed up and let Veronica and Kathleen get in the back seat. She then got in and slammed the door shut firmly. Sergeant Masterson then handed each of them their small bags he had been carrying. He then got behind the wheel and started the jeep. He was about to drive off when Kellie gently put her hand on his arm. "Before we go?" She asked softly and tiredly. "Is Major Morningstar the head nurse and if so is she easy to get along with?"

The smile returned to Sergeant Masterson's face. "Yes," he answered, "she's the head nurse. And, if the Lieutenants will excuse my language, I hear from the other nurses that she's a real bitch of a hard ass." With that he jammed the jeep into gear and took off like they were being shot from a gun.

The drive to the Acre only took about twenty-five minutes, but it was one of the scariest rides of Kellie's life. She felt sorry for Veronica and Kathleen in the backseat, because she didn't know how they stayed in the jeep. Sergeant Masterson had obviously run this route many times before and he took advantage of all his experience. He drove very fast and he wove through traffic just missing cars, jeeps, motorbikes, and bicycle riders by what seemed to Kellie to be bare inches. When his way appeared blocked, he would skillfully turn down another route and maneuvered down narrow streets; some that could barely pass for allies. They finally hit a road that paralleled a beautiful beach that Kellie assumed to be China Beach. The road was fairly smooth and the traffic was sparse. Here, Sergeant Masterson gave the jeep its head and they roared along at a speed Kellie didn't want to know.

After a short while, Kellie could see up ahead what appeared to be a small tent city. Sergeant Masterson drove the jeep off the road and onto the beach. He targeted one of the larger tents and came to skidding halt just a few feet away from the tent's open flaps. He quickly jumped out of the jeep and ran around to open the passenger door.

"Okay, here we are Lieutenants," he said as he signaled for them to get out of the jeep. The nurses carefully climbed out of the jeep onto shaky legs. "Major Morningstar is just inside. While you are meeting with Major Morningstar, I'll take your bags over to the temporary nurse's quarters, which is the tent just behind the mess tent. You can't miss it. But before I take your bags, be sure you have a copy of your orders to give to the Major. Well, I guess that's it. I hope to see you again soon and good luck to you." With that, he jumped back into the jeep and sped off leaving a shower of sand behind him.

The three nurses stood there in silence and watched him speed away and disappear into the tent city. They looked at each other and began brushing themselves off. "Well," Kellie said, looking at Veronica and Kathleen, "I guess we better go inside."

Once inside they looked around at what looked to be one large room. There was a wooden floor and there were desk scattered about tent. People seemed busy and didn't notice them at first. Finally a nurse in fatigues saw them and smiled. She walked over and gave them a short salute. "Hey, you must be the new girls," she said with a chuckle. "I'm sure you'll want to see the Major. Her desk is over there in the far corner." As she spoke, she pointed to a desk sitting catty-cornered at the far back of the tent.

"Thank you," Kellie said with a short salute of her own.

The three tired nurses walked to the desk as indicated by the friendly nurse. There was a sign on the desk that read, 'Major Marjorie Morningstar'. All three looked at the sign in disbelief but said nothing. All three nurses stood before the desk at attention. Kellie had collected all of their orders and held them in her left hand. She saluted smartly as did the other two. "Lieutenants Anderson, Mann, and O'Rourke reporting as ordered, Ma'am," Kellie said as she reached across the desk and handed the Major their orders.

The Major stood up and took the orders with her left and returned their salutes with her right. "Stand at ease," she said curtly. Major Marjorie Morningstar was a short woman in her mid-forties. Her hair was a sandy brown and it had no shades of grey. She had dark brown eyes that darted from nurse to nurse. Her face looked tired and strained, but wasn't unattractive.

"I'm sorry Ladies, but someone has borrowed my chairs so I'll make this brief. You all look exhausted and beat. Bat should have all your bags in place by now. So, I want you to go to the temporary nurse's quarters, get a shower, and then grab some shuteye for about three hours. Then report back here to me at seventeen hundred hours. Understood?"

"Yes, Ma'am," Kellie replied slowly. "But who is Bat?"

The Major smiled. "That would be Staff Sergeant Masterson. We call him Bat. You know for Bat Masterson. Truthfully, I don't know his real first name."

"Yes, Ma'am," Kellie replied again and saluted as did Veronica and Kathleen.

"Okay, then, dismissed. I'll see all of you at seventeen hundred hours."

The Lieutenants turned sharply and left the tent.

As promised, their bags were stacked in the middle of the temporary nurse's quarters. There were eight bunks in the tent and four of them had footlockers at their ends and all four were cleanly made up. The other four had rolled up mattresses with blankets and pillows stacked on them. So, it was assumed by the new nurses that the rolled up mattresses indicated empty bunks. Kellie looked around and said, "Okay Ladies, take your pick."

Kathleen went to the nearest empty bunk, put the blankets and pillow on the floor and unrolled the mattress. She then flopped down on the bunk in exhaustion. But then she started laughing in uncontrollable waves. Tears were actually coming to her eyes.

"What?" Veronica yelled at her.

But the laughter wouldn't stop.

Finally, Kellie yelled at Kathleen, "Come on, Kat, what the hell's so funny?"

Kathleen sat up and bent over. "Can you believe Bat Masterson and Marjorie Morningstar? Can you believe it? Can you?" Then she started laughing all over again.

Veronica and Kellie started to giggle and then burst into full-fledged laughter also.

"Okay Ladies," Kellie was finally able to say. "Let's find the showers, get cleaned up, and grab some sack time."

At seventeen hundred hours, the three nurses entered the administrative tent for the second time. Now, they were showered and cleaned up. They had gotten three and a half hours of solid sleep. They wore olive drab fatigues with army combat boots. On their heads they wore the hated army issued baseball cap. They were clean, rested, and ready for their meeting with Major Morningstar. As they walked toward the back corner of the tent where the Major's desk was, they noted that there were now three cushioned chairs sitting in front of the desk. Upon approaching the desk they removed their caps and placed them under their left arms. As they came to attention and saluted, the Major got to her feet and returned their salute.

"Please, be at ease and take a seat," she commanded in a formal tone.

The three nurses took a seat with Kellie on the far right as the ranking officer. "Thank you, Ma'am," Kellie said as they all sat down.

"Thank you for being on time," the Major started. "We have a bit to go over so I'll just get started straight away." She sat down and picked up three folders that were lying on her desk. "I have your orders right here in these folders. But I'm going to hold on to 'em for a while. First, I want to tell you why you were flown directly here to Da Nang instead of Saigon as is the normal case." She paused for a short moment as if to gather her thoughts. Then, she continued, "The 95th is not up and running as yet. We're in the process of getting everything built and in place. You and a few other nurses are what we can call our 'Advanced Party'. The rest of the staff and support personnel are due to arrive on March 26th aboard the USS Geiger." She paused again and stood up still holding the folders. She cleared he throat and looked intently at the three nurses. "The truth is I had you sent directly to us. I got permission from the Replacement Battalion to hold your orders for four months. It is hoped by that time we will, first have a temporary operation in place over the next several weeks, and second that we will have our permanent facility, which'll be about eight klicks north of here, in full operation in four months; give or take a few weeks."

The Major looked from nurse to nurse but no one spoke. "I understand how you may feel but I need you desperately. There's hard fighting going on just north of us so we'll have to establish defensive positions before we can really start on the hospital itself. Thank God for the Seabees. We're going to have to build and treat at the same time. It's going to be hard. You're all new and you're going to see things that'll shock you. You're going to have to learn the hard way and they'll be no mercy and there'll be no time for sympathy. So, if you get your feelings hurt or the sight of the things you'll see turns your stomach, you're just going to have to gut it up."

She stopped talking and pitched the three folders down on the desk. Then, in a shaking voice she said softly, "I promise to get you to your originally assigned duty stations just as soon as I possibly can. It should be no longer than the four months the Replacement Battalion authorized me." Then taking a deep breath, "As I told you, I need you desperately."

Then, again, she looked from nurse to nurse needing someone to speak; needing someone to say something. Finally, Kellie stood up and snapped to attention. "Being needed desperately is exactly why we came here, Ma'am," she said in a firm and decisive voice. At that moment, Veronica and Kathleen both shot to their feet and also came to attention, and Veronica said in her best Texas drawl, "Just give us your orders, Major, and let's get on with it."

CHAPTER TWENTY-SEVEN

A Marine Recon Team for Khe Sanh

Captain Kyle Collie had arrived in South Vietnam in September of 1967. It had taken him almost a whole month to get to the base known as Cobra Umbrella One. Once there he spend another month getting his crew in place and getting familiar with his Huey 1C Heavy Scout gunship. It was early December 1967 before he was flying actual missions. Things had started out slow for him but now the action was hot and heavy in all directions. It was now late March 1968 and he was still on his first tour of duty, but he had already decided to extend to a second tour unless something bad happened to prevent it.

He now hurried for the operations building. He had received orders to report to the Base Commander Coronel Jeff Keeper. He had no idea what it was all about. In fact, he had only been back from a troop carrier support mission for less than an hour. He reached the operations building and quickly went in. The commander's desk was in an open area just near the back door of the building. He hurried to the desk and gave a quick informal salute that was returned in the same manner by the Commander.

"You wanted to see me, Sir?" Kyle asked briskly.

"Yes, Captain, find a loose chair and have a seat. I have a something that just might make your day." As he spoke, he opened a folder on his desk and started thumbing through its contents.

"Actually, Coronel, I just got my day made a little while ago. I just about got my tail feathers shot off. My crew chief is looking at the rear rotor right now."

The Coronel looked up somewhat surprised. "What happened? I thought the mission to support the 7th Calvary went well."

"It did, Sir," Kyle replied quickly. "It's just that since we retook Hue, the 7th Calvary and the 1st Marines are tryin' to chase the North Vietnamese all the way back across the DMZ. In doin' so, they're, at times, out runnin' our support. I got a little ahead of where I was supposed to be and took some relatively heavy ground fire. Fortunately for me, it was only small arms fire and I think the damage to my ship is minimal. The crew chief should have a report for me very soon."

The Coronel stopped looking at his folder and leaned back in his chair. "Captain, did I understand you to say that you got a little ahead of where you were supposed to be?"

Kyle moved uncomfortable in his chair and replied, "Yes, Sir, that's what I said."

"How do you do that, Captain? How do you *get a little ahead of where you're supposed to be?*"

Kyle didn't like the Coronel's tone. He leaned forward in his chair and spoke very carefully. "With all due respect, Coronel, it's chaos out there. The North Vietnamese and the Viet Cong are movin' as fast as they can to reach their sanctuaries in the DMZ and Laos. And the 1st Marines and 7th Calvary are hot on their asses. We'll get a radio call for support but by the time we arrive the dynamics of the situation has changed. We have to be careful not to fire at the good guys. I got hit tryin' to follow a troop carrier into a zone that had changed hands just as we got there. I'm not the only one that this is happenin' to. The Cobra guys are having it worse than us Heavy Scout guys, because they're faster than us and have to make changes immediately. Some of those Cobra boys have actual dropped fire on friendlies."

Kyle finished talking and realized his voice had elevated to almost a shout and he was sitting on the edge of his chair. Then, more calmly he said, "Sorry, Sir, I didn't mean to be disrespectful."

Coronel Keeper got to his feet and picked up the folder and again opened it up. He took a deep breath and pointed the folder at Kyle. "I'm sorry too, Captain. You've only been flying missions for about four months, but your record has been outstanding. In fact, you and your crew will probably get a commendation for your actions in support of the 1st Marines during the Battle of Hue and there may be a metal in it for you. It's because of that record I want you to handle the mission laid out in this folder. So, maybe we could just start over."

The Coronel was smiling so Kyle returned his smiled and nodded. "Yes, Sir, I'd like that."

The Coronel seated himself again and spread the folder open wide on his desk. "Okay then," he started. But before he could continue a First Sergeant came hurrying up to his desk.

"Begging the Coronel's pardon," the First Sergeant said quickly, "I hate to interrupt, Sir, but the Captain's crew chief is here with his report for the Captain. He said the Captain ordered him to report ASAP."

Kyle spoke up quickly, "I did, Sir, but at that time I didn't know you wanted to see me. But, in any case, we need to know the condition of my ship if I'm to go on another mission."

The frustration on Coronel Keeper's face was evident. "Well, Captain," he said, as he once again slammed the folder shut, "I guess this mission briefing must wait still a bit longer." Then looking up at the First Sergeant and waving his hand, "Okay, First Sergeant, show him in."

The First Sergeant turned and hurry out the door. In a few minutes, he returned with the crew chief close behind him. Staff Sergeant Harvey Milton was a short, slightly overweight man of thirty-years. He was a career military man and one of the best helicopter mechanics in the U.S. Army. Now, he was covered with sweat and grease from working fast and hard on the rotor blade. As he approached the Coronel's desk he stopped and stood to attention and snapped a smart salute. The Coronel returned a half-hearted salute and ordered, "Okay Sergeant be at ease and tells us what you've got to say."

"Well, Sir, it's fairly simple," he replied turning to face Kyle. "She's ready, Skipper," he said in a matter-of-fact tone. "Fueled up and fully armed. And I'll personally guarantee the repairs."

Kyle jumped to his feet and faced the Coronel. "May I, Sir, with your permission?"

"Go right ahead, Captain"

Then, turning to face his crew chief he said, "Good job, Harv. Now, go and find Lt. Denison and you two put yourselves on alert for a new mission. I'll give you all the details just as soon as I get them."

"Roger that, Skipper." With that, Sergeant Milton gave a quick salute and then turned and hurried out the door.

When Sergeant Milton had gone and the First Sergeant had returned to his desk near the door, Kyle faced the Coronel and said, "I think we can proceed with the briefin' now, Sir."

"Do you think?" The Coronel asked sarcastically.

"Yes, Sir, I'm really sorry for all the interruptions and confusion."

The Coronel once gain opened the folder. "Well," he said with a soft chuckle, "at least we know we have a good ship for the mission."

"Yes we do, Sir."

"Okay now listen up, Captain, here's what you've got to do. Your mission is actually two fold. I'll first cover the initial part and that will then flow into the second part." He then paused and looked at Kyle waiting for an acknowledgement. Kyle said nothing but just nodded. "Waiting out by the mess tent is a special team of marines. There are five of them. They're from the 1st Battalion Recon, 1st Marine Division. They're a specially picked team to be inserted to Khe Sanh for a special mission. Now don't ask me anything about the mission because I don't know anything about it. But I do know this, since the siege of Khe Sanh began back in January the 26th Marine Regiment has done an outstanding job of holding Khe Sanh against overwhelming odds. Now that we've retaken Hue and the North Vietnamese and Viet Cong forces are pulling back, the pressure is also easing somewhat at Khe Sanh. The team you'll be escorting to Khe Sanh has been requested by the 26th Marine Regimental command. Their job is important so, it follows that your job to see that they get there is important. I know there's not room on your ship for five guys and all of their equipment. Therefore, I've borrowed a Slick, that's a Huey troop carrier if you're not familiar with the term, from the 7th Calvary with pilot. The team'll go in the Slick and you will cover them all the way to Khe Sanh. You'll see them land and make sure they're safely there. But, *you will not touch down*. Once you're satisfied that they're safely there, you'll then move on to the second part of your mission. Are you still with me, Captain? Have you got any questions?"

Kyle simple said, "No questions so far, Sir. I've flow enough missions to Khe Sanh I can get there blindfolded."

"Let's hope that won't be necessary, Captain."

"Roger that, Coronel, now let's hear about part two?"

"Not so fast," the Coronel said quickly. "I want you to meet the Recon Team, because you may be required to go back in there and get them out and you'll probably need to be able to identify them." The Coronel turned and waved over to the First Sergeant's desk and yelled, "First Sergeant, run over to the mess tent and you should see five marines milling around there somewhere. Gather them up and bring them here and please make it quick."

The First Sergeant shot to his feet and was out the door immediately without replying to the Coronel.

Kyle and the Coronel sat quietly for what seemed like to Kyle an eternity, but it was actually less than five minutes when the First Sergeant returned with the six marines in tow; not five. As the First Sergeant approached the desk, he simply said, "The Recon Team, Sir."

"Thank you First Sergeant that will be all I'll take it from here."

"Yes, Sir," the First Sergeant said with a half salute; then turned and returned to his desk.

The Recon Team was about to stand to attention and salute but the Coronel stood up and waved his hand and said, "As you were, as you were. We can't all be saluting all the time."

"Thank you, Sir," it was the man standing in front who spoke. None of the men had any patches, rank, or name tags on their uniforms. The man who spoke was wearing a very large smile on his face.

"Since I don't know how to address you," the Coronel said, "I guess I'll just point at you." The Coronel pointed at the man in front and continued, "You, what's your name and rank and why're you grinning like that?"

"I'm Sergeant Jordan Costillo and the reason I'm grinnin' is because I'm very happy to see Captain Collie.

Before Jordan could finish speaking, Kyle jumped from his chair and ran over and put a huge bear hug on him. Jordan returned the hug and the two men wrestled around hugging and laughing until the Coronel yelled out, "Gentlemen, please!"

Kyle quickly broke the bear hug and turned to the Coronel. He tried to appear serious but he still wore a small smile. "Beg your pardon, Sir," he said still trying to lose his smile, "but the sergeant here and I go back a long ways. In fact, in some manner we're related. I don't know how the relationship trees work, but my dad's sister is married to this Jarhead's half-brother." Then after a short pause, "And it's been a long time since we've seen each other."

The Coronel was smiling but he slapped his hands together loudly. "Well, I wish we had time for a good old reunion, but we don't. We have to have this Recon team to Khe Sanh within the hour. So, Sergeant Costillo, please introduce your men and tell us what they do. Not so much for me, but specifically for Captain Collie. He may need to know them by name or face or job at a later time.

"Yes, Sir," Jordan said, immediately getting to business. He turned and pointed to the man to his immediate left, who was tall; maybe six feet four. His skin was a brownish red. He had high cheek bones and small dark brown, almost slanted eyes. "This is Corporal Tommy Talltree. He's full bloodied Dakota Sioux. His job with us is trackin' and quiet single man recon. His code name is Tracker. I think I should stop here and tell you that after we leave this room you should all call us by our code names. We don't want anyone knowin' our real names. That's why we don't have any name tags or dog tags. By the way, my code name is Greaser. Is everyone okay with what I just said?"

Both Kyle and Coronel Keeper nodded but didn't speak.

Jordan continued to the next man, who was much shorter than Tracker. His skin was a dark brown. He had wide and dark brown eyes. Like Tracker, his hair was jet black. "This is Corporal Jason Conroy. His mother is full bloodied Cajun and is father is a professor at an all-black college in Louisiana. He speaks fluent French. His job with us is radios. He not only knows how to use any of our radios, but he also knows how to use any of the enemies radios; be they Russian, Chinese, Korean, or whoever. His code name is Breed."

The next man, unlike the other two, was medium height with bright blonde hair. Like all the other men, his hair was cut marine style; very short. He had dark blue eyes set in a pale white face. "This," Jordan continued, "is Private Jeb Dunker. He's from Minnesota. His job with us is sniper. If you're a mile away, you're still not safe from Jeb. His code name is Swede."

Jordan moved to the next man and put his hand on his shoulder. The man was almost as tall as Tracker but maybe an inch shorter. His hair was a brown and red mixture. He had hazel eyes set in a narrow face that featured a tan that couldn't hide his freckles. "This is Private Berry Blackwell," Jordan said patting the man's shoulder, "He's from Oklahoma and he is our weapons man. He can handle any of our weapons as well as anythin' the enemy's got. His specialty is automatic weapons. For this mission, he'll be carryin' one of our rapid fire assault weapons. His code name is Cherokee."

Jordan stopped talking and faced both Kyle and Coronel Keeper. Then he said, "Now as for me my specialty on this mission is as a linguist. I'm fluent in English, Spanish, and four different Vietnamese dialects. I can speak some Russian but I'm not fluent in it."

Turning and looking back to the last man standing by himself behind the others, Jordan signaled for the man to come forward. The man came slowly forward. He was average height but had a thin frame. Unlike the other men, his hair was a sandy-blonde but not cut marine short; instead it was long enough to cover the top of his ears. He had a boyish handsome face with dark brown eyes. As he reached Jordan's side he stopped. "This," Jordan said, "is Staff Sergeant Robert O'Rourke and he isn't with Recon. He's with the Navy Security Group; the NSG. He's top secret and I don't have a clue what he's doin' with us. We were ordered to bring him along, so here he is. He's been workin' with the Army Security Agency; the ASA, over in Phu Bai, who are also top secret. You will notice that he out ranks me. However, for this mission, I have tactical command and the Staff Sergeant will follow my orders in the field. Once we're back, the normal command structure will be back in place. He doesn't have a code name but for this mission we've decided to call him Searcher."

Jordan then shrugged his shoulders and held his hands out and said, "So, that's who we are and that's what we do."

Coronel Keeper looked at all the men and then back to Jordan. "Good job Greaser. Now if you'll get your men going and go get everything you need loaded onto the troop carrier, I'll finish Captain Collie's briefing so you guys can get going. It should only take about ten minutes."

"Okay, guys, let's get goin'" Jordan said as he ushered the men towards the door. But before leaving he turned back and yelled to Kyle, "I'll see you at the chopper before takeoff, Captain." With that he disappeared out the door.

Kyle brought his Heavy Scout to about fifty feet above LZB, or Landing Zone Baker, and hovered there. He watched as the 7th Cav Slick set down gently at LZB. He then watched as the Recon Team quickly got out of the Slick and unloaded all of their equipment. Jordan looked up and gave a quick wave before he gathered up the men and quickly disappeared down a dug out path. Then, the 7th Cav pilot lifted off and made a quick turn south. As he did, he and Kyle could see each other clearly. The pilot gave Kyle a quick snap of a salute and then gunned his Slick and he was off to rejoin his unit. Kyle returned the salute but he was sure the pilot didn't see him.

The trip from Cobra Umbrella One to Khe Sanh had gone on schedule and was uneventful. Before they left, he had a brief discussion with Jordan about home and letters they and written and received. They caught up on how everyone was doing and what they were doing. But the time had been very short so many things remained unsaid. But the short time with Jordan had been a huge moral boost for Kyle. He liked the kid a lot but now, as he gained some altitude, the danger that Jordan was headed into worried him. He couldn't shake the sense of foreboding that lingered in his mind. Khe Sanh was stuck right in the northwest corner of South Vietnam; just below the DMZ and right near the Laotian boarder. Not to mention it was nearly on top of the Ho Chi Minh Trail.

Kyle shook his head as if to clear his mind of unwanted thoughts. He turned his head to face his copilot. "Okay, Denny," he said with a deep breath, "let's get goin' and get part two of this mission out of the way."

"Roger that, Skipper, but what is part two?"

Kyle smiled at him and winked. "I'll tell you on the way there."

"Could I ask where is there?"

"My good man, we're headed for the 95ᵗʰ EVAC Hospital near China Beach. And that reminds me, Denny; to be on the safe side, we'll be goin' to the 95ᵗʰ the long way around via Hue and followin' Route One all the way down. So, when we land at the 95ᵗʰ I'll need you to be sure and get our fuel top off. We probably won't need it but there's no sense in takin' any unnecessary chances."

"It'll be done, Skipper."

CHAPTER TWENTY-EIGHT

The 1066th MASH gets a new Head Nurse

Kyle was cruising along at about four hundred feet and a little over one hundred and ten miles per hour. He had ordered the crew chief to close the waist doors to prevent drag on the chopper thus slowing them down. They had had to keep them open while covering the Recon Team to Khe Sanh. Now, the chopper felt good to him. His crew chief had done an outstanding job with the Heavy Scout. The Heavy Scout usually carried a crew of four; the command pilot, the copilot, the crew chief, and a gunner. However, this Heavy Scout only carried a crew of three; they were minus the gunner. The reason for there being one less crewman was at Kyle's discretion. He decided he wanted extra room for a passenger if need be and extra room to stow their own M16 rifles, which were put underneath the bench seat that the crew chief rode on. The crew chief acted as both maintenance man and gunner. His handheld M60 machine gun was attached to the chopper just above the waist door by a bungee cord that allowed him to move the heavy gun in almost any direction and even allowed him to step out on the skids if he felt the need. Both waist doors had the bungee cord hook up so the crew chief could use the gun at either door. For his safety, the crew chief wore what was called a 'monkey harness', which was a GI safety harness worn on the torso and anchored to the chopper's floor. This harness allowed him much greater movement.

Kyle and his crew had named their chopper, 'Girl Needed'. The name was painted on the door of the left seat in bright red paint. Girl Needed had all the normal weaponry of any Heavy Scout. It had two M60 machine guns on each side operated by the command pilot in the right seat. It had two rocket pods, one on each side mounted just below the machine guns, and each rocket pod held seven rockets, which were operated by the copilot in the left seat. All of this was, of course, was in addition to the crew chief's handheld machine gun.

As they hurried along towards the 95th EVAC Hospital, Kyle heard his copilot speak to him over the intercom in his helmet. "Skipper, when do Harv and I get to know what our mission is?"

"Holy shit, guys, I'm sorry. I just got so involved with gettin' there I forgot to speak up." He paused for a short moment while he adjusted his helmet so the mic was directly in front of his mouth. He made sure his course, speed and altitude was all correct. Then, he started, "You guys know Captain Joyce Willoby?"

"You mean the head nurse at the ten-six-six?" Denny asked.

"Yeah, we've seen her a lot on our trips there," Harv chimed in.

"Okay," Kyle continued, "well, she's gotten herself wounded and wounded pretty bad as I was told."

"What happened?" Denny asked in a worried tone.

"Well, it seems that just after we retook Hue some VC were tryin' to get south and towards the coast but the 5th Marines caught up to them just outside of Phu Bai. The VC let loose with a couple of wild motor rounds that fell into the ten-six-six near the mess tent. Captain Willoby had just finished lunch and was walkin' back to the nurse's quarters when one of the rounds hit about ten yards behind her. She took a lot of shrapnel in the back. One of the bigger pieces lodged near her right kidney. The doctors at the ten-six-six were able to stabilize her and get her on a medivac chopper to the 95th. The doctors there were able to get the shrapnel out without damagin' her kidney. They say she's goin' to be alright but her days in country are over. She's already on her way to Japan."

"I'll be damned," Harv breathed. "She's a real nice lady; always treated me nice. I hope she comes all the way back."

"Ditto for me," Denny said. Then, after a short pause he asked, "But what does that have to do with us?"

"Well, they got a new nurse at the 95th that's got a couple of years of medical school and they want her to take over for Captain Willoby. Our job is to get her to from the 95th to the ten-six-six post haste."

"Why us," Harv asked, "why couldn't she just take one of their medivacs?

"I don't know, Harv, maybe they just want her to be protected," Kyle replied. "I just know we got orders to do the job and so we do the job."

"How long has this new nurse been in country?" Denny asked.

Kyle glanced over to Denny and said with a crooked smile, "As I understand it, she's only been here a couple of weeks."

"What!" Denny yelled into his mic. "What's her rank?"

"She's a 1st lieutenant."

Denny laughed softly, "I bet there're at least three nurses at the ten-six-six that have time and grade on her. I got a feeling this new 1st Louie isn't going to be very well received."

1st Lieutenant Kellie Anderson stood by her duffle bag and several other small bags that were stacked near a helipad that was the farthest helipad from the hospital. That was because it was a utility helipad used for things other than medivac. The medivac choppers used the helipads that were closest to the hospital.

She stood with her arms folded across her chest and with her weight on one leg. Her blue eyes were clouded over indicating that she was angry; very, very angry. She said nothing as the two other members of The Tart Trio tried to calm her down. She only looked down at the ground.

"Come on, Kel," Veronica said in an encouraging voice, "this could be a fast track to captain."

"That's right," Kathleen chimed in as if in high spirits, "you're goin' to do a great job at that MASH unit and the next time we see you, you'll be wearin' captain's railroad tracks."

Kellie raised her head and looked at her two new friends. She stared at them with those cold and cloudy blue eyes. "Will you two cut the crap," she said in a harsh tone. There was a long silence and then she continued, "I was supposed to stay here with you two until the new hospital was up and operational. I was told that by Major Morningstar less than two weeks ago. Now, here I am waiting for a chopper ride to a MASH unit where I'm going to take over the duties of head nurse. Do you hear that; head nurse. I don't know shit about being a head nurse and by all the Saints in Heaven I'm not qualified."

When she stopped talking, she realized she had been yelling at them. She also noticed that she had unfolded her arms and had been waving them about. She flopped down and sat on her duffle bag and let out a long breath. She buried her head in her hands. "I'm sorry," she said softly, "I shouldn't be taking this out on you two. I know you're just trying to help."

Veronica stepped up to her friend and reached down and put her hand on her shoulder. "Look up at me, Kel," she said in a kind voice. Kellie lifted her head out of her hands and looked up at Veronica. When they were looking at each other Veronica continued, "I know you're scared and I know you don't feel prepared. But you're not back at home now. You're in South Vietnam. You're in the United States Army and we're in a war. Your Commanding Officer feels you can do the job that's why she's ordered you to go there. I'm sure she would rather have you stay her as she had planned, but in war things change in a moment's notice."

Then, Veronica removed her hand from Kellie's shoulder and stepped back from her. Kellie watched as Veronica spread her feet apart and put her hands on her hips. "Now," Veronica said as her tone changed from kindly to demanding, "you get your Minnesota ass up to that MASH unit and do your job Lieutenant."

Kathleen hurried over to stand beside Veronica. She nodded her head and said," I ditto everythin' Ronnie said."

Kellie looked at her two friends for several long minutes. Then, a smile slowly started moving across her face and the clouds in her eyes began to clear away and her eyes began to shine again. "You know," she said haltingly, "I've only known you two for about two weeks but I feel like we've been friends since childhood." As she spoke, Kellie got up off her duffle bag. "I'm sure going to miss you gals."

Kathleen gave a little smile and said, "What's to miss? That MASH unit is just a short chopper ride from here. "I'll bet we get to see each other a lot more than you think."

Kellie was about say something else but the sound of a chopper coming in interrupted her. She was surprised that it wasn't a medivac but an assault chopper. It swung around and hovered for a moment and set down gently on the utility helipad. The pilot allowed the engine to run for about a minute and then shut it down. She watched as the rotors slowly stopped their rotation. After what seemed to Kellie to be a long time, the pilot opened the door and climbed out. At about the same time, she saw the waist door slide back and another man wearing sergeant strips climbed out and began stretching and working his legs. The pilot looked around and seeing the nurses he started their way. As he walked towards them, he took off his flight helmet and ran his hand through his blonde hair, which Kellie thought was probably a little longer than regulations. He looked up at them and smiled as he wiped the sweat from his forehead.

Veronica leaned over and whispered in Kellie's ear, "This one's kind of cute, Kel."

Kellie replied without taking her eyes off the approaching pilot, "Maybe you haven't noticed the captain bars on his collar, so behave yourself, Ronnie."

When Kyle reached them, all three nurses stood to attention and saluted. Kyle informally returned their salute and said, "As you were, Ladies. I'm Captain Collie and I'm here to find a Lieutenant Anderson."

"That would be me," Kellie replied as she sarcastically pointed to the name tag on her uniform. Then, turning to the other nurses and pointing to Veronica and said, "This is one of my colleagues, Lieutenant Mann and my other colleague here is Lieutenant O'Rourke."

"Nice to meet you, Ladies," he said tipping his head slightly. He was about to say something to Kellie when he stopped and looked strangely at Kathleen. "I'm sorry, Ma'am, but do I understand your name is O'Rourke?"

Kathleen looked surprised and again stood to attention, "Yes, Sir, that's my name. Is there an issue?"

Kyle waved his hand, "Please, Lieutenant, stand easy. It's just that before comin' here, I dropped of a Marine Recon Team at Khe Sanh and there was a guy in that team named O'Rourke. I think his name was Staff Sergeant Robert O'Rourke. Is this a strange coincident or what?"

Kathleen's face paled and a worried look spread across her face. "Well, Sir, that sounds like my brother, but why would he be with a Marine Recon Team? He's attached to the Navy Security Group."

"I can't answer that, Lieutenant; they just had me flyin' high cover for them as they were inserted into Khe Sanh."

"But Marine Recon at Khe Sanh," Kathleen whispered. "Khe Sanh is a hot spot and Marine Recon must have a dangerous mission. Why is my brother in all of this?"

It was obvious to Kellie that Kathleen was beginning to lose it, so she quickly stepped in. "Hey, Kat, take it easy now. You don't know anything about what's going on. I'm sure your brother will contact you when he can. In fact, why don't you go to Major Morningstar and see if she can contact Khe Sanh for you? Maybe you can get some information."

Kathleen looked at Kellie and her face took on a calmer look. "That's a good idea, Kel," she said. Then, turning to Kyle, she stood to attention again and asked, "Sir, may I be dismissed to go to the OPs tent?"

"Lieutenant, please stop poppin' to attention and salutin' all the time," Kyle said in irritation. "Of course, you're dismissed. But know this; I know the leader of that Recon Team. He's a relative of mine and a good friend. Your brother couldn't be in better hands. Marine Recon is a tough, well trained, and get-it-done outfit."

Kathleen simply said, "Thank you, Sir," Then, she turned and hurried off.

Kyle watched Kathleen basically run back toward the Operations tent. Turning to Kellie he said, "Damn, I'm sorry 'bout all this. I guess I should've kept my mouth shut."

"It's done," Kellie replied simply.

After a long silence, Kyle continued, "Okay, Lieutenant Anderson if you'll give me a copy of your orders we'll get this show on the road. Your chariot awaits you." As he spoke, he waved for Harv to come over. Harv had been watching them and immediately came running. By the time Harv arrived, Kyle was already looking over Kellie's orders. "Harv," he said without looking up from the orders, "get the Lieutenant's gear secured on Girl Needed. Then we'll go over the trip requirements before we dust off."

"Roger that, Skipper," Harv said as he started picking up Kellie's bags.

Kyle folded the orders and put them into his flight jacket. "Okay, Lieutenant, let's get you to your chariot and on your way to the ten-six-six. Please follow me."

As Harv was loading and securing Kellie's bags, Kyle and Kellie walk calmly over to Girl Needed. They walked around to the left seat were Denny was sitting. Kyle knocked on the door and Denny opened up. "Lieutenant Anderson, this is Lieutenant Denison our copilot." The two nodded to each other and gave each other a small informal salute. "Denny, be prepared to wind her up on my signal."

"Roger that, Skipper."

"Were you able to top off our fuel as we planned?"

"Roger again, Skipper, she's full to the brim."

Kyle signaled Kellie with his finger to follow him. They walked around to the left waist door where Harv had already finished loading and securing Kellie's gear and was sitting in his gunner position with the M60 machine gun in place. Kyle turned to Kellie with a very serious look on his face. "Okay, Lieutenant, here's the scoop. The flight isn't a long one but it could be dangerous. We're goin' to follow Route One to almost Phu Bai, and then we're goin' to swing west. The ten-six-six is about eight klicks, or about five miles, southwest of Phu Bai. Now, since we retook Hue, the 5th Marines have secured Route One all the way through Phu Bai to Hue. This ride should be uneventful, but just in case we're goin' to be in combat mode. That means we'll be flyin' with the waist doors open and Sergeant Milton will be at the ready. He's goin' to be set up on the left side and you're goin' to be strapped in on the right side. You can see there's not a lot of room back here. So, should anythin' happen, you have to be prepared to move and move quickly. The sergeant may need to set up on the right side quickly and you'll have to move. He'll show you what you'll need to do and how to do it. Are there any questions?"

"No, Sir, no questions."

As Kellie was climbing in through the left waist door, Kyle stuck his finger into the air and started making circular moves with it. That was Denny's order to start the engine, which he did immediately and the rotor blades were already in motion as Kyle climbed into the right command seat. In seconds, they were airborne.

Kellie sat in the back strapped into the right side and holding on for dear life. Thoughts ran through her mind. Over the last two weeks a lot things had happened to her. She had flow in a large Air Force transport for the first time in her life, she had met two amazing friends, she had taken a wild ride in a military jeep for the first time in her life, and now she was riding in a helicopter for the first time in her life and not just any helicopter; an assault helicopter. Well, this is what she wanted. This is what she had trained for. Now it was all happening. She thought that from here on out things were going to happen fast and furious.

The flight to the ten-six-six was uneventful; in fact they landed a little ahead of schedule. Kellie found Captain Collie to be very nice and helpful. He showed her where to report and had Sergeant Milton take her gear to the nurse's quarters. He told her he was ordered not to fly back to his base at night even though it was a short distance. Therefore, he and his crew would be spending the night at the ten-six-six. He asked her to meet him at the Officer's Club after she had reported. She told him it was fine with her as long as the unit commander didn't have other ideas. So, it was agreed.

Kellie followed Kyle's directions to the Operations tent. There the clerk, a Corporal Hadley, immediately took her into the commanding officer's office. Lt. Coronal Noble Vickers was waiting for her. He was involved with looking over a stack of papers and held a half empty glass of some kind of alcoholic beverage in one hand. He looked up in surprise as they walked in.

"Sir," the Corporal said, "this is Lieutenant Anderson. We've been expecting her."

The Coronal jumped to his feet spilling some of his drink. "Thank you, Jimmy, that'll be all. Jimmy leisurely turned around and walked back out the door closing it behind him.

"Please have a seat Lieutenant. As you can see I wasn't expecting you until a little later."

Kellie sat down in an old wooden chair in front of the desk. "Sorry at the inconvenience, Sir, but we made much better time than we anticipated."

"That is perfectly alright, Lieutenant, perfectly alright. By the way, who brought you in?"

"Captain Collie and his crew brought me in, Sir."

"Oh, yes, Captain Collie. Good man and a good officer. And he's very good at his job. Did you know he hasn't lost a single medivac chopper that he's flow cover for. Not a single one?"

Kellie shook her head, "No, Sir, I didn't know that."

"Well, that's neither here nor there. Right now I'm going to give you a quick synopses of what we've got here and—."

Before the Coronal could finish his sentence Kellie shot to her feet and interrupted him, "Sir, before we go any deeper into this I must tell you that I don't feel qualified to accept the assignment of head nurse. I am—."

Before she could finish her sentence he interrupted her harshly, "You interrupted me Lieutenant. So, we'll do this the hard way."

Kellie was shocked as his whole demeanor had changed. He no longer seemed like a bumbling officer in disarray but now was in complete control. "Stand to attention, Lieutenant," he ordered briskly. Kellie snapped to attention dropping her orders and her cap in the process. He squared himself behind the desk and looked at her intently. "Now, we'll start over. As I was saying, I'm going to give you an overview of our situation here. But first, I'll ask you if you're capable of sitting back down and listening to what I have to say without interruption?"

"Yes, Sir, I most as surly am and I beg the Coronal's pardon."

"Fine, then please pick up your orders and place them on my desk and then pick up your cap and return to your seat."

Kellie did as she was ordered.

"I'm going to make this quick because I'm due in the OR in about fifteen minutes. Our situation here is fluid as well as challenging. We have three doctors of which I'm one. We have eight nurses and you'll make the ninth. The army sent you here to be our new head nurse and that's what you'll be. I know you're worried about acceptance and about being able to do your job with so little experience. But your medical background will be extremely valuable to us and I've already spoken to all the nurses and there'll be no animosity towards you at all. Lt. Clare Mason is the senor nurse now and she'll work directly with you to get you started and make you aware of how we do things here. She, as are all the nurses here, are outstanding people; personally as well professionally. We have two male OR Technicians; a Sergeant Stanley and a Sergeant Morley. There's no one better in the operating room than Sergeant Morley. However, outside the operating room he's a bit of a maverick. We also have two corpsman from the navy and two medics from the army. They're a big help getting stretchers on and off choppers and they do excellent work in triage. You'll find that everyone here goes the extra mile to get things done."

The Coronal paused and relaxed a bit. Kellie continued to watch and listen to him without speaking. "Okay," he said slapping his hands together; I need to finish this up. After leaving here I want you to go to the Officer's Club and wind down. Have a drink and relax and collect your thoughts. The Officer's Club is really just the Club as it's the only club we have and enlisted as well as officers go there. Then, I want you to go to the nurse's quarters and get a good night's sleep; if you can. As head nurse you'll have your own private quarters. They're small but comfortable and private. Then report to me here at oh-six-hundred hours in the morning and we'll finish up. Now, have you got all that?"

Kellie got back on her feet at attention and said with deep sincerity, "Yes, Sir, I understand and I would like to again beg the Coronal's pardon for my first impression."

Coronal Vickers smiled at her and said, "Relax, Lieutenant. We're all going to get along fine. Now, you're dismissed." He stood up straight and gave her a firm salute.

Kellie returned his salute just as firmly and then turned shapely and walked out the door. She walked past the corporal who was still sitting at his typewriter and out of the tent into the evening air. Once outside, she stopped and took a deep breath and let it out slowly. Then the clenched her fist, gritted her teeth and quietly yelled at herself, "Stupid, stupid, stupid."

A little later Kellie was sitting at a table in the Officer's Club and across from her was Captain Collie. The club was a small tent with a bar at one end. It looked like it had been made by the staff themselves out of spare lumber. However, there were about five or six bar stools standing at the bar. The place was dimly lit with a string of lights running crossways near the tent's roof. Scattered about were a number of wooden tables each with four wooden chairs. The floor was wood and uneven in several places. But, as it was, it was still a place to take a break and have an alcoholic beverage. Kyle was sipping on a beer and Kellie was drinking a gin and tonic.

"Well, how'd it go with the commandin' officer?" He asked tipping his beer.

"I certainly could've made a better impression."

"Oh, so things didn't get off to a great start."

Kellie smiled at him, "Could we talk about something else. I'm supposed to be winding down."

Kyle gave a soft chuckle, "Okay, you pick the subject."

"Okay, let's lighten things up a bit," Kellie said leaning on the table with both elbows. "Why do you call your chopper, 'Girl Needed'?"

Kyle chuckled again and gave her his charming crooked smile. "Well," he said, "that's easy. The crew and I are losers when it comes to women. None of us have a girlfriend or a wife. When the opportunity arises for one of us to make it with a woman, we invariably strike out. Thus the name, 'Girl Needed'."

Kellie laughed out loud. "My goodness, Captain, you don't look like you'd have trouble with women."

"That's kind of you to say but let's wait and see how this turns out."

"Captain, I'm only on my second drink and you're already getting fresh with me."

"I'll make a deal with you," Kyle said with his smile again. "If you'll stop callin' me captain and sir, I'll stop callin' you lieutenant. My name is Kyle and I think yours is Kellie. Is that right?"

"That's right, but my friends call me Kel," she said grinning. "And I'll go for that when we're alone but when others are present I think we need to follow protocol. Is that okay?"

"Yeah, that's okay. But that does bring up the question about bein' alone. Are we goin' to get to be alone a lot?"

She leaned back in her chair and looked at him. She pointed her glass at him and said, "I hope so, Kyle. I really hope so."

As she leaned back in her chair and took a sip of her drink, her long black hair fell down across one side of her face. She was smiling and swirling her gin and tonic and didn't notice him staring at her. Her face showed lines of fatigue from the long hard day, but the dim light danced in her clear blue eyes. "I hope so too," he said in almost a whisper. "I really hope so too."

CHAPTER TWENTY-NINE

The Mission at Khe Sanh

When Jordan and his Recon Team ran from the helipad, they entered a dugout path. The path was about six feet deep and each side was lined with sandbags. There they met a marine who said nothing but signaled them to follow him, which they did. They followed the marine down the path carrying all of their equipment with them. After about a fifty yard run, they came to what appeared to be a dugout bunker. It had an opening but no visible door. There were sandbags lining the opening except for the bottom. The marine stood back from the opening and signaled for them to go in.

The inside of the bunker was about twenty-five feet square and deep enough that they could standup with room to spare. It was well lit by powerful lights in each corner, leading Jordan to believe that there must be generator somewhere that was supplying the power. The floor was wood and there were large log supports holding up a wooden ceiling made from the same kind of planking that made up the floor. It was very sparse in the bunker. There was a marine in one corner sitting in a chair facing a small table upon which sat a radio. At the time, he was not using the radio and it didn't appear to be turned on. There was a large table in the middle of the bunker that dominated the space. On it was a map that was being held down on each corner by rocks. There were no chairs in the bunker except for one by the radio being used by the marine that Jordan surmised was the operator.

As their eyes adjusted to the light in the bunker, a tall marine approached them. "Welcome to Khe Sanh," he said smiling. His hair was a light brown with streaks of grey. His physical appearance was muscular and well framed. Dark brown eyes looked out from a tired and ragged face. Jordan estimated his age to be in his early forties. Suddenly Jordan noticed that he was wearing the rank of a major. Jordan quickly came to attention and began the motion of a salute.

"As you were," the Major said, grabbing Jordan's hand and giving it a firm shake.

"Thank you, Sir," Jordan replied while returning the firm handshake.

"Are you the team leader?" The Major asked as he released Jordan's hand.

"Aye, Sir, code name Greaser."

"Okay, Greaser, let's get right down to it. I'm Major Wellman and the short serious man standing behind me is Lt. Myers. We've got a lot to cover so if you and your team will gather around the table I'll layout the mission for you."

Major Wellman went directly to the table and waited until the entire team was gathered around. Lt. Myers didn't come to the table but stood a few feet behind the Major.

Once he was satisfied that he had everyone's complete attention, Major Wellman began, "Okay, I've got a lot say so we can get you on your mission tonight. Greaser, as team leader you may interrupt me at any time to explain something or to insert a comment or opinion. Are we clear on that?"

"Aye, Sir, we're clear."

Major Wellman nodded and continued, "Good. Now, as you may or may not know a new operation started April 1st. If you haven't been able to keep track of the date, that was yesterday. It's in full swing as we speak. The operation is called Pegasus. Its purpose is to reopen Route 9 to supposedly *rescue* us here at Khe Sanh. Nobody here feels that we need *rescuing*, but that's a subject for another time." At this point the Major leaned over the map and pointed to Khe Sanh, he then traced this finger along Route 9. "You can see that Route 9 runs from Khe Sanh to the coast. It's been controlled by the enemy for several months and we've been unable to be supplied via a land route. But a lot of brave chopper jockeys have fought their way in there and helped keep us supplied as well as getting our wounded out. The way Pegasus' works is that elements of the 1st and 3rd Marines are pushing up Route 9 with Army Engineers and Seabees doing patch up work behind them. At the same time, the 1st Air Cav Division is using choppers to skip ahead up Route 9 and secure pockets of resistance."

The Major paused for a long moment, took a breath and then continued, "Now you may be wondering where our mission fits into all this. Well, it's right here." The Major put his finger on the map and made a small circle. "This area right here is what our mission is all about; the area south of Route 9, east of Khe Sanh, and north of the A Shau Valley. We need to know what the enemy's strength is there and, if possible, who they are. Since their defeat at Hue, they've been hurrying to their sanctuaries in the DMZ and in Laos. We know they lost over an entire division at Hue, and we know they've lost at least another division here at Khe Sanh. Their route to get to Laos is between us here at Khe Sanh and north of the A Shau Valley. But the ASA boys at Phu Bai think they've left a sizeable force in the area that I just described as a delaying and harassing force. We want to try and pin point that force and wipe it out." He stopped again and pointed at Jordan. "And that's what you and your team are going to find out for us, Greaser."

There was a long silence as the Recon Team looked at each other and nodded. Then Jordan turned to the Major and said, "Aye, aye, Sir, tell us what you want us to do."

The Major smiled and tilted his head to one side. "Well, as they say, it ain't goin' ta be easy." Leaning over the map again he put his finger at a point just east of Khe Sanh and slightly north of Route 9. "There's a ridge right here. It's barely three hundred yards from our eastern parameter. Every night around mid-night for the last two weeks, the enemy has sent a mortar team high up on the eastern side of that ridge. They obviously have a spotter with them who positions himself on the western side of the ridge so he can look down on us. The spotter radios target information back to the mortar team and they lob rounds into our parameter. We think this mortar team is from that delaying and harassing force. They obviously have a radio to communicate between themselves and their main base. We want to find that main base by getting a fix on their transmissions. I guess you're wondering how you're going to do that?"

"Well," Jordan smiled, "I figured we had a guy from the NSG with us for some reason."

"And you figured right," the Major replied. "Greaser, how you run this mission is your business. Once you're out there all the decision making is on you. But here is what needs to be done. Number one: you'll leave tonight about twenty-three hundred hours. You'll exit under our barbed wire at the southernmost part of our parameter. Number two: you'll quietly and without being seen loop around to the southern end of the ridge I pointed out to you on the map. Number three: you'll maneuver your team into a position that allows you to see clearly the mortar team. You may have to wait until they actually start shelling us before you can locate them. But don't worry about that because stopping the shelling is not our primary on this mission. Number four: you'll have to locate and eliminate the spotter. It'll have to be done very quietly so that the mortar team won't know what happened to him. Number five: Once the spotter has been eliminated, you'll quickly kill the remaining three members of the mortar team starting with the radio operator. He must not under any circumstances get a message off. Number six: your NSG man will contact the ASA at Phu Bai and put them on alert. They're already expecting to hear from you sometime after mid-night and will be listening. Once Phu Bai is ready, your linguist, using the mortar team's radio that should already be set to the correct frequency, will start talking with the mortar team's main base. Your linguist must keep the main base talking long enough for the ASA to triangulate the signal and get a good fix. Number seven: Once your NSG man tells you that Phu Bai has got a good fix, you haul ass out of Dodge. Number eight: here's where Lt. Myers comes in. He'll have two squads at the point where you exited. That's where we expect you to return. One squad will be a machine gun squad and the other will be a rifle squad. On your way back, you'll probably stir up a hornets nest and you'll have bad guys all over you. If you're being pursued as you approach our parameter, say within a hundred yards or less, you can have your team hit the deck and lay flat. While lying flat, you'll fire off a flare that we'll give you. We call 'em 'Daylight Flares' because they'll light up the area bright as day for about thirty seconds. I can't make the point strongly enough that you must be lying down when you fire off that flare, because as soon as that flare goes off, the machine gun squad is going to open up and cut down anything they see standing. And the rifle squad will support them. They'll continue to fire until the flare goes out. Then you can get your team back on their feet and complete your trip back."

He stopped talking and looked at Jordan with a very serious look in his brown eyes. He took a deep breath and asked solemnly, "Does that seem easy enough, Greaser?"

The trip to loop to the south and then back west to the ridge had taken longer than the Recon Team had planned. The distance was about as planned but the need to stay concealed slowed them down. There wasn't as much cover as they had hoped for. The plan had called for an hour to make the trip to a good position on the ridge, then about a half an hour to accomplish the mission, and then another hour for the trip back. They were now at least twenty minutes behind schedule. But at last they reached a position where they could see the mortar team clearly with their Starlight night vision equipment. There was a moon that went in and out behind scattered clouds. It wasn't a full moon but it did provide light and, in addition, the Starlight night vision scopes worked much better with some moonlight. The bad news was that mortar shells were already being lobbed into the Khe Sanh parameter.

The whole team crouched around Jordan waiting for their orders. Jordan handed Tracker a Starlight scope and whispered very softly, "Get over to the other side of the ridge and find that spotter. When you've found him let me know. Get goin' we're behind schedule."

Silently, Tracker moved away from the team and slipped over the top of the ridge. Then Jordan spoke, again in a very low whisper, "We'll use hand signals as much as we can. Now, Cherokee, move over to that high point we passed on our way in and setup your automatic weapon. Depending on how things go, we may need you to cover our retreat." Cherokee said nothing but simply nodded and quietly moved away back in the direction they had come from. "Okay, your turn Swede, setup your sniper rifle right here and sight in on that mortar team. Be sure when things start, you get the radio man first."

Swede quickly and quietly unfolded the bipod on the barrel of his rifle and found a good spot on the ground to setup the rifle. Once the rifle was in place, he stretched out on the ground behind it and began adjusting the Starlight scope attached to the top of the rifle.

Jordan found a good spot to lie down and settled in to wait. With hand signals he told Breed and Searcher to hang loose until they were needed. They followed Jordan's example and found good spots to settle in and wait.

The wait was only a short eight minutes. Tracker came crawling back to the team and gave them a thumbs up. He had found the spotter. Jordan went over to Tracker and whispered, "I'll follow you back to the top of the ridge. There I'll stop. You go on up the ridge and take out the spotter. You know how to do it. Not a sound. When it's done signal me with a thumbs up. I'll be watchin' you with my Starlight. When you see the rest of us head for the mortar team, you come down to join us. Leave your weapon with me and I'll give it back to you when we meet at the mortar team. Have you got all that?"

Tracker simply nodded and immediately turned and started back up the ridge with Jordan close behind. At the top of the ridge, Jordan stopped and watched Tracker disappear into the high grass and small jungle foliage. Jordan used his night vision scope but Tracker could only be seen if he wanted to be seen. Jordan settled in at the top of the ridge and continually scanned the direction were Tracker had vanished. He knew that when the job was done Tracker would become visible again and give him the go or no go signal.

Tracker inched his way back across the spine of the ridge staying invisible at all times. He had found the spotter in an indentation nearly at the top and on the west side of the ridge. He was about two hundred feet directly above the mortar team. High grass and undergrowth concealed him as he crouched in the indentation. He held a small radio in his hand and on his head was a small headset. Because of the headset, he wore no type of head gear. His problem was that to do his job of spotting he had to occasionally stick his head up to see over the grass and undergrowth. And, Tracker thought to himself that would be his undoing.

Moving soundlessly, Tracker positioned himself directly behind and a little above the spotter in his indentation. Tracker reached behind his back and quietly pulled his KA-BAR knife from its holster attached to his utility belt. Then, he waited. He had timed the mortar rounds at being fired about every eight minutes. The last round had been fire just as he was getting into position. He waited patiently and tried to time his movement with the next time the spotter poke his head up. Believing the correct time had arrived, he moved down to within inches of the spotters head. Then, as almost on cue, the spotter poked his head up to look down into the Khe Sanh parameter. The spotter was holding his radio mic in his right hand, so Tracker, faster than any rattle snake, grabbed the spotter around the mouth with his left hand, and at the exact same time, drove his KA-BAR into the base of the spotter's skull with his right. He push the knife hard and fast through the spotter's neck until the point of the blade protruded out the front of his throat just above the Adam's apple. The spotter died within seconds. Tracker quickly crammed the dead man and his radio into the little indentation. He now turned quickly and started back to make himself visible.

Jordan remained at his position carefully scanning the direction that Tracker had vanished into. He was patient because he knew the job had to be done carefully, but he also knew that the mortar attack was simply a harassing maneuver and wouldn't last much more than two hours. It was already after oh-one-hundred hours so he surmised that they only had another hour to get the job done. He didn't want to abort the mission but he had to give Tracker the time he needed. Those twenty minutes they lost on their trip up could prove to be costly. But then he saw what he was looking for. Still quite a distance across the ridge, Jordan saw an arm reaching towards the sky with a thumbs-up signal. He smiled and quickly turned and slid back down to where the rest of team was waiting.

Jordan crawled over to Swede, who was still peering through his scope. He tapped him on the shoulder and Swede looked over to him. Jordan simply pointed three fingers downward towards the ground, which meant for Swede to take out the three man mortar team. Swede winked at him and then went back to his scope.

Radioman Phung Pin sat crouched about two yards from the other two members of the mortar team. He watched as the mortar loader position a shell at the mouth of the mortar ready to drop it down the barrel.

Pin's radio was close by his side. It was turned on and set to the proper frequency in case he needed to contact mission operations. Taped to the top of the radio was his call sign for the night, which was 'Dark Team', and the call sign for mission operations, which was 'Dark Base'. The call signs changed every night so he was given the new names each night on a small card. But the communications frequency was never written down; he was required to memorize it before leaving on the mission.

They had been doing these missions each night for the last two weeks. He didn't really understand the reason for it because they did very little damage and the Americans did very little about them. The Americans did send out a patrol once, but they made a minor effort to locate them. He was told that these missions were to simply harass the Americans and maybe make them lose some sleep, which he doubted it did. He was also told never to use the radio unless in an emergency. Operations wanted radio silence if at all possible.

The other man on the team was the range finder. He wore a small headset and received firing co-ordinance from the spotter. He was now in the process of readjusting the range and distance settings on the mortar.

Pin watched his comrades as they worked and the thought crossed his mind that maybe they could leave early tonight. Maybe they could fire their shells faster and finish up early and get back to the safety of their home base. He breathed deeply and thought what a good thing that would be. That would be the last thought that Phung Pin would ever have, for there was a thud on his chest just below his throat. His eyes shot wide open, he fell backwards, and died immediately.

The loader heard the thud slightly before he heard the distant crack of the sniper rifle. As a result, he had turned to face the noise of the thud and saw Pin on his back with lifeless eyes staring into the sky. He was still holding the mortar shell when there was a second thud; this one was in between his shoulder blades. He had only a short moment to be stunned when he saw the front of his chest explode. He lurched forward and fell with the mortar shell under him.

The range finder saw both of these things happen in quick succession. He realized immediately what was happening. He slung off his headset and started running down the steep slope of the ridge. Had he kept his wits about him, he would've dived to ground and started crawling thus making a shot at him very difficult. But by being upright he presented an easy shot. He had only run a few steps when the third thud caught him in the neck just below his jaw. Unlike his comrades, he didn't die immediately. Although the shot nearly took his head off, he lived several minutes as he bled to death.

After the third shot, Swede looked over at Jordan and again winked. He started to get up but Jordan pushed him back down. "You stay here and watch that slope below the mortar position. If anyone comes up that slope, you take 'em out. Swede nodded and lay back down. Jordan jumped to his feet and picked up Tracker's weapon and then signaled for Searcher and Breed. "Come on you two, you're with me. We got about a hundred yard dash to run. Let's go."

The three started their run across the east side of the ridge. Running against the slope of the ridge was hard going, especially with undergrowth and high grass. When they reached the mortar position they were all breathing hard. Jordan quickly took stock of the situation and started giving orders. "Breed, check that radio and tell me if you can work it." Then pointing to Searcher, "Get on your radio, raise Phu Bai; let 'em know we're in control and ready."

In only a few seconds, Breed said with authority, "This radio's a piece of cake. It's Russian and I know it well. It's already got the frequency set and they were nice enough to put their call signs on it if you can read it."

Jordan leaned down to look at the writing. "Yeah, our call sign will be Dark Team and theirs is Dark Base. Can I use it now?"

"Roger that," Breed replied, "it's a simple push-to-talk operation. Hold the mic and push down on the button to talk and release to listen. But you'll need this headset because there's no speaker. And I guess we can assume that the frequency it's set on is the one we want."

"Well, let's hope so." Then he turned to Searcher, "Is Phu Bai ready?"

Before Searcher could answer, Tracker appeared and scared everyone to death.

"Damn, Tracker, you don't need to sneak up on us. We're the good guys."

"Oops, Sorry," he said smiling as took his weapon from Jordan.

"Phu Bai is waitin' on us," Searcher interrupted.

"Breed you stay by me in case I need somethin' concernin' this radio," Jordan ordered. "Tracker, roll these bodies down the hill or somethin'. Just get 'em away from here."

Jordan squared himself away in front of the radio. He put the headset on and picked up the handset. He took a deep breath and then pushed the talk button and said in his best Vietnamese, "Dark Base, Dark Base, this is Dark Team calling please respond." He released the talk button and waited for a response that didn't come. After waiting what he considered a reasonable time he repeated is call, "Dark Base, Dark Base, this is Dark Team calling please respond."

There was a bit of static and another wait but finally a response came. "Dark Team, why are you violating radio silence? Is there an emergency?"

Jordan gave Searcher the thumbs up and then responded to the question from base. "This is Dark Team, yes, Sir, there is an emergency. We've lost our spotter and cannot find him anywhere. What are your instructions?"

There was another long silence, then another question, "How did the spotter get lost? Was he captured? Have you been compromised?"

Jordan looked at Searcher for information. Searcher said quickly, "Phu Bai got their fix and I've got mine but the third guy in the field didn't get his and we need him to triangulate. You've got to keep them talkin' a little longer."

Jordan immediately went to work again, this time he changed his Vietnamese to a higher more excited tone. "This is Dark Team; our mortar loader has gone up the ridge again to search. Do you want us to continue to fire the rest of our shells in the blind?"

This time the response came back immediately, "This is Dark Base; you are ordered to shut down immediately. Abandon the search for the spotter. Leave the remaining shells. Return now. Shut down your radio and destroy it. This is the end of all communications."

Jordan again looked at Searcher. Searcher smiled and gave the thumbs up sign, "We got 'im."

Jordan jumped up and started giving orders again in rapid fire order. "Okay, guys, let's destroy all this stuff and get the hell outa Dodge. Breed, destroy that radio. Searcher, do you need your radio anymore?"

"No."

"Then, destroy it. Tracker, wait until we're all clear then drop a grenade down the barrel of that mortar and spike it."

As they all were doing as ordered, they heard the crack of Swede's sniper rifle. There were three reports in rapid order.

"Oh! Shit," Jordan breathed. "It looks like they're comin' up here to see what's actually happen. Come on guys let's go, go, go."

Jordan, Breed, and Searcher started running back across the eastern slope of the ridge in the direction they had come from originally. As they ran, they heard the explosion behind them as Tracker spiked the mortar. Jordan never slowed down because he knew that Tracker would catch up with them. As they approached the high point where Swede was, they could still hear him firing shot after shot. Upon reaching Swede's position, Swede swung around and pointed his rifle at them. "Damn," he said in disgust, "you could yell a warning. I nearly shot you. There's no need to be quiet now. You guys must have stirred up the entire North Vietnamese Army. I thought we were just dealing with a mortar team."

"Me too," Jordan replied as he slid in beside Swede. "How many do you think?"

"At first I just saw a few, but now I'm thinking they must have at least a couple of platoons down there, or, hell, maybe even a whole company."

"Shit," Jordan grunted. "I bet this whole mortar team thing was a design to drawn out a patrol from Khe Sanh and ambush them. And we stepped into it."

"At any rate," Swede yelled as he fired again, "we sure can't hold them off with what we got."

Just at that time Tracker joined them. "Well, boys," he said smiling, "I hope the Intel we got is worth all this shit."

"It better be," Jordan said with a trace of anger. "Everybody up and let's hump it to the high point on the southern ridge where we left Cherokee. Swede you drag up the rear and cover us as best you can. Breed; stay back with Swede and help him as much as you can. Searcher, you're with me. Tracker; you take the point but don't out run us too far. Stay close enough that you can still find us in this dark. The moon is still playin' hide-and-seek with those clouds. So, be careful."

After they all had their orders, they took off at a fast pace. They were trying to go back faster than they came out, which made things harder as they weren't able to avoid the natural obstructions as they did on the way out. They were continually stepping into large holes and tripping over large and protruding undergrowth. Swede and Breed were firing as they ran, but it was much to no avail as Breed didn't have a night vision scope on his weapon and they couldn't stop to aim anyway. But they at last reached Cherokee's position. He had been watching for them ever since he had heard the explosion that spiked the mortar.

"What ta fuck is goin' on down there?" He asked as they all gathered around him.

"A lot," Jordan breathed almost out of breath. "Haven't you seen anythin'?"

"No."

"Well, you will," Jordan said sarcastically. "We need to keep movin'. Cherokee, you're goin' to have to handle that heavy automatic weapon of yours as a hand carry. Can you fire it as a hand held?"

"Yeah, there's a handle in my pack that I can attach that'll allow me use it hand held, but the accuracy may not be the best."

"That's okay; we need fire volume more than accuracy right now. Get that handle on and join Swede to our rear and send Breed up here with me."

They were soon on the move again with Tracker still on point. Jordan, Breed, and Searcher were in the middle and Swede and Cherokee brought up the rear. Although they weren't receiving any fire, Swede and Cherokee continually laid down heavy burst of fire to their rear. This went on until they reached the middle of the southern ridge. They were now only about two hundred yards from where they needed to cut back to the north and head down into the Khe Sanh parameter. As they approached the cut back point, all hell broke loose. Bullets started whizzing all around them and were kicking up the earth at their feet. They all automatically hit the dirt.

"Where's that fire comin' from," Jordan yelled back to the rear.

"Not from back here," Cherokee yelled. "It seems clear back here."

"It's coming from south of us down the ridge." It was Tracker yelling at them. He had run back to within about twenty yards of the middle group. "They've loop out wide to our left and they're trying to out flank us. Those little fuckers are trying to cut us off from Khe Sanh!"

"Fuck," Jordan said under his breath. Then he yelled, "Everybody up and runnin'. We've got to get down this slope to the parameter it's only about another hundred yards. Swede, Cherokee change you fire to the south and pour it on. Everybody fire as they run. Let's go, go, go."

They made a sharp pivot to the right and headed down the slope toward the parameter. No one could see very well as they couldn't fire and use their scopes at the same time. Jordan only hoped they would come out close to the entry point. As they went down the slope the fire eased up a bit because the bad guys were on the other side of the ridge but that only lasted a few seconds. The North Vietnamese were now swarming over the ridge and firing down on them. Then, it finally happened; Searcher was hit and went down. Jordan saw Searcher fall and immediately stopped and went to his side. Searcher had been hit high on the collar bone near his neck. The bullet had broken through his collar bone and cut a large gash in his neck. Blood was flowing everywhere.

Jordan jumped to his feet with bullets flying all around him. "Everybody, hold your ground," he yelled as loud as he could. "Turn around and fire everythin' you got."

The well trained Marine Recon Team did as ordered. They stopped running, turned around, and unleashed a hellish barrage of fire at the enemy. Cherokee's heavy machine gun was sweeping the field, Swede's snipe rifle was deadly accurate, and Breed and Tracker fired their weapons until they were empty; then reloaded and started again. But there were just too many. The North Vietnamese kept coming.

But the fire did slow them down; enough so Jordan could get a bandage jammed into the gash in Searcher's neck to slow the bleeding. Once that was done, Jordan reached into his pack and pulled out a couple of the Daylight Flares he'd been given. He had to hope they were close enough to the parameter. With bullets still whizzing by, he shouted another order. "Everybody, cease firing and drop flat, and I do mean flat. And do it now!"

Again, the well trained and disciplined Marine Recon Team did as ordered; they ceased fire and dropped flat on their bellies. Without looking to see if his orders had been followed, Jordan rolled over on his back and pointed the flare gun into the sky and pulled the trigger.

As advertised, the flare rocketed into the sky and at about two hundred feet exploded and turned night into day. Jordan was lying on his back and didn't see what happened, but Lt. Myers was true to his word. He had two squads of marines at the entry point to the parameter; one machine gun squad and one rifle squad. When night turned to day, the

North Vietnamese were caught standing in the open. The machine gun squad opened fire with two heavy sixty caliber machine guns and the rifle squad opened up with semi-automatic rifle fire. The North Vietnamese were cut to pieces.

The flare hung in the sky for nearly a full thirty seconds. When it had died completely out, Jordan was on his feet shouting orders again. "Okay, guys, everybody up and runnin'. I've got Searcher. Go, go, go."

Lt. Myers had turned on a flash light to give them a direction in which to run. As it turned out, the Recon Team was only sixty yards away from the entry point and a little to the east.

Once safely inside the parameter of Khe Sanh, Jordan learned three things. First, their mission had been a success. Artillery from the 1st Marines, the 1st Air Cav, and Khe Sanh itself, had already open up a huge barrage on the co-ordinance given to them by Phu Bai. When dawn broke, marker smoke was fired onto the co-ordinance to guide air strikes in to continue the assault. Second, he found out that two of his team, Swede and Cherokee had been wounded but neither seriously. Cherokee had burns on his hands from continuing to hold his weapon even as it became red hot from continuous firing. Swede had a minor flesh wound in his left thigh. Third, he found out that Searcher had a serious wound. The bullet had indeed broken his collar bone, but, worse it had taken a large chunk out of his neck near his jugular vein. He had been given plasma to hold him over but he needed whole blood or he was going to die. They had to get Searcher to the ten-six-six right away.

CHAPTER THIRTY

Mercy Mission
to the 95th

I t was early morning on April 3rd as a medivac chopper set down gently on the first helipad at the ten-six-six. There were two assault choppers hovering overhead; on the side of one of them read the name Girl Needed. The other assault chopper was one of the new Cobras. There were three nurses, two medics, and one doctor waiting as the medivac chopper settled down. They immediately went to the chopper to help the walking wounded out and to get the stretcher on which the one that was seriously wounded lay. Once everyone was off the chopper, it immediately ok off and headed back north where the 1st Marines and 1st Air Cav were still fighting their way up Route 9. The Cobra peeled off and went with the medivac chopper flying high cover for it. Girl Needed dropped down and landed at the utility helipad.

As Kyle and his crew got out of Girl Needed, they took off their flight helmets and jackets and threw them into the chopper's back compartment. They were all sweating and looked very tired. They had been up since the crack of dawn flying assault support for the 1st Marines as well as high cover for medivac choppers. Then, on special orders from

Cobra Umbrella One, they went back to Khe Sanh to cover the medivac chopper carrying the Recon Team to the ten-six-six. He knew the Recon Team had taken casualties but he didn't know who, how bad, or how many. Their orders also told them to wait at the ten-six-six just in case they were needed to fly cover for any medivacs going to the 95th. They were to stand down until farther orders.

"Am I the only one that wants a drink?" Denny asked bending over and putting his hands on his knees.

"Jesus, Denny, it's only oh-six-hundred I doubt the club is even open," Kyle said as he stretched his back.

"Yeah, I know, but I feel like I've been up for two days. Anyway, who the hell cares?"

"I sure as hell don't," Harv interjected, "I'll join you, Lieutenant."

Kyle looked at his dog tired crew. "You guys go ahead, I'll join you later. I want to go over to the OR and see how bad the Recon Team got hurt."

"Okay," Denny said, waving him on, "when you know something come tell us. We'll be at the club."

"Roger that," Kyle said.

As Kyle approached the OR, there was a nurse standing out front. As he neared the door, she stepped in front of him and held up her hand. "Sorry, Sir," she said in a pleasant but firm tone, "you can't go in there right now. It's very busy in there and you're not scrubbed."

"I just want to check on the guys that just came in on that last chopper," he said, giving her his best hurt look.

"I think some of 'em when over to the operations tent," she replied.

He turned to leave but stopped and turned back. "Excuse me; do you know where I could find Lt. Anderson?"

She smiled at him and pointed to the OR. "She's in there and'll be there for a while yet."

"Understood," he said tipping his head to her. "I wonder if you'd let her know I'm here when she gets out."

She looked at his name tag and said, "And you'd be Captain Collie, correct?"

"That would be me."

"I'll do that, Sir."

"Thank you."

It only took him a few minutes to get to the operations tent where he found three of the Recon Team sitting in some hard backed chairs in a far corner away from the operations activity. He hurried over and as he approached Jordan saw him coming. This time there were no salutes or any military formalities, the two men just hugged each other and slapped each other on the back.

"Man, am I glad to see you're okay," Kyle said.

Jordan stepped back from the hug and replied, "Yeah, I'm okay but three of my guys got wounded; one of 'em bad."

"Who's the bad one?"

"O'Rourke. He got hit in the upper collar bone and neck. He's on the table now. They're tryin' to get 'im stable enough so they can get him down to the 95th where they have more means to fix him up. Last I heard, they expected to have him ready to go in an hour and that was about ten minutes ago."

"And the other two guys?"

"They've already been checked out and are in one of the wards. I thought their wounds were very minor but it looks like they're goin' to want to keep them a couple of days after all."

"Well, what're your plans? Are you headed back to battalion?"

"That's really why I'm here in ops. I used their radio to contract my battalion. I got permission to stay with my wounded until they're ready to travel back to battalion. So, now that the other two wounded are in a ward, I'll be goin' with O'Rourke to the 95th. I'm pretty sure he'll be Japan bound and I'm goin' to see him off. As for the other two guys here, they're goin' back as soon as they can get a ride."

Kyle looked at him with curious eyes and asked, "You mean they're goin' to let you wait around here, and at the 95th, for this guy O'Rourke? Why's that?"

Jordan shrugged his shoulder and replied, "Because I asked them to and they said okay."

"Yeah, I know you asked 'em, but why? Is there somethin' special about him to you?"

Again Jordan just shrugged his shoulders and smiled at Kyle. "He's not Marine Recon but he went on that mission so we could get the job done. And we did get the job done. We put the hurt on 'em, Kyle. We put a real hurt on 'em. So, I guess I feel kind of responsible for him, you know. And he's a good guy and a good marine. I just want to see him all the way through. Can you understand that?"

Kyle just shook his head and smiled, "Yeah, I can understand that; especially since it's you." Then Kyle snap is fingers and pointed to Jordan as if he had some kind of great news. "You know," he said, "I just remembered. O'Rourke's sister is at the 95th. She's a nurse down there. We met a few days ago while I was there pickin' up the new head nurse for here, and I can tell you she was plenty worried about him bein' attached to a Recon Team."

"He's got a sister in country?" Jordan asked surprised.

"Yeah, it's true."

"Well then, while I'm down there I'll look her up and fill her in on what happened to her brother."

"Yeah, you should do that," Kyle smiled knowingly. "You can't miss her. She's got flaming red hair and she's quite a looker."

Jordan laughed out loud. "I hope you find a girl soon, Kyle. I think every girl's 'quite a looker' to you."

"Matter of fact," Kyle said winking, "I'm waitin' for the head nurse to come out of the OR right now. I had a nice little meetin' with her when I brought her here. I like her."

"You like all girls."

Then Kyles smile faded away and he said, "You know, Jordan, I really do like her. I don't get it, but there was somethin' about her that really stuck with me." The two men looked at each other in silence for a long moment and then Kyle repeated almost in whisper, "She really stuck with me."

It was a little over an hour before Kellie came out of the OR and into the wash up and prep area. She was tried and her scrubs were bloody. She was new here and it was her first shift in the OR. She had never seen anything like it. With the fighting along Route 9, they were busy. It was what the nurses here called a 'push'. They had five operating tables but only three doctors. She was amazed at the job the three doctors did. As they finished at one table they moved to another while the table they just left got scrubbed, cleaned and ready for the next patient. There were four nurses and one OR Tech working alongside the doctors. They only had ten recovery beds, so as soon as they could they had to rotate a patient in recovery to the regular ward. The ones that needed to be medevac'd immediately to the 95th were placed in a special six bed ward. Staff Sergeant Robert O'Rourke Jr. was in one of the six beds in the special ward. However, Kellie didn't know who he was or that he was even there.

Kellie was working hard to learn about being the head nurse, but the fact was that everyone worked; no matter your rank or position. She had taken off her bloody scrubs and thrown them into the used receptacle and was leaning over the wash-up sink washing her hands and splashing water on her face when a voice from behind her called her name. "Lt. Anderson."

She continue to lean over the sink using her forearms to prop herself up. She turned her head to look back at the person calling her. It was

Lt. Maxine Worth the Day Nurse. Water dripped off her face as she answered, "Yes."

"Lieutenant, a Captain Collie asked me to tell you he was here."

"He did?" Kellie replied as if not interested.

"Yes, Ma'am, he wanted to go into the OR earlier but I wouldn't let him go in. That was over an hour ago. So, he just left that message."

Kellie straightened up from the sink, grabbed a towel and began drying herself off. "Thank you," she said smiling, "and Lt. Worth, you did right keeping him out of the OR. I'll catch up to him as soon as I can get presentable."

"Yes Ma'am."

Kellie took a deep breath and then started for her quarters.

After Kellie had spent some time in her quarters, she headed for the operations tent to check her roster and to see if she could find Kyle. When she arrived, she didn't see Kyle anywhere, so she went directly to the posting board to check the roster of her nurses. Lt. Clare Mason, who liked to be called May, had been a big help getting Kellie organized on how to run the nursing staff. As Coronal Vickers had told her, there was not any animosity among the staff at all. They had all been very supportive and ready to help in any way they could.

The way they tried to make it work was that four nurses would serve in the OR for one week. The other four, for one week, would be broken so that one would be the Day Nurse and the other three would be divided between the four wards. When the week was up, they would switch. Kellie inserted herself where ever she believed she was needed most. Since the OR wasn't always active, the nurses working the OR would help with the wards during slack time. A shift was normally twelve hours. However, during a push, it could be much longer than that. The really hard part was getting the girls sometime off. To accomplish this, Kellie would have the ward nurses double-up so that one nurse worked two wards. This proved hard at times but everyone pitched in and made it work.

Kellie scanned the roster and found everyone in place. She checked the time from the clock above the posting board; it was eleven hundred hours. She figured Kyle was either at the mess tent or the club. She decided to try the mess tent first and headed in that direction. Upon entering the mess tent, she immediately saw Kyle and another man sitting at a bench table eating an early lunch. She went to the chow line and got herself a hamburger and some fries, then walked over to the bench table and asked, "Are you guys a couple or can anyone join in?"

Both men immediately got to their feet. "Please do join us," Kyle said smiling, "I wasn't sure they'd ever let you outa that OR."

"Well, here I am," she said putting her tray down and sitting down beside Kyle. The men remained standing so she motion for them to sit. "Come on guys set down you're making me nervous."

After they were seated, Kyle made the introductions. "Lt. Kellie Anderson I've the honor to present Sergeant Jordan Costillo of Marine Recon; Sergeant Costillo I've the honor to present Lt. Anderson of the Army Nurse Corps."

Jordan stood up again and saluted. "It's a pleasure to meet you, Ma'am."

"Please set down Sergeant and it's a pleasure to meet you also."

"So, Kel, how're things goin'?"

Kellie looked at him sharply and said firmly, "I thought we agreed to keep things formal unless it was just the two of us."

"Oh, for Christ sakes," Kyle laughed. "This guys a relative of mine. There's no way I can be formal with him."

"That's true Lieutenant, Kyle and I are relation of some sort."

"Okay," Kellie said, "in that case, we can start off by dropping the lieutenant stuff. My friends call me Kel."

"Fair enough, Kel, my friends call me Jordan."

Kellie took a big bite of hamburger and winked at Jordan.

"I hate to start things off by askin' a favor, Kel, but one of the guys that was on my team got hit pretty bad and I wonderin' if you could tell me how he's doin' and when we might be gettin' him down to the 95th?"

Kellie swallowed her big bite of hamburger and squinted at Jordan. "What's his name? What kind of wound does he have?"

"He's Staff Sergeant Robert O'Rourke. He was hit high on the collar bone and the lower neck."

Kellie stopped eating and slowly lowered her hamburger to her tray. Her clear blue eyes began to cloud over. "Did you say O'Rourke?"

Kyle quickly jumped into the conversation. "I'm sorry, Kel," he said quickly. "I was goin' to ask you about it in a more gentle way, but it seems big mouth here spoiled my plans."

Kellie looked at Kyle with those cloudy blue eyes and asked slowly, "I assume we're talking about Kat's brother."

Kyle looked away from her eyes and down at his hands. "Yes," he said reluctantly, "we are."

"What am I missin'?" Jordan asked.

Kyle looked up at Jordan and said, "Kel came over with Robert's sister, Kathleen. They're good friends."

Jordan dropped his head into his hands and moaned, "Aw shit, Kel, I'm sorry. But I had no way of knowin'."

There was a long silence and finally Kellie said softly, "Of course you didn't." With that she stood up and without looking at anyone but just staring down at the table she breathed, "I'll hurry over to the EVAC ward and see what I can find out. You two stay here. I should be right back."

Before either of them could say another word, she was out the mess tent door and gone.

Jordan looked up at Kyle with pleading eyes. "God, Kyle, I'm so sorry!"

Kyle reached over on put his hand on Jordan's shoulder and said firmly, "It's not your fault, kid. It's not your fault."

Kellie ran more than walked around the OR to the special EVAC ward. She quickly went in and found Lt. Sandra 'Sandy' Sanders working the ward. She hurried over to the nurse's station and asked in a whisper, "Sandy, do you have a Staff Sergeant Robert O'Rourke in here."

Sandy picked up her clipboard that held her patient chart and examined it. "Yeah, third bed on the left." She didn't asked Kellie any questions she just went back to her work. Kellie walked slowly down the line of beds until she came to Robert's. She looked down at him and saw he was heavily bandaged and had an IV going, but she could tell he was conscious. She picked up his chart from the end of the bed and read it over.

"How am I doin'?" He asked in very low voice. There was a small smile on the corner of his month.

Kellie mustered her best bedside manner and replied, "Well, it looks like you're off to the 95th here in a little while and then Japan and then home."

"So, I'm goin' ta make it?"

Kellie put the chart back on the hook at the end of the bed and replied smiling, "Yeah, you're going to make it."

He closed his eyes and a small tear ran out the corner of his left eye. "You know," he continued in his broken and low voice, "I sure wish I could've thanked Greaser for gettin' me outa there. You know he carried me over a hundred yards with bullets buzzin' all around us. I owe my life to 'im."

"Greaser! Who's Greaser?" Kellie asked.

"Oh, that's the code name for Sergeant Costillo. That guy's a great marine."

At that point, Robert began to cough and choke a little.

"Hey, that's enough of this chit chat," Kellie smiled. "Now, you lay back and wait for your ride out of here."

"Yes Ma'am."

Before Kellie started back to the mess tent, she made a couple of more stops to check up on the other two members of the Marine Recon team. Both were doing well and were expected to be release back to their battalion in a couple of days.

As she entered the mess tent, the two men were sitting impatiently staring down at their empty trays. They immediately looked up as she entered. They jumped to their feet but didn't say anything. They just looked at her and waited as if they were children waiting for Santa Claus.

As she walked up to them she signaled for them to sit back down. "Relax and take it easy. O'Rourke's doing fine and is scheduled to go out to the 95th on the next medivac chopper." Then, pointing to Jordan, "Your other two guys are doing just fine and are scheduled for release in a couple of days."

Both men looked relieved but only of a few seconds. "When is this medivac chopper due in?" Kyle asked suddenly.

Kellie looked confused and said, "I'm not sure but I think within maybe fifteen minutes or so."

"Do you know if it's got high cover to the 95th?"

"No, I don't." Kellie now knew what Kyle was thinking.

"Okay, I'm goin' over to OPs I'll see you guys shortly," Kyle said as he hurriedly started to the door."

"You're not goin' without me," Jordan yelled as the started after Kyle.

"Well, don't leave me behind," Kellie said tagging after Jordan.

Two medivac choppers arrived about fifteen minutes after Kyle had put in his call to Cobra Umbrella One. He had asked permission to fly cover for the medivacs going to the 95th. His permission had been granted but he was order to return to base immediately after the medivac choppers were safely at the 95th. What that meant to Kyle was that he wouldn't see Kellie for who knows how long.

Kyle pulled Kellie aside behind his chopper as the two medivac choppers were being loaded with three stretcher cases each; one of which was Robert O'Rourke.

"Listen, Kel," he started with a halting stutter, "I guess I won't be seein' you for who knows when." He looked around to see if they were being watched. Satisfied of their limited privacy, he put his hands on her shoulders and continued in a soft voice, "In this short time, I've become very attached to you. I mean, I think I like you very much." Kyle paused and looked into her clear blue eyes. A flush came over his face. "I guess I'm not sayin' this very well but I'd like to see you again as soon as I can. I'd like to spend some time with you. Would that be okay with you?"

At first Kellie was taken aback by his sincerity and stood somewhat ridged as he gently held her shoulders. But, then, she relaxed and smiled up at him. She tilted her head to one side and took off her cap. Her long black her tumbled out onto her shoulders coving his hands. Continuing to smile up at him she said, "Of course we've only known each other a very short time and we are in the middle of a war. And we have to be careful to not move things too fast under these circumstances. But, having said all that, I think I'd like to send some quality time with you, Captain Kyle Collie."

She had barely finished speaking when the rotors of Girl Needed started to rotate and Harv was yelling at him to come on; they had to go. The medivac choppers were already loaded and waiting for their high cover to dust off.

He looked back at his chopper and then back to Kellie. He couldn't resist the unbelievable urge to kiss her, so he leaned forward quickly before she could move and gave her a quick, warm kiss on the lips. He then turned quickly and started running for his chopper putting on his flight helmet as he ran. But about half way to the chopper door, he stopped and turned back to face her and shouted, "Can I change the name of my ship to Kellie?"

Kellie didn't hesitate, "Sure," she yelled waving to him.

He waved back and was then at the controls of 'Kellie'. He dusted off and got up high so the medivac choppers would be below him. In minutes, the three choppers had banked to the south and were headed for the 95th.

Kyle kept the newly christened Kellie hovering at about two hundred feet above, as the medivac choppers each set down and were unloaded. Kyle watched as the well trained personnel removed the stretchers, did standard triage, and then hurried them off of a ward were they would be treated in the order of the triage. Once he was satisfied all was well, he dropped down and set down on the utility helipad. He never cut his engine as his passenger jumped out. Jordan gave a quick salute and then started to turn to go to the OR, but Kyle signaled for him to come over to his open widow. Jordan, instinctively ducking to avoid the rotor blades, ran up to the window. "What's up?" He yelled over noise of the engine and rotors.

"Just thought you'd like to know that Kellie has radioed Robert's sister, Kathleen, and that she's aware that he's in this group we just brought in."

Jordan shook his head but didn't say anything.

"Take care of yourself, Marine," Kyle shouted as he waved Jordan away. After Jordan was clear, Kyle opened up the throttle and the crew of the Kellie was on their way back to their base at Cobra Umbrella One.

Jordan waved again then turned and started for the OR but he stopped. He doubted they would let him in and he wasn't sure Robert was there anyway. So, he decided to go to the ward were he had seen them take all the stretchers. As he walked in, no one stopped him immediately. He looked up and down the ward that had twenty beds on each side. Shortly he spotted a nurse wearing a cap but her flaming red hair could be seen tucked under the cap. He started down the aisle, but was stopped quickly by a nurse carrying a clip board.

"Excuse me, Sergeant," she said politely, "but this ward is off limits. These men are going to be prepped for OR."

"I'm sorry, Ma'am, but I need to see Sergeant O'Rourke just for a minute."

"Well, I'm sorry too, Sergeant, but you'll have to leave."

Then, Jordan got an idea. "But, Ma'am, Lt. O'Rourke asked me to drop by for just a few minutes. I see her down there right now."

The nurse stood up straight and looked down the row of beds and saw Kathleen standing at the foot of a bed. "Kat asked you to come by?" She asked suspiciously.

"Yes, Ma'am," Jordan replied holding up his right hand as if to swear.

The nurse took a deep breath and said in a commanding tone, "Okay, you can go down there but you can only stay a few minutes. I'll be watching you and when you see me signal you must leave."

Jordan smiled his best smile, saluted, and said, "Thank you, Ma'am."

As he approached the bed, Robert recognized him and weakly lifted his left hand and gave a limp wave. "Well, if it's not my babysitter come callin'."

Jordan smiled and took Robert's hand out of the air and placed it by his side. "I don't think you should be movin' around much," Jordan said quietly.

"Hey, Sis, this Jarhead here is the one that saved my bacon out there. He must've carried me over a hundred yards with bullets flying everywhere."

Kathleen turned to face Jordan and held out her hand, "Hi, I'm Rob's sister, Kathleen."

Jordan ignored her hand and stood up straight and saluted. "Yes Ma'am. And thank you Ma'am. I'm Sergeant Jordan Costillo of the 1st Battalion Marine Recon."

Kathleen smiled and held her hand out again, "Take it easy, Sergeant, we're not so formal here and my name is Kathleen but my friends call me Kat."

Relaxing only a little bit, Jordan took her hand held it. "Thank you, Ma'am, I mean Kathleen, no, I mean Kat."

Kathleen continued smiling at him and then politely asked for her hand back.

Jordan immediately dropped her hand. He hadn't realized he was still holding it. "I'm sorry, Ma'am," he said with his face flushing a bright red.

Jordan looked down the aisle and saw the nurse frantically signaling him to leave. He turned to Robert and said hurriedly, "Okay, Searcher, you take care now, and don't give those nurses in Japan a hard time. You did a good job for us. You'll always be an honorary Marine Recon as far as I'm concerned. Maybe I'll see you again someday; you never know." With that he waved and hurried away up the aisle and out the ward door.

After Jordan was gone, Robert asked his sister in a raspy voice, "What'd you think of 'im?"

Kathleen looked down at her brother and said firmly, "What I think of him is of no concern of yours at this point. You just need to get fixed and get on that plane to Japan. They won't let me work on you but I've a good friend, Lt. Mann who'll be sure you get taken care of properly. And don't be given her any of your Irish Blarney. Just lay there and let them get you ready for the flight."

"Yes Ma'am. Lieutenant, Ma'am," Robert replied mockingly.

Kathleen softened and said, "Really Rob, be serious for just a minute. You know Mom'll be glad your home."

Robert's faced turned serious and he said slowly, "Sis, this wound doesn't mean I'm leavin' the Corp. I'm a marine until the end or until I retire. And that's the truth. Nothin' has changed."

"That's a subject for different time," she said patting his leg. "I gotta go now. They'll be comin' for you here in a minute." She turned to walk away but had only taken a few steps when she stopped and turned back. "You know," she said with her green eyes shining, "your friend seems like the bashful type. And man I'm a real sucker for the bashful type." Then she turned and hurried down the aisle just as they were coming to take Robert to the OR.

CHAPTER THIRTY-ONE

Kathleen and Jordan

When Kathleen came out of the ward, she looked around briefly for Jordan but didn't see him. Since she was on duty in Ward 1, she returned to her duties. She had been given a short break to see her brother by Major Morningstar. Her shift was a twelve hour shift and it was now sixteen hundred hours so her shift was almost over. She was due to be relieved at seventeen hundred hours.

When Jordan left the ward, he had gone straight to the operations tent. There, he made contact with his battalion which was now based just west of Hue. According to his battalion headquarters, his best route back would be to catch a ride on a convoy going up Route 1 to Hue. There he could catch a Slick from Hue to his battalion. But since he was at the 95th almost right at China Beach, he was given a two day pass to enjoy life for a short while before returning to battalion. So, now Jordan wondered what to do with himself for two days.

Kathleen came off her shift exactly as scheduled. She walked outside into the evening breeze and removed her cap and shook her hair out. She leaned forward and put her hands on her knees. Her hair fell forward and she ran her fingers through the thick red tangle. There was no use trying to untangle it out here; she would need a comb and a brush to accomplish that task. Straightening up, she started for the Officer's Club to get a nice Irish whiskey with ice before going to the mess tent to eat. She put her cap back on and pushed her hair up underneath it as well as she could and then started out for the club. As she neared the Officer's Club, she saw Jordan setting on the ground near the enlisted quarters with his back to her. He appeared to be sipping on a bottle of beer.

"Hey, you," she shouted.

He quickly turned around then got to feet and saluted.

She returned his salute as if she was annoyed by the whole thing. "What're you doin' sittin' out here on the ground?"

"Well, enlisted aren't allowed in the Officer's Club. So, I had a nice army guy bring me out a beer."

He was still standing, while not at attention, very stiff.

"Will you relax, Jordan? That is your name correct?"

"Yes Ma'am. Sergeant Jordan Castillo."

"Jordan, why're you so tense?"

"It's military protocol, Ma'am. We marines live by it,"

"Well, come on inside with me and I'll buy you a drink."

She started towards the door but Jordan didn't move. She turned and looked at him in surprise. "Aren't you comin'?"

"But, Ma'am, I'm not allowed."

"So, you'll be my guest. That's allowed you know."

"Yes, Ma'am, but…."

"Don't you like me, Jordan?"

"Oh! Yes Ma'am of course."

"Do I have to make it an order, Sergeant?"

"No, Ma'am. Lead on I'm right behind you."

Kathleen slipped under the tent flap and pushed open the door to the Officer's Club. She went in with Jordan close behind her. She stopped and looked around until she found a small table they could use. She approached the table and was about to sit down when Jordan ran up and grabbed the chair and pulled it out for her. She smiled softly and took her seat which he gently pushed under her. Jordan then hurried around to the other side of the table and took his seat.

Kathleen smiled softly at him and said, "This isn't a first class club, Jordy, we have to go up to the bar to order. They don't have table service. I'll go get us some drinks. What would you like?"

She started to get up but Jordan grabbed her arm. "No, Ma'am you remain seated, I'll go get the drinks. What would you like?"

She settled back into her chair and looked at him intently. She removed her cap again and laid it on the table and then said, "I'll have a double Jamison on the rocks if you don't mind?"

"A double Jamison it is," he replied as he got up and walked to the bar.

The bar was a simple structure of lumber and some kind of metal that Jordan didn't recognize. There were several bar stools standing empty in front of the bar. In fact, most of the club was empty. But Jordan did see a few enlisted men sitting over in a corner drinking beer. The floor was made of wood but was uneven in many places. Jordan leaned over the bar where the bartender was standing cleaning a glass. The bartender wore the uniform of the Navy. If Jordan knew his Navy ranks, the bartender was a Seaman 2nd Class.

"Could I get a couple of double Jamison's on the rocks please?" Jordan asked politely.

"You got it, Marine, comin' right up."

The bartender built the drinks and set them in front of Jordan.

"How much do I owe you?" Jordan asked pulling out his wallet.

"Is this your first time here? And are you with Lt. O'Rourke?"

"Yes to both questions," Jordan replied carefully.

"In that case, the drinks are on me, Marine. Go enjoy yourself."

Jordan stood up straight and replied, "Thanks, Navy, I won't forget it."

Jordan gathered up the drinks and went back to the table where Kathleen was waiting patiently. "Ah, that looks good," she said as he set the drinks on the table.

After he had taken his seat he said suddenly, "My name's Jordan."

"Yes, I know," she said in a curious tone and small frown on her face. "You called me Jordy."

"Yes, I did. Hasn't anyone ever called you Jordy before?"

"No," he said shaking his head, "never."

She pushed back in her chair and took a long pull on her drink and then pointed the glass at him, "Then I'll be the first," she said smiling. "Hello Jordy."

Jordan couldn't help but laugh, "Hello Kat."

Then Jordan turned serious. "You know we both could get in trouble for violatin' the non-fraternization policy?"

Kathleen threw her back and laughed a little too loudly. But it didn't seem to bother her. She took another swig of her drink and said firmly, "Didn't Rob tell you? We're from Hell's Kitchen. We've be gettin' in trouble all our lives."

"Yeah, he told me you guys are from Hell's Kitchen, but I'm from Marfa, Texas and I only get in trouble every-now-and-then."

They were both laughing when she turned serious. "I'll take care of myself, Jordy. If I want to fraternize, then that'll be on me."

"Fair enough," Jordan replied.

She looked down at her glass that was now empty. Jordan noticed her staring at her empty glass. "I guess I better go and get some refills," he said getting up and heading to the bar again. He returned shortly with two freshened glasses.

"Thank, you," she said softly. "Now, I have a question to ask you."

"Fire away."

"How is it that a boy from, excuse me where is it in Texas you come from?"

"A little place called Marfa."

"Where's that exactly?" She asked mockingly.

"It's a way out in far West Texas near the Davis Mountains."

"Well, that doesn't help me much but I'll continue with my question. How is it that a boy from Marfa, Texas ends up in the Marine Recon and then ends up here in Vietnam? How'd that happen?"

"That's a fair question and I'll answer it on one condition."

"And that condition is what?"

"That you then tell me how a girl from Hell's Kitchen ends up in the Army Nurse Corps and then ends up in Vietnam, and her brother to boot no less."

"That's fair enough, but you have to go first."

"Okay, I'll go first but I'd like to get one thing straight before we start."

"And what's that?"

Jordan took a deep breath and then slugged down his drink. "I don't want to make you mad or hurt your feelin's but I want one thing clear."

Kathleen set her drink down and leaned over the table closer to his face. "What're you goin' ta drop on me, Jordy?"

"It's about me and your brother," he started, then paused, and then forced the words out. "I want it understood that if anythin' should happen between you and me that it has nothin' to do with what I did for you brother. Your brother was runnin' close to me when he was hit. I stopped and helped him the way any other member of my team would've if he had been near one of them. Marine Recon *DOES NOT* leave anyone behind. We're a team and we fight like a team and help each other like a team." He stopped and took his eyes away from her and looked down into his drink. Then, without looking back up he continued. "I just want to be sure that anythin' that you and I may have or may develop doesn't have a pity or gratefulness part to it. I want it to be what we fill for each other and not anythin' else. I hope you understand what I'm tryin' to say. I may be takin' too much for granite but I think you're a great person and I want to know you for you; not for anythin' I did for your brother. I also know we've only known each other one day. But one day in a war like this can be a long time." He stopped talking and was trying to think of something else to add. He still hadn't looked up at her.

She pushed herself back from the table and took a long swig of her drink. She put the glass on the table and said, "Jordy...."

But he interrupted her. "There's one other thing I forgot to tell you. Battalion has given me a two day pass before I have to report back. That means I have all day tomorrow to myself. I was hopin' you could find a way to get free to spend the day with me at the beach. That'd really be nice, it really would. I guess now I'm finished. Maybe I'm really finished."

She moved back to the table and put her hands on his arm. "Jordy, I don't think there's any way I can get free tomorrow. I'm the new kid on the block here and I haven't earned any points or rights yet. I don't know how I could get free, but we can meet for drinks again and even have evenin' mess together."

He stood up in frustration. "No, that's okay, Lieutenant, I really dumped a lot of pressure on you. I shouldn't've done that. Sometimes I let things get away from me. I think I better go now." He turned and started for the door.

"Jordy, wait," she yelled.

She jumped up to try and catch up to him but he turned back and held up his hand. "No, Lieutenant, it's really okay. It really is. Sometimes things just don't work out. I assume too much a lot of times. I've got that kind of heart. It's kind of strange it doesn't affect me in my job; but it doesn't. Go figure that!"

With that he hurried out the door leaving her standing by the table. As she stood there she heard something clinking, looking down she saw it was the ice in her glass because her hand was shaking so badly.

But, then again, sometimes things do work out. As soon as Kathleen got over her shakes, she finished her drink and then went straight to Ward 2 where her good friend and fellow Tart Trio member was working the noon to mid-night shift. It was now nineteen hundred hours and

Veronica still had five hours to go on her shift. Kathleen found her sitting at the nurse's desk at the head of the ward. Veronica smiled as she saw her friend approaching.

"Hey, girl, I thought you'd be gettin' some sack time by now. Is there anythin' goin' on?" Veronica asked when Kathleen got close enough that she could talk in a moderate whisper.

"Yeah, Ronnie, I need a favor and it's a big favor."

Veronica's face showed a worried frown. "Like, I asked, is there somethin' goin' on?"

"I've got to ask you to do somethin' for me, Ronnie, and I'll owe you big time and I swear I'll pay you back."

Veronica pulled her over by the door for more privacy and asked, "Okay, shoot. What's goin' on?"

Kathleen looked Veronica straight in the eyes and said, "I need to you take my shift tomorrow. I know it means you'll have to pull back-to-back double shifts and I know that's goin' to be an ass kicker, but I need it Ronnie, and I'll pay you back the very next day. I swear it."

"Sure I will," Veronica said simply. "That's what The Tart Trio is for." Then after a pause she asked matter-of-factly, "Is it a guy?"

Kathleen didn't move her eyes from Veronica's as she answered, "Yeah, it's a guy and he's enlisted."

Veronica rolled her eyes, "Be careful girl. I'd hate to see you get busted. Are you goin' to tell the Major?"

"Yes I am, just as soon as I leave here."

"Well, get goin'. I got my rounds to make. And let me know how it all turns out."

Kathleen reached over and gave Veronica a big hug. Then, without saying anything else she turned and hurried out of the ward and headed straight for Major Morningstar's quarters. When she got there, she took a moment to compose here self and then knocked firmly on the Major's door.

"Come," was the simple reply from the other side of the door.

Kathleen went inside and saw the Major sitting on the edge of her bunk. She was still in uniform but her cap was removed and her hair was in a mess. She was holding a small glass of something that Kathleen assumed was a drink of some kind.

"Well, Lt. O'Rourke, to what do I owe the pleasure of this unexpected visit?"

Kathleen stood to attention and said bluntly, "I have a request, Ma'am."

The Major got up from the edge of the bed and took a few steps to the small desk that stood just beyond the end of her bunk. She pulled the chair out and sat down. She placed her drink on the desk and turned back and looked hard at Kathleen. "You can stand at ease, Lieutenant, and proceed with your request."

Kathleen stood at the position of at ease and tried to gather her words.

"Well, Lieutenant, I'm waiting. I'd like to have a little private time sometime tonight."

"Ma'am, I've arranged for Lt. Mann to take my shift tomorrow. She's doin' me a favor that will cost her a lot of sleep but I intend to make it up to her the very next day. I'm doin' this so I can spend some time with a sergeant in the marines. He has one day before he has to return to his battalion and I'd like to spend that one day with him. And that's my request."

Major Morningstar studied Kathleen closely, and then asked, "Why're you telling me this? If you've already arranged things with Lt. Mann you could've done this and I probably would never have found out about it."

"Yes, Ma'am, I know, but that's not the way I am. I couldn't do anythin' behind your back. If you order me to not do this, I'll cancel the whole thing. The sergeant doesn't know I'm doin' this, so he'll not be hurt and I can easily stop Lt. Mann from goin' on my shift. I know I'm breakin' the officer and enlisted rules, so I couldn't go on with this without tellin' you first and askin' your permission."

Major Morningstar stood up and pushed her chair back. "Stand to attention, Lieutenant," she said gruffly.

Kathleen snapped to attention and waited for the boom to be lowered on her.

"Lieutenant, as far as your arrangements with Lt. Mann to cover your shift, I couldn't care less, unless it has an impact on our performance here or our moral. As far as the other thing, I don't think I heard it. Therefore, there is no other thing. So, you're dismissed, Lieutenant. Please leave so I can get some private meditation time."

Kathleen was stunned but she managed to pop off a sharp salute, do an about face, and quickly leave the Major's quarters. She smiled as she hurried towards the enlisted quarters to tell one Sergeant Jordan Costillo that she would meet him for morning mess at oh-seven hundred hours and then spend the rest of the day with him on China Beach and swimming in the South China Sea.

So as things happened, Lieutenant Kathleen O'Rourke and Sergeant Jordan Costillo spent the whole next day together; lying on the beach, swimming in the sea, and telling each other the story of their lives. They were honest with each other in all things except one. Jordan didn't tell her that he was a multi-millionaire. He wanted to wait for another time for that.

After that wonderful day and early the next morning, Jordan was on a troop convoy headed up Route 1 to Hue. There he would catch a flight on a Slick headed for his battalion and he would be back in the war.

CHAPTER THIRTY-TWO

The Relatively Quiet Time

I f it could be said that there was a 'relatively quiet time' during the Vietnam War, it would arguably be the late summer of 1968. Most of the fighting had been relegated to the southern part of South Vietnam near, or around, the capitol of Saigon. The northern part of South Vietnam was in a somewhat stable condition, due mainly to the heavy defeat of the North Vietnamese and Viet Cong (South Vietnamese guerillas know as VC) forces during the Battle of Hue (better known as the Tet Offensive), and the heavy loses they endured during the Battle of Khe Sanh. Between the two battles the North Vietnamese and the VC lost over two full divisions, which numbered somewhere between 10,000 and 13,000 troops. They spent the rest of the spring and summer of 1968 hurrying to their sanctuaries in Laos and in the DMZ (Demilitarized Zone) where the American forces were not allowed, by rules of engagement from Washington D.C., to pursue them. There they would lick their wounds, resupply and reinforce their loses via the Ho Chi Minh Trail, which the American forces were also not allow to attack because the trail ran from

North Vietnam through Laos and Cambodia; two countries that were supposedly neutral and not involved in the war, which, of course, was a joke to everyone except the American forces doing the fighting. Taking all this into account, there was limited offensive action in the northern part of South Vietnam by either side during this time.

Kyle sat at the small desk in his quarters at Cobra Umbrella One. He stared down at the one sheet document that lay on the desk. He held a ballpoint pin in his hand clicking the open and close button at the top over and over again. The document that lay before him was his request for an extension for another tour in South Vietnam. It was now the middle of August 1968 and his tour of duty was due to end on September 24th. He had always had it in his mind to sign up for another tour but now he hesitated. There were several things that weighed heavy on his mind.

First there was Kellie. Over the quiet time, he and Kellie had been able to spend a lot of time together. In July, Kellie had even gotten a three day pass and they had spent the whole time at the Rest and Relaxation (called R & R) quarters near China Beach. It had been a wonderful three days. Kellie had even gotten to visit her friends, Kathleen and Veronica, at the 95th. Kyle found himself falling very hard for Kellie and he could see that she felt the same way. But they spoke very little of their feelings. They both were afraid to go too far at this point in their lives. He knew that she had already planned to extend when her tour was up, but he didn't know if she still felt that way. Her tour wouldn't be up until March of next year. He wanted to make sure he wasn't extending just to be near Kellie, but for the right reasons.

Second there was Harv. He thought back to the day last week when Harv had knocked on the door to his quarters. He had opened the door to find Harv standing there nervously holding his flight helmet. And he remembered the conversation.

"Excuse me, Skipper, but could I have a few words with you in private?"

"Sure, Harv, come on in and have a seat." The room was small so Kyle went over and set on the edge of his bunk offering the desk chair to Harv.

Harv nodded his head and took a seat in the chair and placed his flight helmet on the floor. "I hope I'm not interfering with anything, Skipper."

Kyle could see that Harv was very nervous and tried to put him at ease. "No, not at all, Harv, what can I do for you?"

"Well, Sir, I've been over here for two tours and I've got to decide if I want to stay for a third tour. They've already promised me another stripe if I extend. Can you believe they'd make me a Sergeant First Class? But I wanted to talk to you first before I make up my mind."

"Sure, Harv, I'm happy to do what I can. What is it you want to talk about?"

"Well, Sir, I've been over here almost two years now and I've been pretty damn lucky. I mean I've been flying gunner for a long time. I'm way past the odds of me getting it. Most gunners are hit during their first tour and now I'm looking at three. And I've been really lucky to have you as my Skipper and Lt. Denison as our left seat."

"So, Harv, you feel like you're pushin' the odds by going for a third tour."

"That's only part of it, Sir." Harv paused and clenched his hands together and looked at Kyle in desperation. "The main thing is winning."

Kyle looked confused. "I guess you need to clear that up for me, Harv."

"Captain, you're an officer and I'm sure you're much smarter than me. So, I would just like for you to confirm some of the things that we enlisted, especially the Non-Coms like myself, have been wondering about. And I might include several officers as well."

"Harv, I think I'd like all this a lot better if you'd just come out say want you're goin' to say."

"Okay, Sir, the fact is they're not going to let us win this war are they?"

Kyle was taken aback. "What're you tryin' to say, Harv?"

"It's simple," Harv replied as his voice got louder and he stood up, "back in March and April and even in May, we had those bastards on the run. We kicked 'em out of Hue and chased them all the way to the DMZ and the Laotian border. We wiped out over two divisions and crippled two others. They ran for their sanctuaries across the border and we weren't allowed to pursue them. On top of all that, in June we abandon Khe Sanh after all that fighting and the retaking of Route 9. Khe Sanh is in easy striking distance to the Ho Chi Minh Trail. All we had to do was cross the border into Laos and cut the damn trail off and deny them a place to rest, resupply, and reinforce. We had 'em where we wanted 'em but we weren't allowed to go finish the deal. I'm not saying we could've won the war then and there because the same damn thing is happening down south except it's the Cambodian border we can't cross. The poor guys fighting in the south have got the same stupid problem we have up here. *They won't let us finish the job.*" Harv paused and took a deep breath and said in frustration, "And, Sir, those bastards in Washington have no intention of letting us win this war do they? Just tell me what you think, Captain, do you believe they're goin to let us win this fucking war?"

Kyle stood up and turned his back on Harv. He pushed his hands in his pockets lowered his head. And without turning to face Harv said, "Harv, you're the best chopper mechanic in the whole damn army, and you fly gunner with the best of 'em. I'd hate to lose you. But I can't tell you what they're thinkin' in Washington. I know this war is a lot more political now than it was when I first got here and surely since you got here. I think it stinks, Harv. I really truly think it stinks. As I said, I don't know exactly what to tell you except I'd sure hate to fly missions without you. That scares me." Then he turned and faced Harv and looked him hard in the eyes. "I guess I haven't helped you much, Harv. But I know you'll do what you believe you have to do."

Then Harv reached down and picked up his flight helmet, put it under his left arm and stood to attention. He snapped a rigid salute to Kyle and said, "Thank you, Sir; I know you've told me the situation as well as you can. All I can say is that I don't feel up to putting my life on the line anymore for a war that we're not going to be allowed to win. But, Sir, from my heart it's been an honor serving with you. You're the best of the best, Sir."

Kyle stood to attention and returned the salute and said with all sincerity, "Please believe me, Harv, when I tell you that the honor has been all mine."

Harv then turned smartly and left the room.

After Harv left, a small tear had trickled down Kyle's cheek.

As Kyle came back to the present, he looked down at the extension document again. Instead of seeing the document, he saw the face of Lt. 'Denny' Denison. For extending for another tour, Denny had been promised a promotion to captain and a ship of his own; one of the new Cobras. Denny had accepted and was being transferred down south to the 281st Assault Helicopter Company. They were stationed at Nha Trang and their specialty was flying Black Ops missions for the Special Forces (better known as the Green Berets). Denny was due to ship out to the 281st on August 29th.

As for Kyle, there'd been no promises for him to extend. He was told that by the time he finished his second tour he would be up for promotion to major. But that was all he was promised. If he extended, he was faced with getting a new crew and getting them trained in the way he wanted things done. There would be no Harv and no Denny. He'd still be flying the old Heavy Scout. It was a bleak prospect.

But, in the end, and after much soul searching, he did the very thing he had determined he shouldn't do; he extended so he could be near Kellie.

CHAPTER THIRTY-THREE

Lt. William Barnett joins the 187th Regiment

I t was now August of 1968 and Lt. William Barnett was wadding through a rice paddy in the coastal lowlands of Thua Thien Province. The coastal lowlands were between Hue and the South China Sea coast. They ran north to almost the DMZ and south to just below Phu Bai. The rice paddy he was sloshing through was full of mud and water that came nearly to the tops of his boots.

It had taken William almost two months to catch up to the 101st. He had arrived at Cam Ranh Bay on March 15, 1968. Cam Ranh Bay was far south of where he was now. The 101st had arrived four months earlier in December of 1967 and had moved on before he got there. Plus, he was held in a replacement battalion before he got an assignment. Finally in late May he got assigned to be the commanding officer of the 2nd Platoon in Company C of the 3rd Battalion, in the 187th Regiment of the 101st Airborne Division "Screaming Eagles" or in military terms the 2/C/3/187. He had reported to Camp Eagle which was not far from Phu Bai and Hue. But his time there was short, as he barely got to know the men in his platoon before they move out of Camp Eagle in June to participate in Operation Nevada Eagle along with the South Vietnamese Army.

The objective of Nevada Eagle was to make a large swing through the coastal lowlands and try and pacify the villages and to prevent the VC from stealing all the rice. It was believed that if they could prevent the VC from stealing all the rice in the region, it would limit the food supply to the North Vietnamese Army. For years, the VC had been intimidating the local villages with terror, torture, and outright executions to get the rice. The hope was that Operation Nevada Eagle would prevent that from happening.

His platoon was somewhat unusual because it was made up of various squad types. Most platoons had specific jobs to do. Some were rifle platoons, or mortar platoons, or machine gun platoons. However, his platoon was made up of five squads; three rifle squads of ten men each, one mortar squad of three men, and one machine gun squad of five men. Each squad was led by a Staff Sergeant and William had a second in command to help him. His second in command, or Platoon XO, was 2nd Lt. Joe 'Mac' Macland. Including himself, that made his platoon forty-four men strong. This made it a few men more than the normal size platoon.

Now as they sloshed their way towards their objective, William had his platoon in a standard combat deployment. He had his rifle squads up front with him and spread out slightly so as not to be bunched up. He had his XO about fifty yards behind him with the mortar and machine gun squads. Their objective was to secure the south bank of a small river that ran through the rice patty. William couldn't help thinking that back in Texas they'd call it a creek instead of a river. These little rivers were all over the lowlands, and even though they were small they sometimes could be deep. A trooper had to be careful when crossing one of these rivers or he could find himself in over his head. In addition, the current was always moving eastward towards the South China Sea. Fortunately, his orders were to secure the bank and not cross the little river.

As they approached the river, William was being very careful because intelligence had informed them that there was a very high probability that the village on the other side of the river had been occupied by the VC. The village was about a hundred yards from the river just at the edge of the rice paddy. Far down the river to their right, a company size force of South Vietnamese troops had been sent across the river to flank the village to the far right and check it out. If any VC were flushed out, they would probably head straight across the rice paddy and right at William and his platoon. At least, that was the plan.

William signaled a halt at nearly the very edge of the river bank. Using hand signals, he had his men take the prone position with their weapons at the ready and to fix bayonets. He signaled for his radioman to come up. When he arrived, William took the handset and clicked the talk button twice.

"Okay, Mac," he said, speaking softly into the handset, "hold your guys back behind us around thirty yards. I want you to set up your mortar team in our center and have them mark their range at about ten yards on the other side of the river. Then, I want you to split your machine gun squad. Put one machine gun to our far left flank and the other to our far right flank. And don't fire until you see or hear us firing. Now, remember, we're between you guys and the river. I don't want anyone hit by friendly fire. You need to get ready fast because I expect those South Vietnamese boys to make contact anytime now. Also, don't worry about your back. 1st Platoon is about a mile back holdin' in reserve."

There was only a short silence before Mac replied, "Roger all that." That's all he said as the handset went silent.

Things were quiet for what seemed like a long time. The men lay sweating as ordered but they held their positions without moving. It only had seemed like a long wait but it really wasn't, when William heard weapons fire coming from the village. The fire was followed by shouts and a few explosions. William surmised that the South Vietnamese troops had made contact with some VC elements, and he hoped his men had the discipline to hold and wait. They did. No one fired or exposed himself until the VC became clearly visible. They were running hell bent to get away from the pursuing South Vietnamese troops. As always the VC were readily identifiable by what they wore. Their unofficial uniform was what looked like black pajamas, a sampan hat, and flip-flops on their feet. But they all carried the deadly Russian made AK47 assault rifle.

William held his fire until he felt sure that most of the VC was now exposed in the rice paddy and none, hopefully, were still in the village. To his concern, there only appeared to be fifty or sixty of them. But he didn't feel safe waiting any longer; he opened fire and his men followed suit. As the rifle squads laid down a heavy and accurate volume of fire, the first of several mortar rounds exploded just on the other side of the river as ordered. This turned the running VC away from the center and ran them directly into the waiting machine guns. They were cut to pieces.

The battle only lasted about ten minutes and it was over. William ordered one rifle squad across the river to check for survivors. His men waded across but by the time they got to the other side, the South Vietnamese troops were already there going from body to body shooting them; the dead and the wounded. His men stood back as per their rules of engagement. The rules stated that all prisoners were to be handed over to the South Vietnamese. William didn't much care for this stupid rule but he followed orders and watched as the South Vietnamese took no prisoners. He assumed that the South Vietnamese were getting some payback for the terrible way the VC treated the villagers.

William then started taking stock of his entire platoon. They had suffered five wounded; two seriously. All the wounded had been in the rifle squads. He again signaled for his radioman and he again used the double click on the handset. "Mac, are the medivac choppers on their way?"

"Yes, Sir," Mac replied quickly, "they should be here in a few minutes."

"Good, I'm putting down some red smoke at the LZ for the wounded. So, be sure the choppers know about that and ask them if they've got high cover to the ten-six-six and get back to me."

Again the answer was short, "Roger to all that."

William stood in the LZ with his wounded men. Red smoke bellowed into the sky marking their location. He wondered how long this operation was going to last. These types of encounters had been going on over the last month and it appeared they would continue for some time as they worked their way down from north of Hue through the lowlands to south of Phu Bai. He had no way of knowing how long it was going to take. During these encounters, they rarely encountered North Vietnamese Regulars; just VC gorilla's. He also didn't know how effective this operation was being. Once a village was cleared of VC, 101st medics would go in and try to help the villagers with medicine and care. The South Vietnamese would try and insure the villagers that they could keep their rice or sell it to the government, but they could *NOT* sell it to the VC or North Vietnamese. The villagers seemed to be grateful, but he suspected that would last only until the VC came back.

As he thought all these things, he watched as the medivac choppers picked up his wounded. Actually, all the wounded were place in one chopper. The second chopper was dropping off ammunition and other supplies.

As the red smoke died away and he could see the choppers more clearly as they rose into the sky carrying his wounded men to the aid and care of the 1066th MASH just outside of Phu Bai. He cocked his head to one side and took a long look at the chopper flying high cover. It was heavily armed with machine guns and rocket pods. When it peeled off to cover the medivac choppers, he saw the name on its side. He smiled and thought what a nice name and that it must have a meaning to the chopper crew; it read, 'Kellie'.

CHAPTER THIRTY-FOUR

Kathleen, Veronica, and the 95th

It was late July 1968 when Major Morningstar called Kathleen and Veronica to her quarters for a private meeting. The meeting had to be arranged around the schedule of both nurses, which was hard to do because twelve hour shifts were still the standard. But the Major got it all worked out and both nurses came to her quarters one early morning before Kathleen would start her shift in Ward 1, and Veronica in Ward 3.

Major Morningstar was sitting at her desk when a soft knock came at her quarter's door. "Come," she called out.

The door opened and Kathleen and Veronica came in. They were tired and the Major could see it in their eyes. And they both were about to start twelve hour shifts. As they both started to come to attention, the Major quickly stopped them. "Forget the military stuff and set down."

The Major's quarters had improved greatly since the early days at Red Beach. They were now in the new facilities at the bottom of Monkey Mountain; just about eight klicks north from Red Beach. Almost the whole staff had now moved to the Monkey Mountain facility. The two nurses quickly found a couple of chairs and set down.

The Major turned in her chair to face the two tired nurses. "I guess you're both wondering why I called this little meeting."

Kathleen and Veronica looked at each other and then back to the Major. "Yes, Ma'am," Veronica answered for both of them.

"Well," the Major started slowly, "I owe you two a bigger debt than I can repay. When you two first got here I asked to hold your orders until we could get the 95th up and running. In fact, I told you I'd release you back to your original orders sometime in late May when we were supposed to be at full capacity. Lo and Behold, now here it is July 25th and you're both still here, even though we have a nice new facility with an almost adequate staff. I've worked you both hard; and I mean really hard. And I don't recall a single complaint." The Major paused and looked down at the floor. She seemed ashamed. Then she continued without looking up, "On my desk here I've got your original orders but I'm afraid they're kind of out dated. It seems the war has moved on and things have changed. So, battalion has given me the prerogative to cut you new orders. They're allowing me to keep you here or transfer you to another assignment. But it has to be to an assignment that is in great need; not just a fun spot." At this point, she stopped talking and just looked at the two tired nurses.

Kathleen and Veronica again looked at each other. There was a long silence then Veronica looked at the Major and said sternly, "I'll say to you what I said to you back then at Red Beach, just give us your orders, Major, and let's get on with it."

Kathleen reached over and slapped Veronica on the back. Then she look at the Major with a big smile on her face and said with a laugh, "You've gotta have a Texas girl to tell it like it is and put it on the line. That's what I say, Major, that's what I always say." She giggled a bit and then turned serious, "So, Major Marjorie Morningstar, what're our orders?"

The Major stood up and folded her arms across her chest. She smiled down at the two smiling nurses and said simply, "That's up to you. You two busted your asses for me and I'm not one to forget things like that. As a result, I'm going to let you pick your next assignment. You can stay here, or you can go someplace else. It's up to you. But you have to tell me now; I'm not going to sit on this longer than today. So, shoot, what's it to be?"

"Can we have a few minutes to talk this over?" Kathleen asked surprised.

"I'll give you ten minutes. You two step outside, come back in ten minutes, and let me know."

When the two were outside the Major's door, they just stared at each other of several minutes. Then, Veronica blurred out, "Shit, we're burnin' time here. What'd you want to do?"

Kathleen put her hand on Veronica's shoulder and said softly, "I want to stay here, Ronnie."

Veronica smiled at her and took Kathleen's hand from her shoulder and held it tightly. "It's your marine isn't it?"

Tears formed in Kathleen's eyes as she looked into Veronica's eyes. She breathed deeply and said, "Yes, it is. He goes on missions all around here and I get to see him at least once a month. I care for him, Ronnie, I really care for him."

"I know you do, Kat," Veronica said as tears began to form in her eyes also. "But I think I'll be movin' on to some other place that needs a crazy Texas girl."

"But, Ronnie, you know nothin' can break up The Tart Trio," Kathleen said as she had gone past tears now to full crying.

"Nobody knows that better than me, Kat. Come on let's get back inside and set the Major straight."

When they reentered the quarters, both girls were wiping their eyes. The Major knew immediately that the girls were about to split up. "So, what's the verdict? What do you two want to do?"

Kathleen spoke first. "If it's okay with you, Major, I'll be stayin' on here at the 95th?"

"Are you asking if it's okay with me?" The Major asked mockingly. "Nothing could make me happier. Your experience and work ethic make you valuable beyond words and I promise to get you that silver bar as quick as I can." Then, after a short pause, she turned to Veronica. "And you Lt. Mann?" She asked softly.

Veronica straightened up and smiled at the Major through new tears that were forming in her eyes. "Well, Major," she started, "whata you got out there that needs someone with my unique talents?"

"Well, Lt. Mann, you may not believe this but I happen to know that the 1066th MASH has a shortage of two nurses who just rotated out. And I believe you know the head nurse at that particular unit."

Veronica's eyes lit up. "You mean I can be back with Kel?"

The Major's eyes sparkled as she spoke, "Yep, that's what I mean. I'll cut your orders today and we can have you there by August 1st. Just give me the go ahead."

"The go ahead is given, Major."

But at this point the Major became serious. "Okay, Lt. Mann, but I have to be sure you're aware that you'll be going into a hot zone. We've had it rough here at times but up there it's just about twenty-four by seven. I need you to know what you're getting into. They need you desperately up there, but you don't have to go. Remember that, Ronnie, you don't have to go."

It was the first time that Veronica could ever remember the Major calling her, 'Ronnie'. She looked at the Major and said with conviction, "It's understood, Major," she said with deep emotion, "but it's like what Kel said that first day at Red Beach, 'Bein' needed desperately is exactly why we came here, Ma'am'."

So, as the events of war and destiny continued to turn, on August 1, 1968, Kathleen waved good-bye to her Tart Trio sister as Veronica climbed aboard a medivac chopper headed for the ten-six-six. There were no more tears as each Tart Trio sister was completely cried out. But they did make imaginary plans to all get together sometime before they all went home. Kathleen's last words to Veronica were, "Could you please keep that Texas ass of yours down. It would be such a disappointment to so many of our fightin' boys if you got it shot off."

CHAPTER THIRTY-FIVE

Veronica and William

It was the day before Thanksgiving and after three months of sloshing through rice paddies and fighting constant fire fights, the 187th Regiment of the 101st Airborne made their way back to Camp Eagle and Phu Bai. They were tired, dirty, and used up. William's 2nd Platoon was down to twenty-one men of the original forty-four that started with him back in August. And about half of them were replacements. All he had now was rifle squads; the mortar and machine gun squads had been moved to other platoons.

As bad as they may have looked, they gave a lot worse than they got. Operation Nevada Eagle was still in progress with other units of the 101st and 82nd Airborne, but what was accomplished in their three months was nothing short of amazing. They killed or captured nearly a thousand VC and over eight hundred North Vietnamese Regulars. They captured from the enemy large amounts of weapons and tons of rice. Now, other regiments and battalions were still pushing across the lowlands, and were still killing the enemy and capturing his supplies. How long the operation would continue was unknown as was the final tally of enemy dead and supplies captured.

But as for their casualties to this point, they had lost ninety-eight men killed and two hundred and ten wounded. As for William's 2nd Platoon, he had four men killed and sixteen wounded. William intended to get permission from the Company Commander to go over to the ten-six-six and check on his wounded. But for now, he just settled into his tent on 'Officer's Row' to get cleaned up and catch up on his sleep. He shared the tent with another officer who had not showed up yet. There were rumors going around that tomorrow, on Thanksgiving Day, they were to receive a hot meal of turkey and dressing. As William threw his gear on the floor and flopped down on his bunk, the thought of turkey and dressing sounded very good. It sounded very good indeed.

As it turned out, they did have turkey and dressing and it was very good. William walked along towards the Company Commander's tent patting his full stomach. As he reached the captain's tent, the flap was open and he peeked inside. "Captain," he said softly.

The Captain looked up from his small desk in surprise and then a huge grin spread across his face. He was still holding the remains of a turkey sandwich. "Oh, sure, Barnett, come on in."

William pushed his way through the opening and went inside. Military formalities were not much in place so he just stood loosely holding his cap. "I'm sorry to bother you at this time, Sir, but I've got a request to make if I could?"

Captain Jamie Mackey was a short man in his late twenties. His brown hair was longer than normal because he hadn't yet been able to get it cut since getting back to base. He had large brown eyes set in a narrow face accented by a small turned up nose. No matter his looks, William thought he had done an outstanding job leading the company the last three months.

Captain Mackey put down his sandwich and looked at William smiling all the while. "What's this request?" He asked. "I mean it is Thanksgiving and all."

"Sir," William began awkwardly, "I like to requisition a jeep and go down to the ten-six-six and check on my wounded guys."

The Captain simple stared at him for a short moment and then said, "I know it's only about eight klicks over there but it could still be dangerous. Is this something you feel you have to do?"

William nodded his head, "Yes, Sir, it is. I'd really like to do this today since its Thanksgiving."

The Captain continued to look at William intently but then suddenly said, "Okay, but take a driver with you. I don't want you going alone. And plan on staying the night over there because I don't want to take the chance of you coming back in the dark," then after a short pause when William didn't reply, "Is all of that okay with you?"

"Yes, Sir," William stammered.

The Captain started writing on a piece of paper on his desk. When he finished he handed it to William. "Take this to the motor pool and they'll give you a jeep and a driver. And please come back in one piece, Barnett, you did a good job for me out there and I don't want to have to replace you. Rumor has it that we'll be headed back to the A Shau Valley soon. You weren't with us when we were last there, but believe me it's no picnic. So, I'm going to need my best and most experienced officers. Roger that?"

"Roger that," William replied taking the paper with a smile. He then turned and hurried out of the tent. On his way to the motor pool, he thought about the A Shau Valley. He had heard about it from some of the other guys who were there. He guessed soon he was going to learn about it firsthand.

The drive over to the ten-six-six only took about twenty-five minutes. The driver they gave him was very careful and took no chances. He checked every bump in the road and every spot that looked like it might be mined. The driver's name was PFC Jack Kingsley. He was actually with the 82nd but was assigned to William anyway. Jack was a hardcore country boy from Arkansas. He had short cut blonde hair and deep brown eyes set in a very round face. William figured Jack was only about five-foot-five. No matter how William tried, he couldn't make Jack fit the profile of an airborne trooper.

They literally bounced into the ten-six-six around fourteen hundred hours. Earlier they had been stopped by a patrol from the 5th Marines, but were allowed to proceed. Jack brought the jeep to a halt just outside what looked to William like an administrative area.

"This is what they call the Operations Tent," Jack said turning to look at William. "But they don't do any operatin' in there it's just a glorified administration tent. Most of the time you can find the commandin' officer in there."

William jumped out of the jeep and looked back at Jack. "I'll tell you, Private, I don't know if you have anythin' to do around here but whatever it maybe, see that you're done with it by seventeen hundred hours. Meet me back here at the jeep at that time and we'll make arrangements to spend the night here. You got that?"

"Roger that, Lieutenant, I'll entertain myself until seventeen hours."

William took a quick look around and then headed for the operations or administrative tent, whichever. He pushed the flimsy door open and walked in. As he entered, he heard loud noises coming from another room on the far side of the tent. The door to the room was closed but there was a sign on it that read, 'Coronal Vickers, CO'. He started for the door but was stopped by someone speaking to him.

"Excuse me, Sir, may I help you?" The question was being asked by a tall soldier sitting at a desk just to the left side of the door. William could tell he was tall because his legs were jammed underneath the desk and the rest of his frame towered over the desk surface. He was wearing the two stripes of a corporal and the brass of the Medical Corp. He had curly black hair and small brown eyes set in a long narrow face. He had a long neck but his most outstanding feature was a large hawkish nose that dominated his face.

William caught himself staring and quickly answered, "Yes, I'd like to see the Commanding Officer if I could." And before the corporal could answer he added, "It'll only take a minute."

"Well, Sir, as you can hear, the CO is currently with someone. However, if you'd like to wait you can take a seat here by my desk." As he spoke, he pointed to a small folding chair that was positioned almost directly in front of his desk.

"Thank you," William said. But before he could take his seat, the door flew open and an officer wearing the rank of lieutenant coronal was holding it open.

"Okay, Lieutenant, you can go now," he said in frustrated voice, "and as I told you I don't care how you arrange the wards. You're the head nurse, you arrange them anyway you want. The last head nurse had her way and I'm happy for you to have yours."

Shortly a nurse wearing an Australian bush hat walked out of the office. But once outside the door, she turned and faced the Coronal, who was still holding the door open. Her face and neck were red. "Sir," she said through gritted teeth, "thank you for your time. I will see to the rearrangement of the wards at once."

The Coronal said nothing else. He simple turned back to his office closing the door behind him.

The nurse wasn't finished. She quickly turned to the corporal and said in a control and level voice, "Jimmy, I want you to get me some Seabees or Army Engineers or somebody ASAP. Have them report to me. I need some work done post haste."

The corporal was taken aback but didn't dare make an argument. "Yes, Ma'am, I'm on it this very minute."

"Good," she said as she turned to walk away. She nearly bumped into William as she did so. "Oh, I'm sorry, Lieutenant, please excuse me."

William bowed slightly and said, "No problem, Ma'am."

She looked at him briefly and started for the door.

"Ma'am," William called after her.

She was almost to the door but stopped and turned and looked back at him, "Yes."

William took a few steps towards her and said, "You know I was thinkin', since you're the head nurse, you might be the person I want to see instead of the CO."

She put her hands on her hips and asked in a puzzled voice, "And how can I help you, Lieutenant?"

He took a few more steps towards her until he was standing right in front of her. "Well, you see I'm with the one-oh-first and you have some guys from my platoon here and I just came by to check on their status. I mean I'd like to know who's gone on home and who might be available to return to duty in the near future. And, you know, it is Thanksgiving."

"So," she said slowly, "you'd like for me to take you to your guys."

"Yes," William responded smiling.

She looked down at his name tag and asked in a more friendly tone, "What's your name, Lieutenant?"

William pointed to his name tag and said, while continuing to smile, "Barnett, Ma'am."

"Yes, I see your name tag. But what's your first name?"

"William, Ma'am, I'm Lieutenant William Barnett."

"And you're with the one-oh-first?"

"Yes, Ma'am, I am."

Her face showed complete surprise and she stepped back from him and looked him over up and down. "Well, I'll be damn," she breathed as a smile crossed her face.

William didn't know what to think. "Is there a problem, Ma'am?"

"No, William, there's no problem," she said turning and walking towards the door, "please just follow me." William started to follow her but she stopped and turned to face him. The big smile crossed her face again as she said, "You know Lieutenant William Barnett this isn't such a big war after all. In fact, it's getting to be really damn small."

William followed Kellie as they walked pass the OR and towards Ward 1. As they approached Ward 1, Kellie stopped causing William to nearly run into her. "Oops," she laughed as they pushed apart, "before we go in, I'd like to apologize to you, Bill, you haven't seen me at my best."

William simply smiled at her and said, "Two things, Ma'am. First my name's not Bill; it's William. And second you've done nothin' to apologize for."

Kellie stepped back and folded her arms across her chest. "Okay, *William*," she said stressing his name, "but I feel the need to talk and you'll understand as I go along. First, let me explain about the yelling in the CO's office." She paused and pointed to the Australian Bush hat she wore on her head. "You see this hat."

William only nodded.

"Well, it was given to me by a dying Aussie. He knew he wasn't going to make it and he wanted me to have it to remember him by. He seemed to think I was some kind of angel." She stopped talking and took the hat off and held it in her hand. She looked down at it and then continued, "He was hit while working liaisons between the 5th Marines and his own 1st ANZAC division along Route 1. We tried our best but we couldn't stop the internal bleeding. So we moved him to what we privately call the 'Terminal Ward'. He was in with three other guys. The guys in that ward aren't stupid. They know the score. He died just this morning leaving me this hat." She stopped talking again and looked up from the hat to William's eyes. Getting herself together, she put the hat back on and continued, "I hate that ward. Guys shouldn't be put in a place where they know they're going to die. I hate it. That's what I was yelling at the CO about. I want to do away with that ward and merge it back in with the other wards. I don't know why I was yelling at the CO, it's not his fault. The last head nurse made that arrangement and now I'm going to change it. And that's the story about the yelling."

William didn't say anything he just waited for her to continue.

"Second," she said as a small smile returned to her face, "a very close friend of mine was supposed to join me today for a little Thanksgiving dinner and drinks later, but he got put on a mission alert and won't be able to make it. I hate that because I really like the guy. And do you know who that guy is?"

"No, Ma'am, I don't," William replied. "Should I?"

"No, I guess not. But I can tell you his name; it's Captain Collie."

William's face changed first to a very puzzled look and then to look of wonderment. "You don't mean Captain Kyle Collie do you?"

"That's exactly who I mean."

"This is unbelievable; Kyle is a good friend of mine. For Christ sakes, his father is married to my aunt. I don't really know what that makes us but we're related somehow. Damn I hate that I'm going to miss him."

Kellie laughed, "That's how I knew your name. Kyle talks about Coalville, Texas a lot and you're always part of the conversation."

"Son of a bitch, I wish he could've been here."

"You and me both," Kellie said, "but it's not to be. So we must press on. I'm going to introduce you to the nurse on shift in Ward 2. She'll be able to help you find out the status of your guys." As she spoke, she turned and started walking toward Ward 2. "And by the way, she's a Texas girl so you two might have something in common."

William smiled and followed her into Ward 2.

Veronica looked up from her small desk at the front of the ward when she heard the door open. She saw Kellie and an officer approaching her desk. She stood up to greet them as they arrived.

"Ronnie," Kellie started as she and William arrive at Veronica's desk, "I've got one of your fellow Texans from the one-oh-first who's here to check on some of his wounded men. I was hoping you could help him out. This is Lt. Barnett, who incidentally, is a friend of Kyles." Then turning to William said, "This is Lt. Mann."

Both William and Veronica nodded to each other.

"Okay, then," Kellie said as she padded them both on the shoulders, "I'll leave you in Ronnie's capable hands, Lt. Barnett. If you need anything else you can find me in my quarters."

William grabbed Kellie's hand as she started to leave and gave it a soft squeeze. "Thank you, Lt. Anderson for all your help as well as all the information."

"No problem," she said as she extracted her hand and turned and left the ward.

"How exactly can I help you, Lt. Barnett?" Veronica asked quietly.

"Oh," William said as if being awakened, "I'm from the one-oh-first and I have some guys here. I'd like to visit with them if I could and then find out if any of them will be returned to duty anytime soon."

"Do you have their names and rank?" Veronica asked, again quietly.

"Yes, I do." He reached into his back pocket and produced a list of names on a small piece of paper, which he handed to her.

She took the list and sat down at her desk and started checking his list against her chart, which was attached to a clipboard. After only of few seconds, she looked up at him smiling and said, "You're in luck, Lieutenant; we have all five of these men in our ward. But before I let you go talk to them, I need to go and check their charts and make sure they're not due any treatments and to make sure they're status is good enough for a talk. Okay?"

"That's absolutely okay," he said quickly and tried to match her quiet voice.

Veronica got up, and carrying her clipboard, started down the row of beds.

William watched her walk away for a few seconds and then quietly called after her, "Excuse me, Lt. Mann, I think Lt. Anderson said you were from Texas."

Veronica stopped and looked back at him, and still smiling said softly, "Yes I am."

"Could I ask where in Texas?" He whispered back to her.

"Sweetwater," she replied and then turned and continued on down the row of beds.

Over the next hour, William visited with his five wounded men. They were all in good spirits and earlier had completed a nice Thanksgiving Day lunch. As it turned out, two of the men had bad enough wounds that they were scheduled to be moved down to the 95th the next day. The other three were being watched and should be able to return to duty over the next two weeks. William was doing what he considered a good officer should do and that was to take care of his men as best he could. He got so involved in talking with his men that he let the time get away from him. He looked and noticed it was almost seventeen hours; the time he was to meet Private Kingsley back at the jeep. He quickly and politely closed out his meeting with the men hurried back to the nurse's desk at the front of the ward. Veronica was still there but had made several rounds of the beds during his hour long chat. Veronica was busy working her way through some paper work when William appeared at her desk. He didn't say anything; he just stood there as if waiting for her to reach a breaking point before he spoke.

She finally broke the silence, "Is there somethin' else I can help you with, Lieutenant?"

"Yes," he stammered nervously, "yes there is."

"And what would that be?"

"I was kind of wonderin' what time your shift was over," he said quickly, almost too quickly.

Through years of experience, Veronica knew what was coming so she went into her tease mode. "Well, Lieutenant, why would you wonder that?"

William was beginning to feel like a high school kid. He put his hands behind his back and said brokenly, "I was kind of thinkin' you might like to join me at the club when your shift is over. I mean if it's not too late and you can make the time."

Veronica leaned back in her chair and removed her hat. Her blonde hair tumbled out. She continued to smile her best and most charming smile. "My shift ends at eighteen hundred hours. I then will probably hurry over to the mess tent to get some chow. After that, I'll probably go to the nurse's quarters and shower and get cleaned up. I would say that by twenty hundred hours I would probably be at the club for a relaxin' drink. How does that fit with your schedule, Lieutenant Barnett?"

"I think," William said as he turned towards the ward door, "that I'll probably be in the club havin' a drink at twenty hundred hours."

As William reached the door and started to leave, Veronica called to him softly, "Don't they call you boys in the one-oh-first, 'Screamin' Eagles'?"

William pushed the door open slightly and looked back at her and said proudly, "Yeah, they do."

Veronica leaned forward on her desk and in a soft tone asked, "I was just wonderin' what that little old eagle is screamin'?"

William smiled at her and replied, "I'll tell you all about it over a drink at the club at twenty hundred hours." With that, he disappeared through the door.

Once outside it was only a short walk to where the jeep was parked. Private Kingsley was already waiting for him. "Everything go okay, Lieutenant?" He asked.

"Indeed it did, Private Kingsley, indeed it did."

Private Kingsley reached over and patted the hood of the jeep and said, "I got quartered in with a couple of army medics so I'm fixed for the night. But they want me to move the jeep to over behind the utility helipad to keep it out of the way. So, I'll be doin' that if it's okay with you, Lieutenant?"

"Yeah, I got no problem with that."

"Okay then, I'll do that now. Are you all set with your quarters for the night?"

"Uh, no, not yet," William replied putting his hands on his hips, "but I'm goin' to take care of that right now."

Private Kingsley jumped into the jeep and gave William a halfhearted salute, "Roger that. So, what time do you want to leave tomorrow?"

William smiled at Kingsley and said, "I'm not sure. We'll talk about it after mornin' mess tomorrow, I'll let you know then."

"You sure you're okay, Lieutenant? You look kind of strange."

"No, I'm fine, Private. You go ahead and I'll see you at mess in the mornin'."

Kingsley gave William another quick salute and then jammed the jeep into gear and took off. William watched him go and then turned and started for the Operations Tent to secure quarters for the night. As he walked, he smiled and muttered to himself, "As Shakespeare would say, 'Me thinks I may be in love'."

And as events happened on Thanksgiving Day in 1968 at the 1066th MASH unit in South Vietnam, 1st Lieutenant William Barnett met and became acquainted with 2nd Lieutenant Veronica Mann.

CHAPTER THIRTY-SIX

The New Year's Eve Gathering

It was now the 30th of December and Lt. Kathleen O'Rourke was working hard to finish the plan she'd been working on since just after Thanksgiving. Her plan was complex and took all her spare time. Mixing her work on the plan in with her scheduled shifts and other duties was difficult, but she was slowly getting it done. But now it was nearly New Year's Eve, so the plan had to come together today.

The plan called for getting The Tart Trio and their dates to the 95th for New Year's Eve, and it had to be done without causing issues with anyone's duty or military orders. As for herself, Kathleen had covered for several other nurses over the last two weeks including Christmas Eve and Christmas day. She had done that so she could then get them to cover for her on New Year's Eve and New Year's Day. Now as for Kellie and Veronica, Kathleen had been in communications with Kellie ever since December 1st. With Kellie being the head nurse, she was able to secure a schedule for herself and Veronica that would allow them to come down to the 95th for New Year's Eve and half of New Year's Day. At the same time, Veronica was able to get her new boyfriend, Lt. Barnett, who was still just a few klicks down the road at Camp Eagle, to free himself up to go with them. The problem was how to get them all down to the 95th from the ten-six-six. That's where Captain Collie came into play. Kathleen had told Kellie to talk to Kyle about it and see what he could do, which she did just after Christmas on Kyle's last high cover mission to the ten-six-six.

Kyle was all for the get together, but for him to leave Cobra Umbrella One on New Year's Eve, go over to the ten-six-six and pick up the two nurses and Lt. Barnett, and then fly down to the 95th, he first had to be able to stand-down from mission alert, and second, he had to have a reason to go down to the 95th. The first thing turned out to be the easy part. He didn't have to ask to stand-down, as he was taken off mission alert. The newer Cobras were doing most of the assault work now and with both sides not mounting any major offenses, Kyle spent most of his time just being on ready standby. He had a new crew now. Denny had taken promotion and had been sent down south to fly a Cobra for the Special Forces. Harv had refused to stay and risk his life in a war that he was convinced he wouldn't be allowed to try and win. So, he rotated out and went back to the States. As a result, Kyle had a new crew chief and a new copilot.

The second thing was harder to accomplish. He had to find a way to convince the Base Commander that he needed to go down to the 95th, and that he needed to use his chopper to get there. He went over several different plans in his head. But none of them made any sense to him. In the end, he decided to simple go and tell the Base Commander the truth; that he wanted the use of his chopper to fly down to the 95th to spend New Year's Eve with his girlfriend.

To Kyle's surprise, Coronal Keeper had simply said okay but it was on the condition that he would be back on the afternoon of New Year's Day and that he couldn't take any of his crew with him, which was all just fine with Kyle.

So, Kathleen had all but one of her little group accounted for, and the unaccounted for person was her own date, Sergeant Jordan Costillo. Since their first meeting, they'd only seen each other two other times and both times were for less than a day. But the time she did get to spend with Jordan she treasured because she was really falling hard for him. The problem was that Jordan was always off somewhere on a Recon mission. She never knew where he was or what he was doing. She knew it was dangerous and it worried her, but her work kept her mind occupied most of the time. But during her off shift hours and alone in her bunk, all kinds of bad things went through her mind.

She'd been able to get word to Jordan about the planned get together through Captain Collie. Kyle had flown escort for one of Jordan's missions just after Christmas and filled him in on the plans. Jordan had promised to get in communication with Kathleen sometime on the 30th. It was now late afternoon on December 30th and she had heard nothing from Jordan. In her heart, she knew he would come if he could.

She walked down the beach and then turned and walked a short distance inland. There, standing in a small clump of trees was a small hut. She had succeeded in renting it for New Year's Eve night from one of the male operating room technicians. In the terms of the military personnel the hut was called, a '*hootch*', or a place where a guy could keep his Vietnamese girlfriend. But for New Year's Eve night it belonged to her, and this was where the planned gathering was to take place.

After walking up to the hootch, she peeked in the window and saw that no one was there. She guessed that the occupants had already left. The door was pad locked and she had the key in her pocket but she didn't go in. She leaned her back up against the door and folded her arms across her chest. Closing her eyes, thoughts ran through her mind. What a crazy set of circumstances she was involved in. Being a girl from Hell's Kitchen, she never believed in coincidences or luck. She thought that things happened for a reason or were caused by something or someone. And she believed you made your own luck. But the whole thing with

The Tart Trio and the guys they had met made her wonder. It was strange enough that three girls from vastly different walks of life could end up being such good friends in such a short period of time. But even stranger were the guys; all three of them were from Texas, and were good friends or related to each other in some way; two of 'em were even from the same hometown. What were the odds of all three of them entering different braches of the service, then all ending up in South Vietnam fighting in a war, then meeting up with each other through a trio of nurses. Maybe there were such things as coincidences. She smiled to herself and then said out loud to no one, "But I'll bet Father, no I mean Bishop, Conway would say that it's not a coincidence but rather divine intervention."

Then, she pushed herself away from the door to the hootch, unfolded her arms, and started back to the 95th where her swing shift in Ward 2 would soon start. As she walked she said loud, again to no one, "I don't care if its coincidence or divine intervention, I just want my guy to be here."

It was near fifteen hundred hours on December 31st, when Captain Kyle Collie set his chopper gently down on the utility helipad at the 95th EVAC Hospital. After the blades had stopped, he got out and walked around to the left side of the chopper and pulled open the waist door. His three passengers chambered out of the chopper and onto the helipad. Kyle then slammed the waist door closed and joined the other three. Except for Kyle, they were all wearing civvies. William was in jeans and wearing a wild looking Aloha shirt. He had sneakers on his feet with no socks. Kellie was wearing a pair of cut-off fatigue shorts and a sleeveless white shirt. She was also wearing sneakers with no socks. Veronica was more formal. She wore a short skirt that came to mid-thigh and a red sleeveless blouse. On her feet, she had pair of flip-flops that had red rhinestones set in them. Unfortunately for Kyle, he was required to be in uniform because he was flying an armed assault helicopter. The four seemed lost as they scanned the area with worried looks. But then smiles replaced the worried looks when they saw Kathleen walking towards them wearing a huge smile on her face. She was dressed in a pair of white short-shorts and a pull over white T-shirt. On her feet were the standard sneakers with no socks.

When Kathleen reached the group, The Tart Trio immediately went into a group hug. They laughed and searched each other over. Kyle and William smiled at each other as they stood back and watch the three nurses go through their greeting ritual. Finally, Kathleen pulled free and said loudly, "Come on you guys, follow me." She turned around and pointed to a jeep that was waiting for them about twenty yards away. "Everybody pile-in we've got a short drive to our hootch."

"Wow, a jeep," Kyle exclaimed. "How'd you manage that?"

"I've got a lot of pull around here," she replied laughing.

Everyone had piled into the jeep except for Kyle. He stood back as Kathleen got behind wheel and was about to start the jeep. She looked at him still smiling and asked, "What's the matter, Kyle?"

He looked at her deeply and asked, "Still no word from Jordan?"

The group went quiet. Kathleen gripped the steering wheel and looked straight ahead. "No," she said softly, "I've not heard anythin'. I'm sure he would've made it if he could've." There was a long silence and then the smile returned to her face and she continued, "I'm sure he'd want us to ring in the New Year in true Marine Recon fashion. And that's what we're goin' to do."

Kyle leaned over and planted a huge kiss directly on her lips. "Let's get to that hootch and see if we can Recon the hell outa this place."

Kyle was still climbing into the jeep when Kathleen jammed it into gear and took off like a shot. Everyone was laughing and talking again as they sped down the beach.

It was now twenty-two hundred hours; just two hours away from midnight and the ringing in of 1969. Kathleen sat in a chair at the small table in the middle of the hootch. She smiled to herself, which she was convinced was a victory smile. The little party had turned out better than she could've ever imagined. Even though the food was sparse and consisted only of sandwiches and chips that Kathleen could pilfer from the mess hall, everyone seemed to be having a good time. The one thing that was in abundant supply was alcohol. The Officer's Club at the 95th and been nice enough to supply her a good amount of all kinds of alcohol and she had been able to obtain even more at the Post Exchange or in army terms, 'the PX'.

She sat at the table drinking a Jamison on the rocks and watching all her friends. Kyle and Kellie were over by the record player going through a stack of records and sipping on drinks. William and Veronica were both stretched out on the floor lying on pillows. They sipped on dinks as they laughed while they talked.

It had been a long evening of drinking, joking, and telling stories. If anyone had secrets, they were now common knowledge. Kathleen had made a valiant effort to not seem alone. She laughed and drank with everyone. She accepted the heartfelt thanks from all her friends for her efforts in organizing the gathering. Although she did indeed feel alone and kind of like a fifth wheel, she was extremely happy to see everyone and to be with them. Kyle and Kellie had just put on some loud Beach Boys music, when a hard knock came at the door. No one seemed to hear it except Kathleen. At first she thought she had imagined it, but then it came again and louder. She sat up straight and looked around. If anyone else heard the knocking, they were ignoring it. She put her drink down, pushed herself out of the chair, and went to the door. At first, she cracked the door open slightly and peeked out. Then she recognized Captain Marley. He was one of the doctor's at the 95th. He was wearing his white surgeons coat and his stethoscope hung around his neck. He had the bad luck to be in charge of the OR on New Year's Eve.

"Hey, Lt. O'Rourke," he called through the small opening.

Kathleen pulled the door open wide and asked in an amazed tone, "Captain Marley, what're you doin' here?"

He unceremoniously pushed his way into the hootch. "You need to come back to the OR with me," he said harshly.

By now everyone in the room had noticed Captain Marley and slowly started to form a semi-circle behind Kathleen.

"What's going on, Kat?" Kellie asked as she stepped up alongside her friend.

Kathleen shrugged her shoulders and looked back to Captain Marley and asked. "What can I do for you, Sir?"

The doctor looked around at all the people staring at him intently. "Look, I'm sorry gang, but I've got a hard headed Jarhead that refuses to leave the triage area unless he can talk to you, Lt. O'Rourke." He paused and then in frustration yelled, "And can someone turn that damn music off."

Kellie left her friends side and went over to the record player and turned it off.

Kathleen looked at Captain Marley in wonderment. "You mean we have wounded in the triage area *NOW*?"

"Yeah, we do," he replied, "they just arrived in an ambulance that came in from somewhere on Route 1." He paused for a moment and when everyone just stared at him and didn't speak he continued, "What I've got is three wounded marines; none of them serious. But one of them refuses to leave the triage area so we can treat him in OR until he talks to you, Lt. O'Rourke." He then changed his tone to be much more angry and demanding. "I don't need this on New Year's Eve, Lieutenant. Could you please come with me back to the triage area and talk to this guy? It should only take a few minutes and then you can get back to your party."

"But, Sir, how did you know I was here?"

Captain Marley looked at her in disbelief. "Lt. O'Rourke, everybody knows you're here. This little get together isn't a secret. Now, can we go?"

"Yes, Sir," she said as she turned to face her friends, "I'll be back as quick as I can."

"Hold on a minute," it was Kyle speaking, "maybe we all should go."

"For God's sake, why is that?" The doctor asked in frustration.

Kyle turned to Kathleen and asked in a suspicious tone. "Kat, is there any other marine that knows you personally enough to ask for you by your name? I mean any marine except for Jordan."

Kathleen's eyes widened as she turned back to the doctor. "Do you know this marine's name?"

At this point, the doctor was losing control. "No! All I know is that he's a Staff Sergeant. Now, all this shit is over. Lieutenant, I'm ordering you to come with me."

"That won't be necessary, Captain," came a voice from the door.

Everyone turned their attention to the door and standing there in the doorway and leaning against the frame was Staff Sergeant Jordan Costillo. He was in his combat uniform except he was bare-chested and hatless. There was a bandage that ran from his left arm pit to over his left shoulder and back down to his arm pit again. He was dirty and sweaty but he had a joyous smile on his face.

"Christ Almighty!" The doctor yelled. "What is going to happen next? How'd you get here Sergeant?"

"Jordy", Kathleen yelled as she ran over to him. But she stopped before he touched him because she was afraid he was hurt.

Then all hell broke loose as everyone started to talk at the same time. William went to the door and grabbed Jordan by the arm and pulled him into the hootch and guided him to a chair at the table and pushed him down into it.

Then Captain Marley started waving his arms and yelling, "Okay, everybody just hold on here. Everybody stop. I mean it. I don't want to have to call the MPs and ruin your party. But I will if I have to."

Everyone calmed down and backed away from Jordan. "Okay," he said in a calmer voice. "Now, I'll ask again, Sergeant, how'd you get here?"

Jordan stood up and faced the Captain and stood at an informal attention. "I'm sorry, Sir," he said in a true military voice, "I've been disrespectable and I beg the Captain's pardon."

Captain Marley looked around the room and, now feeling more in control, said to Jordan, "I understand, Sergeant. So, please continue."

"The truth is, Captain, I followed you."

"How could you follow me, Sergeant, I'm in a jeep."

Jordan stood uneasy moving from side to side on his feet. "Well, Sir, the ambulance driver brought me. I don't want to get him in trouble because I kind of ordered him to follow you. He's a private and I guess I was able to maybe intimidate him."

Captain Marley nodded his head and asked, "Where's the ambulance now?"

Jordan shrugged, "I told him he could go. I think the Navy is goin' to put on a fireworks display at midnight and he wanted to see it."

Captain Marley let out a long breath, "Well, now that you've seen the Lieutenant here can we get you back to the OR so we can take a look at that wound."

"Sir, I'd really like to say with my friends and this wound is hardly a wound at all. The truth is I faked most of it so I could get here to be with my friends. Please, Sir."

"Please, Sir," came another plead from Kathleen.

Captain Marley wavered for a moment and shouted an order. "Sit down in your chair, Sergeant, and let take a look at that wound and I'll decide."

Everyone was quiet while the doctor removed the bandage from Jordan's shoulder. He put the bandage on the table and bent over and studied the wound carefully. "Who patched you up, Sergeant?"

"It was done by our corpsman in the field, Sir."

Captain Marley stood up and smiled. "Well, he did a pretty damn good job. I see he even put in a couple of switches. I'd say this wound was made by shrapnel."

"Yes, Sir, it was."

"It's still a little red and might get infected." Then Captain Marley looked around the room. "Could someone bring me that bottle of vodka over there and some napkins?

Kyle hurried over and got the half empty bottle of vodka. He also grabbed a handful of napkins that were lying next to the sandwich tray. In seconds, he was back at the table and placed everything within the doctor's reach.

"Thanks." Captain Marley said simply, as he continued to study the wound. "Okay," he said carefully, "I'm going to bath this little wound in some of this wonderful 100 proof vodka." He then soaked down a napkin with the vodka. Gently he began cleaning the wound with the saturated napkin. He worked for almost five minutes making sure the wound was completely cleaned and the vodka had soaked down into the wound. He used several soaked napkins as he worked. "Well, I think that's pretty good," he finally said. "Now, can someone run out to my jeep and get the first aid kit?"

No sooner had he spoke the words before Kathleen was running out the hootch door. She was back in less than a minute and handed the kit to the doctor.

Again, he simply said, "Thanks." He opened the kit and took out some disinfection salve and rubbed in gently around the wound. When finished he stood back with a satisfied look on his face. Then, he took out four large band aids and carefully crisscrossed them on the wound. He finished his work and closed the kit and picked it up. He started for the door but stopped just short of it turned around and pointed to Jordan. "You can stay here with your friends tonight, Sergeant, but you're to report to the OR tomorrow morning for some antibiotics. Is that clear? Because if it's not you can come with me now."

Jordan got to his feet and again took the informal attention stance. "It's clear, Sir, and you've got my word on it. And, Captain, thank you, and have a happy New Year."

Kathleen ran up and took the doctor's hand. "Thank you, Captain Marley. I owe you one."

The Captain just smiled, gave a mock salute and walked out the door.

The group spent the next half hour talking, laughing, and sipping drinks. Soon it was only twenty minutes until midnight and the New Year. Kathleen was now involved with everyone else; now that Jordan was there. They went around the small room and each one told what they looked forward to after they got out of Vietnam. They all had a wish but it was easy to tell that none of them wanted to reveal their deepest wishes to the entire group. Kathleen was the last one to tell her wish. She held up her hands to get silence. Once the group was quiet and listening, she said, "I can tell you what I wish could happen but I know it won't happen."

Everyone just watched her waiting for her to continue.

"I have enjoyed this get together so much that I wish I could own a place somethin' like this, but it would be on a beautiful stretch of beach somewhere in Hawaii. But my place would be huge. It would be large enough so that all of us could have our own rooms, and each room would have its own bathroom. And there would be a large livin' area where we could all be comfortable. There'd be an extra-large kitchen with all the food and drinks any of us would ever want. I'd live there but I'd insist that all of you would promise to come and visit once each year." She paused and looked around at the group grinning and said, "Now, isn't that a great wish? If only I could make it come true."

"You can, Kat," Kyle said with a mischievous smile, "you just need to ask Jordan."

Jordan's head snap around to Kyle and the look on his face was one of shock and disbelief. Kyle knew immediately that he had made a mistake; a mistake that had violated the trust of a friend. He quickly got up off the floor where he and Kellie were lying. He reached down and took Kellie's hand and pulled her to her feet. "Come on, Kel, we need to go for a walk on the beach and find a place to watch the fireworks display. And I want to talk with you in private anyway." With that, Kyle and Kellie were quickly out the door.

"What the hell was that all about?" Kathleen asked in wonderment.

At that moment William, who was seated on the floor with Veronica, jumped to his feet pulling Veronica to her feet with him. "Kyle's got a good idea there, Ronnie. We should find us a spot on the beach also. Come on let's go."

Veronica nodded and followed William as they quickly went out the door.

Kathleen's look of wonderment was now gone. She turned her gaze to Jordan, who was looking down at the table. She leaned back in her chair and stared hard at Jordan, who wouldn't return her gaze. They were quiet for several minutes and then Jordan said, "I wish there was somewhere I could take a shower. I bet you're tired of seein' me dirty like this."

Kathleen leaned forward and put her elbows on the table, folded her hands together, and placed them under her chin. Her eyes showed hurt. "Jordy," she asked softly, "what is it that everyone knows and I don't know?"

"Well," Jordan started, "I was...."

"Stop," Kathleen interrupted him sharply, "Jordy, please look at me when you speak to me."

Jordan raised his head and looked her straight in the eyes. "As I was sayin'", he continued, "I was plannin' on tellin' you tonight after the fireworks, but Kyle had to shoot of his month. So, here goes. The first thing is that if you don't know that I've fallin' completely in love with you, then you've not been payin' attention. I had a whole lot of things rehearsed to say to you but that's kind-of all changed now. The second thing is that I'm rich, Kat. I'm very rich. That's what you didn't know and everybody else did."

He started to continue but she again interrupted him. "Rich?" She asked him in surprise. "How rich are we talkin' about?"

He shrugged his shoulders, made a funny face and then stammered, "The last numbers I got from home said I was worth about six and a half million, but that's been over six months ago."

Kathleen's eyes widened and she breathed, "Six and a half million dollars?"

"Yeah, I'm pretty sure it's in that general neighborhood."

"For God sakes, Jordy, that's a pretty nice neighborhood."

He smiled, "Yeah, I guess it is."

Kathleen didn't know exactly what to say next. Finally she just blurted out, "But how does a multi-millionaire get to be a sergeant in the marines? And, in addition, get his rich ass sent to Vietnam?"

"That's a different and long story involvin' my perceived obligations to my family. I'll be happy to go over that with you at another time. But, for now, just know that it's true."

"But…" she started but now it was his turn to interrupt.

"You hear that," he shouted, "they've started the fireworks. Come on let's go out and watch." As he spoke, he grabbed her hand and pulled her out the door. Once outside, he ran through the trees to the beach pulling her along behind him. At the beach, they stopped and looked up at the grand display being put on by the United States Navy.

They were standing there looking up, when she asked softly, "Why didn't you tell me Jordy? Were you afraid that I would be with you just for your money?"

Without looking down from the sky, he said, "No, that's not it at all. I knew from the first five minutes on China Beach with you durin' our first meetin' that you weren't that kind of person. It's just that when people know you're rich they tend to treat you differently. Not on purpose but without knowin' it. Like Kyle and William, they do it sometimes without even knowin' it. I just wanted our startin' to be absolutely pure. Can you understand that?"

"I don't think I do completely, but I think you do."

He turned and reached down and put his finger under her chin and tilted her head back. He looked down into those beautiful green eyes with the fireworks reflecting in them. Then he bent down and kissed her. It was a long, hard kiss. In the process, he had pulled her tightly to him. When he realized what he had done, he looked down at the all dirt and mud he had gotten on her from his still dirty body. "Christ, I'm sorry, Kat. It looks like I got you just about as dirty as me."

She just chuckled and turned back towards trees. Still holding his hand, it was her now that pulled him along. "I know where we can go and take a shower," she said through a smile.

"Did you say we?" He asked.

"We," she replied simply.

It was a slow moving partially hung over group that gathered at Kyle's chopper on New Year's morning 1969. Kyle was back in full uniform now, and was desperately trying to round everyone up so they could get started back to the ten-six-six. He needed to be back to his base by noon so he had to get everyone moving. Just as he thought he had everyone in tow, Kathleen came running up with Jordan in tow. She also had with her another nurse carrying a camera.

"Hey, gang," Kathleen yelled as she approached, "we can't breakup without some pictures." Then pointing to the nurse, she continued, "This is Lt. Bailey and I've asked her to take a few pictures."

Kyle rubbed his head, "Come on, Kat, we've got to go."

"It'll just take a minute," she insisted. "This is probably a once in a life time thing so come on."

Kyle relented and they all six lined up in front of the chopper, with Kyle and Kellie on the far left, William and Veronica in the middle and Jordan and Kathleen on the end. Lt. Bailey then quickly took a series of pictures. When she was finished, Kyle started to move everyone to the open waist door of the chopper.

"Wait," Kathleen yelled, "I need one more shot. I want a shot of The Tart Trio. Come on over here girls and we'll get a shot of us standin' together."

Once again, Kyle yielded and simply leaned back against the chopper. Veronica and Kellie joined Kathleen and they stood together with their arms around each other's necks. Kathleen was in the middle with Kellie on her left and Veronica on her right. Knowing the urgency of the situation, Lt. Baily quickly got in position and started snapping a series of pictures. When she finished, she held the camera up high and laughed, "I'm sure I got some good ones."

"Now, we have to go," Kyle insisted as he ushered everyone towards the chopper door. Kellie, Veronica, and William all climbed into the chopper, as they waved and shouted their good-byes.

Jordan stopped at the door of the chopper and held out his hand to Kyle. "I won't be goin' with you guys. I need to find that ambulance driver and get a ride back up Route 1. He'll know how to get me back to my unit."

Kyle took his hand, gripped it hard and shook it vigorously. "You take care out there, Jordan," he said sincerely.

"I can say the same to you, Kyle." Then after a short pause he smiled and added, "And you and Kellie make a good team. I think you should stay with her, Kyle. You don't need to search for girls anymore."

Kyle laughed and said, "My searchin' days are over."

Jordan walked back to join Kathleen as Kyle slid the waist door shut. He then walked around to the right side and climbed into the command seat. In a short few minutes, the chopper was 'dusting off'. It was a termed used by all the military to describe a medivac chopper taking off with wounded. But, in this case, the wounded were simply hung over and it was an assault chopper; not a medivac.

So, the year 1968 in South Vietnam came to a close and the year 1969 began. The year 1969 in South Vietnam would hold the destiny of all six of the little group in its hands, as the ever turning and changing events of war would continue.

CHAPTER THIRTY-SEVEN

The Ten-Six-Six Gets a New Commander

It was now early February of 1969, as Lieutenant Kellie Anderson sat in the front passenger seat of an army jeep speeding down a dirt road outside of Phu Bai. She wore combat boots and camouflage fatigues with her lieutenant rank on one collar and the Army Medical Corps emblem on the other. As the jeep bounced over the rough road, she held on to her Australian bush hat. "Shit, Sergeant," she yelled. "Do we have to go so friggin' fast?"

"You said you had to be to the airstrip before fourteen hundred hours, Ma'am," the sergeant yelled back with a smile on his face.

Sergeant Tim Morely was a short timer with less than a month to go in country and even less respect for officers. He was tall and skinny and probably wouldn't weigh one hundred and fifty pounds soaking wet. He had blonde hair that peeked out from under his army helmet. His dark brown eyes were accented by heavy dark eyebrows that seemed to come together between his eyes. His current goal in life was to return to his home town of Panama City, Florida and become a beach bum. "Do you want me to slow down, *Ma'am?*"

"No, Sergeant, just get me there. But preferably in one piece."

A short time later, Kellie was standing near the operations gate at the Phu Bai Airstrip. She was waiting for the new commander of the ten-six-six, whom she was ordered to pick up. She knew the new commander very well; it was her father Lt. Colonel Jacob B. Anderson. She watched as new personnel streamed through the gate until, at last, she saw him walking across the tarmac. It was the first time she had seen him in his uniform since the Korean War when she was barely five years old. As he approached, she saluted smartly, "Lieutenant Anderson reporting to pick you up, Sir."

He returned her salute, "Very good, Lieutenant. Have the sergeant pick up my gear at the drop off point. They're all marked."

"Yes, Sir", then turning to Sergeant Morely, "You heard the colonel, get it done, and then you're dismissed. I'll be driving the colonel to the ten-six-six."

"Roger that, Ma'am," the sergeant said as he saluted and hurried off to retrieve the bags.

After the sergeant had gone, they both stared at each other for a long moment. Then, they broke out into loud laughter. "My God," Kellie said still laughing. "I'm looking at an honest-to-gosh Korean War retread. How in hell did they get you back in?"

"Well, the truth is," he said slowly. "I volunteered. I was inspired by the way you dropped out of medical school, against my wishes I might add, to come over here and do this."

"Medical school will still be there when I'm through here."

"I hope so, Kel," he said turning serious. "I like the sound of Doctor Kellie Anderson better than Lieutenant Kellie Anderson."

"It'll happen, Dad," she replied just as serious. "Not to worry. Come on now; let's get you to your new command."

"Is that bush hat regulation?" He asked as they started across the airstrip.

"No, but then not much is at the ten-six-six."

By the time they reached the jeep, Sergeant Morely was struggling to get all of the bags into the back seat. "I think that's all of'em, Colonel," he said saluting.

"Thanks, Sergeant," Kellie said returning his salute. "Have you got transportation back to the ten-six-six?"

"Yes, Ma'am, I do," he replied hesitantly. "But I've got a few stops I need to make first if the Lieutenant has no objections?"

"What kind of stops?" Kellie asked suspiciously.

"It's just personal stuff, Lieutenant."

"This personal stuff doesn't involve any of the local working ladies, does it?"

"Like I said, Lieutenant, it's just personal stuff."

"Okay, but don't catch anything we can't cure, Sergeant Morely," Kellie said firmly. "You're a damn good operating room technician and I don't want to lose you to some incurable kind of Vietnamese crouch rot. Be sure you're back before curfew."

"Yes, Ma'am," he said smiling and giving a half-hearted salute, "before curfew."

As the jeep bounced down the jungle road, Jacob watched his daughter closely. They had been diving for several minutes before anyone spoke. Finally, Jacob broke the silence. "So, tell me Lieutenant, what do you do at the ten-six-six?"

She kept her eyes on the road as she spoke. "At present, I'm the head nurse."

"Are you enjoying your work?" He asked. "I mean is this what you came here to do?"

"Yes, I'm enjoying my work. But I can't say I like the circumstances. Nobody in their right mind would enjoy seeing the things I've seen. But I do feel I'm making a major contribution. And, I like and respect the people I work with; including Sergeant Morley. You're going to be taking command of a damn good outfit, Dad. I mean a really damn good outfit."

"I'm glad to hear that, Lieutenant," he said slowly. "But I promise you I'll find out for myself."

"We wouldn't have it any other way, Colonel," she replied smiling. "But, trust me you're going to like everyone you meet."

"Speaking of liking people I meet, tell me about this chopper jockey you've been writing me about. It sounded serious in your letters."

She was silent for a moment and then she pulled the jeep to the side of the road and stopped. She turned and looked at him with the concern in her deep blue eyes that he had grown use to over the years. "It is serious, Dad," she said softly. "We love each other." When her father didn't answer, she lowered her head so as not to meet his eyes and continued. "Kyle wants me to marry him."

Jacob reached over and put his hand under her chin and lifted her face. He looked deep into her eyes. "And how do you feel about that?" He asked carefully.

Without moving her eyes from his, she answered in a firm voice. "I feel like it's what I want, Dad."

"So, you really love this guy, uh!"

"I do, Dad! I really do. More than you can ever believe."

"Oh! I can believe it," he said, lowering his hand from her chin and leaning back to look at her. "I was just wondering when you were intending to tell me. If I hadn't of asked, I still wouldn't know."

"I'm sorry, Dad."

She removed her bush hat and her hair dropped down to almost her shoulders. He stared at her for a long moment, thinking back to her childhood. She practically looked the same; with her dark black hair and cloudy blue eyes. She had the same serious look on her face that she seemed to always carry.

"But, why so secret?" He finally asked, breaking his train of thought.

"To tell the truth," she replied slowly and uncomfortably. "I knew you would start on me again about medical school and I wasn't ready to handle it."

"But you are now!" He challenged.

"Yes, I am. Kyle and I have it all worked out. I'll leave the army and finish medical school when my second tour is up."

"What about Kyle?"

She moved uneasily in the jeep seat. "He's a career man, Dad. He's going to stay in."

"And, you two think you can make this work?" His voice had a tired tone.

"Yes," was her simple reply, "don't you?"

Jacob wasn't sure if her challenge was a question or a demand. He looked at her carefully again. "If it were anyone else, I'd certainly say no. But since it's you, Kel, I have to believe you can do it. In any case, you'll have my complete support."

"Now, that's the Dad I grew up with," she said smiling and putting her hat back on. "When do I get to meet this chopper jockey?" He asked.

"Soon," she replied happily, as she jammed the jeep in gear and pulled back onto the road.

As the jeep bounced down the dirty jungle road, he gave a chuckle and held his fist up and gave the thumbs up sign. "Thumbs up," he yelled at her.

She laughed and returned the sign to him, "Thumbs up, Colonel, thumbs up."

CHAPTER THIRTY-EIGHT

March, the Month of Decisions

It was March 6, 1969 as Kellie and Veronica sat in the club at the ten-six-six. They each held a drink in their hand. They were exhausted. They had both just come off long shifts in the OR. In January, the 9th Marines had gone on the offensive into the Song Da Krong Valley and the adjacent A Shau Valley and started an offensive push along the border with Laos. At times, using loosely defined words in the Geneva Convention, they executed ambushes inside of supposedly neutral Laos with great success. They were still there and the fighting was intense. As a result, there was a big push and casualties were flowing into the ten-six-six from several Marine Field Hospitals. The staff at the ten-six-six was working around the clock to take care of the in rush of casualties. Medivac choppers were coming in two or three at a time and mostly without high cover. Two medivacs had been hit by VC ground fire and brought down. The VC had also sent several mortar rounds into the ten-six-six but hadn't hit anything or anyone. Quick reaction by the 5th Marines had eliminated the VC threat to everyone's relief. To make things worse, monsoon type rains had been pouring down. Only the extreme bravery of the medivac chopper pilots was getting the wounded through to the ten-six-six. The rains had even caused problems with the generators that kept the unit supplied with electricity. But some Seabees had stayed on the problem keeping the OR and other essential areas operating without interruption.

Kellie set her drink down and leaned back in her chair. She ran her fingers through her hair, which was matted with sweat and rain. She looked over at Veronica and reluctantly said, "I'm sorry, Ronnie, but I've had to put you back on OR shift in about three hours. I think you should go hit your bunk and try to grab some sack time."

Veronica looked at her and gave her a crooked smile. "Yeah, I guess I will," she replied. She slugged down her drink and then stood up to leave but stopped after only a few steps. She put her hand on Kellie's shoulder and asked gently, "Have you heard anythin' from Kat? How's it goin' down at the 95th?"

Kellie looked up at her with weary eyes and replied, "Yeah, I heard from her briefly this morning around oh-seven hundred. They're about like us the push is on them too. Would you believe they found her asleep on an OR gurney? She'd been working OR and ward shifts for twenty hours. She's doing her job but she's also worried sick about Jordan. She knows he's somewhere out there. Everybody knows that a full company of Marine Recon went into the valley with the 9th Marines."

"Well, how're you doin', Kel?" Veronica asked softly. "Have you heard anythin' from Kyle?"

Kellie took a deep breath and let it out slowly and said, "I guess I'm doin' just like Kat. I'm working my ass off to keep my mind busy, because all I know is that Kyle's been pulled from high cover duty and is now flying assault missions only. That's all I know."

Veronica patted Kellie's shoulder and started for the club door, but Kellie called after her, "And what about, William? Have you heard from him?"

Veronica turned back and looked at Kellie and shrugged her shoulders. "Yeah, I've heard from 'im. I've even seen 'im a couple of times.

He manages to get down here once-in-a-while. He's still at Camp Eagle but I can tell somethin's up. He can't tell me anythin' except that they're gearin' up for a move. So, that's what I know, he's gearin' up for a move." She stopped talking, lowered her head and put her hands on her hips. Then she asked with mock anger, "Why'd you and Kat let me fall for a guy like William? I blame the two of you for this roll-a-coaster ride. I was perfectly happy bein' the town flirt. Now look at me." With that, she smiled, waved her hand at Kellie and then walked out the door.

It was now March 18th and the marine offensive push had ended and the casualty flow had now returned to normal. Kellie found she could actually give the nurses some leisure time and gave out some R&R, which she did at every opportunity. Now, she and Veronica sat in the CO's office. They had been ordered to be there at their earliest availability. They had only been waiting for a little over ten minutes when Colonel Anderson came through the door in a hurry.

"I'm sorry for being late," he said as he hurried around his desk to his chair. "I got caught up in OR but now I'm here." Both nurses started to their feet, but he waved them back down. "I'll try and make this brief. I've got some paperwork here for you two. It's your extension papers. If either, or both, of you want to extend for another tour, I need you to fill out this paperwork so I can get it up to battalion. If you don't want to extend, then your tours will terminate tomorrow on March 19th and I'll make arrangements for you to get transportation down to Da Nang. I know this is short notice and battalion is really on my ass about it. They need to know how to cut your orders. They'll accept a verbal answer via our squawk box but I have to get this paperwork out to them today." He paused for a moment and Kellie started to speak but he held up his hand to stop her. "Just a minute, there's more. I've been authorized to tell you, Lt. Anderson, that if you extend you'll get your railroad-tracks and that you'll remain here at the ten-six-six as a captain and the official head nurse and not just as a fill in as you've been this last year. And as for you, Lt. Mann, you'll get your 1st lieutenant's silver bars and the assignment as Kellie's XO. Now, if you two need some time to talk this over, step outside and take about ten minutes then comeback inside with your answers."

The two nurses looked at each other and smiled. Then Kellie spoke, "There's no need for a conference. All three of us who came over here together, me, Ronnie, and Kat, have all committed to two tours. So, just tell us where we sign."

Colonel Anderson stood up and looked down at the two nurses. He let out a long breath and said, "Both of you have gone above and beyond. You've got nothing else to prove. I wish you would reconsider. Of course, I'm speaking now as Kellie's father and not the CO, which could get me in a world of shit, but I need to say it."

Veronica stood up and looked at Colonel Anderson with tired eyes. "A good gentleman friend of mine in the one-oh-first just extended for another tour," she said softly. "I want to be here. I've got no reconsiderin' to do. However, if you wish to discuss this with your daughter in private, I'll wait outside for Kel."

At that, Kellie stood up. "Sir," she said, "I don't need any time to reconsider. That answer comes from your head nurse as well as your daughter."

"Okay," the Colonel said pushing the papers across his desk, "just sign on the dotted line and we'll go out and get Jimmy to raise battalion on the squawk box."

Both nurses signed where designated. Then, before they left the office, Kellie asked, "Sir, while we're on the squawk box, could we get Jimmy to also raise the 95th so we could have a quick conversation with Lt. O'Rourke?"

"I don't see why not," was the reply. "Come on let's go get it done."

After Jimmy had reached battalion and Colonel Anderson had spoken with the correct people and had given verbal confirmation that Lieutenants Anderson and Mann had signed extension papers, he raised the 95th. It took the radio operator at the 95th several minutes to find Kathleen. In fact, they had almost given up waiting when the radio operator finally returned. "This is nine five are you guys still there."

"Roger that nine five, we're still here," Jimmy responded.

"Okay, I've got Lt. O'Rourke on her way here. I had to awake her from a dead sleep. She's pretty pissed off. I hope this is important."

There was a long pause with only static coming across the squawk box, when finally Kathleen's voice broke through the static. "This is Lt. O'Rourke, over."

Kellie took the mic away from Jimmy and quickly started talking, "Kat, this is Kel and Ronnie can you read me okay, over?"

"Roger that, Kel, I read you five-by-five. What' goin' on?"

Before Kellie could reply an irritated voice said, "Hey, will you guys cut the 'Roger' and 'Over' stuff and just get done. We need this radio, okay?"

"Understood," Kellie replied apologetically. "Kat, Ronnie and I just wanted to know if you extended or not."

There was a short silence then Kathleen replied, "Yes, I did. But it wasn't easy."

"Why, what's the matter?"

"Jordy didn't want me to. He wanted me to go home and wait for him. It was hard to tell him no, but I did. I couldn't break my word to you guys."

"Oh, Kat, you should've talk to us first! We would've understood!"

"It's okay, Kel, Jordy's tour is up this July but he's tryin' to get an eight month extension so we can leave at the same time next year."

"Will they let him just pick how long he wants to extend? Doesn't it have to be a full tour?"

"I don't know. We'll just have to wait and see. Anyway, I'm on board for another full tour. I got my silver bars so I'm a 1st lieutenant now."

Then came the irritated voice again, "Okay, girls, this all very touching but I've got to clear this frequency. I'm going to have to shut you down."

Quickly Kellie said, "Okay, Kat, we'll get in touch with you again later. Take care."

Then the static returned and the conversation was over.

CHAPTER THIRTY-NINE

They Called It Hamburger Hill

O n May 10th of 1969, the move that 1st Lieutenant William Barnett had been gearing up for finally took place. He was on a Slick with eleven other men headed for the A Shau Valley. His platoon had new replacements and was now at full strength. He had four squads and each squad had the full complement of ten men giving a total of forty men. Adding to that, himself, his XO and the Platoon First Sergeant his platoon was forty-three men strong. However, this time all his squads were rifle squads; he had no machine gun or mortar squads. The good news was that he still had 2nd Lt. Macland as his XO and he had been given an experienced platoon sergeant in Sergeant First Class Mickey Morrison. In addition, of the four squads, two of them still had their veteran staff sergeants leading them.

As he sat in the doorway with his feet dangling over the side, he looked down at the dense jungle below. It made him wonder what he had gotten himself into. But, he knew they were headed for the A Shau when he signed up for a second tour. So, he had no complaints, and anyway this is why he became an officer in the 101st Airborne. He tried to put his worry for Veronica out of his head and his heart. He had wanted her to go home, but she extended anyway. Pushing the issue would've been useless, because her bond with her two nurse friends was as strong, or stronger, than any love she might have for him. In his heart, he knew he had no right to ask her to leave; so he didn't.

His thoughts were interrupted as the Slick pulled its nose up and started its descent. His worries for Veronica would now have to be put after his worries for his platoon. He looked down at the small LZ that would become their base camp. It was a small clearing surrounded by heavy jungle. The Slicks barely had room to put down. As his Slick touched down, William jumped out and kept his head low in respect for the rotor blades. He ran quickly to a spot in front of the Slick and held his fist high above his head. As soon as all the men were out of the Slick, it immediately was airborne again. Slick after Slick came in and dropped off their troops and then shot back up into the air. Soon there were over a hundred men milling around the small LZ. William wondered if it was going to be possible to get the entire company into this small area.

Still holding is fist high, William yelled as loud as he could, "2nd Platoon on me." He started pumping his fist up and down and yelling, "2nd Platoon on me, on me, on me."

Soon all of his guys had gathered around. "Okay, this is goin' to be home for a while." Then he found his XO and grabbed him by arm, "Mac take Sergeant Morrison and go find 1st Platoon. We're supposed to bivouac just to their right. As soon as you do that, get the men over there and start setting up, but first be sure you get a defensive parameter in place. I'm goin' to find the Captain and see if he's got any new orders. You got all that?"

Mac didn't speak; he only nodded his head and left to find the platoon sergeant. When Mac was gone, William started walking at a brisk pace towards where he thought the Captain should be. The Captain's Slick had landed exact where it was supposed to at the very far south end of the LZ. As a result, William had no trouble finding him. William wasn't the first platoon leader to find the Captain. By the time William got to there, the Captain was already surrounded by three of the other platoon leaders.

As William approached the small group, Captain Mackey yelled at him, "Barnett, I've been hearing firing. Are we under attack?"

William was startled but was pretty sure of his answer. "No, Sir, I don't think so. I think it's just some light resistance we're gettin' as we set up our defensive positions. I'm pretty sure we won't get any real resistance until we start up that hill because they hold the high ground."

Captain Mackey nodded his head and said more calmly, "Okay men, get your platoon's organized and the defensive parameter secure then meet me at my tent. I'll have it set up by then and we'll have an officer's call."

The platoon leaders nodded and then hurried off to get the job done. As William hurried back towards his platoon, he looked up at the tall hill that towered above him. The base camp they were setting up was almost exactly at the base of the hill. The whole thing gave William a feeling of dread.

The hill that towered above William's base camp was technically named Hill 937. However, it was known locally by the Vietnamese as Ap Bia Mountain. The number was derived from the fact that the hill was 937 meters (or 3,074 feet) high. It stood just over a mile from the Laotian border. It was covered in thick jungle and, in places, high elephant grass. The North Vietnamese had occupied the hill since 1966 and had established a network of caves at the summit. In addition, they had built several levels of defensive trenches and bunkers that circled the hill just below the summit. The hill was important to the North Vietnamese because it was very close to their sanctuaries in Laos and a gateway into the A Shau Valley and then on into South Vietnam.

The LZ where William's company set up its base camp was near the base of the hill on the northwest side, which put it, roughly, between the hill and the Laotian border.

When the 9th Marines had stopped their offensive push along the Laotian Border, they left a Marine Recon Platoon in a position just north of Hill 937. The job of the Recon Platoon was to make reconnaissance probes towards the hill and to the west towards the Laotian border, and if possible, to locate and identify any North Vietnamese units in the area. They were instructed not to engage but only report their information back to Battalion HQ. In charge of the 3rd Squad of that platoon was Staff Sergeant Jordan Costillo.

At Cobra Umbrella One, Colonel Keeper had called a meeting of all pilots in the ready room. Leaves had been canceled and passes revoked. All the pilots were seated murmuring to each other waiting for the colonel to arrive. They'd been waiting almost an hour when the colonel finally showed up. As he walked in the door he was followed closely by the base XO, Lt. Colonel Lesley Baker, the pilots started to their feet but he waved them down, "As you were, gentlemen."

Colonel Keeper walked to the front of the room and looked out across at his pilots, who all wore worried looks on their faces. "Okay, gentlemen, here's the scoop," he started in a strong voice. "From this moment on you'll be on ready alert at all times until farther notice. You can expect to see a lot of action over the next couple of weeks. So, listen carefully while I fill you in. When I done, there'll a short question and answer session but the key word here is short. To start with, there'll be no more high cover missions. Since that has basically already stopped, that should be no surprise. Now, for what this is all about. As I speak to you, elements of the 101st Airborne Division and ARVN units are being helicoptered into the A Shau Valley. Their main objective is to capture Hill 937. After this meeting, Colonel Baker will go over the exact location on the maps. He will also give you the rules of engagement concerning the Laotian border." At this point, Colonel Keeper took a short pause and clasped his hands together. He looked around the room as if looking into each man's face. Then, he continued, "Gentlemen, this is going to be a tough one. That hill is covered in dense jungle, undergrowth, and tall elephant grass. That means you're going to have a hard time seeing your targets. It also means that the little shits can see you much easier than you'll be able to see them. So, you can expect small arms fire and RPGs from almost anywhere. And *MOST* important, you'll have a hard time recognizing the friendlies. You *MUST* be sure who you're shooting at before you open fire. I can't emphasize this enough. Now, Colonel Baker has a few words before the Q and A begins."

Colonel Keeper didn't sit down but only stepped aside as Colonel Baker stepped up front. "Gentlemen," he started, "you'll not be going out as a single assault mission, but rather as a group. When we get a fire mission, you'll all be going. Now, when you make your attack runs, the Cobras must be first in because they're faster. If the Scouts went first, then the Cobras would be running up their asses. So, the Cobras make their run first, then the Scouts. Your formations will be given to you by your group leaders. In this case, Captain Ranson will lead the Cobras and Captain Collie will lead the Scouts. After you leave our map meeting, you're to get with your crews and fill them in just as we've told you." Colonel Baker then stop, looked at the pilots, smiled and said, "And that's it. I now turn you back over to Colonel Keeper for the Q and A."

Colonel Keeper retook center stage and asked, "Okay, any questions, Gentlemen?"

There was a brief silence and then one pilot asked in a deep sarcastic voice, "I know that area Colonel, I've been there before. I mean that hill is barely a mile from the Laotian border. Are we goin' to be allowed to violate Laotian air space?"

Colonel Keeper rocked back on his heels and then reluctantly said, "Colonel Baker will cover all of that in your mapping session, but I can tell you that you can't expect to be allowed to do that."

There was groaning across the room. Shortly another pilot spoke up, "Then there's no need for anymore talking is there, Colonel?"

"I guess not," the Colonel replied sharply. "I'll be leaving now." Then, turning to Colonel Baker, "You may proceed with the mapping session, Colonel."

With that, Colonel Keeper quickly left the room. Then, slowly, all the pilots began to gather around a long table at the front of the ready room that had a large map spread out on it.

The mapping session took about an hour. After it was over, a group of disgruntled pilots left the ready room. Kyle was no different than the others. He hated having his hands tied by stupid rules of engagement. Not that rules of engagement were always stupid; just these rules of engagement. Shaking the doubts out of his head, he went about finding his crew. Unlike his first crew that he was able to hand pick, his new crew had been assigned to him. His new crew chief and gunner was a young twenty-eight year old fresh from the States. His name was Sergeant Billy O'Brian from Boston, Massachusetts. Kyle didn't like him. It wasn't that he didn't do a good job; he did. It was just that he was so damn cocky and sure of himself. His new copilot was 2nd Lt. Berry Clyde and he was fresh from Camp Walters. Kyle liked the twenty-two year old, but felt uncomfortable with his inexperience. But both men had performed well so far and Kyle couldn't think of any real complaints.

Kyle was unable to find Sergeant O'Brian right away but he did find Lt. Clyde at the Officer's Club. Lt. Clyde was standing at the bar about to take a drink when Kyle reached up and took the glass out of his hand. He set the glass down on the bar with a bang. Then, putting on his most authoritative face he boomed, "Okay, Lieutenant, we're on ready alert around the clock, so you get your ass out there and find Sergeant O'Brian. When you find him, you two get out to Kellie and check and double check her out. Make sure she's fueled to the max and that she is armed to the max. You have O'Brian check every single mechanical thing about her from the motor to all her electronics. Then you get inside and make sure everythin' works exactly right. If I get in there and she won't start up immediately, I'm holdin' you responsible. Is all of that clear, Lieutenant?"

"Yes, Sir," the Lieutenant replied in shock, "I'm on it right now." With that he grabbed his hat and hurried out the door.

It was now May 12th as William and Charlie Company pushed their way up the hill. For the last two days, William's 2nd Platoon had been engaged in several fire fights. Most of the fighting had been to their flanks and behind them, as the enemy used the dense jungle to their advantage to sneak down the hill and flank them. While Charlie Company was engaged in keeping the enemy from coming up behind them, Bravo Company was pushing up the hill about 150 meters to Charlie Companies left, and Alpha Company was making a wide swing up the hill to their right.

Bravo Company was on the point and encountered heavy resistance about half way up the hill. The fight raged until late afternoon when Bravo was ordered to dig in and setup defensive positions for the night. Charlie and Alpha Companies moved back down the hill to their original starting point before digging in for the night. Once settled in, William checked his men to see how they had fared. So far things were not as bad for his platoon as for others. William's 2nd Platoon had suffered only two wounded and they had already been medevac'd out. But, at this time, there were no replacements so the 2nd Platoon was now two men short of full strength.

That evening, just before dark, air strikes were called in to hit the top of the hill. William and his men could see the heavy bombs and napalm exploding on the top of the hill. They wondered if anyone could survive that bombing. They got their answer early the next morning as they once again started up the hill. Again Bravo was on the point. It didn't take long for Bravo to make contact with the enemy. A ferocious fire fight erupted. Charlie, who was still on Bravo's right and about 50 meters behind them, moved up to try and support them. At the same time, assault helicopters began making strafing runs in close support of Bravo. To make matters worse, there had been torrential downpours that had turned the landscape into a muddy quagmire.

William was desperately trying get his men to move up the hill, when Mac came running up and dived into the mud beside him. Mud splashed up into William's face. "Mac," he shouted above the roar of battle, "what the hell're you doin' here? Why aren't you with 3rd and 4th Squads?"

"Sir," Mac shouted, "we need to get on the radio to battalion. Those choppers are shootin' up our guys. They've hit Bravo bad. We've got to stop 'em somehow. Bravo's lost their radio. We gotta do somethin' they're killin' friendlies."

William pause for only a second or two before slapping Mac on his helmet, "Okay, Mac," he shouted firmly while pointing off to his left, "our radio's with 1st Squad. They're over there just to our left; see them? Do you see the radioman?"

Mac nodded his head.

"Get goin' over there and get that shit stopped. Now go, go, go."

As bullets kicked up mud all around him, Mac got to his feet and ran to 1st Squad. He made it and waved back to William as he was talking on the radio.

William turned back and looked up the hill. His men were slipping and sliding in the mud but still continued to push forward. Then, suddenly Mac was by his side again. "Any luck?" William asked in frustration.

"Yes, sir, we got it stopped," Mac replied, "but too late for a lot of guys."

William looked into Mac's muddy face and saw the anger boiling inside him. "Okay, Mac, you did a good job." He then patted Mac on the helmet and ordered, "Now get back down to 3rd and 4th Squads and see how bad we've been hurt."

"Yes, sir," Mac replied. "But while I was on with battalion we got some new orders. We're to stop our advance and hold the line here and cover Bravo as they pull back. Between the PAVN and friendly fire, they took a lot of casualties." With that, Mac turned quickly and started back down the hill.

William rolled over in the mud and slammed his fist into the muddy ground. "What the fuck is goin' on here," he screamed as loud as he could. "We've got a well dug in enemy, rain and mud, and now friendly fire. Friendly fire for God's sake. What the livin' fuck is goin' on."

Unfortunately for the men of the 101st Airborne Division, this wouldn't be the last of the friendly fire episodes.

Kyle had just landed back at Cobra Umbrella One after a tough assault mission over Hill 937. He had no more than stepped out of his chopper when he was met by an orderly who told him to report immediately to Coronal Keeper's office. Kyle stared at him for a moment and then nodded his head okay. He pulled off his flight helmet and looked back at his crew, who were just getting out of the chopper. Sergeant O'Brian dropped to his knees, pulled off his flight helmet and slammed it to the ground. He said nothing as he just knelt there breathing hard. His copilot, Lt. Clyde, staggered up to him after dropping his flight helmet to the ground. "What the hell was that all about", he breathed in anger. "Going in there without being told that the 1ˢᵗ Air Cav would have Cobras there free lancing without any group integrity. Fuck, they nearly shot our asses off up there."

Kyle took a deep breath and nodded. "I know, I know," he said softly. Then after a long pause, he straightened up and looked hard at Lt. Clyde. "Berry, I need you to keep it under control. You got me?"

Berry reached down and picked up his helmet, looked at Kyle and nodded, "Yes, sir."

"Good," Kyle replied. "I need you to get O'Brian goin' on refuelin' and rearmin' Kellie. Then, I need you to go to the other ships in our group and get me a status report on their availability. I need to know if they lost anybody and how bad they may be shot up. It's important I know how many we can put up on a moment's notice. Can you do all that for me?"

"I'll get it done skipper," Berry replied seriously. "What about you, Skipper?"

Kyle looked at him with a small grin, "I gotta report to the CO and it's not goin' to be fun. I'll get back as soon as I can." With that, Kyle turned and started for the CO's office at a fast trot.

As he approached the CO's office he could hear the sound of the Coronal yelling through the walls. Kyle still carried his flight helmet under his left arm. He was soaked in sweat. It rolled down from his hairline into his eyes and down to his mouth. Before entering he quickly wiped as much sweat as he could from his eyes using his shirt sleeve. He took a deep breath, knocked gently and pushed the door open. Captain Ranson, who was standing before the Coronal, turned his head to look at Kyle as he entered the room. Captain Ranson had a look of pure anguish on his face, which, like Kyle's, was covered in sweat.

"Come in and join us Captain Collie," the Coronal said sarcastically in a pleasant voice. "We were just discussing some simple things like friendly fire. Are you aware of what friendly fire is Captain Collie?"

Kyle didn't know rather to answer or not, but he forced out, "Yes, sir, I know what friendly fire is."

The Coronal waved his hand at Kyle and said, "Come on over here and join us Captain Collie. I'd like your input on this."

Kyle walked over and stood by Captain Ranson who seemed happy to have someone else in the line of fire. "Yes, sir," Kyle said softly, "how can I be of assistance?"

"Assistance," the Coronal said mockingly. "How can you be of assistance?"

"Yes, sir," Kyle repeated.

"Well, maybe you can start by helping Captain Ranson here clear up this friendly fire mess," the Coronal said with his voice rising again. "I thought that during our briefing I made it very clear about being sure of your targeting. Do you recall that Captain Collie?"

"Yes, sir," Kyle replied, "I remember it quite clearly."

The Coronal spread is arms out as if questioning and said, "So, what's your explanation? In about an hour I'm going to have a general here from I Corps no less. He's going to be all over my ass about this friendly fire situation. Since Captain Ranson seems to have no answers, maybe you can help me with this?"

Kyle's voice became very cold and steady as he answered, "Yes, sir, maybe I can."

The Coronal was somewhat taken aback. His face was red as he said, "Then, by all means, Captain Collie, please enlighten us."

"May I speak freely, Sir?" Kyle asked in a stone cold steady voice.

The Coronal put his hands behind his back, took a deep breath, and said, "Yes, speak freely. I want this thing cleared up."

"First, sir," Kyle began, "I think it would be a great help if you'd believe a bit more in your officers." The Coronal brought his hands from behind his back with clenched fist but didn't speak. "Havin' said that, Sir," Kyle continued, "I'm of the opinion that Captain Ranson is a fine officer and did his job exactly right. You see, Sir, Captain Ranson and his Cobra group went in ahead of my Scouts. I was right behind them. I watched them all the way through their run before I lead my Scouts on our run. It wasn't Captain Ranson's Cobras that shot up our friendlies and it wasn't my Scouts." Kyle took a short pause but no one spoke so he continued, "The ground forces identified the assault choppers as Cobras but couldn't see their markings so they didn't know which group they were with. So, it clearly wasn't my Scouts. And I'm tellin' you, Sir, it wasn't Captain Ranson's Cobras either, because I was right behind him and I saw everythin'. In between Captain Ranson's run and my run, several free lancing Cobras from the 1st Air Cav came in without group integrity and began strafing everywhere. Since they nearly shot down a couple of my Scouts just as we started our run, I'm pretty damn sure it was the Cobras from the 1st Air Cav that caused the friendly fire. I can't say for sure of course because I was kind of busy up there. But I can say for *DAMN* sure it wasn't our Cobras."

There was a long pause before the Coronal spoke. He finally clasped his hands in front of him and asked, "Captain Collie, would you be willing to repeat all of this before a board of inquiry if need be?"

"Yes, sir, I would," Kyle replied simply. "That is I would if you, Coronal, would stand with me."

The Coronal seemed to relax and leaned over his desk putting his hands on the edges of the desk. He raised his head slowly and looked up at Kyle. "If it comes to it, I'll be right there with you, Captain." He then straightened back up and said briskly, "Okay Captains, you're dismissed. Be sure your ships are ready at all times. There's a big push coming to take that damn hill and we need to be ready at any time."

Kyle and Captain Ranson both stood to attention and saluted. When their salute was returned, they turned and hurried to the door. As they reached the door and Captain Ranson had exited, Kyle turned back to the Coronal and said softly, "You're a good CO, Sir. I know how much those men on the ground mean to you. I know how all of this hurts. It hurts us all even if we weren't involved." Then he hurried out the door.

Coronal Keeper stood at his desk for a short while unsteady on his feet. Then, with the palms of both hands, he reached up and dried the wetness from his eyes.

At the ten-six-six the push was on, triage was swamped with wounded. Medivac choppers had been coming in two or three at a time every hour. Kellie had Veronica and two other nurses working non-stop now for the last eight hours. Casualties from the battle at Hill 937 were mounting by the hour. The push was on again. Veronica knew that William was somewhere in that battle but she tried to keep it out of her mind so she could concentrate on her job.

As Veronica was working with an army medic on a casualty, Kellie came up and tapped her on the shoulder. Veronica turned quickly as if startled. "Damn, Kel," she yelled, "don't sneak up on me like that."

"Sorry," Kellie said, "I need to talk to you for a minute. Can you break away?"

Veronica looked around. "Wait for me over by that ambulance," she said pointing to an ambulance several yards away that had a couple of flat tires, "I'll be there as soon as I get this guy turned over to the medic."

Kellie nodded and hurried off to the crippled ambulance. It was only a short while before Veronica joined Kellie at the ambulance. She wiped her forehead with her arm as she approached. "What's up, Kel?"

"We got problems, Ronnie," Kellie answered in a worried voice. "We gotta get more of the seriously wounded outa here and down to the 95th. We've call the 95th for some extra medivacs but they've already sent all they have available. I'm not sure what we're going to do."

"Have you thought about a temporary ward somewhere?" Veronica asked looking around the area.

"Yeah, I thought about that," Kellie nodded, "but even if we could, we're running low on supplies. We did get a medivac chopper filled with supplies from the 95th, thanks to our sister, Kat. But if this push keeps up and things don't slow down it won't be enough."

"Well, you must have somethin' in mind," Veronica signed, "else we wouldn't be standin' here talkin'". Kellie put her hands on Veronica's shoulders and pushed her back a few steps. Her stare burned into Veronica's eyes. "Oh, shit," Veronica breathed. "What's comin' my way?"

"I'm a captain now", Kellie said firmly, "I might be able to pull some rank at the 95th. I'm going to hitch a ride on the next medivac headed down to the 95th. Once there, I'm going to beg, borrow, or steal everything I can get my hands on and get it up here post haste. And that means that you're going to be in charge while I'm gone."

Veronica's eyes widened. "Oh, no you don't," she yelled in shock, "I'm just a trooper. I don't give orders. You can't leave me in charge. Kel, I'll fuck things up for sure. I will."

Kellie, still holding Veronica's shoulders, shook her hard and pushed her up against the ambulance and held her there. "Now you listen to me, 1st Lieutenant Mann", she growled, "you're my XO and you *WILL* take charge and you *WILL* get the job done. Do I make myself perfectly clear?" Veronica simple stood there against the ambulance without speaking. She was shocked at Kellie's tone. "I say again, 1st Lieutenant Mann, do I make myself perfectly clear?"

Veronica reached up and pushed Kellie's hands off her shoulders. Then she leaned forward and got face-to-face with Kellie, "Roger that, Captain Anderson, I'm in charge until you get back."

Kellie stepped back and folded her arms across her chest and said, "Good. Now, I recommend rearranging the triage area so that you can keep the less seriously wounded outside and ask one of the doctors if he can come out and work on them."

Veronica pushed passed Kellie and looked intently at the triage area. Then, turning back to Kellie she said in a more controlled tone, "That might work for a while, but I'm pretty sure the doctor's not goin' to be able to stay out here very long."

Kellie smiled, "You're right he probably won't. So, then you just keep moving things around as best you can."

Veronica smile back at her and laughed, "Well, I'll try and see that we're all still here when you get back, but no promises."

"Okay, let's get going," Kellie said quickly, "I'm going to head over to the helipads and grab the first medivac headed to the 95th. And I'll let you go do your thing."

"My thing," Veronica laughed, "yeah, my thing." She then started walking away from Kellie back towards the triage area.

"Hey," Kellie yelled after her, "have you heard anything from William."

Veronica turned back and shook her head, "No, not a thing. I just know he's on that fuckin' hill somewhere. I don't think about it. I got work to do." Then she started to turn back towards the triage area but stopped and asked, "And Kyle? You got any word from Kyle?"

Kellie just shrugged her shoulders and said, "No, not from him personally. I just know his group is flying fire missions on that hill. That's all I know."

Veronica gave her a small wave and said, "Well, have a good trip and hurry back." With that, she turned and hurried back to the triage area.

On May 14th and 15th the Air Force dropped tons of bombs and napalm on the top of Hill 937. By May 16th the top of the hill was practically barren of any vegetation. It looked bald headed. During this time, William's 2nd Platoon had been in the fight every day. They would fight their way up the hill, and then near dark would retreat back down. By May 18th, the platoon was now down to eighteen men. Nearly every officer in Charlie Company was either dead or wounded; including the Company Commander. William was the only officer in Charlie Company that was still standing. Mac had been wounded and sent back by medivac. William had lost his platoon sergeant as well as most of his squad leaders. Even with all of this, preparations were underway for a final assault on the hill on

May 20th. New companies from other battalions were being brought in to reinforce the assault. But there was no relief for the 3rd Battalion. All four of its companies; Able, Bravo, Charlie, and Delta would be part of the assault.

By now the hill had a new name. It was no longer designated just as Hill 937, but was now being called 'Hamburger Hill'. The men of the 101st considered the hill a meat grinder. Casualties had now reached over sixty killed and over three hundred wounded.

On May 20th, the Air Force once again poured bombs and napalm onto the top of the hill and this was joined by a heavy artillery barrage. All of this lasted nearly two hours. Then, the men of the 101st started up the hill for what they hoped was the last time. The PAVN had mostly left the hill but had left suicide platoons behind to fight to the end. It was Alpha Company who first reached the summit of the hill followed closely by Charlie Company. As William and his platoon neared the top of the hill, he signaled a halt to the advance. He stood up and looked around at the twelve men who were left in his platoon. He was filled with anger and pride at the same time. He took a deep breath and then he shouted, "Fix bayonets". His men did as ordered. Each man now stood with their platoon leader with fixed bayonets. "Okay, guys let's take the top of this fuckin' hill and nobody stays alive except Screamin' Eagles."

So, the remaining men of the 2nd Platoon, Charlie Company, 3rd Battalion, 187th Regiment, of the 101st Air Borne Division charged to the top of Hamburger Hill and killed every living thing that didn't have a Screaming Eagle patch on their shoulder.

When it was all over, 1st Lieutenant William Barnett sat on the top of a cave entrance at the very top of Hamburger Hill. His feet dangled down over the entrance to the cave as he looked down into its dark entrance. Just moments before, some of his men had thrown several high explosive and napalm charges down into the cave; killing all the remaining defenders of Hamburger Hill. He sat there swing his feet back and forth as if he didn't have a care in the world. He pulled out his canteen and shook it for signs of water. There wasn't any, so he unceremoniously tossed his canteen down into the cave. He chuckled to himself as he watched it disappear into the darkness. He had removed his helmet and it lay by his side. His rifle, with the bayonet still fixed, he used to prop himself up. His hair was all matted with sweat, dirt, and mud.

He seemed to be trying to figure out what to do now that the fighting was over, when someone gently laid a hand on his shoulder and said, "Sir, you better let me have a look at your wound and then we can get you over to the medivac LZ."

William looked back over his shoulder to see a young medic looking down at him. "What wound?" He asked surprised.

"The one on your back, Sir," the medic replied simply.

William turned his head back and looked down into the cave entrance again. "Sure," he said, "take a look at it."

"This may hurt a little, Sir," the medic said in a sorry tone, "there's a slash across your back about a foot long and maybe a quarter inch deep. I'll need to get some Sulphur in there and then put some heavy gauze on it to help stop the bleeding then we need to get you to the medivac LZ and get you out of here. But we'll start with getting your shirt off so I can wrap bandages around your chest."

"You do what you gotta do," William said turning his head to look at the medic again. He was stunned when he saw the medic clearly. He was just a kid. To William he looked about twelve years old. "For God's sakes, how old are you?" William asked with a small chuckle.

"Nineteen, Sir," was the reply as he removed William's shirt and started to work on his back.

"Are you with Charlie?"

"No, Sir, I'm with Alpha Company, 3rd Platoon."

"What's your name?"

"Corporal Bobby Miles, medical corps."

William groaned a bit as he felt Corporal Miles firmly push the heavy gauze into his wound. "Sorry, Sir, but I've got to get that gauze in as tight as I can to stem the bleeding."

"You're doin' fine corporal, I got no complaints."

"Sir, if you'd hold your arms up so I can run these bandages around your chest, we'll almost be done here."

William did as instructed. "You know Corporal Miles," he said in all seriousness, "that was a pretty brave thing you did. I mean climbin' that hill under heavy fire armed only with your medical kit."

"Oh, shoot, Sir, that's my job. It wasn't anything special. The guys say I'm just a dumb farm boy from Missouri and I don't know any better." Then he gave a soft laugh, "You know what; they're probably right." After a short pause, he started helping William to his feet and continued, "Come on now, I'll get you over to the medivac LZ and I want to get some plasma going into you until you can get some whole blood and you're going to need some stiches when you get to the medivac hospital."

William got to his feet and gingerly followed Corporal Miles to the medivac LZ. There the corporal helped William onto a stretcher, pushed a needle into his arm and hooked up a bottle of plasma. "That should do it, Sir," Corporal Miles smiled, "one of these choppers will get you to a medivac hospital where they can fix you up good." The young medic gave William a small salute, then turned and headed back to the top of the hill.

William watched him for a moment as he started to disappear into the smoke and haze that still dominated the battlefield. Then William propped himself up on his stretcher and yelled, "Hey, Corporal Bobby Miles from Missouri." Corporal Miles stopped and looked back with an unsure look on his face. "I think it was special, Corporal Miles," William said in earnest, "I sure as shit think it was very damn special. And you know what; I don't think you're so dumb either."

Corporal Bobby Miles a medic from Alpha Company, 3rd Platoon, gave William a young childish smile and then disappeared into the smoke and haze.

Kyle had his group of Heavy Scouts, which numbered five counting him, hovering just below the summit of Hamburger Hill so they couldn't be seen clearly from the top of the hill. They were on the west side of the hill between the hill and the Laotian border. He was part of a new plan that would make the assault helicopters more effective and less likely to be involved in friendly fire. The plan called for the Cobras to make their run from west to east as usual pouring fire on the top of the hill. But then the Scouts were to wait, hovering as they were now, just below the summit. The idea was that the defenders on top of the hill would believe that the Cobras were the only attacking craft. And they would believe this because, normally, the Scouts would immediately follow the Cobras. But this time no Scouts showed up. As a result, the plan worked perfectly, as the defenders came out of their caves and bunkers and were headed for the trenches to pour fire down on the men of the 101st. To their surprise, five Scouts came up from below and caught them in the open.

Kyle's Scout was the first one to rake fire across the top to the hill. As he gunned Kellie to gain speed, he and Lt. Clyde unleashed all their fire power. All four sixty caliber guns raked the top of the hill and rockets fired from their mounted pods exploded among the defenders as they reversed their course and ran back toward the cover of the caves and bunkers. Crew Chief O'Brian was firing his waist mounted sixty caliber non-stop. As the Scouts finished they first pass over the summit, the top of the hill was littered with dead and wounded defenders. Kyle knew this attack was very important because down below the 101st was about to makes its final assault on Hamburger Hill.

Kyle had his group wheel around and prepare for their second pass over the summit of the hill; this time the run would be east to west. "Okay, group," Kyle yelled into his mic, "this'll be our last pass so let's make it a good one. Here we go!" With that, Kyle pushed Kellie forward and gained speed. Once again, they unleashed all their fire power. There weren't as many targets on the second pass, but there was one too many for Kellie.

"Skipper, RPG at two o'clock low," O'Brian yelled frantically.

Kyle saw the RPG just as it was fired and took evasive maneuvers immediately. Those quick maneuvers probably saved Kellie from being blown out of the sky. The RPG exploded just above Kellie and towards the rear. Kyle could feel the shrapnel banging against the skin of Kellie. Then, he felt the loss of power as Kellie began of spin on its rotary axis. Kyle fought the controls to try and keep Kellie from going down in Laos. He forced Kellie to bank hard right and started down the north side of the hill. But no matter how hard he tried, Kellie was drifting west towards the border.

"How's everybody doin' so far, "Kyle yelled into his mic."

"I'm still in one piece, Skipper," O'Brian responded.

"Me too, I'm okay," Lt. Clyde said giving Kyle the high-sign as he spoke.

"Good," Kyle yelled back, "everyone hold on tight because I think this is goin' to be a rough landin'. I'm goin' to try and auto-rotate us down but the response to the controls isn't very good and I'm havin' a hard time changin' the rotor blade pitch. So anyway, here we go. O'Brian, make sure you're fully inside the ship; don't be sittin' in the door."

"Not to worry, Skipper, I'm buckled in tight back here."

Kyle fought hard to keep Kellie from drifting west towards the border but he felt he was losing the battle. So, in his best judgement, he felt he should go down now before it was too late. So, he pushed the controls forward and down. Just before they hit the first tall tree, Kyle tried to pull the nose up so they would hit more on the belly of the craft. But the controls didn't respond and they went into the jungle almost nose first.

Two medivac choppers landed at the ten-six-six. But they weren't carrying wounded from the battlefield, they were stuffed full of medical supplies. As the two medivac choppers touched down, Kellie jumped out the side door and, keeping low, she ran around to the pilot's widow and beat on it with her fist. The pilot nodded and opened the widow. Kellie yelled in at him, "I'm going to get some help over here to unload this stuff. You guys hang on here."

The pilot nodded again and shouted back to her, "Sorry I can't help you unload but I've got to keep my ship ready for an instant dust off. That means the rotor blades will be going, so remind your people to keep their head down as they unload."

Kellie nodded and then asked, "Once we get you unloaded, can you take some wounded back to the 95th with you?"

The pilot gave her the high-sign and simply said, "Roger that."

Before Kellie could start looking for some help to unload, Veronica was there with two other nurses and two army medics. Kellie smiled as she saw Veronica. "I see things are still here."

"Barely," Veronica shouted.

"Okay, Ronnie, you supervise the unloading and show everyone where all this stuff goes. Once you've finished, these guys say they can take some wounded back to the 95th, so get six or so of the next guys in line and get them onboard."

"Roger that," Veronica yelled.

"I've got to go report all this to the CO. He's going to be pissed I didn't tell him what I was doing."

Veronica just waved at her and then turned to start getting the supplies unloaded and stored. Kellie took one last look as how things were going and then hurried off to the operations tent. As she entered the operations tent, Jimmy was sitting at the squawk box looking at a Playboy. He looked up as she entered and quickly hid the magazine under his small desk. "Not to worry, Jimmy," she said smiling, "I've seen those mags before."

"Yes, Ma'am," Jimmy responded as he stood up. "But, Captain, be careful going in there. He's kind of mad. He's been looking for you the last couple hours and no one could find you."

Kellie slowed her pace down as she approached the CO's door. She couldn't help but wonder why he would be mad. She gently knocked on the door and waited for the reply. It came almost immediately.

"Enter."

Kellie walked in and closed the door behind her. She started for his desk but he stopped her with a wave of his hand. "Just sit down, Kel," he said softly.

Kellie took a chair as a worried look crossed her face. He had called her 'Kel', which met this was going to be a personal meeting.

"Where've you been?" He asked nonchalantly. "I've been looking for you for over two hours."

Kellie moved uneasily in her chair. "I went on a shopping spree down to the 95th to get us some extra supplies. I was very successful. I was even able to get some whole blood."

The Coronal nodded his head thoughtfully and said, "You could've let me know. After all I am supposed to be in charge around here."

Finally, Kellie couldn't stand this cat and mouse game any longer. She got to her feet and asked bluntly, "What's this all about, Dad? You called me 'Kel'. I guess that means we must have a personal problem."

Coronal Anderson waved her back to her chair. "Well, I've got two things to tell you," he said. "One is as your father and the other is as your CO. I expect you to handle them both as an officer in the United States Army Nurse Corps. Is that understood?"

Kellie was seated again as she looked up at him and nodded without speaking.

He put his hands behind his back and said, "There's no good way to say this so I'll just come right out with it." Then, after a short pause, he continued, "Kyle has been shot down. He was hit on a fire mission over Hamburger Hill. He was last seen going down near the Laotian border. The other pilots in his group say he went down hard. At this point, that's all I know."

Kellie stood up and turned her back on her father. She asked softly, "Do we know if he and his crew survived the crash?"

"No," was the simple reply.

"Do we know which side of the border he went down on?" She asked still standing with her back to her father.

"No, we don't."

Kellie slowly turned and faced her father. Her eyes had changed over to the cloudy blue that her father had seen so many times before. "I guess that's the thing you had to tell me as my father? Now, what's the thing you wanted to tell me as my CO?"

He looked at her hard and said with no trace of mercy in his voice, "I need you to get back out there and be my head nurse. We've all got a job to do here; personal things aside. Can you do that or do I need to get Lt. Mann in here?"

She straightened herself and came to the position of attention. "No, Sir, she said firmly, "you'll not need to get Lt. Mann in here. I'm completely capable of continuing to perform my duties. And if that will be all, Sir, I'll leave now and go do just that?"

"Fine," he shot back, "you're dismissed, Captain." As she had the door open and was leaving his office, he yelled, "And the next time you go on a shopping spree, you let me know."

Kellie slammed the office door behind her and stormed by Jimmy and out of the operations tent. She forced herself to calm down as she walked over to the triage area, where she found Veronica talking to a wounded man using her best smile and Texas drawl. As Kellie approached, Veronica stood up, still smiling, and asked, "How'd it go with the CO?"

"Fine," Kellie replied simply. "Did you get all the supplies stored away and did you get some of the wounded out on those choppers to the 95th."

Veronica sensed something was wrong but she kept it to herself. She replied to Kellie in a firm and to the point tone, "Yes, the supplies are all stored away where they go and we were able to get six wounded out on the two choppers. Things have slowed down and are almost back to normal. The four guys you see here in triage are all we have left to process and their wounds are minor and have been attended to by nurses."

Kellie finally let some of her tension out and smiled at Veronica. "Good job, Ronnie, I don't know what I'd do without you."

Veronica cocked her head to one side and asked, "Is everythin' okay, Kel?"

Kellie clasped her hands together and frowned at Veronica. "Well, yeah, I guess so," she said in a voice that reflected fear, "if you don't count the fact that Kyle has been shot down and crashed somewhere along the Laotian border and I don't know if he's alive or dead."

Staff Sergeant Jordan Costillo watch as the helicopter spun around its rotor axis. Smoke belched out of the rear of its engine. He knew the pilot was fighting for control of the chopper as he tried to force it to stay on the north side of Hamburger Hill. But he could see the pilot losing the fight as the chopper drifted more and more to the west and the Laotian border. Finally, in desperation, the pilot forced the chopper down hoping to crash land on the South Vietnamese side of the border. From Jordan's position, he couldn't tell on which side of the border the chopper crashed. But Jordan did know one thing; he knew the pilot. The chopper had the name 'Kellie' on its side. The pilot in that chopper was his friend and relative, Captain Kyle Collie.

As Jordan watched the chopper go down into the jungle, he took a quick compass reading. He would need the compass reading because the jungle hid the exact crash site from his vision. However, the smoke that could be seen rising from the crash site did give him a relatively good location.

Jordan's squad was on the point for the platoon that was left behind to probe the PAVN lines and locations. The rest of the platoon was about 150 meters behind him. They had been moving carefully to the southwest towards the Laotian border so they could monitor the PAVN troops as they abandon Hamburger Hill and rushed towards their safety areas in Laos. Jordan now worried that the crash site was directly in the path of the PAVN troops retreat. Quietly, Jordan held up his fist to stop his squads advance. His seven man squad just as quietly stopped their advance and melted into the jungle. Using hand signals, Jordan called for the radioman. Quickly, the radioman was at his side.

"Sparks," Jordan said in a whisper, "get hold of the Lieutenant and tell him we're holdin' our position here and waitin' for them to catch up. If he has any questions, tell 'im I'll fill 'im in when he gets here."

"Roger that, Sarge," Sparks replied.

It only took the rest of the platoon twenty minutes to reach Jordan's position. The Lieutenant disbursed the other three squads quietly into the jungle and then located Jordan. 1st Lieutenant Jason Parker was a short and stocky man. His brown hair was cut so close he appeared baldheaded. The thing Jordan liked most about Lt. Parker was that he was an all business type of guy when on a mission. Lt. Parker crouched next to Jordan and asked in a whisper, "Okay, Sergeant Costillo, why're we stopping?"

"No need to whisper, Sir," Jordan said in a normal voice, "my squad has secured this area. The nearest PAVNs are at least two klicks west of us."

"Okay," Lt. Parker said casually, "I'll ask again. Why're we stopping? I don't know about you, but I'd like to get to the 9th Marine fire base at the Laos border and finish his mission."

"Yes, Sir," Jordan replied, "I feel the same way but somethin' has come up that I feel we need to attend to."

"And what would that be?"

"I saw a chopper go down just west of us near the Laos border. It went down hard so I'm not sure about the condition of the crew. But since we're goin' in that general direction anyway, I wanted to get permission to take a small squad and branch off to go investigate the crash site and see if the crew needs help."

"You say, 'general direction'," Lt. Parker said mockingly, "just how far would you think you'll be branching off."

"Well, that's kind of unknown at this time, Sir, but it can't be too far. I'm thinkin' it might only be five or six klicks south of the 9th Marine fire base. All I need is about three volunteers to come with me and you and the rest of the platoon can continue on to the fire base. It shouldn't take me very long and I'll meet you at the fire base."

The Lieutenant studied Jordan for a long minute and then asked, "Sergeant, if you were me, would you consider this little branch off to be off mission? You know that Marine Recon doesn't take kindly to going off mission?"

Jordan wouldn't lie to his lieutenant. "Yes, Sir, they might consider it to be off mission. But we're finished with our mission and we're headin' to a marine fire base where we'll be helicoptered back to our battalion. Except for gettin' to the fire base, our mission is over. I'm just askin' to try and save a chopper crew if we can."

The Lieutenant lowered his head and removed his jungle hat. Sweat rolled down his nearly bald head. He looked up at Jordan and asked in a point blank tone, "Is this particular chopper crew something special to you?"

Jordan pause for a moment and then answered firmly, "Yes, Sir."

The Lieutenant put his jungle hat back on said, "Okay, Sergeant, you can pick your volunteers, but be sure they're volunteers. I don't want anybody going on this branch off against his will. Is that clear, Sergeant?"

"Yes, Sir, it's clear. May I ask for my volunteers from the entire platoon?"

The Lieutenant chuckled to himself and said, "I suppose you have some particular volunteers in mind?"

"Yes, Sir, I do," Jordan replied smiling.

"Okay, okay, you can get your volunteers from the entire platoon. When you're finished getting your volunteers, tell Sergeant Sanders that his 2nd Squad will take the point and that we'll be heading straight for the fire base. Put your second in command in charge of your squad. And good luck, Sergeant Costillo, I hope your chopper crew is still alive."

"Thank you, Sir."

Jordan had gotten his volunteers and the rest of the platoon had moved out for the fire base with 2nd Squad on the point. It was quiet in the jungle, as four men knelt in a close circle. No one spoke for a long while, then it was Tracker who was first to speak. "So, what the hell did we volunteer for?"

"Yeah, Sarge, what the hell did we volunteer for?" Swede asked laughing.

"Come on, Greaser, let us in on it," Breed chimed in.

A wicked smile spread across Jordan's face. "You guys are goin' to love this one."

The chopper had crashed through a heavy canopy of jungle. The rotor blades had been ripped off and the tail section dangled loosely hanging onto the crafts fuselage by several cables. The chopper had come to rest at about a forty-five degree angle with the nose buried into the soft jungle floor and its fuselage being held up by broken branches. Smoke still came from the engine but not nearly as much as before. All the cockpit glass was shattered and broken. Both cockpit doors dangled open. Fortunately, they had fired their entire ordinance, which probably kept the chopper from blowing up.

As Kyle tried to move, he couldn't help but think how strangely quiet it was, it seemed an eerie silence hung over the crash site. Slowly, Kyle's consciousness began to stir his brain back to life. He reached down to break lose his seatbelt and harness but part of the console was pushed across his chess blocking his reach, which may have been a good thing because the chopper was tilted to the right and had he popped open his harness he may have fallen out the open door. Before trying anything else, he stopped to take stock of their situation. He removed his flight helmet and yelled, "Head count."

"I'm still buckled in back here, Skipper, O'Brian yelled. "I don't think I'm hurt. It'll be easy enough for me to get out of my safety belt and slide out the waist door."

"Okay, Sergeant." Kyle replied. "You go ahead and try that. If you're successful come around over here and give me a hand."

"Roger that, Skipper, but I think we may need to hurry and get away from Kellie 'cause I see dripping fuel."

"Okay, let's get outa here," Kyle shouted.

Kyle had started to work on getting free when Lt. Clyde said softly, "I think I'm still here, Skipper, but I don't think this tree should be growing out of my shoulder."

Kyle immediately jerked his head up and stopped what he was doing. He looked over to the copilot seat. Because of the tilt, Lt. Clyde was leaning towards Kyle. Like Kyle, he was being held in place by his harness, but there was something else holding Lt. Clyde in place. There was a thin tree branch that ran through Lt. Clyde's back and came out of his left shoulder. The branch was about five feet long with three feet of it still attached to another tree branch behind Lt. Clyde and two feet of it sticking out of the front of his shoulder. Lt. Clyde looked as though he was impaled. Strangely enough, there was very little blood flowing, but blood did drip from the end of the branch.

"Jesus, Berry," Kyle breathed. "Just hold on until I can get freed up, then me and O'Brian will get you out of that mess."

"Roger that, Skipper, I don't think I'll be going anywhere."

As they spoke, O'Brian came along side of Kyle, "Okay, Skipper, how can I help?"

"I need some help getting' this console pushed up enough so I can get out of my seatbelt and harness."

O'Brian stepped up and got a grip on the console. "Okay, Skipper," he said through gritted teeth, "you get a good hold and we'll both push on the count of three. Are you ready?"

"Yeah, I'm ready but be sure you're set to get out of the way because when I get out of the harness I'm probably goin' to fall out on top of you."

"Here we go, Skipper. "One, two, three, *PUSH*!"

Both men pushed hard, but it took less effort than expected. The console gave way almost immediately. Quickly, Kyle worked his hands down and broke free of his seatbelt and harness. And, as expected, he fell from the shattered cockpit and landed roughly on the ground. O'Brian had stepped back to get out of the way. Immediately upon hitting the ground, Kyle jumped to his feet. He quickly took stock of himself to make sure he had no unseen injuries. Satisfied he was okay he turned to O'Brian and shouted, "Come on, we've got to help get Berry out he's been impaled by a tree branch."

O'Brian walked over and peered into the cockpit and saw Lt. Clyde with the tree branch running through him. "Christ All Mighty," he moaned, "how in shit did that happen?"

"How it happened isn't our issue now," Kyle growled as he started back into the cockpit. "Our issue now is gettin' him out. You go back and see if you can find the first aid kit".

"I'm on it," O'Brian yelled as he hurried back to the rear of the chopper.

Once inside the cockpit again, Kyle began to assess the situation. He knew that time was limited because of the dripping fuel. Finally, after several moments of indecision, Kyle spoke to Lt. Clyde in a commanding voice. "Berry, here's what we're goin' to do. I'm goin' to use my K-BAR to cut that branch off as close to your shoulder as I can. Then, I'm goin' have O'Brian hold you from the other side while I release your seatbelt and harness." At this point, Kyle paused and wiped sweat from his eyes then he continued, "Now comes the hard part. I'm goin' to take hold of both of your shoulder and pull you forward. That should pull you away from the part of the branch still inside your shoulder. Then, hopefully, O'Brian and I will be able to lower you out of the cockpit without hurtin' you too much. But there's no use in shittin' you, when I pull you away from that branch, it's goin' to hurt like a son-of-a-bitch."

Lt. Clyde looked up at Kyle and smiled, "It sounds like a plan, Skipper, let's get on with it."

While Kyle was carefully removing Berry's flight helmet, O'Brian arrived with the first aid kit. Kyle took the kit, opened it and looked inside. "Well, there's not a lot in here," he said in disgust. "But we'll just have to make due."

"Skipper," O'Brian urged, "we need to hurry this along. We don't know when the bad guys are going to show up, and then there's that fuel leak."

Kyle knew he was right. "Okay, O'Brian, you go around to the other side and get behind Lt. Clyde. Once you're in place take hold of his shoulders and hold him steady."

When O'Brian was in place and holding Lt. Clyde's shoulders, Kyle reached down to his boot and pulled out his K-BAR. "Are you ready, Berry?" He asked softly.

"Ready, Skipper."

Kyle put the K-BAR as close to Berry's shoulder as possible and began to cut the branch. He had to use a sawing motion to get the quickest results. Berry moaned and gritted his teeth but didn't yell out. It only took a couple of minutes to cut through the small thin branch. When the job was complete, Kyle could see the remainder of the branch in Berry's shoulder. Kyle had done a good job, as less than a half an inch of the branch still protruded from Berry's shoulder. Kyle gave a sigh of relief as he slipped the K-BAR back into his boot. "Berry, are you still with me?" Kyle asked.

"Still here, Skipper."

"Well, hang tough because now comes the hard part." Then, looking behind Berry to O'Brian, he said, "O'Brian, I'm goin' to pop Berry's harness and seatbelt now so hold on to 'im."

"I got 'im," O'Brian replied firmly.

When Kyle popped the harness and seatbelt, not much happened. It was because of the tilt of the chopper and Lt. Clyde was already leaning against Kyle pilot seat.

"Hey, O'Brian," Kyle shouted, "comeback around to this side and give me a hand. I need you to be right behind me to break our fall when I pull Berry loose."

When O'Brian was back around front with Kyle, he squeezed himself into the cockpit just behind Kyle. Kyle put his hands on Berry's shoulders and held them very tight. Kyle reasoned that he shouldn't warn Berry about when he was going to pull, so he just quickly pulled Berry forward as hard as he could. Berry gave out a loud shout as he came loose from the branch and collapsed into Kyle's arms. O'Brian steadied Kyle to keep them from falling out of the cockpit. Then, as gently as possible, O'Brian and Kyle pulled Berry from the cockpit and laid him on the jungle floor.

Where before there didn't seem to be much blood, blood now flowed freely from the wound. Quickly, Kyle got what he could use from the first aid kit. There was some kind of powder to sprinkle on the wound, which he did. Then, there was some gaze and bandages to try and stop the bleeding. There was barely enough gaze to stuff into the wounds front and back side. Through it all, Lt. Clyde stayed conscious and didn't make any more shouts or sounds.

When it was all over, Kyle had removed Berry's shirt, sprinkled the powder on the wound, stuffed gaze into it, ran bandages around Berry's chest to hold the gaze in place, and used the last of the bandages to immobilize Berry's arm across his chest.

Kyle smiled down at Berry, "I guess we got you all fixed up."

"I guess you did," Berry smiled back. "Thanks guys, but I hope I'm not going to be a burden to you."

"Can you stand up?" Kyle asked.

Berry started to struggle to his feet and Kyle and O'Brian were quick to his aid. They steadied Berry, who momentarily wavered. "I can walk, Skipper, don't let me hold you guys up."

Kyle gave a quick smile and then started shouting orders. "O'Brian, how much ammo do you have left for your M60?"

"I only got two belts left."

"Can you hand carry the M60?"

"I've already got the hand carry attachment on it, Skipper, and I can put the two belts over my shoulders."

"Good work, O'Brian," Kyle said slapping him on the back. "Now, how about our M16s, did they survive the crash?"

"I'll have to look but they still should be secured in the bench holding area."

"Go find them and bring them to me," Kyle ordered.

While O'Brian was off getting the M16s, Kyle pulled Berry's army 45 automatic from his side holster. He levered a round into the chamber and handed the pistol to Berry. "I know this is only good for close range," Kyle said, "but, God willin', you won't have to use it." Berry grinned and saluted Kyle with the pistol.

Soon, O'Brian was back carrying two M16s. He handed them to Kyle. "I'm sorry, Skipper, but there's only two clips each for the M16s."

Kyle took both M16s. He slung one over his shoulder and the other he carried at the ready. He stuffed the four ammo clips into his belt. He turned and looked at his crew. Lt. Clyde was wounded but able travel. He had the 45 automatic pistol pushed into his belt. Sergeant O'Brian was hand carrying the heavy M60 and had the two belts of ammo criss-crossed over his shoulders. They awaited his orders.

Kyle looked at his crew and decided to tell them the truth. "Okay, guys," he started, "I'll tell you what I know and what I'm plannin' on doin'. I don't know if we're in Laos or not. But no matter where we are, we need to head east; away from Laos and hopefully towards our own guys. I still have my distance and direction compass so we should be able to set a course headed east. I know it's not much help but that's all we got at this point. Now, there's one other thing we need to discuss before we get started. And that one thing is surrender. If things get bad, we'll have to make the decision to surrender or not. This is one thing I'll not make into an order. It'll be up to each of you to make that decision. But I hope we can all agree on what we'll do. So, I'm goin' to ask each of you what you'd prefer to do. We'll start with you, O'Brian. What's your opinion?"

O'Brian nervously held his machine gun close to his body. He moved from one foot to the other trying to stay calm. "Well, Skipper," he finally said, "I'm not going to speak for anyone else. I mean I'm just a sergeant. But, as for me, I don't want to send the rest of my days in some Laotian shithole prison; being a slave or whatever. So, if it comes to it, I'd just as soon go out fighting." He stopped talking and continued to move nervously. He then waved his hand and stated, "And that's the way I feel."

"Good enough," Kyle said nodding his head. Then, pointing to Lt. Clyde, "Okay, your turn, Berry. What say you?"

"I don't need to say anything. Sergeant O'Brian took all the words right out of my mouth."

Kyle grinned and waved his M16, "Okay, then, let's head east as fast as can."

"What about you, Skipper, you didn't vote?" O'Brian asked. "I'm not moving until you get to vote."

"Come on, O'Brian," Kyle shouted, "the vote is unanimous. Now, no more votes, I'm in command again and I ordered us to head east as fast as we can."

The work volume at the ten-six-six had dropped off considerably since the battle for Hamburger Hill ended. The triage area was empty and the nurses had gone back to their normal schedules. However, the wards remained full, mostly due to the fact that many of the wounded were being held for return to duty because their wounds were not of a serious nature. Most of the seriously wounded cases had been medevac'd to the 95th. Medivacs were still coming in from Hamburger Hill, but they were now only a few at a time as they were getting the last of the wounded off the hill.

1st Lieutenant Maxine Worth, better known as Max, was working triage duty but because triage was empty at the present time, she spent much of her duty time helping in the wards. However, she kept a sharp ear out for the sound of incoming choppers. Even if she didn't hear any choppers, on occasion, she would walk out to triage and scan the skies just to make sure she didn't miss anything. Currently, she had just finished scanning the skies and was turning to return to Ward 4 where she was helping out when she heard the familiar sound of rotor blades beating against the air. Quickly, she turned back, shaded her eyes, and searched the skies again. There, just coming into view, was a single medivac chopper. She immediately, yelled for the medics and corpsmen that were busy in the supply tent. In seconds, she and the medics and corpsmen were at the helipad waiting for the chopper to touch down. No sooner had the chopper touched down, than they had the three wounded out and into the triage area. Once the chopper pilot saw everyone was clear, he gave a quick salute and dusted off.

Of the three wounded, two were walking wounded and didn't require immediate OR assistance. However, the third one was on a stretcher with a plasma bottle hook up to him. Max immediately began her triage routine on the stretcher case. He was lying on his side but to her relief he was conscious and smiling up at her. "Where's your problem, Soldier?" She asked returning his smile.

"My back," he replied simply. "The medic in the field said I'd probably need some stiches and whole blood."

Max went around to his back and began examining the wound. Blood had now soaked through the gaze and was now tricking down his back and onto the stretcher. She carefully cut some of the bandages away so she could remove the gaze and take a look at the wound. "You say a field medic patched you up?" She asked as she continued to study the wound.

"Yes, Ma'am," he replied with a flinch as he felt her probing around his wound. "He's a nice young kid from Missouri."

"What's your name, Soldier?" Max asked in a business-like manner.

"Well, Ma'am, first thing is that I prefer to be called a trooper; not a soldier. I'm with the one-oh-first and we prefer trooper. My name is Barnett, First Lieutenant William Barnett."

Max gave a short laugh and said, "Well, I'd say your kid from Missouri did a pretty nice job," Max said patting him on the shoulder. "And he was right; you'll need some stiches as well as some good ole whole blood. So, we'll get you into OR right now." As she finished speaking, she signaled for two medics. As they approached she ordered, "Get him into OR and cross match his blood with his dog tags so they can start some whole blood. The doctor can take it from there."

The medics said nothing they just nodded, picked up the stretcher and hurried off to the OR.

As coincidence would have it, Kellie was working a shift in OR when William was carried in and placed on an operating table. She was busy cross matching his blood type with his dog tags when she noticed the name. It was William Barnett. She hurried over to the table he was on and looked down at him. He had been rolled over on his stomach so the doctors could work on his back. She bent down and looked into his face. He knew who she was even through the surgical mask. He smiled at her but didn't say anything.

By now a doctor was standing over him examining his wound. The doctor only took a few seconds before he started shouting orders. "Okay, nurse, I'll need some clamps to stim this bleeding and you need to start some whole blood. This is going to take a lot of stiches so get the needles and tread ready. And I guess we better give this guy some of our joy juice to override the pain. I don't think we need to put him completely under."

"Excuse me, Doctor," Kellie said quickly, "I know this man personally and I think it would be better if another nurse could take over for me."

The doctor looked at her in surprise. "Well, do it fast, Captain, I need to get started."

Kellie turned and signaled for 2nd Lieutenant Michele Martin to come to the table. "Marty, did you hear the Doctor's orders?" She asked firmly.

"Yeah, Kel, I got it. You can bug out."

"Thanks, Marty," she said as she hurried out of the OR.

Kellie quickly got out of her scrubs and went as fast as she could to the triage area, where she expected to find Veronica. But the triage area was empty and Veronica was nowhere to be found. She stood there wondering where to look next when she saw Maxine coming back to the triage area. "Max," she yelled.

Maxine looked around and saw Kellie. She smiled and started in Kellie's direction. "Yeah, Kel, what's up?"

"Have you seen Ronnie anywhere?"

"Yeah, just a little while ago, she's helping out in Ward 2."

Kellie turned and started running to Ward 2, "Thanks, Max," she yelled back as she ran.

Ward 2 was full. This was the ward where the less seriously wounded were waiting to be released back to their units. Kellie weaved her way through men who were standing up and talking and nurses who were checking charts until she finally saw Veronica near the back of the ward. She pressed through a small group of men and finally made it to where Veronica was standing at the foot of a bed talking and smiling at the wounded man occupying the bed. The man happily smiled back at her.

"Hey, Ronnie, I need to see you if I could?" Kellie asked in a cold tone.

"Sure, Kel," Veronica said surprised. She waved a good-bye to the man in the bed and turned her full attention to Kellie. "What can I do you for?"

"Let's go outside," Kellie said, as she took Veronica's hand and began pulling her down the ward isle. Veronica followed her without any arguments or questions.

Once they were outside and alone, Veronica asked in a somewhat irritated tone, "What the hell's this all about, Kel?"

Kellie nervously looked at her dear friend and then said bluntly, "It's William. He's in the OR as we speak."

Veronica staggered backwards a few steps. Her face, with the Vietnam suntan, turned pale. "What…" she stammered, "What's happenin'?"

Kellie kept her composer but just watched her friend.

"It was that fuckin' hill wasn't it?" Veronica shouted. "That Goddamn fuckin' useless son-of-a-bitchin' hill." Tears began to run freely from her eyes down her pale cheeks. Then, she managed to gain some control and asked in a shaky voice, "how's he doin'? Is it bad?"

Kellie ran to her and put her arms around her neck. Leaning close to Veronica's ear, she whispered, "I'm sure he's going to be okay. He's got a bad gash down his back. When I saw him he was conscious and smiling. He's getting whole blood and the doctor is stitching him up. He's under the joy juice right now."

Veronica's first reaction was to pull free of Kellie and run to the OR, but she fought that off and wrapped her arms tightly around Kellie and held on as if her life depended on it.

The battle for Hill 937, better known as Hamburger Hill, lasted for eleven days; the 10th of May through the 20th of May 1969. It was a ferocious, bloody, and costly battle for both sides. The 101st Airborne Division would suffer 72 killed and over 370 wounded. Most of those casualties were among the men of the 3rd Battalion, 187th Regiment. It was the 3rd Battalion that took the brunt of the fighting. They would suffer more than sixty percent casualties and nearly every officer in the battalion was either killed or wounded.

The PAVN, or the North Vietnamese Army, would suffer more the 630 killed and an unknown number of wounded. It would also be learned later that as many as another 1,100 were found dead across the border in Laos. That means that as many as two complete PAVN battalions were completely wiped out.

But the real tragedy of the battle would come two weeks later, when the powers that be decided to abandon the hill on June 5th 1969. So, after all the bloody cost, the hill was only occupied by American forces for two weeks. This caused a storm of outrage in the United States. The political backlash would cause President Nixon to declare the 'Vietnamization' of the war, which meant that the Vietnamese would be required to begin taking over all the ground fighting in South Vietnam. Shortly thereafter, Nixon started withdrawing American Forces from South Vietnam. So, in truth, the Battle of Hamburger Hill was the beginning of the end of American involvement in South Vietnam.

But none of the political maneuvering, or the outlandish lies of the press, or the actions of those in congress can take away from the outstanding courage, valor, and dedication demonstrated by the men of the 101st Airborne Division Screaming Eagles during the battle for Hamburger Hill. Nothing can take away from the honor and dignity they earned on that hill. When the 3rd Battalion returned home from Vietnam it was awarded its 4th Presidential Unit Citation and became the most highly decorated battalion in any airborne division.

CHAPTER FORTY

Running Through the Jungle

Kyle pushed his crew hard. They had been walking through dense jungle and tall elephant grass for the last two hours. He was trying desperately to stay on a due east course, but it was difficult because of having to winded around trees and, at times, thick undergrowth. He tried to keep the crew in single file with him in front, Lt. Clyde second, and O'Brian bring up and covering the rear. His original idea was to keep a twenty-five meter gap between each of them, but he had to scrap that idea because he didn't want to lose eye contract with his crew. At times, the jungle, undergrowth, and elephant grass was so dense that being just ten meters apart would put them out of sight of each other.

As they reached what amounted to a small clearing, Kyle took a reading on his compass, and then he held up his hand to order a halt. Kyle took a knee and signaled the others to do the same. When they were all kneeling close to each other Kyle said in a tired voice, "Well, guys, we've been walkin' for a little over two hours and the best I can tell is we've barely made it three klicks. And, to make things worse, I can't be real sure we've been goin' east all the time. But the good news is that at some clear areas I've been able to still see the hill to our right, which means that we must still be north of the hill."

Then, after a long pause in which no one spoke, Kyle put his hand on Lt. Clyde's good shoulder and asked, "How're you doin', Berry."

Lt. Clyde looked at Kyle with a pained expression. "I'm holding you guys up," he said in desperation, "You need to just give me an M16 and some rations and leave me here. You can take a reading on this spot and send help when you get clear. I mean it, Kyle, it has to be done."

Kyle was about to speak but O'Brian beat him to it. "Look at me, Lt. Clyde, I'm just a lowly sergeant but I'm telling you that that's simply not going to happen. Nobody is leaving anybody. Isn't that right, Skipper?"

Lt. Clyde dropped from his knee down to a sitting position. "Can't you shut him up, Kyle?"

Kyle got to his feet and towered over Lt. Clyde. Then in a harsh voice he said, "Now hear this, Lt. Clyde, this is still a military operation and I'm in command. You'll not be so flippant as to call me by my name. To you I'm either Sir or Captain or Skipper. Do you read me, Lieutenant?"

"Yes, Sir, I'm sorry, Sir," Lt. Clyde mumbled as he struggled to his feet. "What're your orders, Sir?"

A huge smile crossed Kyle's face. "My first order is for you to let me check out those bandages and see how they're holdin' up."

As Kyle was about to reach over and examine the bandages, they all heard a very faint crunching sound coming from the direction they had just come from. O'Brian spun around quickly with the M60 at the ready. They all strained to hear another sound but none came. Quietly, Kyle whispered softly, "Everyone find some cover."

Finding cover was about the easiest thing they had been asked to do since this mission started. Each man found a tree and melted into the undergrowth behind and around it. There was total silence as the crew waited for whatever was coming. Finally the silence was broken by the sound of movement through the jungle and tall elephant grass. The sounds were soft and suppressed but, none the less, they could be heard.

Kyle gripped his M16 tightly as he strained to see or hear something; anything. Then, his heart skipped a beat as someone behind him placed a hand on his shoulder. Kyle spun around quickly but the hand grabbed his M16 and pushed him down deeper into the undergrowth. "Please, Captain," a voice said softly, "you best let us handle this,"

As Kyle recognized Tracker, he started to speak. But Tracker put his hand over Kyle's mouth and put a finger to his own lips; indicating that Kyle should be silent, to which Kyle complied. Using hand signals, Tracker had Kyle follow him. As Kyle followed, Tracker was constantly signaling him to be silent. They had only gone a short distance when they came to another small clearing were the rest of the crew was waiting for them. There were smiles all around, but Tracker was still deadly serious. He signaled for them to lay down flat on their bellies, which they did. Tracker gave them the signal to stay put, as he quietly move away and disappeared into the jungle.

It seemed like an eternity had passed as they lay on the jungle floor staying as quiet as they could possibly be. Then, just ahead of them, maybe only ten meters away, five VC came moving through the jungle in single file. They each carried a Russian made AK47 assault rifle. They moved ever so carefully and quietly thinking they were unseen. Suddenly, all hell broke loose. There was the sound of a high powered sniper rifle firing. It fired three times, and starting at the rear of the line, three of the VC fell dead immediately. Then the sound of a M16 was heard and another VC went down dead. The last VC turned to run but Tracker put a K-BAR through his neck before he had taken a single step.

It was all over in a matter of seconds and Staff Sergeant Costillo was standing over the helicopter crew with a smile on his face. He looked down at them and laughed, "Those guys have been followin' you since you left your chopper. We picked 'em up about an hour ago. I think they wanted to capture you; not kill you. I guess their bosses in Laos are goin' to be really pissed off, because they'll have to find some other poor slobs to put on display."

Kyle rolled over onto his back, propped himself up on his elbows and said unceremoniously, "Gentlemen, I'd like for you to meet a distant relative of mine, Staff Sergeant Jordan Costillo of Marine Recon."

When they were all on their feet, smiling and shaking Jordan's hand, the rest of the Recon team showed up. Kyle introduced Tracker, Swede, and Breed to his crew. It seemed to be a happy time, but Tracker made a signal to Jordan. Jordan nodded his head and cut the celebration short. "Okay, guys, I know we've got officers here, but I'm assumin' tactical command. Do we have any disagreements?" There were no challenges. "Good, then we've gotta move. Tracker says there's maybe a whole platoon of PAVN regulars on our ass. Just for everyone's information, we're in South Vietnam but only about four klicks from the Laotian border. We need to turn north to get to a marine fire base. It's almost right on the border and it's about ten klicks from where we stand now. Now those PAVN assholes are goin' to chase us all the way to the fire base and they'll be weavin' back-and-forth across the border. They've got the advantage of bein' able to travel faster and more freely, but we have the advantage of a good head start. So, come on we need to get movin'."

As everyone geared up and got ready to move, Kyle asked, "Jordan, have you guys got a medical kit or somethin'? Lt. Clyde has got a bad wound that needs more attention than I could give it."

Jordan turned and yelled, "Hey, Breed, grab your medical kit and go take a look at Lt. Clyde. See if you can help. But make it snappy and check him as we move. Okay, people let's go, go, go."

CHAPTER FORTY-ONE

Good-bye to Major Morningstar

First Lieutenant Kathleen O'Rourke hurried to the nurse's quarters. She had just finished a long shift in the OR and she was tired, but she had been ordered to report to the head nurse's quarters on the double. So, she had gotten out of her scrubs and washed up as fast as she could. As she hurried along, she wondered about being ordered to the head nurse's private quarters. Normally, she would meet with Major Morningstar at her desk in the operations building. She smiled to herself as she remembered her first meeting with Major Morningstar. That was over a year ago and the operations area was a tent at Red Beach not a nice building below Monkey Mountain.

All of these thoughts left her mind as she walked through the nurse's quarters and stopped at the door to the head nurse's private quarters. She knocked gently and then waited politely for a reply. There was a short pause and then a weak voice said, "Enter."

Kathleen pushed the small wooden door open and went in. The head nurse's quarters were a bit larger than she remembered. Unlike before, there was room for a full sized desk and a couple of extra chairs to go along with the bunk. As she entered, Kathleen was prepared to come to attention but she didn't. Major Morningstar was sitting at her desk holding large glass of whiskey. An almost full bottle of Old Grand Dad bourbon stood on her desk. She had a small smile on her face but her eyes told another story. The Major wasn't drunk but she was very somber. She titled the glass towards Kathleen and ordered, "Please take a chair, Kat." Then, after Kathleen and taken a chair, she asked, "Would you like to join me in a drink?"

Kathleen was surprised by being called by her nick name rather than simply lieutenant. It was unlike the Major to be so informal. "Yes, Ma'am," Kathleen finally spoke, "I'd think I'd enjoy one. It was a hard shift in the OR."

"Good, good," the Major said as she took out an extra glass and poured a healthy sized drink and handed it to Kathleen. She then leaned forward and held her glass up. "A toast," she said in an almost whisper, "to The Tart Trio."

Kathleen couldn't hide the surprise on her face.

"Oh, my goodness, Kat, did you think I didn't know about The Tart Trio?"

"I guess I'm just a little surprised," Kathleen said as she clicked her glass against the Major's. "To The Tart Trio," she repeated. Then both women took a large swallow from their glasses.

After the Major had digested her drink, she leaned back in her chair and asked, "You're probably wondering why I sent for you?"

"Yes, Ma'am, I am."

The Major leaned forward again and asked softly, "For this meeting, why don't you just call me Marge. And would it be okay if I just called you, Kat?"

"I have no problem with any of that, Marge," Kathleen said smiling and then sipping a little more whiskey.

The Major leaned back in her chair again. A very studious and serious expression came over her face. "What would you say if I sent you to the ten-six-six on Temporary Duty assignment?"

Kathleen tried to hide her surprise by saying, "Marge, I think we've had this discussion before. Remember, you, me, and Ronnie. Ronnie went to the ten-six-six and I opted to stay here."

The Major nodded, "Yes, I remember. But that was then and this is now."

"What does that mean?" Kathleen challenged.

The Major didn't answer but laughed out loud, took a sip of whiskey, and asked, "Do you remember when you girls first got here and reported to me at Red Beach? And then I dropped it on you that I was keeping you all here to help me. Do you remember that?"

"I remember that, Marge. But what's that got to do with me goin' TDY to the ten-six-six?"

The Major still didn't answer Kathleen's question, she just said, "I bet I can tell you something you don't know."

"What would that be, Marge?"

The Major took another sip of whiskey, looked at Kathleen with compassion and asked, "I bet you don't know that I really liked you three girls then, and I still do now? You three represent not just what is best in the Army Nurse Corps, but what is best in people. I love how you treat each other. I love how you love. I know you've all got guys that you care for; maybe even love." She stopped talking and took another small sip of whiskey. Kathleen didn't know what to say, so she just stayed quiet and let the Major continue, "You know, Kat, I was in love once? I bet you didn't know that?"

"I guess everyone's been in love at one time or the other," Kathleen said gently.

The Major chuckled, "Yeah, someone like you would guess that everyone has experienced love. But you'd guess wrong, Kat. Not everyone has and that's a damn shame because it's really something to treasure. Do you want to know who my love was, Kat?"

"Sure, Marge, I'd really like to know."

"His name was Captain Lawrence Billings. He was a doctor at the 1107th MASH in Korea. And me, I was a young twenty-two year old 2nd lieutenant nurse. For almost two years we worked together at that MASH, and during that time we really fell hard for each other. In our spare time, we made plans for when we would get married and what our life would be like back in the States." She stopped and took another sip of whiskey. Then, she took a deep breath and let it out slowly. "We almost made it," she continued. "But three days before the cease fire, one of our choppers got hit and spun out of control. It crashed into our OR killing two doctors, one nurse, and three wounded. Lawrence was one of the doctors." She stopped again and drained her glass of whiskey. She looked at Kathleen and smiled, "So, I made a career out of the army and here I am now. At least here I am for today."

"I'm sorry to hear that, Marge," Kathleen said slowly, "it must've been a terrible experience. But what did you mean by the last part? The part about 'at least here I am for today'. What does that mean?"

The Major poured herself another drink. This time it was smaller than before. Then, looking at Kathleen sadly, she said, "I've been relieved."

"Relieved?" Kathleen asked. "Whata you mean?"

"It's very simple, Kat, they've replaced me with a much younger head nurse. She's a captain and she'll be here tomorrow."

"Are you bein' relieved or is it that your tour's up?"

"Oh, it's about one in the same. They want me to rotate out and I guess it's for the best." After a short pause, she laughed and continued, "The good news is they're kicking me up to lieutenant coronal. I got my silver oak leaves."

Kathleen studied her longtime head nurse and asked carefully, "Marge, don't you want to go home? Don't you want the promotion?"

Major Morningstar took small sip of her whiskey and smiled at Kathleen and said, "No I don't. You see they're sending me back to go around to different colleges and universities to help the recruiting effort." She shook her head, "I'm going to hate that. Can you imagine what it's going to be like? I mean after working over here with great people like you and all the other nurses, people who're so unselfish, so dedicated, so loyal, and who'll give their all without complaining, people who'll put their life on the line." She stopped again and laughed, "Do you remember when we found you asleep on an OR gurney after you'd put in nearly twenty hours?"

Kathleen smiled, "I remember."

"Oh, well," the Major sighed, "it is what it is. But I want to do one more thing before I leave and that's to help you, Kat, if I can. I know Ronnie's airborne lieutenant got wounded at Hamburger Hill and that he's waiting at the ten-six-six for a decision on if he can go back to duty or if they're going to send him here. If I know airborne lieutenants, he's going to be fighting coming here because he's afraid we'll send him back to the States, which we probably would. And I know that Kel's chopper jockey has been shot down and is MIA. She's doing her job but, at the same time, she's worried sick." The Major paused again and in a more gentle tone, "I guess I'm not telling you anything you don't already know."

Kathleen took a deep breath and drained her whiskey glass. "Yeah, I know all that," she said. "But how can sendin' me up there help?"

Major Morningstar look amazed. "My God, girl, you can be there for them. You can help them and still do your job. They've had two nurses rotate out in the last month. They've got enough work for you up there, and, Kat, what about that enlisted marine of yours? He may end up at the ten-six-six anytime."

Kathleen stood up. "What enlisted marine? What're you talkin' about?"

The Major waved her hand at Kathleen. "Come on now, Kat, sit back down. I know all about it. You know I know. It was me that looked the other way while you spent a night on the beach with 'im remember."

Kathleen slowly returned to her chair. "Yeah, I remember. It's just I guess it has to come out sooner or later. It's lasted longer than I'd hoped for."

Again Major Morningstar's face took on a look of shock and amazement. "For Christ sakes, Kat, you don't think I'd squeal on you do you?"

Kathleen clasped her hands together and shook her head as moisture formed in her eyes. "No," she said, "I really know better than that. I just don't know how long I can keep this up. Since the battle at that stupid damn hill, I've heard nothin' from 'im."

"So," the Major said drawing out the word for impact, "why not let me help this one last time? Kat, go to the ten-six-six. Up there you'll be in the thick of things. And The Tart Trio can be together and draw strength from each other."

Kathleen picked up her empty glass and handed it to the Major. "You might give me another little slug," she said with the moisture now turning to tears. "God, we're goin' to miss you around here, Marge, but you go back home and you get us some good nurses. I'll tell you though; I'm goin' to pray every day and every night that this damn thing gets over before you have to send anymore nurses over here."

Major Morningstar smiled at Kathleen and took her glass and poured her another small shot of whiskey. Then, she held her glass up and said happily, "Another toast, to you and all the others I've served with. I'm going to miss all of you." They both took a long drawn off their drinks and then the Major reached into her desk drawer and pulled out some papers. She handed them to Kathleen and said slyly, "Here're your TDY orders. I took the liberty of getting them done ahead of time."

CHAPTER FORTY-TWO

The Fast Team and the Slow Team

They'd been traveling for over two hours when Jordan called a break. The men were tired but Lt. Clyde was the worse. They had stopped the blood flow as much as possible but now, with all the hard work of hurrying through the jungle, the blood flow had increased. Jordan figured they were still about seven klicks from the marine fire base. He wasn't sure if Lt. Clyde could make it. During the break, Breed once again attended to Lt. Clyde as best he could.

As the men took the much needed break, Jordan waited impatiently for Tracker to show up as he was supposed to do at every two hour interval. Jordan's patients were beginning to wear very thin, when Tracker finally appeared. Tracker looked very tired and worried. Jordan knew that the continued excursions through the jungle to keep track of the PAVN following them and then reporting back would soon ware down even Tracker. When Tracker was kneeling by his side and panting, Jordan asked, "Okay, Tracker, what's the scoop."

"Not good, Sarge," Tracker panted. "The little assholes are makin' better time than we are. They're mostly stayin' on the Laos side where they have no fear of runnin' into any of our guys. Plus they don't have any wounded to slow them down."

"How many do you think?" Jordan asked.

"Oh, it's a full platoon; about forty or so."

"What's your best bet?"

Tracker shook his head and replied solemnly, "It's hard to say for sure, Sarge, but at the pace we're goin' and if our estimate of seven klicks to the fire base is good, I'd say they'll probably be able to cut us off about three klicks from the fire base."

Jordan was silent for several seconds. "Roger that, Tracker, now go and get Captain Collie and Breed and bring them over here. Have Breed bring his radio and you come back with him."

Tracker simply nodded and hurried off to gather up Captain Collie and Breed. Breed was putting on some final touches to Lt. Clyde's wound when Tracker found him. Tracker relayed his instructions to Breed and Captain Collie who was with Lt. Clyde. Shortly, they were all kneeling forming a circle around Jordan.

"I'm not goin' to mince words, "Jordan started, "Tracker figures the PAVN shits are goin' to be able to cut us off about three klicks short of the fire base. So, we gotta make an alternate plan."

"Would they attack us that close to the fire base?" Kyle asked.

"I don't know but we can't take a chance."

Kyle nodded, "Okay, what's your plan?"

"We split up," Jordan said simply.

"Well, I hope there's more to it than that?" Kyle asked.

"There is," Jordan replied sarcastically. "First, Breed, can we raise the fire base on your radio?"

"No, not now, Sarge, I've got power issues. My batteries are low. I figure we need to be at least three klicks closer before they can read me."

"Are you sure you got their frequency correct?"

Breed simple looked down and asked, "Do I need to answer that?"

Jordan smiled, "No, sorry about that, Breed."

Breed simply waved it off.

"Okay, guys, here's what we do," Jordan began, "we split into two teams. One we call the fast team and the other we call the slow team. The fast team will consist of Breed, Tracker, Captain Collie, and Sergeant O'Brian. The slow team will consist of Swede, Lt. Clyde, and me. The fast team will move ahead as fast as possible to try and beat the PAVN to the fire base. You should be able to make it at least pass the three klick cut off point. After that, you should be okay. All along the way, Breed will continue to try and raise the fire base. When you do get them, Breed, tell them what's happenin' and to try get a rescue team out to us. Let them know that the PAVN are about forty men strong. Now, we on the slow team will move ahead at our best speed. When we get to a position where I believe we're about to be cut off, we'll set up defensive positions and try and hold until we get some help from the fire base. O'Brian, I'll need to swap weapons with you. I'll need that M60 more than you." Jordan stopped giving orders and looked around, "Everybody got that, 'cause we gotta get goin'."

"I like your plan, Sergeant Costillo, except for one thing," Kyle said standing up. "I'll be takin' the M60 and stayin' with the slow team."

"The plan stands as I described it," Jordan said firmly.

"I'm the rankin' officer here and at this point I'm takin' command and I'm stayin' with the slow team."

Jordan was now on his feet. "Kyle, we agreed that I'd have tactical command and you can't change that."

"Stop it!" A shout came from outside their circle. "There's not going to be a slow team," Lt. Clyde demanded harshly. "Because some fuckin' body is going to give me a fuckin' M16, prop me up against a fuckin' tree, and leave me the fuck behind!"

Jordan now became very angry. "This shit has gone far enough," he shouted as his face turned crimson red. "We don't have time for any of this bullshit. We've already wasted too much time now. They are lives at stake here. Tracker, get the fast team together and lead them out and do it *RIGHT FUCKIN' NOW!*"

Tracker did as ordered. "Please, Captain, let's go for everybody's sake," he begged. As the fast team hurriedly left the others, Kyle looked back with rage showing in his face.

Jordan waited until the fast team was out of sight and then called the slow team together for a short meeting. "Okay, here's how it works," he said, "we're goin' to continue on right behind the fast team. I hope we can make maybe three more klicks before we get cut off." Then pointing to Swede he said, "As we go, Swede, I want you to keep a sharp eye out for a good spot for us to setup an ambush. When you see it, let me know and we'll stop no matter how far we've gone. It needs to have a decent clearin', it needs to give you a good place with cover to setup your sniper rifle, and it needs to give me some space for this M60. I would prefer that you be setup somethin' like twenty meters behind me. I'll try and setup directly in front of them. But a lot of this depends on exactly which direction they come from."

"Is that all you want, Sarge?" Swede asked jokingly. "Are you sure you don't want me to guide them straight into our ambush?"

Jordan grinned at him, "Well, if you could, that would be nice."

"What about me?" Lt. Clyde asked. "What do I do in all this?"

"You're with me," Jordan answered turning serious again. "I want you on my right because Swede is goin' to be behind me on my left. Now this next part in important for both of you. Swede, don't fire at the first two you see because that'll be their point men. Be sure and let 'em go by. Then, when you see the main body, start at the back and pick them off. Lieutenant, you'll be on my right and I want you to keep your eyes on the point men. Once you hear Swede open up, you take out the point men. When they hear the shootin' they'll probably turn back towards you makin' your shot easier. But in any case, those point men belong to you. Be sure you stay with them and take them out 'cause while all of that is goin' on, I'm goin' to open up with the M60 right into their faces." Jordan pause and both men nodded to him but didn't speak. "And in conclusion," Jordan said jovially, "if all goes well, we should be able to hold out until some relief from the fire base reaches us."

"It sounds to me like a lot of shit has to happen just right and in just the right order for us to make this work," Lt. Clyde said nervously.

Jordan winked at him and said confidently, "That's what Marine Recon does. We make things happen just right and in just the right order." Then with a wave of his hand he said, "Let's move out. Take the point, Swede, and find us that ambush spot. One more thing guys, I'll be goin' on mostly hand signals from now on so keep an eye on me. I know that'll be hard for you, Swede, so if need be I'll catch up to you so you don't have to keep lookin' back."

Unfortunately, the plan didn't follow just the right order. They had only gone a little over one klick when Swede appeared out of the jungle and stood before Jordan and Lt. Clyde gasping for breath. "What the hell happened, Swede?" Jordan asked in confusion. "Did you find a suitable clearin'?"

"We're not going to get a clearing, Sarge," Swede said in between gasps.

"Okay, talk and talk fast," Jordan ordered.

"They've already cut us off and are moving south towards us. They can't be more than five minutes behind me."

"Do you think they saw you?" Jordan pressed.

"Well, nobody shot at me so I guess not."

"And we haven't heard any shootin' at all, so I have to believe that the fast team must've made it through," Jordan surmised.

"That makes sense," Swede breathed.

"Could you tell what kind of formation they were in?" Jordan asked hurriedly. "I mean were they fanned out, bunched up, or in single file?"

Swede shrugged his shoulders in frustration. "I'm sorry, Sarge, but I'm not sure. As soon as I saw 'em, I took off running, but if I had to guess, I'd say they were fanned out."

Jordan let out a long breath and started issuing orders. "Okay, guys, we'll follow our original plan as close as we can. Swede, you flank out to left as far as you think it's safe and setup. I want you to start things off, so as soon as you get a target start shootin'. Maybe they'll look in your direction and I can take 'em by surprise with the M60. I'm goin' to move up to that big tree on the right up there about twenty meters and set up the M60. Lt. Clyde, we're goin' to take the chance that they're goin' to be fanned out, so you can forget about any point men. You stay here and cover my back cause as soon as I open up with this M60 they're goin' to be comin' after me. You got that?"

"I got it," he said, "but can somebody help me out of this damn sling so I can at least have some use of my left arm?" Jordan pulled out his K-BAR and quickly cut away the bandages that immobilized Lt. Clyde's left arm. Once the job was done, Lt. Clyde nodded a thank you and quickly found a spot and got down on his belly to position his M16 from a prone position. It wasn't an easy thing to do with only one good arm.

Jordan started to run for his position but Swede reached up and grabbed his shoulder. "Sarge," he said, "you know I'm not going to be much help with this sniper rifle. I know I'm fast at firing and reloading but at these close quarters, well, I'm not that good. Plus, I've only got thirty rounds left and I know you only have two belts of ammo for that M60 and the Lieutenant has only got two full M16 clips."

Jordan slapped him on the back and said, "I know, Swede. You just do the best you can and that'll be good enough for anybody. I'm just hopin' the fast team is as fast comin' as they were goin'."

Swede nodded, smiled, and then turned and ran to find the best spot he could and as far out on the left flank as he dared.

Seeing his men were getting in place, Jordan bent down to Lt. Clyde and said in a soft whisper, "Good luck, Sir."

Lt. Clyde smiled back up to Jordan, "Same to you, Sergeant."

With that, Jordan ran to his tree and setup the M60.

CHAPTER FORTY-THREE

The Tart Trio at the Ten-Six-Six

The club was almost completely empty as Kellie sat alone at a table. Her bush hat was cocked back on her head. She toyed with a glass that held a double Jack Daniels. It was her third double during the half hour she had been sitting in the club. She put the glass to her mouth and took a small sip. A frown crossed her face as the drink tasted weak. She smiled as she realized that the ice had melted making the drink taste like water. She reasoned she had been toying with glass too long. Pushing herself up from the table she walked tiredly over to the bar. She placed the glass on the bar and asked the bartender softly, "Could you please sweeten this up for me. It seems I've let the ice melt."

"Yes, Ma'am," the bartender replied politely. He took the bottle of Jack Daniels off the shelf and poured a shot into the glass. "Would you like some more ice?"

"Yes," she answered, again softly. "And you might want to put just a little more Jack in there also, and just keep my tab going if you would."

The bartender smiled and did as requested and then asked, "Captain, are you tryin' to get a load on?"

"I might be," she replied, "I just might be." She tipped the glass to the bartender and turned and walked back to her table.

She sat back down and stared into her glass. Kyle had now been MIA for over a full day. She knew that with each hour that went by the chances of getting him back grew smaller and smaller. This was her first chance to really think about it. She had been trying to keep busy so as to block it out of her mind. But as the sun began to set and darkness settled over the ten-six-six, Veronica grew tired of her volunteering to take shifts for everyone, and threaten to go to the CO if she didn't take some time off. So, she had come straight to the club without showering or changing clothes. The bad news was that now she could think and she could be afraid.

She had intentionally avoided her father and he had not tried to talk to her. She knew his solution would be a 'thumbs up' and a 'good cry'. But she wouldn't cry. She and Kyle knew the dangers of their affair when they started it. They knew that one or the other of them could be killed at any time, but mostly it was Kyle because he was up in his chopper almost every day; especially since the battle for that God forsaken hill had started. In her heart, she had been expecting the news her father had given her about Kyle being shot down to come sooner or later. Now it had finally come and she was disgusted with herself because she was having a terrible time handling it.

She again stared down into her glass. She frowned and said to the glass, "You're not helping me much, Jack. I expected more from you." When the glass didn't respond, she swirled the liquid around and said mockingly, "Not talking, uh. Well, I don't blame you. There's not much to say." Then she chuckled softly, "I guess talking to a glass of booze means I'm getting a buzz on."

"That's generally what it means." It was the bartender talking to her. He was now standing by her table looking down at her. "I'm goin' off shift in a few minutes and I was wondering if there's anything else I do for you, Captain, before I leave?"

She looked up at him and replied, "No, Sergeant, this'll be my last drink, but thanks for asking. Do you want me to pay my tab now?"

"Not necessary, Captain, I'll leave it for my relief." He turned and started to leave but stopped and turned back. "They'll find 'im, Captain," he said gently, "you need to have faith in our guys. They'll find 'im."

She watched as he turned and walked to the door. As he opened the door to leave, she shouted, "Thank you, Sergeant, thank you a lot."

Except for Kellie and the new bartender, the club was completely empty now. Kellie thought this to be strange for this time of the evening and the fact that the casualty flow was now far less than normal. Maybe all the nurses were taking advantage of the situation to grab some shut eye and do some personal things. At any rate, she was sipping her last drink very slowly. She had removed her bush hat and put it on the table. Her long black hair now hung to her shoulders and down into her face. She turned her chair away from the table and pulled another chair up close so she could prop her feet up on it. The thought of taking her boots off crossed her mind but it was quickly discarded. So, she settled back in her chair with her feet propped up and nursed her drink.

"Hey, you, are you drunk?" The question came from behind her. Without taking her feet down, she bent her head back to see who was talking. "I asked if you're drunk," the voice asked again.

Kellie sat her drink down, pulled her feet from the other chair and put them on the floor, and turned in her chair to see who was talking. To her shock standing just a few feet from her were Veronica and Kathleen. They stood with their arms around each other's necks. They both had huge grins on their faces.

Veronica pointed to Kathleen and said, "Look who I found wonderin' around the operations tent."

"Kat," Kellie shouted joyfully as she jumped to her feet. "What're you doing here? How'd you get here?"

"Questions, questions," Kathleen laughed.

Kellie ran to her two friends and threw her arms around both of them. After hugs all around, Kellie said, "Well, tell me. Answer my questions."

Kathleen took her by the arm and guided her back to the table. "Come on," she said pulling out a chair, "everyone sit down and I'll start talkin'. We'll need some drinks 'cause it's a long story involvin' Major, and soon to be Lt. Coronal, Morningstar."

As they all got settled at the table, Veronica jumped up and said, "I'll get the drinks. What does everyone want?"

Kellie waved her hand and laughed, "Nothing else for me. I've had my limit for tonight."

"I'll have what you're havin', Ronnie," Kathleen said smiling.

"Okay," Veronica said, as she started for the bar, "I know you like that Irish whiskey. Jamison, I think it is. I bet we still have some of that stuff here somewhere."

"Not to worry, Ronnie, whatever you got will work."

Soon Veronica came back carrying two glasses full of Jamison Irish Whiskey. She put one in front of Kathleen held the other for herself. "Now, Kat, spill the beans."

Kathleen put her hands on the table and said softly, "Before I get started on how I got here and why, I just want you guys to know how happy I am to be here."

They all smiled and grasped hands at the table. "You can't believe how great it is to see you here, Kat," Kellie said with deep emotion.

"Kel, I know you're hurtin' right now," Kathleen said gently. "But you're not alone. I haven't heard anythin' from, or about, Jordy either. It's hard to keep my mind on work. But it's what we do and we do it well. You're the head nurse, you put me where I can do the most good and know that I'm here for you personally whenever you need me."

There was a long silence as the girls just looked at each other. Then, Veronica said, "That's a ditto for me. At least my guy is in Ward 4 and is goin' to be okay. But he's chompin' at the bit to get back to his platoon. But I'm not sure the doctors are goin' to let him go. They're still worried about his spine. That cut ended up very close to his spine and they're worried about some possible nerve damage. They want to make sure that area heals completely before they'll release him. It's goin' to make him really mad but I think they're goin' to send him down to the 95th."

"I hope they do," Kellie said with anger and looking Veronica directly in the eyes. "I don't care if it makes him mad as hell. He needs not just to be down at the 95th, he needs to be home. He's done his share in this place at least five times over."

"You'll get no argument from me," Veronica said. "You're preachin' to the choir."

"You know, Kat," Kellie said as she squeezed Kathleen's hand, "not so very long ago a very wise sergeant told me that we need to have faith in our guys. I think that sergeant was right and that's what I intend to do from now on. I think you should too."

Kathleen smiled at her friends and said with a laugh, "Let me take a shot of this Jamison and then I'll tell you the story of how I got here and the story of soon to be Lt. Coronal Morningstar."

CHAPTER FORTY-FOUR

The Alamo in the Jungle

The slow team didn't have long to wait. Jordan had barely gotten the M60 setup when the PAVN began to appear through the trees and undergrowth. Jordan immediately noticed two things that were in their favor. First, the PAVN were fanned out just as Swede had suspected. They appeared to be at intervals of about three meters but it was hard to tell as they weren't in an even line, but it meant that they had no backup behind them. They were strung out. Second, they started to appear far to his left, which meant they were first appearing near Swede. So, Swede would be able to get the first shots off as they had planned.

Jordan tried to be patient as more and more PAVN began to appear through the trees and undergrowth. They drew closer and closer to him. Since they we were fanned out, they were coming towards him from both sides of his tree. His trust in Swede paid off as he finally heard the crack of the sniper rifle. The first crack was followed quickly by two more. As Jordan had hoped, the fire from the sniper rifle got the attention of nearly all the PAVN. They turned towards the sound of the rifle. One of the PAVN started shouting orders and pointing in the direction of the rifle fire. Jordan was momentarily taken aback because the man wasn't speaking Vietnamese but Laotian. Under his breath, he growled, "These sons-of-bitches aren't PAVN, they're Laotian Army."

Jordan determined that now was the time for the Alamo in the jungle to start. He got to his knees and held the M60 steady, since he had no tripod for it. Then, he open fire. He sprayed the nearest fanned out group to him. The enemy, who had their backs to him, began to fall. Taken by surprise, they began to fade back to the jungle seeking cover. Jordan, knowing he had to conserve ammo, took his finger off the trigger and dropped back down. He heard three more reports from the sniper rifle then it fell quite. Quietness settled over the small battleground, but that was only temporary as Jordan heard the report of the M16 from behind him. He spun around to see two enemy lying dead just to the right of his tree. Lt. Clyde was doing his job.

Jordan checked the ammo belt in the M60. He had fired over two-thirds of the belt in just the opening moments of the battle. He would have to be more conservative. As he was going over all this, the Laotians made a charge. He again opened up with the M60 and Lt. Clyde opened up protecting his right. It was a quick skirmish, as the Laotians moved backed into the trees after taking several casualties. There were only a few rounds left in the M60 ammo belt so Jordan opted to change to his last belt while he had the chance. As he was in the process, a grenade bounced off the tree trunk above his head and landed about ten feet behind him. "Grenade!" he shouted as loud as he could and he dove to the right side of the tree. The explosion sent shrapnel flying everywhere, but he wasn't hit. Although he couldn't see anyone, he quickly started firing wildly into the trees. While he was firing, another grenade sailed over his head and exploded several meters behind him.

The grenade went too far behind him and again he wasn't hit. But unfortunately, the Laotians followed the grenade with another charge. This time they were effective. Jordan felt a sharp pain in his left calf and he went down. He rolled over to see four Laotians charging him with weapons firing. He then saw the four Laotians explode before his eyes. He heard large amounts of shooting and shouting. Reaching down to his boot, he pulled out his K-BAR. It was his last means of defense. He tried to get to his feet but his left leg didn't want to work. As he struggled, a strong hand grabbed his shirt collar and helped to his knees. Looking up, he saw towering over him a tall marine wearing the patch of the 1st Battalion, 9th Marines; better known as 'The Walking Dead' Battalion. They were called that because the PAVN had promised that every single marine in the 1st Battalion 9th Marines would be dead by the end of the battle in the rice paddies. That was over a year ago and the 1st Battalion was still standing. So they started calling themselves the "Walking Dead", because they guessed hey were supposed to be dead.

"Hey, Grease Ball," the Marine said, "I got word from some of your squad that you'd be out here, but ain't it just my luck to find you. And to top it all off, I probably saved your sorry ass. If I hadn't of blasted those PAVN shits, they were sure to waste you."

Jordan blinked his eyes and said automatically, "They're not PAVN; they're Laotians."

"Don't matter," the Marine said, "they still would've wasted you."

"Yeah, it does matter," Jordan replied still waving his K-BAR around, "we need to report this to intelligence."

The Marine caught Jordan's hand and roughly took the K-BAR away from him. "You're goin' to hurt someone with this thing if you're not careful."

The stunning effect of his wound was wearing off somewhat and he struggled to recognize the marine that towered over him. The voice sounded familiar but he couldn't place the face. "Do I know you?" Jordan stammered.

"Yeah, you do, Grease Ball," the Marine laughed. "I'm surprised you haven't picked up on it by now."

Jordan managed a small smile and said, "Well, I am under a certain amount of duress here."

Before anything else could be said, a Navy Corpsman pushed Jordan down to the ground on his back and started examining his calf. After a short time, the corpsman said, "Well, Sergeant, we got good news and we got bad news. Which do you want first?"

"I'll take the bad news first," Jordan said bracing himself.

The corpsman shrugged and said, "The bullet went all the way through your calf breaking your shinbone along the way.

"And what's the good news?" Jordan asked.

The corpsman put on a broad smile, "The bullet managed to miss your arteries so you're not going to bleed to death."

"How 'bout that," the Marine laughed. "Come on, Doc; put somethin' on him so I can carry him back to the stretcher area."

The corpsman put a tight bandage around Jordan's calf and said to the marine, "Okay, you guys can start back now, but don't let him put too much pressure on that leg."

"I'll treat him like he was made of gold."

The Marine helped Jordan to his feet, or his foot as it were, and wrapped his strong arm around Jordan. Jordan was able to hop along with just barely putting his left foot down at all. They had only gone a few steps, when Jordan yelled back to the corpsman, "Hey, Doc, I had two other guys with me. How'd they make out?"

"The marine made out okay. He just has a few cuts and scratches. But, the army guy didn't make it. A grenade must've landed right next to 'im because he's messed up awful bad."

Jordan lowered his head and ran his hand through his short hair. He looked up at the marine and said, "His name was 1st Lieutenant Berry Clyde. He saved my ass. He covered by back."

The Marine just nodded his head and said, "Yeah, I know how it is. It seems to happen that way a lot." Then, as if shaking his head clear, he said softly, "Come on, Grease Ball; let's get you back to the stretcher area."

Jordan noticed the corporal strips on the marine's sleeve. "Okay, Corporal Kellen, let's get goin'."

"Oh, so you finally figured out who I am?"

"Sure, it was just a matter of time before the Grease Ball thing came back to me. Tell me, you said you'd been told I was out here, who told you?"

"It was one of the guys from your squad. He mentioned your name. Our Captain had hell tryin' to keep those guys you sent on ahead from comin' back with us. But the Captain just wanted his guys on this mission. So, here we are."

"Well, I'm really glad to see you Corporal Gerald Kellen."

"Ah, you even remembered my first name."

"I could never forget."

They hobbled along in silence for a while before Jordan finally asked, "When's the last time you been home to Marfa?"

"About eight months ago," Gerald replied. "They gave me thirty days leave before I started my second tour. I went home and spent some time with my wife and daughter. After this tour I'm taken off this uniform and becomin' a civilian again. And you?"

"Aw, shit, I guess it's been near on three years since I been to Marfa."

"Really, three years."

"You really got a daughter?" Jordan asked. "I mean I'm a little surprised that anyone would marry you."

"Don't be a wise ass, or I'll drop you right here," Gerald said jokingly. "She's three years old."

"What's her name?"

"Christina. We named her after my mother."

Jordan could see the stretcher area up ahead, "Can we slow down just a minute?" He asked.

"Sure."

"Since you've been back home much more recently than me, I was wonderin' if people still come to Marfa to see the Mysterious Marfa Lights?"

Gerald laughed, "Yeah, they do. They really do. Those lights are even more popular than the hotel where all the movie stars stayed while makin' the movie, 'Giant'."

"No shit," Jordan chuckled shaking his head.

"No shit," Gerald repeated.

"You know, Gerald, I know a way a guy could make a lot of money off those lights."

"Oh yeah, and how would that be?"

"He could buy a little patch of land just off the highway were you can see the lights. Then, you setup a little park of some kind with a parking lot. And you have restrooms, and you sell cold drinks, and you have a bunch of those mechanical binoculars that you put a dime in to see. That way people can see the Mysterious Marfa Lights without any discomfort and they don't even have to bring their own binoculars or drinks, and they don't have to park alongside the highway."

Gerald thought for a minute then said, "Why're you tryin' to think up ways to make money in Marfa? I hear you're the richest marine in history. You probably own most of Marfa by now."

"No, the only thing I own in Marfa is my house," Jordan corrected him. "Anyway, you didn't answer my question. What'd you think of my idea? Do you think anyone will ever do somethin' like that?"

Gerald was quiet for a moment and then said, "Come on, Jordan, let's get you to the stretcher area so we can get you to the fire base so, then we can get on a chopper, so then we can get you to a real doctor who can fix that leg of yours."

"But, Gerald, you still haven't answered my question."

"Okay, okay," Gerald said in frustration as he coached Jordan along, "yeah, I think somebody will do that someday. But I'm not sure we'll live to see it."

As evening settled over the 9th Marine's fire base, Jordan stared across the small base at a lone medivac chopper. Jordan was still on a stretcher and was in an area that was designated by a sign that read, 'Medical

Evac Area'. The sign was a simple piece of board and the writing on it looked as though it had been done with a crayon. The chopper he stared at looked very lonesome out there by itself. The Base Commander had order that there would be no flights out until morning. He wanted no one flying out in the dark and he deemed it too late in the evening to start a flight now. So, Jordan would have to wait until oh-six hundred hours in the morning before he would be on his way to the ten-six-six. Although, Jordan was still on his stretcher, he now sat up and leaned back again a stack of sandbags that ringed the area.

Jordan was jockeying around trying to get his leg in a comfortable position for the night, when a figure approached him out of the semi-darkness. The figure was walking with a crutch. It was Kyle. He maneuvered himself next to Jordan and the sandbags. Using the crutch, he gently slid down the sandbags to a sitting position next to Jordan.

"How's it goin', Sergeant Costillo? Did they give you some morphine?" He asked.

"It could be better, Captain Sir," Jordan answered. "And yes I got some morphine but the corpsman told me that's the last I can have until I get to the ten-six-six tomorrow mornin'."

"Look at it this way, Jordy; you got the million dollar wound. They're goin' to send you home for sure. It's goin' to take quite a while for that leg to heal up. The corpsman tells me the docs'll probably have to put a medal bar or somethin' like that in there."

"Yeah, I guess so," Jordan replied slowly. "You know, Kyle, I'm a little surprised that you're speakin' to me."

"Well, that leads into why I'm actually here," Kyle said softly. "I'm here to make an apology. I didn't make things easy on you back there. I was so tied up with savin' my crew that it blurred the big picture. I had no business tryin' to take command away from you at that time. In a chopper, I'm your man, but in a ground battle you're the man for the job. And the results proved it."

Jordan reached over and put his hand on Kyle's shoulder and said gently, "You're the man for a lot of things, Kyle. You're like a brother to me and I'm sorry for doin' things the way I did."

"You couldn't've done it any other way, Jordy. There just wasn't time to be nice about it. We had to move. Anyway, I just stopped by to tell you I got no hard feelings and that I know you did what you had to do for the whole group."

Kyle started the struggle to get up but Jordan held on to his shoulder and stopped him. Then in a pleading voice said, "I can't tell you how sorry I am about Lt. Clyde."

Kyle lowered his head and replied, "I know, Jordy. I really guessed he wouldn't make it from the time I took that branch outa his shoulder. I just wanted him to make it so bad that I just couldn't let go."

Jordan smile and said, "You know what you just described? You described exactly how a good officer should act. You care for your men. There's nothin' wrong with that. And I'll tell you somethin' you may not know. Lt. Clyde saved my life. He stayed behind me and covered my back. He had me cut his bandages off so he could use his left arm as best he could. When the fight was over, there were four dead Laotians lying behind me. Lt. Clyde took them out. I'm goin' to find an officer somewhere that'll put him in for a metal. I was present and I'll give the testimony."

Kyle reached over and gave Jordan a gentle slap on the face, "You just found your officer."

Kyle once again started his struggle to get to his feet. This time Jordan helped him as well as he could. Once Kyle was standing with his crutch, Jordan asked, "By the way, what happened to your foot?"

Kyle looked down and pointed to his right foot. "Actually it's my ankle. I broke it."

"How'd you do that?" Jordan asked with a small chuckle.

"It was very heroic," Kyle said seriously. "Your guy Tracker was drivin' us through the jungle so fast that I got my foot tangled up in some heavy undergrowth and I tripped. I went down but my foot turned at a ninety degree angle and my ankle didn't like that. Breed grabbed me and half dragged and half push me the rest of the way to the base."

"Well, that's goin' to make for a really good war story," Jordan laughed.

"Do you think there's a purple heart in it for me?" Kyle asked still using a serious tone.

"I don't know, Kyle, but why not?"

Kyle turned and started walking away but yelled back, "I guess I'll see you in the mornin' on the medivac flight. I think there'll be six of us goin' over to the ten-six-six."

"What about Lt. Clyde?" Jordan shouted. "Will we be taken his body back with us?"

Kyle stopped and looked back at Jordan. It was dark now and he could barely see his friend and relative, but he knew pain was in Jordan's face because he heard it in his voice. "No," Kyle said simply, "they have his body in a make shift morgue. They'll be flyin' all the dead out in two other medivacs tomorrow sometime. We won't see Berry again."

The battle would become known in the Marine Recon as the Alamo in the Jungle. Marines are a tight brotherhood but they respect all those who fight with them. For that reason, and if for no other, the marines saw to it that 1st Lieutenant Berry Clyde was posthumously awarded the Silver Star for valor.

CHAPTER FORTY-FIVE

A Time to Cry

Kellie sat in her small head nurse's quarters working on the nurse's roster. She was now very thankful for having Kathleen here at the ten-six-six for reasons other than personal. Just over the last month two nurses had rotated out back to the States and she was having trouble covering all her bases. She was also thankful for the slowdown in casualties, but that couldn't be counted on to last much longer. Now, as she checked the roster, she found that all the wards were covered, including the fact that Kathleen was covering both Wards 3 and 4, and triage was covered. However, she was coming up one nurse short for OR. But as long as the casualty flow stayed low, she could get by.

She was deep in thought when a soft knock came at her door. "Come on in," she yelled.

2nd Lt. Michele 'Marty' Martin stuck her head in the door. "We got a chopper coming in, Kel. According to the squawk box, we got six wounded."

Kellie looked at her roster again and then said, "Okay, Marty, I see you're already scheduled for triage so can you handle it?"

"Roger that," came the reply.

"And, Marty," Kellie said quickly before Lt. Martin left, "go over to Ward 2 and tell Ronnie to go and prep OR and be ready to assist and I'll cover her ward."

"Yes, Ma'am, I'm on it." With that, Lt. Martin quickly disappeared.

Kellie checked her roster one more time then folded it and put it in her top left shirt pocket. She quickly grabbed her bush hat, pulled it snuggly on her head, and hurried out of her quarters. As she double-timed for Ward 2, she saw the medivac chopper starting it decent to the helipad. There was one thing different today; the medivac chopper had high cover, as a Heavy Scout gunship hovered high above. It had been over two months since their medivacs had high cover. She was really glad to see it back in action.

By the time Kellie reached Ward 2, Veronica had already gone. She quickly went to the nurse's station and checked the log to see if anything needed to be done. But, as she suspected, Veronica had everything under control. Rather than sit at the nurse's station, she calmly started down the row of beds checking the charts as she went. Though she tried not to, seeing these wounded boys made her think of Kyle. Maybe he was hurt somewhere. She prayed that if that were true, there was someone there to help him.

While Kellie was making her rounds in Ward 2, Kathleen had just finished hers in Ward 3 and was starting on Ward 4. Ward 4 mostly contained seriously wounded that were being schedule to be sent down to the 95th. About halfway down the row of beds, was William. She tried to hurry by his bed to avoid conversation, but it was no use.

"Hey, Kat got a few seconds," William called out.

She turned back to face him and smiled, "Yeah, I got a few seconds. But understand I can't talk about what you want to talk about. And please don't call me Kat. I'm here in a professional standin'. It's Lt. O'Rourke, please."

His face took on a look of desperation and he sat up in his bed. "Come on, Kat, we're friends and Ronnie won't tell me anythin'. Can't you just help me out a little?"

"William, you've asked every nurse that has worked this ward the same question and you get the same answer. Why don't you give it up?"

"But, Kat, you guys can't let them ship me down to the 95th. You know that. You know they'll send me home. They've got to let me get back to my platoon. Somebody has got to tell me somethin'."

Her Irish anger began to bubble up, "Somebody will tell you somethin', but it'll be a doctor not a nurse! And you give us nurses too much credit, none of us knows anyway!"

He took a deep breath and let it out slowly. Then he smiled and said softly, "You know, I see why Jordy likes you so much. You sure are pretty when you're mad. With that red face matchin' that red hair."

There were some cat calls and some hand clapping in the ward.

She stood in the middle of the row with her feet spread apart and her hands on her hips. "Okay you guys, you can just knock it off. I've gotta finish my rounds here and I don't want to have to report any of you to the doctors."

"There's no need for reporting anybody," a weak voice said from the end of the row.

The voice was that of Major Stalls. He was suffering from a very serious chest wound. When he talked, it mostly came out as heavy wheezing. He was high on the list to be sent down to the 95th but the doctors were having a very hard time stopping the internal bleeding. Each time they thought they had him stable enough to put on a chopper for a trip to the 95th; the internal bleeding would start again. He had been in the OR three times and each time he came out he was weaker.

Kathleen slowly walked down the row of beds until she reached the end. At Major Stalls' bed, she procedurally looked at his chart. Then she walked around his bed and checked the IV that was dripping whole blood into him. After she had put on the display of doing necessary things, she bent over and whispered to him, "I'm not goin' to report anybody, Major." Then smiling she continued, "I just have to keep these characters in line or they'll take advantage of me."

He forced a smile and wheezed, "You know you look a lot like my daughter. She's got red hair too, and sparkling green eyes. I don't think her hair is as flaming red as yours, but it's a pretty red. And she's got a little pug nose kind of like yours. Of course, she's only seventeen years old, so she's got some cute freckles across her nose. I bet you did too once upon a time."

"Yes, I did," she replied, "once upon a time."

Then, in a wheezing whisper, he asked, "Lieutenant, would it be too much to ask you to take your cap off so I can see your red hair and green eyes clearly?"

Kathleen looked around the ward. There were several of the wounded watching her quietly. After hesitating for a few moments, she reached up and took off her cap. She held her cap in one hand and shook her hair out with the other. Her hair now only came down to just above her shoulders, as she had cut it for convenience, and because there was a loosely enforced guide line for hair length.

Major Stalls didn't say anything; he only looked at her with a gentle smile. There was complete silence in the ward. Then, he closed his eyes and turned his head into his pillow. Kathleen saw a tear rolling down his cheek. She reached over and patted his shoulder and said softly, "Now you get some rest, Major. The doctor'll be makin' his rounds in a little while and I want you to be at your best."

He didn't say anything; he only nodded his head slightly.

Kathleen turned and stepped back out into the aisle. Carrying her cap in her hand, she walked slowly back up the aisle towards the nurse's station. She knew all eyes were on her, but no one said a word; not even William. About halfway down the aisle, she stopped and began putting her cap back on and pushing her hair up underneath it. She stopped what she was doing when someone yelled, "Lieutenant, Ma'am, could you please leave your cap off just this once for us." Looking around, she saw the young soldier who spoke was a burn victim and was bandaged all across his torso. Kathleen paused momentarily, removed her cap and shook her hair out again. Then, slowly she continued down the aisle. When she reached the nurse's station, she pitched her cap on the small desk. She then went around behind the partition that divided the station from the door to the ward. There, no one in the ward could see her. She clinched her hands into fists and leaned her forehead again the partition wall. Putting her fists against the wall above her head she whispered a little prayer, "God, please let this end. Please, God, please let this end."

Veronica and 2nd Lt. Sandra 'Sandy' Sanders had just come out of the OR and were standing outside. Lt. Sanders was out of her scrubs and had cleaned up before going outside. However, Veronica was still in her scrubs. Her surgical mask still hung around her neck and there was blood on her scrubs. "Well, that one wasn't so bad," Lt. Sanders said as she pushed her hands above her head and stretched.

"No, that one wasn't so bad," Veronica agreed. "Say, Sandy, would do me a real favor?"

"Sure, Ronnie, if I can."

"Would you go over to Wards 3 and 4 and take over for Kat. Ask her to meet me here in front of the OR. I'll clear all this with Kel and make sure you get some extra break time."

"No problem, Ronnie, I'll head over there right now."

"Thanks, Sandy, we'll owe you one."

It was ten minutes before Veronica saw Kathleen walking towards her. In the meantime, Veronica had gotten out of her scrubs and cleaned up. Kathleen was walking slowly with her head down. As she approached, Veronica asked, "Hey what's wrong with you?"

Kathleen looked up, shrugged her shoulders, and said, "Oh, nothin' much. It's just been one of those days. You know you get 'em sometimes."

Veronica smiled and replied, "Yeah, but I think your day's about to get better."

"Really, well how's that?"

"Jordy's in the OR," Veronica blurred out.

Kathleen's eyes widened and her face turned pale. She immediately turned to go into the OR, but Veronica quickly stepped in front of her and stopped her.

"I'm goin' in," Kathleen said with determination and fear.

"Okay," Veronica said, "but first you need to hear me out. You can do that can't you?"

Kathleen paused and looked at Veronica more calmly and asked, "Okay, Ronnie, how bad is it?"

"He's goin' to be alright, Kat. That's the first thing you need to know. He's goin' to make a full recovery."

"I'll ask again, how bad is it?"

Veronica relaxed a bit and said, "He took a bullet through his left calf. The bullet went through clean and didn't hit any arteries. However, it did shatter some of his tibia. We've been in surgery cleaning up the wound and picking out pieces of bone fragments. He's goin' to have to have a metal rod put in to reconnect the tibia. We can't do that here. So we've stabilized him to move him to the 95th. They may be able to do it there but I'm bettin' they'll send him on to Tokyo. The important thing now is that the doctors tell me he's goin' to be fine. He won't even have a limp. But the healin' time will be around six months."

Kathleen took a few steps back from Veronica and asked suspiciously, "You're shootin' straight with me, right Ronnie? You're not feedin' any bullshit just to spare me are you?"

Veronica straightened up and looked hurt. "How can you ask me that? I'm your Tart Trio sister. I gotta tell you that cuts me. That cuts deep." Then stepping aside she said in anger, "Okay, I've told you everythin'. Go on in. He still on the OR gurney. He's probably still recoverin'. We had to put him completely under. Our joy juice just wouldn't cut it."

Kathleen started for the OR but when she got to the door she stopped and turned back to face Veronica, who was starting to walk away. "Wait,

Ronnie," she yelled. Her face was no longer pale but flushed red with embarrassment. "I'm sorry," she stammered, "I had no right to talk to you that way. Can you please forgive me?"

Veronica smiled at her, "I've already forgotten all about it. But as your XO I'm orderin' you to get him in a bed in Ward 4. We want him to go down to the 95th on the next chopper. Okay, Kat?"

"Okay, Ronnie." With that Kathleen turned and entered the OR.

Veronica watched her go inside, then turned and started for Ward 2. She walked fast as if on a mission. It only took a minute to get to Ward 2 where she found Kellie sitting at the nurse's station. "Here I am ready to take my shift back," she announced as she tapped her knuckles on the desk.

Kellie looked up and smiled, "It's almost twelve hundred hours now and your shift is over. It's time for your break. Anyway you should've been working in OR."

"It's okay; I'll take the next shift. As XO I've had to change a few things around and it'll work out better if I just hang around her for a while. And I was workin' in OR. We're all done there. Not much to talk about."

Kellie looked surprised, "Change a few things? What kind of things did you change?"

"I'd like to tell you all about it, but I don't think you have time. You see the CO sent me here. He wants to see you post haste."

Kellie's eyes narrowed, "What's going on, Ronnie?"

"I think you should hurry, Kel. The CO seemed especially excited about somethin'. I hope you're not in trouble again."

"Why should I be in trouble?"

"Kel, you really should go," Veronica said trying to rush her. "If you don't show up PDQ, you're goin' ta get me in trouble."

Kellie grabbed her bush hat and jammed in on her head. "Okay, I'm going, but this better be important and you'd better not've messed up my roster."

Veronica watched as Kellie hurried out the ward door. She sat down at the desk and took her cap off and hung it on the chair back. Leaning back in the chair, she allowed a huge smile to spread across her face. She looked down the row of beds at the wounded boys getting ready for their lunch. Ward 2 contained mostly men who were not seriously wounded and were waiting to be released back to their units. Then, unexpectedly, she yelled out to them, "You know guys, somedays you get to give good news to someone and that makes you feel wonderful, but, then somedays you get to give good news to two someones and that makes you feel even more wonderful."

The men in the ward just looked back at her and smiled.

As Kellie hurried across the compound, she couldn't help but wonder what this was all about. She knew that Veronica wasn't telling her the whole story. It was easy to tell that Veronica knew something that she wasn't telling. At any rate, she wondered if this meeting was with her CO or with her dad. When she entered the operations tent, Jimmy was at his little desk fiddling with the squawk box. "Hey, Jimmy, how is he today? You got any idea what this is all about?"

At first Jimmy said nothing but only pointed at his sleeve. Then he said in a very uppity tone, "You'll note, Captain, that I now have another stripe on my sleeve. Simply calling me 'Jimmy' will no longer suffice. I think to follow proper protocol you should hence forth address me as Sergeant Hadley."

"That's a very nice speech, Sergeant Hadley," Kellie said with authority. "But you didn't answer my question. Do you know what this is all about?"

"No Ma'am, the Coronal didn't inform me of the subject of your meeting. However, I've been instructed to tell you to enter as soon as you arrive. You've arrived, so you may enter."

Kellie rolled her eyes as she walked to the CO's office door. "Thank you, Sergeant Hadley," she said mockingly over her shoulder. She gently knocked on the door and waited for the reply.

"Enter," was the simple reply.

Kellie pushed the door open and stepped inside. She immediately froze in her tracks. Her father was sitting at his desk with a large smile on his face. Standing next to the desk and leaning on a crutch under his right arm, was Kyle.

"Look who came in on that last medivac chopper," her father said pointing at Kyle.

Finally Kellie managed to yell, "Kyle!"

"Yeah, it's me," he replied with a grin, "but I expected a little more reaction from the woman I intend to marry."

Kellie ran to him and threw her arms around his neck. She nearly knocked him off his crutch. He staggered but managed to stay upright. They locked in a long, hard, and passionate kiss. When their lips separated, Kellie put her chin on Kyle's shoulder and continued to hold him tight. As she held Kyle, she was able to look over Kyle's shoulder and back at her father who was now standing behind his desk watching them happily. Suddenly, her father leaned over the desk and intently looked at Kellie's face, as it rested on Kyle's shoulder. "Kel, are those tears in those bright blue eyes of your?" He asked carefully.

Kellie released Kyle and pushed back a short distance and said softly, "It's nice to see you, Captain Collie."

"Now that's the kind of reaction I was hopin' for," he said with that crooked smile of his.

Kellie stood before her father and Kyle crying. Tears rolled freely down her cheeks, and her eyes were a very bright blue. Her father sat back down in his chair and asked gently, "Is this the time to cry, Kel? You've always told me that there would be time enough to cry later. Is this later? Is this the time to cry?"

She slowly lifted her right hand up and gave him the thumbs up sign. "Now is the time, Dad, now is the time." Then with a soft chuckle, she said, "And you know, it's not as bad as I thought it would be. I guess you've been right all along."

Kyle reached his hand out to her and she took it. He pulled her to him and lifted her chin so he looked down into her eyes. He bent down and kissed her again, but this time softly. Then, struggling with his crutch, he turned to face her father. Holding Kellie in one arm, he stood up as straight as he could. "Coronal Anderson, Sir," he said, "down in Texas we believe in doin' things the honorable way. So, I'm formally askin' you for the hand of your daughter in Holy Matrimony."

Coronal Anderson once again got to his feet. He looked seriously at Kellie and asked, "And what say you, Kel?"

Kellie looked at her father with moisture still sparkling in her eyes. She moved even closer into Kyle's arm. "I say, yes, Dad. Your daughter says yes."

Coronal Anderson nodded his head and addressed Kyle. "I give you my consent to marry my daughter." He paused for a moment and looked hard into Kyle's eyes and then continued, "But you must know this, if you hurt her in any way you'll answer to me. And that answer can be very harsh. Are we clear on that, Captain Collie?"

"Yes, Sir, we are clear. And, Sir, I wouldn't have it any other way. In addition, I swear to you on my honor that Kellie will finish medical school. No matter how long it takes or how hard we have to work, you'll be able to see that MD behind her name."

Coronal Anderson nodded again, put his hands behind his back, and cleared his throat. He quickly changed his mood to be much more military. "Okay, now that we've settled all of that, we need to attend to that ankle, Captain Collie. I believe we did the preliminary setting in the OR, but we need to get a temporary cast on it." He paused, looked at Kellie and asked, "Can you take care of that, Captain Anderson?"

Kellie moved from Kyle's arm and answered, "Yes, Sir, I'll see to it personally."

"Okay then, let's get moving. Captain Anderson you help Captain Collie to the OR. Be sure the cast is a temporary one. We want the doctors at the 95th to check the setting and do any adjustments that may be required. They can apply the permanent cast. And assign him to Ward 4 so we get him out of here as quick as we can. Have you got all that, Captain Anderson?"

"Roger to all of that, Sir. And I'm on it."

CHAPTER FORTY-SIX

A General Comes to the Ten-Six-Six

Kellie had given Kathleen an extra-long break so she could spend some time with Jordan in Ward 4. When Jordan had recovered enough that he was lucid, Kathleen found a wooden folding chair and set it down next to Jordan's bed. She took his hand and quietly asked, "How're doin', Marine?"

"Well, my leg hurts like hell," he answered, "but I feel better just lookin' at you."

"Your leg is goin' to hurt for a while. They had to dig a lot of bone chips outa there and they had to stabilize your shinbone enough so they could keep it from floating around until they can get a metal rod in there."

"Am I headed to the 95th?" He asked cautiously.

"Yep," she replied smiling, "and then probably on to Japan and then home."

"Home," he whispered, "sounds kind of funny when I say it. I sure wish you were comin' with me."

She squeezed his hand tightly. "I will if you want me to, Jordy," she stammered. "I'll resign my commission and they'll send me home."

Jordan looked at her in surprise. "You don't mean that."

"I do mean it. You just say you want me to be your wife and I'll do it."

Jordan pulled his hand away from her. He struggled to propped himself up on his elbows.

Kathleen shot to her feet. "Stop, Jordy," she almost shouted, "you need to lie down and stay still."

He ignored her and said with passion, "I love you, Kat. And one day in the near future you're goin' to be my wife. But I've known from our first time together on China Beach that you're a kind, lovable, honorable, and loyal person. And I know very well what quittin' your responsibility here would do to you. Do you think that I'd ask you to violate all the things you believe in; all the things that make you the wonderful person you are? I won't do that. When we're husband and wife, I don't want anythin' hangin' over us. And if you quit now it's goin' to follow you the rest of your life. I know you, Kat. Sometime down the road, you're goin' to start askin' yourself if you did the right thing. It'll always haunt you and in turn it'll haunt me too. I *WILL NOT* do that to us, Kat. I hope you understand what I'm sayin'. Please tell me you do?"

Kathleen slowly sat back down in her chair. Her love for him was almost ready to explode out of her. "Jordy please lay back down," she whispered softly.

This time he did as he was asked. He straightened his arms and he flopped back down on his back. She took his hand into both of hers and she held it for several minutes without speaking. Then, she patted his hand and looked deeply into his eyes. "Yes," she said smiling, "I under-stand. And you're right. So, I'll finish my tour over here. But when it's done I'm comin' for you. You got that?"

"I got it," he laughed softly, "but you won't have to come for me. All you'll have to do is come home to Marfa. I should be all healed by then, and your mom and I'll be waitin' for you."

Kathleen straightened up and said in surprise, "My mom!"

"Yep, I'm goin' to have her moved down to Marfa lock, stock, and barrel."

Kathleen laughed, "You know my mom might have somethin' to say about that."

"Gettin' her to agree isn't my job; that's your job. I just do the haulin'."

Jordan and Kathleen were laughing together when Kathleen felt a hand on her shoulder. It was Veronica. "Okay, Kat, that's all for now. He needs rest and anyway Kellie wants to see you."

Kathleen got to her feet with a large smile on her face. "Roger that, Ronnie," she said, "I'm on it."

Kathleen and an army medic stood near the helipad impatiently waiting for Major Smith. Major Smith was the doctor who was to bring her the list of six wounded that were to be released and sent down to the 95th. Kellie had put Kathleen in charge of getting the wounded that were on the list from Ward 4 to the medivac chopper, which was due at any moment. The chopper pilot was going to be very upset if he arrived and they were no wounded to pick up. She was about to start for the operations tent to find out what was wrong, when she saw Major Smith approaching from the OR.

When he reached her, he handed her a clipboard and said apologetically, "Sorry I'm late. We had to make a last minute change."

Kathleen glanced at the list, as Major Smith turned to go back to the OR. "Wait, Doctor," she yelled after him.

He stopped and looked over his shoulder without turning around, "Yeah, what?" He yelled back.

She walked towards him slowly still studying the list. "Why isn't Major Stalls on the list? She asked puzzled. "I thought we had him stable enough to travel."

Major Smith slowly turned back to face her. He jammed his hands down into the pockets of his white lab jacket. "We thought so too," he said sadly. "But he died on us about an hour ago. That last patch up job we did was just too much for him. Why, was there something personal?"

Kathleen looked up at the doctor and let out a long breath. "No, I just reminded him of his daughter. That's all. I just reminded him of his daughter."

Major Smith nodded and said, "It's rough sometimes." With that, he turned and again headed for the OR.

"Yeah," Kathleen whispered to herself, "sometimes it can be rough."

After he was gone, Kathleen checked the sky for the chopper but she didn't see or hear anything. Looking down at the list again, she saw that Jordan and Kyle were both on the list but William wasn't. It was strange that all three of The Tart Trio's guys were in the same ward at the same time. This was the first time since New Year's that they had all been in the same place. She turned and handed the clipboard to the medic and ordered, "Here, go to Ward 4 and have the ward nurse help you get these guys on stretchers and then get some help to carry them out here to the helipad. And you better hurry I'm expectin' that chopper anytime."

The medic didn't say anything; he just took the clipboard and hurried off.

Kathleen was alone now so she scanned the sky again for the chopper. This time she heard the sound of rotor blades beating against the air and finally the chopper came into view. Kathleen quickly looked around for the wounded but she didn't see them yet. The chopper brought its nose up and began to settle onto the helipad. To Kathleen's dismay there was still no sign of the would-be passengers. Then, to Kathleen's surprise, the pilot shut down the engine and rotors slowly came to a stop. That wasn't normal. She started walking towards the chopper when people started climbing out of the waist door. There were four of them. Two of them were women in the uniform of the Army Nurse Corps. They were both wearing 2nd lieutenant's bars on their shoulders. After them, came an army officer in jungle fatigues and he was wearing the gold oak leafs of a major on his shoulder. And last but certainly not least was another army officer but this one had a star on his shoulder.

"Christ Almighty," Kathleen whispered under her breath, "it's a fuckin' general."

While the major and the general were talking to each other, the two nurses walked up to Kathleen, who had not moved. They each snapped off a smart salute. It was a few seconds before Kathleen got her wits about her and returned their salute. "Who're you guys?" She stammered.

"I'm 2nd Lieutenant Baylen Bankston," the taller of the two said, "and this is 2nd Lieutenant Karen Whitewater."

"What're you doin' here?"

The two nurses looked surprised. "We're here as replacements for the two nurses that rotated out," it was the taller one speaking again.

"Oh, yeah, sure," Kathleen was still stammering. "It's just that I wasn't expectin' anyone on that chopper. And who're those two guys?"

Lieutenant Bankston smiled a wicked smile and said, "Maybe you should go over and ask 'em. But before you do that could you point us to the operations area?"

"Sure it's right over there," Kathleen responded as she pointed toward the operations tent, "you can't miss it. It has a sign above the entrance."

"Thanks," was the simple reply. Then, the two nurses picked up their bags and walk off towards the operations tent.

No sooner had the two nurses walked away, when the two officers came walking over. As they approached, Kathleen snapped to attention and gave them a sharp salute. "As you were, Lieutenant," the General said smiling. "I guess you're a bit surprise, uh, Lieutenant?"

"To say the least, Sir," Kathleen spat out.

"I'm Brigadier General Nathan Blackwell. This is my aid, Major Clarkson. We had to get here today and the day is almost over so I commandeered this medivac. I hope I haven't screwed with anyone's plans. Have I?"

"To be truthful, Sir, we have six wounded scheduled to go down to the 95th on this medivac."

"That's okay; you can still use this chopper. I'll just call for another one." Then turning to the Major he said, "While I'm doing my thing, see if you can stir up another chopper for us." Then, turning back to Kathleen he said, "Can you show us where we might find the Commanding Officer."

"Yes, Sir, he'll be in his office at the operations tent if he's not in the OR."

As they were speaking, the wounded began to arrive. There were three stretcher cases and three walking wounded. Jordan was a stretcher case and Kyle, on his crutch and wearing a cast, was one of the walking wounded.

"It looks like you're about to get busy, Lieutenant," the General smiled. "So if you'll just point us to the operations tent we'll be on our way."

Kathleen pointed in the direction of the operations tent and said, "Yes, Sir, it's right over there. You can't miss it. It has a sign over the entrance."

"Thank you, Lieutenant; I'll have Major Clarkson inform the pilot of the change in plans so you can begin loading your wounded."

"Thank you, Sir."

The General whispered something into the ear of Major Clarkson and then walked off towards the operations tent. Major Clarkson went back to the chopper and had a brief conversation with the pilot and then followed the General to the operations tent. The pilot fired up the chopper engine and the rotors began their rotation.

Veronica was walking along with Kyle when they arrived at the chopper. "Are you shittin' me, is that a general?" She asked.

Kathleen stood back away from the chopper and took her field cap off. "No Shit it is. And I think our CO is in for a big surprise."

Once all the wounded were on board and just before they closed the waist door, Kathleen smiled at Jordan and gave him a little salute.

As the door was closing, Jordan yelled, "See you in Marfa."

Then the door was closed and the chopper was dusting off.

Brigadier General Nathan 'Blackie' Blackwell was sent from I Corps to the ten-six-six for two reasons; to evaluate moral and to give out some promotions and metals. The High Command at I Corps had already made the decision to abandon Hamburger Hill on June 5th after occupying it for barely two weeks. They were trying to prepare for the backlash that would surely come after all the blood the hill had cost. The mission that General Blackwell was on didn't set well with him. He was a soldier's general and didn't like the idea of leaving Hamburger Hill after such a sacrifice. But he was a soldier in the U.S. Army and he would follow his orders.

Along with Coronal Anderson and 1st Lt. Veronica Mann as escorts, General Blackwell and Major Clarkson slowly worked their way through each ward talking to the men and giving out some promotions and a lot of Purple Hearts. He was now in Ward 4, the last ward. Ward 4 was mostly empty now as most of the men had been sent down to the 95th or been moved to other wards to await release to their units.

As General Blackwell approached the bed of 1st Lt. William Barnett, he paused and took some paperwork that was handed to him by Major Clarkson. William climbed out his bed and stood to attention as the General reached his bed. "Lieutenant, it wasn't necessary for you to stand up," General Blackwell said politely.

"That's okay, Sir, I've been ready to report back to my unit for some time now."

The General glanced down at the paper he was holding and then looked up at William and said, "Yes, I can see by this doctor's report that you've been very troublesome in that area."

"I'm sorry, Sir, I don't mean to be troublesome."

"I'm sure you don't," the General chuckled. "But that's neither here nor there; I have four things for you, Lieutenant. However, before we start please stand at ease."

William relaxed and stood at ease. Veronica and Coronal Anderson moved in closer to listen and watch.

"First, I have here the Purple Heart for your wounds incurred on Hill 937." The General reached over and pinned the Purple Heart to William's pajamas just over his heart. "Second, I have these for you." He handed William a small square box, which William took and opened. "Those are your railroad tracks. You're now Captain Barnett." William started to speak but the General held up his hand and stopped him. "You can speak when I'm finished," he said quickly. "Third, you'll be happy to know that you can report back to your unit in a few days. The doctors have released you but they want a few more days of healing before you go. Your unit, I believe, is the 3rd Battalion, 187th Regiment of the one-oh-first. They're back at Camp Eagle and preparing to be shipped back to the States. You'll be taking over Charlie Company for that preparation. And you'll return to the States with your battalion."

William's eyes were wide with disbelief but he remained silent until the General finished with the fourth item. "And last but certainly not the least I have this for you." General Blackwell leaned over and pinned another metal on William's chest right next to the Purple Heart. Then he stood back and saluted. William didn't know what was happening but he came to attention and returned the General's salute. "What I've just given you, Captain Barnett is the Distinguish Service Cross. It's the second highest award for valor that our country can give. It normally takes months and sometimes years to get this metal processed. But yours was accomplished in less than two weeks. The men in your platoon spoke very highly of you. And it's my honor to pin it on your chest." There was a long pause of absolute silence in the ward. General Blackwell smiled and said, "Now, Captain, you may speak".

"Sir," William started, "I don't know what to say. This is a great honor, but the truth is, Sir, I don't deserve this honor. You see, Sir, I started up that hill with forty-three men and only eight of them were able to walk back down. That's thirty-five men killed or wounded. I'm gettin' this honor because of the courage of the men in my platoon. I honestly don't feel worthy of it. Do you understand what I'm tryin' to say, Sir?"

General Blackwell looked at William with sympathy in his eyes. "Maybe I can answer your question with a short story." He paused and folded his arms across this chest and then continued, "Back in 1952 I was a young captain in charge of a company in Korea. It was a company in the 23rd Regiment of the 2nd Infantry Division. Much like your company, Captain, we were given the job of taking a well defended hill. So, along with several other companies, we assaulted that hill. It took several assaults and lots of support from our air power and artillery, but we finally took the hill. It was a long, hard, and bloody battle. I had assaulted that hill with a re-enforced company of 162 men. When it was finally over, only sixteen of us walked back down that hill. Like your hill, Captain, my hill was given a name; they called it Heartbreak Ridge. You can find it in the history books. Just like you, I was wounded, and just like you, I was given a metal. Mine was the Silver Star. And just like you, I felt unworthy to wear that metal. But in time I came to realize that I just did what had to be done, as the men in my company had. Today, I wear that Silver Star with a lot of pride and honor; not just for me but for the men who were with me in that company on Heartbreak Ridge. And you, Captain, will wear that Distinguish Service Cross with pride and honor for yourself and for the men in that platoon you lead up Hamburger Hill. And that's my story. Now you get back to your unit and do your job." He then turned to Major Clarkson and asked sharply, "Did you procure us a chopper, Major?"

"Yes, Sir, and as a matter of fact, it's already here."

"Good, then let's get going and let these people continue with their jobs." With that, the General turned and shook hands with Coronal

Anderson and Veronica thanking them for their help. Waving, he started hurrying down the aisle.

"Sir," a loud shout came from behind him.

He stopped and looked back to see William standing in the aisle at attention. "I will wear this metal with pride and honor for the men who went up that hill with me. And thank you, Sir, for helpin' me understand."

General Blackwell only smiled and gave William a quick little salute. Then he and Major Clarkson hurried out of the ward.

Veronica walked over and took William's hand. She gave it a tight squeeze and said softly, "You know, it makes you feel good to know that there are generals out there who actually do give a shit."

While General Blackwell was going through the wards, Kellie was in the CO's office getting her new nurses signed in. She was sitting at the CO's desk going over their orders and their profiles. The two nurses sat in chairs across from the desk. Kellie smiled and said, "Well, ladies, it looks like you're both qualified to…"

Before Kellie could finish her sentence Lt. Bankston shot to her feet and interrupted her, "Ma'am, before we go any farther into this, I think it only fair to warn you that I was ordered to this assignment. My first choice was the 91st EVAC Hospital at Chu Lai. I…"

Now, before she could finish her sentence Kellie interrupted her harshly, "You interrupted me Lieutenant and you *WARNED* me. Okay, so we'll do this the hard way."

Kellie whole demeanor quickly changed. She no longer took the friendly approach but now it was strictly military. "Stand to attention, Lieutenants," she ordered briskly. Both new lieutenants snapped to attention dropping their caps in the process. She squared herself behind the desk and looked at them intently. "Now, we'll start over. As I was about to say, it appears you're both very qualified for this job. Now, I'm going to give you some orders. But first, I'll ask you if you're capable of sitting back down and listening to what I have to say without interruption?"

"Yes, Ma'am," it was Lt. Whitewater speaking. "And I would like to beg the Captain's pardon."

"And you, Lt. Bankston?" Kellie asked pointedly.

"Yes, Ma'am, I was out of line. It won't happen again."

"Fine, then please pick up your caps and return to your seats."

They did as they were ordered.

"I'm going to make this quick because the CO will be back here in a few minutes. I'm going to send you over to the club where you'll meet my XO, Lt. Mann. She'll get you settled in and brief you on our situation here." Then, slapping her hands together, she continued "I need to finish this up. After leaving here I want you to go to the Officer's Club and wind down. Have a drink and relax and collect your thoughts. The Officer's Club is really just the club as it's the only club we have and enlisted as well as officers go there. Then, I want you to go to the nurse's quarters and get a good night's sleep; if you can. Then report to me at the head nurses quarters at oh-six-hundred hours in the morning and we'll finish up. Now, have you got all that?"

They both got back on her feet at attention and Lt. Whitewater said with a deep sense of urgency, "Yes, Ma'am, I understand and I would like the Captain to know that I'm a full blooded Choctaw from Oklahoma. My brother, Jamie Whitewater, is fightin' over here with the 4th Infantry Division. I'll do anythin' you ask of me. I'll bust my ass for you, Captain."

Kelly smiled at her and said, "Relax, Lieutenant. That goes for you too Lt. Bankston. We're all going to get along fine. You'll find that we all have nick names around here. For instance, I'm Kel and my XO is Ronnie. We have a Max and a Marty and a Sandy and others. If you have no objections, Lt. Whitewater, I think we'll call you Choctaw. And Lt. Bankston, since your first name is Baylen, I think we'll call you Bay. Now, you're dismissed." She stood up straight and gave them a firm salute. They returned her salute just as firmly and then turned shapely and walked out the door.

After they were gone, Kellie smiled to herself. She looked up and pointed her finger into the air and whispered quietly, "Thank you, Coronal Vickers, where ever you are."

CHAPTER FORTY-SEVEN

The Tart Trio Goes Home

It was now mid-afternoon on March 19th 1970 and Kathleen sat at a table in the Officer's Club at the 95th. She sipped on a drink of Jamison Irish whiskey while she waited for her two friends to join her. Kellie and Veronica were due in from the ten-six-six at fourteen hundred hours. It was now fifteen hundred hours and Kathleen was becoming concerned. Over the last seven months since she reported back from her TDY assignment to the ten-six-six, things had gotten worse in South Vietnam. More and more American troops were being pulled out of Vietnam as the so call 'Vietnamization' of the war proceeded. It was obvious to anyone that really looked at the situation that things were deteriorating. The Vietnamese simple didn't have the will or the military experience to fight. As a result, getting into and out of Da Nang wasn't as easy as it used to be. In fact, many times it could be downright dangerous.

As the time inched on towards fifteen-thirty hours, Kathleen's tensions grew. She decided to go over to Operations and see what she could find out. She had just started for the door when her two friends entered. They all saw each other at the same time and they rushed together immediately. Hugs, kisses, and slaps on the back when on for several seconds before Kathleen finally broke away and asked, "Where've you guys been? I was startin' to really worry. Was there somethin' wrong with the flight?"

"No, the flight was okay," Kellie said, "it's just we had a hard time getting a couple of spots in the Temporary Officer's Quarters. It looks like our flight tomorrow is going to be full. There're lots of people leaving."

"Yeah, I know. Come on over here I got a table," Kathleen said pointing to the table. "I'll get us some glasses and a bottle."

"You mean a whole bottle?" Veronica asked.

"Sure, why not. We're short timers."

Kathleen went to the bar and signaled the bartender, "Hey," she said, "give me that bottle of Jamison and three glasses of ice."

"You can't have the whole bottle," the bartender laughed. "I can only sale it to you a shot at a time."

Kathleen gave him a vicious look and growled, "Give me that fuckin' bottle. My two friends over there and me are short timers. We ship out tomorrow. You can report me if you want. Whata you think they're goin' to do; keep me here?"

The bartender gave a small laugh and pushed the bottle to her. "Hang on while I get you the glasses and ice." Soon he was back with the glasses and ice. "You go on to the table. I'll bring the glasses and ice."

"Thanks," she said smiling and winked at him. She dug into her fatigue pocket and pulled out some money to pay and placed it on the bar.

He pushed her money back to her. "Keep it, short timer," he said. "I only got thirty-one days left myself. Nobody's going to miss that Irish shit anyway."

She laughed and rejoined her friends at the table. As promised the bartender brought over the glasses and ice. "Enjoy," he said.

Once they all had a drink, they just sat there staring into them. Except for the other noise in the bar, there was only silence at their table. Finally, Veronica spoke up, "Well, doesn't anybody have anythin' to say. I mean after two years in this place doesn't anyone have a comment."

Still no one spoke, so Veronica continued speaking slowly, "I just hope we didn't waste two years. I hope we did some good and I hope to God I can sleep at night when I get home. I mean after all the things I've seen."

Kellie reached over and grabbed Veronica's chin. She turned Veronica's head so that Veronica looked into her eyes. "Don't you dare talk like that," she scolded. "You're damn right we did some good and they weren't wasted years. Lots of those guys we treated made it back. And we learned a lot about our work and about people. I wouldn't trade the look on those guys' faces when we helped them, or watched over them in the wards, for anything. So, don't you dare let me hear you talk like that, Ronnie, because you are one of the best of the best! And if you have any trouble sleeping, you just call me. I'll be there for you."

"And we can't forget," Kathleen added with a smile and a tilt of her glass. "We got three pretty good guys outa the deal."

Veronica sighed heavily and slapped herself on the forehead. "Sorry, gang, I guess I just got the short timer's blues."

"And speakin' of guys," Kathleen continued, "how's everybody doin' and what're your plans? I don't ever want to lose contact with you two. I know we all must have accumulated some substantial leave time over two tours. How're we goin' to use it?"

"Those're good questions, Kat," Kellie replied. "Since we've been mostly out of touch these last three months, why don't we go around the table and each of us gives some answers? And I say we start with the one with the short timer blues."

"Okay, I'll start," Veronica smiled taking a sip of her whiskey. "I don't have as much leave time as you two because I spent a lot of time up at Eagle Beach with Bill. I think I've got about thirty-five days left. So, with that, first, I'm goin' home to Sweetwater and visit my parents and friends. Then, I want to spend some time at Jodie's grave tellin' her about all I've done. And I want to see Mr. Conners and tell him the same thing and I want to tell him about you two and the new Tart Trio. He'll get a real kick out that. I figure to spend about two weeks in Sweetwater, and then I'm goin' to Coalville and meet Bill at his farm."

Kellie held up her hand and stopped her. "So it's Bill now; not William?"

"Oh, yeah," Veronica laughed, "we got that straight while he was still at the ten-six-six. I told him if his dad was Billy and that was good enough for the Metal of Honor, then Bill should be good enough for the Distinguished Service Cross."

They all had a good laugh and then Kellie said, "Okay, go on, go on."

Veronica took another sip of whiskey and continued, "Well, I'll meet Bill's mother and we'll all sit down and plan our future. When my leave is up, I have to report to Fort Sam Houston. But my enlistment is up in August and I need to decide if I'm goin' to say in, or resign my commission, or go to the reserves. Plus, Bill is a West Point man so he's still got about five years of commitment." She stopped and smiled a knowing smile at them and then said, "But the bottom line is we're goin' to get married sometime over the next two years and we have to see how we're goin' to get it into the mix. But I promise we will. The rest of it is to be continued."

Again there was silence at the table as the others waited to make sure Veronica was finished. After what seemed a long time, Kellie finally said, "That all sounds wonderful, Ronnie, I hope it all works out for you because you deserve it."

"Enough of that," Kathleen chimed in. "It's your turn now Kel. Let's hear it."

Kellie clasped her hands together, took a deep breath, and said, "Okay, here goes. I've got thirty-nine days of leave coming. I'm going to go home to St. Paul and visit Dad. You all know he rotated out in February. He's back home trying to decide rather to renew is practice, or retire. He staying in the reserves and they gave him his bird, so he's a full coronal now. I'll spend time talking a lot of things over with him before I head down to Texas to meet Kyle's parents. Kyle's back at Camp Walters.

They gave him his gold oak leaf so he's a major now. He's in charge of an assault helicopter training battalion. Kyle will be there at his parent's place when I get there and he wants to get married right away and I feel the same way, but, like Ronnie, my enlistment is up in August and I've got the same decision to make as she does. And Kyle is still wrestling with staying in the army. After being over here, he's not sure. Then, if you tie all that in with me returning to medical school, there's a lot on the table. Over these last seven months, Kyle and I have been working on getting me accepted into medical school at Southern Methodist University in Dallas. And I've been accepted, but it's a lot of money, so we have to work that out also. But Kyle promised my dad, and he's not going to back off that promise. After my leave is up, I've been ordered to Fort Hood, Texas. That's not far from Kyle's home. Again, like Ronnie, I guess a lot of things are to be continued."

Veronica held her hand up to be recognized but she didn't wait for recognition she asked simply, "You mean you've been accepted into medical school at SMU?"

Kellie nodded yes.

"Holy shit, Kel, that's great."

"Yes, it's great," Kellie agreed, "but SMU is a parochial school and it's damn expensive. I tried to get Kyle to let me go to a state school but he wouldn't hear of it. His promise to my dad means a lot to him."

"Anyway," Kellie said ending her turn, "there's a lot to be continued."

After another short silence, Veronica pointed to Kathleen, "Okay, Kat, it's your turn. Let's hear it."

Kathleen shrugged her shoulders and said, "I feel kind of bad because my situation isn't as nearly complex as yours. I've got thirty-four days of leave coming and after it's used up I'm to report to Fort Sam Houston; just like you, Ronnie. But first let me update you on Jordy. His leg is completely healed and he doesn't even have a limp, and he didn't reenlist in the marines. At this very moment, he's back home in Marfa waitin' for me. He's purchased a condo in Dallas for us to use while he's in school at

SMU. His goal is a law degree. I'll commute between Dallas and Marfa while he's in school. Once he's out of school, he intends to setup his law practice in Marfa. As for me, I'll be goin' straight to Marfa to burn up my leave time. Jordy has already moved my mom to our new home in Marfa. Then, I'll report to Fort Sam Houston for the remainder of my enlistment, which will end in August; just like you two. Jordy and I talked about it and I've opted to go into the reserves."

She paused and looked at her friends, "There's a lot more but I thought I give you a chance to ask questions. Are there any questions so far?"

Veronica and Kellie looked at each other and smiled. "No, I guess not," Kellie replied.

Kathleen nodded and continued, "Good, so now on to the second part. Jordy and I plan to be married in our home in Marfa. We hope this will happen sometime in November of this year. Now, you all know I'm a great planner. Remember the great New Year's Eve party I put together. Now, while we're on that long flight back to the good ole USA, we, the three of us, are goin' to plan my weddin'. The key to this plannin' will be the fact that you two will have to attend as my bridesmaids and that Kyle and Bill will have to attend as best men. There are no options here; all of you have to attend. So, that means you've got to get yourselves and your guys to Marfa on the date required. If that means gettin' everyone some leave, then you need to get to work on it as soon as you get back. Now, is all of that clear?"

Veronica and Kellie simple sat there staring at her. Kellie took a big gulp of her whisky and Veronica drained her glass. Then, as Veronica poured herself another drink, she asked shyly, "Do you think we can pull all of that off? I mean there's goin' to be a lot of shit happenin' in our lives about that time."

Kathleen grinned broadly and said, "As I said, there's no option. You *WILL* be there and you *WILL* have Kyle and Bill in tow. How you manage things, I leave to you."

"Well, thank you, Kat," Kellie said mockingly. "I guess if there's no option, we don't have much choice do we?"

"Now you're gettin' the picture," Kathleen laughed.

"Is there anythin' else?" Veronica asked.

"Now that you mention it," Kathleen replied, "there is. But first, Ronnie, why don't you fill mine and Kellie's glasses before I continue. Do we need any more ice?"

"I'm on it," Veronica said as got up went to the bar. She returned shortly with a small bucket of ice. "Who needs ice?" She asked. Everyone nodded yes, so she unceremoniously scooped ice into their glasses using her hand. When she was finished, she looked around and said, "Well, I guess we're ready, Kat. I hope this next part is a little easier on us."

"I hope it is, Ronnie, I really hope it is." Kathleen reached into her back pocket and pulled out what looked like a small wallet. She opened it and took out two slips of paper. She handed one to Veronica and the other to Kellie. Then she sat back and waited.

It took several seconds before her friends realized what was before their eyes. When they did, they both shot to their feet. "What's this all about, Kat?" Kellie asked seriously. "Is this some kind of joke?"

"It's no joke," was the simple reply.

"But, Kat, this is a check for three hundred thousand dollars! It's made out to Veronica and William Barnett. This can't be real."

"Yes, it is, Ronnie, it's real, and, Kellie, yours is made out to Kellie and Kyle Collie. You'll notice that both checks have an expiration date of January 1, 1972. You can cash them any time after you're married up until January 1, 1972. After that, the checks are no good."

"But, Kat, I can't accept this," Kellie breathed, as she put the check down on the table and pushed it towards Kathleen. "I just can't. And even if I could, Kyle wouldn't."

"I have to ditto that," Veronica echoed and she also put her check down on the table and pushed it towards Kathleen. "Bill would never buy into it."

"Please sit back down," Kathleen said in a dead serious tone, "and I'll tell why you can and must accept them."

Veronica and Kellie both slowly sat back down. Kellie started to speak but Kathleen held up her hand and cut her off. "Please listen to what I've got to say. Can you both do that?"

They nodded yes.

"Okay, here it is in a nutshell," Kathleen began. "Over these last seven months, we've all kind of kept to ourselves. I don't think I talked with you two more than a couple of times. I guess we all were tryin' to work out what we're goin' to do and at the same time do our jobs to the best of our ability. I understand all that. But now we're back together and we've got to remember how we all got started in this; I mean bein' nurses and comin' to Vietnam, as well as bein' the best of friends. We all had different reasons for bein' here. And the same thing goes for our guys. They all had different reasons for bein' here. We've been blessed because we all came out of it alive."

Kathleen stopped and took a sip of her whiskey. She looked at the other two women but she couldn't read their expressions. It seemed she wasn't making a lot of progress so she decided to get straight to the point. She set her drink down, let out a long breath and then continued, "When we had that New Year's Eve party and I found out that Jordy was rich, at that time he told me the last time he checked he was worth around six million dollars. Well that's changed a bit. When he got back home he found out he's worth around ten million dollars now."

Veronica and Kellie looked at each other wide-eyed. "Ten million dollars," Kellie whispered. "Did you say ten *MILLION* dollars?"

"That's what I said and it's still growin'. He's even been offered over a hundred million if he'll sell all his oil holdings and natural gas lease rights."

"What's he goin' to do?" Veronica asked.

"We're workin' on that right now," Kathleen said with a trace of frustration, "but that's not the issue here. The issue here is those checks. I don't know if you've thought about it, but once we're all married to our guys, we're goin' to all be related in some tangled fashion. Jordy and I talked for nearly an hour on the overseas phone line at the exchange. It cost me over two hundred dollars. But Jordy made it clear what he wanted to do. He says he has more money than he'll ever spend and he wants to share some of it with the guys that are part of his family and brothers of war who fought by his side, risked their lives for each other, and would've died for each other if need be. But he doesn't want to just give it to them. He wants us to be part of it. That's why the checks are made out to married couples rather than individually. You two have got to understand how much this means to Jordy. He sees us all as friends for life. If you don't accept your check, it's goin' to crush Jordy and, in turn, me. You can consider it a weddin' gift or anythin' else you might want to call it." She paused briefly and lowered her head. Tears formed in her eyes and she said in a soft whisper, "Please don't let me down, please don't."

Kellie could stand it no longer; she got up from her chair and hurried around to Kathleen, who remained sitting. She took Kathleen's head her hands and pulled it to her and held it tightly to her waist. "Stop you're crying, Kat," she said haltingly. "I'm not going to let you down." Then she laughed, "Even if it means I have to accept three hundred thousand dollars." Kellie reached down and picked up her check and smiled sheepishly, "now all I have to do is get this by Kyle."

"I bet you can," Veronica said with a laugh. "I bet you can sell it to Kyle just like I'm goin' to sell it to Bill." As she spoke, she reached down and picked up her check.

Kathleen pulled away from Kellie and stood up. She dried the tears from her eyes. Looking at Veronica she laughed, "You know, Ronnie, I firmly believe that you put the tart in The Tart Trio."

"I think you may be right, Kat," Veronica said in a serious tone. "But for now, I think we should finish off this bottle of Jamison. We've got to be at the plane tomorrow mornin' at oh-seven hundred. Then the long ride home and we can talk our heads off just like we did when we came here oh those many months ago."

Kellie was about to propose a toast, when a lieutenant coronal dressed in an Air Force uniform approached their table. All three nurses started to their feet, but the Coronal signal them to remain sitting. "As you were," he said with a tired smile. "If I could, I'd like to join you for a few minutes. I'm Lt. Coronal Chris Nolan and I have some things to give you along with some information."

The nurses all looked at each other with dumbfounded expressions on their faces. Kellie, as the ranking officer, gathered herself together and asked, "Beg your pardon, Sir, but we don't understand what this about. Could you fill us in?"

Coronal Nolan pulled up a chair and sat down. He placed a briefcase he was carrying on floor next to him. "I understand. Let me explain. I'm your pilot for tomorrow's flight. I was supposed to do this little chore tomorrow before the flight, but we have a full flight and time is going to be factor so I decided to get it done now. I've had a hard time finding you. It wasn't until I spoke with the CO of the 95th that I decided to come here. He said if you weren't in the Temporary Officer's Quarters, then you might be here. And here you are; all three of you."

"Sir," Kellie pressed again, "you still haven't told us anything. Why're you looking for us?"

"I Corp sent down some things to add to your orders and I have them in my briefcase." As he spoke, he opened his briefcase and took out several sheets of paper. He thumbed through them and, checking each nurse's name tab, he handed them each a single sheet of paper. "These are to be added to your orders. They authorize and award you the National Defense Service Metal. Present these orders at your next duty station and you'll be presented your metal."

"Sir," Veronica said in amazement, "You mean you chased us down just to give us this? Everyone gets this medal."

He sighed and said, "No, Lt. Mann that's not the only reason." He then handed her another sheet of paper. "You, Lt. Mann, have been awarded the Meritorious Service Metal. Congratulations, that's quite an honor."

Veronica stared at the paper and slowly got to her feet. "But, Sir, there must be some mistake. I didn't do anythin' for this."

The Coronal started to speak, but Kellie politely spoke first. "Sir, if you'll allow me, I'm sure I can clear this up."

The Coronal smiled and nodded. Then Kellie look up at Veronica and said softly, "Please sit down, Ronnie."

Veronica put the paper on the table and keeping her eyes on Kellie she slowly sat back down. Kellie leaned forward on the table and said in a commanding tone, "I put you in for that metal, or rather my dad did. I could've done it myself but I'm just a captain. So, I asked my dad to do it for me because he's a field grade officer and I thought that might make the difference in it getting approved." Then leaning back and shrugging her shoulders she added, "And I guess I was right."

At first Veronica was speechless, but then she got angry. "Did anybody else at the ten-six-six get one of these?"

"Not that I know of," Kellie answered simply.

"Okay. I don't get it. Why am I so honored?" Veronica shot back.

The Coronal simply sat there watching and smiling, but Kathleen was becoming worried. "Come on," she said, "let's not lose our cool."

Veronica turned to Kathleen and said in an almost shout, "Well, I think I should know why. All it says on this piece of paper is I got it for meritorious service while serving as XO to the head nurse at the 1066th MASH unit in South Vietnam. I guess I can accept that. But who in hell didn't serve meritoriously there." Then turning back to Kellie, she asked sharply, "You're tryin' to tell me that Marty, or Max, or Sandy, or anyone of those nurses didn't deserve this just as much as me?"

"You know who you sound like, Ronnie?" Kellie asked in a soft but steady voice.

Veronica was taken aback. Her face took on a puzzled look and she asked, "What'd you mean?"

"I mean doesn't all the things you're saying sound familiar?"

"No, should it?"

"Well," Kellie continue, "I wasn't actually there, but I was told that a certain Lt. William Barnett didn't think he deserved the Distinguished Service Cross for what he did at Hamburger Hill. He felt he was getting a metal for what his men did. But in the end, he was made to realize that he was wearing that metal not just for himself, but for all the men that went up that hill with 'im." She stopped talking and there was a long uncomfortable silence. "Do you remember that?" She added.

The tension seemed to flow out of Veronica and her face became relaxed. "You're sayin' that I should wear this metal for all of us?"

"Yes, I'm saying that," Kellie answered, "but I'm also saying that you did an outstanding job as my XO. I could've never made it without you. As I told you before, you're one of the best of the best. And, as Kat ask of you and me, I'm asking of you; don't let us down."

Veronica looked at her two friends and said softly, "Thank you, Captain Anderson. I'll be wearing this medal for every nurse that has served or will ever serve at the ten-six-six."

Kellie turned to Coronal Nolan and said, "I'm sorry, Sir, for this little scene and we all appreciate you efforts to get these medals to us."

Coronal Nolan closed his briefcase and got to his feet. "It was my pleasure, Captain. And, if I'm busy tomorrow and don't get to speak with you again directly, God speed." He started away but turned back and said, "There is on last thing that'll be covered tomorrow but I'll tell you now. Everyone is being told that they should probably not be wearing their uniform when they get off the plane. There're a lot of protesters outside the gates at Travis these days and they're saying a lot of nasty and ugly things. Guys have been spit on and sometimes they're even physical. It's not an order; it's just a kind of warning." He nodded and turned again and walked away.

Kathleen's face turned red and she yelled after the Coronal, "Fuck the protesters. I'm wearin' my uniform. I'm not ashamed of it, as a matter-of-fact, I damn proud of it."

Kellie and Veronica both smiled at Kathleen and nodded in the affirmative. Then they filled their glasses again. The bottle was now empty. Kellie held her glass high and yelled for all to hear, "A toast." She waited until Veronica and Kathleen were holding their glasses high. "A toast," she repeated, "to the good ole USA. And watch out! The Tart Trio is coming home! And they'll be proudly wearing their uniforms!"

PART SIX

The Autumn of 1970
The Weddings

CHAPTER FORTY-EIGHT

Veronica and William

It was August 16, 1970 as Veronica stood with Kathleen in front of the main gate to Fort Sam Houston in San Antonio, Texas. It was a boiling hot Texas summer day and they tried to find some shade near the small guard post at the entrance. Veronica was in civilian dress. She wore a brown skirt that came to her knees and a sleeveless white blouse. Her legs were bare and she wore a pair of black high heeled shoes. There was nothing on her head to protect her from the sun. She carried a medium sized purse on a strap over her shoulder. On the ground next to her were two large bags; one an army duffle bag and the other a civilian suitcase. In her hand she still held the orders that honorably discharged her from active duty in the United States Army Nurse Corps and assigned her to a Troop Program Unit, or TPU, just west of Dallas. She was now officially in the Army Nurse Corps Reserves.

"Have you got everythin'?" Kathleen asked.

"Yeah, I think I got everythin'," she replied looking down at her bags. "The big stuff I had shipped to Bill's place. It's amazin' what all you collect over three years."

"It is indeed," Kathleen replied, "I've already shipped most of my stuff to Jordy in Marfa."

"How much longer you got?" Veronica asked.

"I still have twelve more days to go before I can get out of this uniform. Strange as it may sound, I'm goin' ta miss this old army garb."

Veronica looked down at her attire and smiled, "Yeah, I know what you mean." There was a long and nervous pause and then she said, "Look, Kat, you don't have to stand out here in this heat with me. Bill's goin' to be here to pick me up any minute. I phoned him just before we left the Administration Buildin'. He's got a motel room less than a mile from here."

"I don't mind, Ronnie. I don't mind at all, unless it would make you more comfortable if I were to leave."

There was another long nervous silence, when William pulled up to the entrance. He saw the two women and maneuvered his brand new 1970 Ford Fairlane 500 up next to them. Bringing the car to a skidding stop, he jumped out and ran to Veronica. Kathleen watched smiling as the two embraced for several long minutes. Finally, William looked up from the embrace and smiled at Kathleen. "Hello, Kat. Sorry, I didn't mean to ignore you."

"Not to worry, Bill, I'm not offended."

Breaking away from Veronica, he said, "Hey, let me get these bags into the trunk and we can get started."

While William was attending to the bags, Kathleen and Veronica just stood there in the heat staring at each other. Then, suddenly, Kathleen launched herself at Veronica. She threw her arms around Veronica's neck and held on to her for dear life. Veronica dropped her purse and wrapped her arms tightly around Kathleen. Both women began to cry uncontrollably. When William had loaded the bags and closed the car trunk, he walked around the car to see the two friends holding each other and crying. He simply smiled and leaned back against the car. He didn't want to interfere.

Finally, Kathleen pushed herself away from Veronica. Straightening her uniform and drying her eyes with the palms of her hands, she said chokingly, "I don't know why we're doin' this. We're goin' to be seein' each other again in a few months. And Kel'll be there too. So, you two go on now. Go on." Kathleen began stepping backwards as she spoke.

William open the passenger side door for Veronica and started to help her in but Veronica stopped. She stood halfway in the car and halfway out. "You take care, Girl," she yelled still crying. "And watch out for any incomin' rounds. You hear me. Keep that Hell's Kitchen ass of yours down. Keep it down."

They had been driving for almost twenty minutes when William glanced over to Veronica and asked, "You're awfully quiet. Is there somethin' wrong?"

"No, not really," she replied with a smile. "But I'd like to ask a favor."

"Ask away," he said keeping his eyes on the road.

"I was wanderin' if we could break up our trip to the farm?" She asked carefully. "I know we planned on gettin' there today, but I'd like to stop at a nice hotel and spend one night alone together. I've got a couple of things I'd like to talk to you about."

"I don't see why not. We can stop in Waco. We should be able to find a nice hotel there. I'll call Mom and tell her we've been delayed and won't be there until tomorrow. But, you know, you've got me worried. Can't we discuss these things while we drive?"

"We could."

"Then, why don't we. I promise we can still stay at the hotel."

"Okay," she said as she slid across the seat to cuddle next to him. She remained silent for several minutes as they rode along.

"I can't stand this," William laughed, "could you please get on with it?"

She seemed to gather her thoughts and then she asked, "Do you remember when you proposed to me at Eagle Beach just before you shipped out?"

"Yes, I remember it very well."

"Do you remember the plans we made about when and where we would be married?"

He slowed the car down and said softly, "I feel somethin' comin'. I hope you haven't changed your mind."

"Absolutely not," she purred as she punched him in the arm, "I'm not lettin' you get away."

"Then, what is it?" He asked in frustration. "Maybe I should pull over to hear this."

"Maybe you should. Remember my original plan was to go over all this in a nice hotel room."

He let out a long sigh, "I think you're right. Hold on we're goin' to get to Waco as fast as I can get us there safely." He pushed the gas pedal down and the new Ford Fairlane 500 roared ahead. As they sped down the highway, they said very little to each other.

Once in a beautiful suite at the Waco Hilton, William dropped the bags he was carrying on the floor, checked the air conditioning and then kicked off his shoes and flopped down onto the large king size bed. He fluffed up a pillow and propped himself up on it. He pointed to Veronica and announced, "Okay, I'm ready. Hit me with it."

Veronica smiled sarcastically and kicked off her high heels. She then slipped out of her skirt and blouse. Dropping everything on the floor, she walked over to the air conditioner and stood in front of it in only her panties and bra. She spread her arms out and soaked up the cool air. After what seemed to William a very long time, she reached down and picked up her purse. She opened it and pulled out Jordy's check. "There're several things but we'll start with this."

"What's that?" William asked frowning.

Veronica walked over to the head of the bed and handed him the check. "It'll explain itself."

William took the check and looked at it. He then sat up straight in bed and bellowed, "This is a check from Costillo Enterprises to Veronica and William Barnett for three hundred thousand dollars." After a long pause he asked loudly, "Is this some kind of joke?"

"No," she replied simply.

"But why would Jordy want to give us three hundred thousand dollars?"

Veronica sat down next to him on the bed. "I'll explain it the best I can," she said putting her hand on his shoulder.

Over the next half hour, she told him about her last night in Vietnam, about the meeting with Kellie and Kathleen, about the money, and about their long flight home. As she ended her story, she said, "It's what Jordy and Kat want. I couldn't say no to Kat the way she put it. But the check is made out to both of us, so you can stop it if you want."

William stood up and walked a short distance from the bed and, still holding the check; he turned and looked back at her. "And you say Kel and Kyle got a check just like this?"

"Yes."

"Does Kyle know about it?"

"Yes, Kel told him about it while she was on leave with Kyle in Coalville."

"And Kyle accepted?"

"Yes, he did. It just made sense. It'll help a lot with Kel's medical school cost at SMU."

He walked over to her and gently put his hand on her cheek and asked, "Why'd you wait until now to tell me? Why didn't you tell me while you were on leave with me at the farm?"

She lowered her head and replied, "At the time, I didn't know Kel had told Kyle. And I guess I was afraid you might turn down the check. I didn't know what to do. I was originally goin' to keep it from you until after we were married. But things changed for me while I was on leave at home in Sweetwater. That's the other thing I wanted to talk to you about. The reason I want us to get married within the next two weeks."

He slowly sat down on the bed again and took her into his arms. "We're goin' to be husband and wife, Ronnie. I want us to be able to tell each other everythin'. I love you, Girl, I love you."

"I know you do," she moaned, "that's why this is so hard."

As he continued to hold her, he said softly, "So, tell me."

She didn't move from his arms and she didn't raise her head as she spoke, "While I was home in Sweetwater, I found that my parents are havin' a real hard time. My dad's workin' himself to death tryin' to keep the bank from forclosin' on their mortgage. Dad's worked hard all his life and the oil fields have taken a real toll on him. He's only fifty-eight years old but he looks seventy. And Mom does the best she can by doin' housework for other people. But she's beat down too. I didn't know it but over the years they've fallen farther and farther behind in their mortgage payments. Now the bank is givin' them until the end of September to catch up or their goin' to foreclose and make them move out." She paused and looked up at him, "That's the house I grew up in, Bill. It's not much, but it's their home and they've got no place else to go. What I'm askin' is for us to get married earlier than we planned so we can cash that check. Then, I'd ask you to let me take fifty-thousand of that money to help my parents. They've been in that house a long time so their mortgage is only about twenty-five-thousand. I want to pay their mortgage off and give the other twenty-five to my friend Michael Conners. He's a big business man in Sweetwater and I'll have him set up a small monthly income for them. By doin' those two things, they'll be able to get by okay and Dad won't have to work so hard and Mom can stop doin' housework for other people. I hate bringin' this to our marriage. But they're my parents, Bill. I love 'em so much."

She was on the verge of breaking into tears. William stood up and took her hands and pulled her to her feet. He then took her face into his hands and kissed her gently on her forehead. "Here's what we'll do," he started, "we won't give 'em fifty-thousand, we'll give 'em a hundred-thousand." She started to speak but he put his finger on her lips and continued, "Then I want you to take another hundred-thousand and fix up the farm house however you want, but I will insist that two extra rooms be added for our children. If my mom or step-dad gives you any shit, just let know. How does that sound?"

She smiled up at him with moist eyes. "That all sounds great, Captain Barnett."

"Do you think you can organize our weddin' in just two weeks?" He asked.

"Maybe not me alone, but I know this girl named Kathleen that'll help me and she's one hell of an organizer."

"Well you'll have to do it all without me. I've got to be careful with my leave time. I need to be back at Fort Campbell in two days. I'm plannin' on flyin' back to Fort Campbell and leavin' the new car with you. Let me know when you get all the plans in place so I can get back down here. I've already used up most of my leave for this year. But I think they'll give me an extension to get married. But our honeymoon will have to consist of a weekend at a super nice hotel in Dallas. I promise you we'll have a really nice belated honeymoon next year."

"Honeymoons are the least of my worries" she said emotionally. "I've got you, I've got good friends, and your mom and step-dad love me; even those two step-brothers of yours love me. And anyway, your mom and I will have a ball makin' plans to renovate the farmhouse. And after we're married, when you have to go back to Fort Campbell, I'll take our new car and drive to Sweetwater and take care of business. When that's done, your mom and I will put our renovation plans to work. Then, where ever the military sends us, no matter what we have to do, it's my plan to be at your side and make you a happy man the rest of your life."

William put his hands on her shoulders and push her back a few steps. He looked at her with a naughty grin and said, "I was just thinkin' that if you could slip out of those panties and bra, you could make me a happy man now."

Veronica smiled that wicked smile of hers and reached behind her back and unsnapped her bra and let it drop to the floor. Next she slipped her thumbs under the waist band of her panties and pulled them down to ankles. She stepped out of her panties and using one foot flipped them across the room. Turning away from him, she walked to the bed and climbed onto its far side. Laying on her side and propping her head up with her elbow and hand, she reached over and patted the other side of the bed.

And so on September 16, 1970, Veronica and William would become the first of the three couples to be married. The wedding took place at the farm. Kathleen, who on August 28th had been honorably discharged from active duty and assigned to a TPU in Abilene, Texas, was there to help put things together. A small platform was built about twenty yards from the Barnett Cemetery. It was painted white and decorated with flowers of all kinds. Folding chairs were brought in and setup in front of the platform. They were arranged so as to form an aisle the bride could walk down. The reception was held in the farmhouse itself.

Veronica's bridesmaids were, of course, Kathleen and Kellie. At Fort Hood on August 29th, Kellie had resigned her commission and was honorably discharged and didn't go into the reserves. She was busy buying furniture for her new home in Coalville; a house that Kyle had surprised her with. He'd been building on it secretly ever since he'd gotten back home from Vietnam. It was finished except for the furnishings, which Kyle insisted Kellie pick out.

William's best men were, of course, Jordan and Kyle. Kyle had driven down from Camp Walters in his new car; a 1970 Lincoln Continental. Jordan had flown into Dallas and rented a car to drive to the farm.

The ceremony was a simple one but a beautiful one. The only problem was there were many more people at the wedding than had been expected or invited. The overflow had to stand in the back behind the folded chairs and food ran short at the reception. Michael Connors had made arrangements for Veronica's parents to ride with him in his limousine. As a result, Veronica's father was there to walk her down the aisle. And to Veronica's shock and great happiness, Michael Connors had found original Tart Trio member Margie Mason, now Margie Hightower. With Margie were her husband and two children brought to the wedding via special limousine from Houston. In attendance was the entire Collie family as well as the entire Jordan family. Jordan's benefactors, as well as unofficial relatives, Jimmy and Judy Orland were there. Many uninvited people from Coalville came to simply show their respect for the Barnett family.

Veronica was beautiful in a wedding gown that Kellie had helped her pick out at a bridal boutique in Dallas. William wore his army dress blue uniform. Kyle was also in his army dress blues. With special permission from retired Marine Brigadier General Dick Jordan, Jordan wore his marine dress blues.

After the announcement of, 'With the power vested in me by the State of Texas, I now pronounce you husband and wife. You may now kiss the bride', William did just that; he kissed the bride. And Veronica Leigh Mann and William Clyde Barnett were husband and wife.

Then as many as could, got into the farm house for the reception. During the reception, Kyle and William pulled Jordan aside to a private area behind the house. There, they both thanked him profusely for what he had done for them and promised that they would always be there to help him in any way they were needed and at any time.

Jordan only said, "It's me that's thankful. I hope this is only one of many happy days to come for all of us. We, and I mean all of us, earned it the hard way."

CHAPTER FORTY-NINE

Kellie and Kyle

It was exactly one month to the day, October 16, 1970, since Veronica and William got married, that Major Kyle Collie stood in front of the altar at the Coalville First Baptist Church in his army dress blues waiting for his bride to be to come walking down the aisle. Standing at his side as his best men, were Captain William Barnett, in his army dress blues, and Jordan Costillo, in his marine dress blues, again with the permission of retired Brigadier General Dick Jordan. Standing as brides maids were, of course, Veronica Barnett and Kathleen O'Rourke.

With a few exceptions, the church pews were filled with many of same people who attended Veronica and William's wedding. The Collie Family was there. This time it was the entire family as Kyle's little sister Lilly Jo was there with her boyfriend. The Jordan Family was there and with them were Jimmy and Judy Orland. To Kellie's great surprise and amazing delight, her old high school friend, Mike Linsberg was there. He and his wife, Ellie, and small son, Tyler, had flown down from St. Paul with Kellie's dad.

As Kyle stood there waiting, there was a moment of sadness. For out there in the church, was his entire family; except for his grandfather, James Collie, who had passed away in 1967 just as Kyle was shipping out to Vietnam. Kyle always carried a heavy burden in his heart for having to miss his beloved Grandpa's funeral. Now, he felt a true sadness that his Grandpa wouldn't be here for his wedding. But his grandmother, Mary, was out there sitting with her Granddaughter, Lilly. His sadness faded as he remembered how quickly and sincerely his family had accepted Kellie and fell in love with her. Kellie had won them over by simply being herself. It had been Kyle's mother, Sue Ann Collie, who had surprised Kellie by taking her to her brand new home. Kellie was stunned that Kyle could've managed to get so much done in such a short time. He had designed the house using the many conversations he had with Kellie about her dream home. She loved the house and wanted her father to come live with them. But he declined. He wanted to stay near his late wife and wanted to be laid to rest next to her when his time came.

Now, the wait was over. As the organist began playing, 'Here Comes the Bride', everyone stood up and looked back at the approaching bride. At her side and holding her arm, was her father, Coronal Jacob Anderson wearing his army dress blues. Walking in front of Kellie and dropping rose petals, was her little flower girl. She was seven year old Betsy Lee Jordan, the daughter of Dick Jordan's second son, Clint Thomas Jordan.

Kellie's beauty took Kyles breath away, as he watched her slowly approach. He could see a nervous smile through the thin white vale that hung over her face. Upon arriving at the altar, Coronal Anderson gave his daughter's hand to Kyle and then he stepped back. Then, the marriage ceremony of Kellie Jean Anderson and Kyle Gene Collie began.

The reception was held at Kyle's grandmother's house. Mary had been alone in the house since James' death. Mary fought many battles with depression at being alone in the big house. At times, she had illusions of seeing James sitting in his favorite easy chair or seeing her twins, Daryl and Cheryl, running through the house. But Daryl and Cheryl were both married and living their own lives. But her twins had given her several wonderful grandchildren; like Kyle. Though the house was empty and lonely most of the time, her family was nearby in Coalville and she was always having her grandchildren and great-grandchildren over to visit and spend the night. Daryl and asked her many times to sale the old house and come live with him and Sue Ann, but she always declined.

But, now, the house was a beehive of activity as people pushed into the house and overflowed out onto the back porch and backyard. Kyle walked through the house working the crowd and trying to talk to everyone. Kellie, spend most of her time talking with her friend Mike and her father. Suddenly, Kyle saw his grandmother standing by herself near the kitchen sink. He immediately went to her and tapped her on the shoulder. She jumped as if being brought out of dream. "God, Kyle, you scared me," she said laughing.

"How could I scare you with all this goin' on?"

"Well, I was in deep thought."

"I'd like to ask you what you were thinkin'," he said thoughtfully, "but first I'd like to thank you for all this."

"Oh, this was my absolute pleasure and anyway I got a lot of help from your mom and dad as well as your Aunt Cheryl."

"I just want you to know how much Kel and appreciate all you've done." Then after a short paused he continued, "So, what were you in such deep thought about?"

Mary pointed out to the porch were Lilly was standing and talking to her Aunt Cheryl, "I was thinkin' about your sister. You know her young man has asked her to marry him?"

Kyle jerked up in surprise, "No, I didn't know that. I guess I better go have some words with her young man."

Mary quickly grabbed his arm before he could leave. "No you don't," she said harshly, "You let her come to you. She thinks the world of you, Kyle, and she'll come to you. Now, you'll let her do that won't you?"

Kyle relaxed and give his grandmother that cute grin of his, "You know I will Grandma." He then bent down and kissed her on the forehead and said softly, "I've always said that you're the smartest Collie of all."

Kyle started to leave but she stopped him again. "Kyle, I've been thinkin' about givin' this old place to Lilly when she's married. Would that upset you? I mean you're the oldest and all."

Kyle took her hands in his and said, "That wouldn't upset me at all, Grandma. We've all got nice homes, so I got no problem with you givin' this beautiful old place to my little sister. But I would make one requirement."

"And that would be?" Mary asked suspiciously.

"That would be that you get to live here with them. I know Dad as asked you over and over again to move in with him and Mom, but you always have insisted on stayin' in your own house. Well, now I'll do the insistin'. You stay with the house or it's no deal. Okay?"

"I think Lilly'll go for that," Mary said with a knowing smile. "Now you go on and mix about. I got things to do."

Kyle did as he was told and started looking for Kellie. He saw her in the living room talking with Veronica and Kathleen and he started in that direction, but someone grabbed his arm and stopped him. He turned to see Jordan standing there holding a drink in one hand and holding Kyle's arm in the other. He was wearing a worried look on his face. "Jordy, is somethin' wrong?" He asked with a half-smile.

"Kyle, is there some place we can go and have a short talk?" He asked. "And I'd like to get Bill and bring him alone too."

"Sure, Jordy," Kyle said slowly, "but we'll have to find Bill."

"No we won't. He's out in the backyard chewin' on a sandwich."

"Alright then, let's go."

Jordan and Kyle went through the kitchen, out the backdoor, across the crowded porch, and into the backyard. They found William browsing a picnic table filled with food. "Hey, Bill," Kyle yelled.

William looked up and smiled, "Hey, guys. I'm just checkin' out this great grub."

Kyle waved him over, "Come on. Jordy wants to talk with us about somethin'."

"What?" William asked.

Kyle looked at Jordan who didn't say anything. Turning his look back to William, he said, "I don't know."

William walked over to them and asked, "Where're we goin'?"

Kyle again looked at Jordan and asked, "You want quiet and privacy?"

"Yeah, that would work. You got a place in mind?"

"Yes, I do," Kyle replied, "you two just follow me."

The three of them had just started walking away with Kyle in the lead when they were stopped by a yell that said, "Hey, Big Brother!"

Kyle turned to see Lilly walking towards him hand-and-hand with a man who looked like he didn't want to be there. The man was tall, maybe six feet two. He had well-groomed sandy-brown hair. His eyes were a deep brown set in what could be called a handsome face, which was clean shaved. He wore a dark blue suit with a white shirt and a soft yellow tie. On his feet were highly shined black shoes.

As they arrived in front of Kyle, William and Jordan took a few steps back. "Big Brother," Lilly said smiling and pointing to the man, "I'd like for you to meet Professor Luke Crane."

Kyle held out his hand, which Luke took, and the two had a firm handshake. "It's nice to meet you, Professor Crane," Kyle said in a serious tone.

"The pleasure is mine, Major Collie."

Lilly looked at them in frustration. "Okay, enough with the formal stuff. Kyle, this is Luke. Luke this is Kyle."

Kyle smiled down at Lilly, "Do you have somethin' to tell me, Little Sister?"

"A few things to tell you, but, more importantly, I have somethin' to ask you." Lilly didn't waste words. She went directly to the matter. "I've been datin' Luke for over a year. We've fallen in love over that period of time. Luke has asked me to marry him. I told him he had to ask my parents and, if he got by them, he had to ask you. He got by Mom and Dad, so now he's here to ask you."

"You're doin' this on my weddin' day?" Kyle asked with a small growl.

"I thought it was a perfect time. I mean with the atmosphere and everythin'."

There was a short silence as Kyle stared down at his sister. "Has he been honorable?"

"When you left for Vietnam, I promised you no one would touch me without your permission. We Collie's keep our promises. Luke has been more than honorable. In fact, he's been too honorable for my part. I'll admit that it's been a hard challenge to keep my promise but Luke helped me and here we stand."

Before Kyle could reply, Luke quickly interjected, "I love your sister, Kyle. We Crane's keep or promises also and I promise I'll love her, keep her, and protect her for all our lives."

Kyle smile down at his sister and asked softly, "Do you love 'im, Little Sister?"

"I do, Big Brother, I really do."

Kyle turned and signaled for Jordan and William to join him, which they did immediately. Then, turning back to face Luke, he said, "Okay, Luke, you've got my permission to marry my sister." There were smiles all around until Kyle held his hand up and added, "But know this, Luke, the two gentlemen standin' with me love Lilly almost as much as me. Captain Barnett here is with the 101st Airborne Screamin' Eagles, and my other relative here is Jordan Costillo and he was with the 1st Battalion Marine Recon. Both of them fought in Vietnam. I tell you these things, Luke, because if you ever hurt my sister in anyway, mentally or physically, you'll have to answer to all three of us. With all that said, do you still want to marry my sister?"

Luke reached over and pulled Lilly to him and held her tightly. Then he looked Kyle straight in the eyes and said firmly, "I do indeed, Kyle, in fact, now even more so."

Kyle reached over and pinched Lilly's cheek, "I like 'im, Lilly Jo, I like him a lot."

Lilly jumped up and kissed Kyle on the cheek, then took Luke's hand and started pulling him away. She and Luke had only taken a few steps when she turned back to face Kyle and said in a matter-of-fact tone, "Oh there's one thing I forgot to tell you. Luke has only had his full professorship for about two months. Back in sixty-five and sixty-six, Luke was in Vietnam with the Special Forces. Yeah, that's right Big Brother, Luke was a Green Beret." With that, she took Luke's arm and they waded back into the crowd.

Kyle folded his arms across his chest and watched them walk away. Then with a big smile on his face, he turned and asked, "Okay, guys, where were we?"

"You were goin' to take us to a private place to talk," William answered.

"Oh yeah, just follow me."

Kyle took them up to the park on Lonesome Hill. It was a short walk from the backyard where they were. Kyle fought of the melancholy feeling he had because this was the same spot he last saw is good friend Bennie. Except for a few people walking the trails, they were alone. Kyle and William sat down on a cement bench and looked at Jordan, who continued to pace back and forth in front of them.

"Okay," William finally said, "let's have it. What's this all about?"

"Yeah," Kyle chimed in, "let's hear it. After all this is my weddin' day and in a couple of hours my new wife and I will be headin' out for Dallas Love Field to catch a plane for the Virgin Islands and a full week of honeymoonin'."

Jordan stopped pacing and stood before them with his hand behind his back. "I need some advice. You two guys are college educated and a lot smarter than me. Here I am, for God's sake, a twenty-six year old freshman at SMU tryin' to get a law degree."

Kyle and William looked at each other. Kyle cocked his head to one side and asked, "Has this got somethin' to do with you goin' to college?"

"No, not really," he replied in irritation. "It has to do with an offer I've received from an oil and natural gas consortium to sell all my holdings. They've offered me a hundred million dollars for everythin' I own except for my house in Marfa and the five acres it sits on."

William whistled and said, "That's a lot of money, Jordy. Are you goin' to take it?"

"That's just it. I don't know what I should do. Of course, I'd love to have all that money but…." He stopped talking as if he were having trouble finishing his sentence.

"Yes, but what?" Kyle asked.

Then Jordan blurred out, "But I've already got over twelve million dollars and it's still growin'. I'm havin' a real hard time sellin' my holdings. My mom and Jimmy Orland worked hard to put Costillo Enterprises together and I feel if I sell out I'm betrayin' them in some way. The holdings and my house are all I have left of my mom." He took his hands from behind is back and held his fist in the air. "Can you guys see where I'm comin' from?"

"Take it easy, Jordy. Take it easy," William said softly.

"Jordy, why would havin' the money instead of the holdings be any different?" Kyle asked. "You can still have Costillo Enterprises. You could do different things with it. And I'm sure what your mom wanted for you was security and you'll have that either way."

"Yeah, I know all that," Jordan said a bit calmer now. "If it were just the gas leases it would be one thing, but all that oil land is another. I told 'em I'd sell all my gas leases all over the state to 'em. I told 'em I wanted to keep my oil lands. But they told me it's all or nothin'. I don't like people dictatin' terms to me."

Kyle stood up and went over and put his hand on Jordan's shoulder. "You know, Jordy, I think you already know what you're goin' to do. I think you've known all along. You just wanted me and Bill for a soundin' board. Me personally, I think you should do three things: first, I'd wouldn't sell to the consortium; that would make you very unhappy, second, I'd take some of the money in Costillo Enterprises and expand your investments into things other than oil and gas; things you'd enjoy more, and third, I'd go down and enlist in the Marine Reserves. You can still get credit for your time in the Corp and they'd make you and officer in a heartbeat. Your whole last tour in 'Nam they tried to get you to take a commission."

William jumped to his feet. "Holy shit, I agree with all of that." He went over and slapped Kyle on the back. "Good thinkin', Kyle. Damn good thinkin'."

"Whoa, whoa, just a minute here," Jordan said with a stunned look on his face. "What was that last part? I mean the part about enlistin' in the Marine Reserves. You're tellin' me you not only want me to be a twenty-six year of freshman, but now you want me to be a twenty-six year old 2nd lieutenant?"

"No, no, no," William shouted. "With all your background you'll go in as a 1st lieutenant. I can almost guarantee it. And you know your hearts in the Corp and always will be. So, why fight it. My God, Kat's in the reserves."

"He's right, Jordy," Kyle said with his cute grin, "you're a United States Marine through and through and you know it. And I know that Kat will be very relieved to not have you mopin' about it."

Jordan stood there looking expressionlessly at his two friends and relatives for a long minute. Then a smile started to form on his face. "Well, shit, why not," he said laughing. "And I won't have to get permission from a retired general to wear my dress blues at my weddin'. Come on, Bill, we need to get this newly wed back down to his wife so they can go on their honeymoon."

CHAPTER FIFTY

Kathleen and Jordan

I t was exactly one month to the day, November 16, 1970, since Kellie and Kyle got married, that Marine Reserve 1st Lieutenant Jordan Costillo stood in front of the altar at St. Mary's Catholic Church in Marfa, Texas wearing his marine dress blues waiting for his bride to come walking down the aisle. Standing at his side as his best men, were Captain William Barnett, in his army dress blues, and Major Kyle Collie, also in his army dress blues. Standing as brides maids were, of course, Veronica Barnett and Kellie Collie.

This day had purposely been selected by Kathleen for her marriage to Jordan. For this was the anniversary of the death of Jordan's mother. In Kathleen's mind, the best way to remember Rosa Costillo was for Jordan to start a new life in Holy wedlock. At first, Jordan didn't like the idea, but while in Coalville for Kyle and Kellie's marriage he spend some time at his mother's grave. It was then that he agreed to the date. It was just a matter of coincidence that the date fell exactly one month after Kyle and Kellie got married.

The pews in the old church were not greatly occupied. In fact, the attendance to the wedding was very small. Because of the distance and isolation of Marfa, most of the Collie and Jordan families couldn't make the trip. However, Jordan's half-brother Retire Brigadier General Dick Jordan and his wife Cheryl did make the trip. And this time he didn't have to give Jordan permission to wear his dress blues. Of course, Kathleen's mother was there since she had moved into the Costillo home almost a year ago. Gerald Kellen, now a civilian and his wife Millie were there. Judy and Jimmy Orland were present. Judy had flown them there in their private plane. They were a few local citizens of Marfa that attended uninvited just to see the very rich Jordan Costillo.

To Kathleen's undying gratitude, Jordan flew His Excellency Bishop Kevin Conway all the way in from Washington D.C. by private charter plane, to perform the ceremony. When asked, His Excellency's only said, "I wouldn't miss it for the world."

As the wedding march began, the little flower girl, in the person of five year old Christina Kellen, started her trip down the aisle spreading rose pedals on her way. The bride followed a short distance behind dressed in a beautiful white bridal gown. Walking her down the aisle and holding her arm was her brother Gunny Sergeant Robert O'Rourke Jr. wearing his dress blue marine uniform. Robert had been flown in on the same chartered plane as Bishop Conway; they had a wonderful time catching up with each other on the long flight.

When the bride and her escort arrived at the altar, Robert gave Kathleen's hand to Jordan and stepped back. The couple turned to face Bishop Conway who was standing on a small platform in front of them. The small platform elevated him slightly above them. He looked out at the small gathering and raised his hands over the heads of the couple and said in a loud voice, "Before I start the marriage ceremony, I would like everyone to know that I have known Kathleen Finoa O'Rourke since she was born at Roosevelt Hospital in Hell's Kitchen, New York City. I christened her and I watched her grow into a young lady. I watched her as she worked her way through Boston College. Then, I watched the young woman join the United States Army Nurse Corps and serve two tours of duty in Vietnam. Now, I have the pleasure to stand here before the full grown woman and her chosen mate for life to join them in Holy Matrimony. This I do with a happy heart.

After his short speech, His Excellence Bishop Kevin Conway performed the marriage ceremony in the Catholic tradition, and married Kathleen Finoa O'Rourke and Jordan Orland Costillo.

The reception was held at the Costillo Estate. The house was no longer Jordan's house but was now the Costillo Estate. Over the last year, Jordan had been busy remodeling the house. He added four new bedrooms and three new full baths. One of the new bedrooms was specifically for Kathleen's mother. She designed it and furnished it to her own desires. The existing three bedrooms were remodeled and new furniture added. The existing two baths were expanded to include large Jacuzzi tubs and everything was done in beautiful marble and granite. He remodeled the three living rooms and refurnished them. The five acres the house was on was re-landscaped with green grass and three large water fountains. The entrance to the estate had a large cast iron gate that lead onto a small road that wound around to the house. Out to the side of the house was a large parking area that had two three car garages.

Kathleen's mother had seen to the organization of the reception. It was held in one of the large living rooms. Tables were brought in and food in large amounts was catered in from the best Tex-Mex and Bar-beque restaurants in Marfa. Champaign, wine, beer, and whiskey was readily available as was water and a variety of soft drinks.

Jordan and Kathleen spent time with everyone that came to the wedding. Kathleen especially enjoyed talking with Bishop Conway and her brother Robert.

Bishop Conway asked her, "What is the first thing you intend to do on this beautiful estate?"

Kathleen gave him a wicked smile and said, "I hope this doesn't shock you, Your Excellency, but I intend to make some babies."

The Bishop laughed and replied, "Well, you're an O'Rourke and I wouldn't expect anythin' else. But I demand that when they're born, you notify me so I can bless 'em and christen 'em."

"You got a deal, Bishop. You got yourself a deal."

Kathleen felt a tap on her shoulder and she turned around to see her brother, Robert, smiling down at her, "Well, Sis," he said, "I'm really, really happy for you. That guy you married is really somethin'." Then reaching up pulling his collar open, he pointed to the scar on his neck. "I wouldn't be here to give you away if weren't for him. I'm glad you guys got together over there and it turned out this way."

Kathleen put one hand on Bishop Conway's shoulder the other on her brother's shoulder. Then, without lifting her head, she said softly, "You know, as bad as things were over there, I got a lot out of it. I learned a lot about people, I worked with women of great courage and commitment, I saw so many acts of courage you couldn't put 'em all in a book. I found a man I want to spend the rest of my life with and have my children with. I found four of the best friends I'll probably ever have in my life; Ronnie, Kel, Bill, and Kyle. I've been blessed Bishop, and there're many times I wonder why God pick me to bless so much."

Bishop Conway reached up and put his hand on Kathleen's and said with conviction, "You're blessed, Kat, because you're a child of God. You always have been. You may wander at times, for we all sin. But you're a child of God. You've never left your beliefs."

Kathleen looked up and smiled at two of the wonderful men in her life. "Thanks, Father, oh, I mean Bishop. Old habits are hard to break."

Jordan had found Gerald and his wife Millie and thanked them for coming. He especially thanked little Christina and planted a kiss on her forehead. Next, he found his half-brother Dick and his wife Cheryl and thanked them for making the long trip because he knew that Dick's wounds from World War II were coming back to haunt him. Jordan knew that the trip was hard on Dick. "Thanks, Brother, for makin' this trip. I know you're hurtin'." Then, looking at Cheryl he said, "If there's anythin' you need, Cheryl, you call me." Cheryl only nodded so Jordan reiterated what he had said more forcibly, "I mean it, Cheryl. Don't just nod to me. I mean every word of it. You call me if you need anythin' at all."

Cheryl looked at Jordan with frustration in her eyes, "I'm sorry, Jordan. I didn't mean to be so stand-offish. I know you mean it and I may take you up on it."

"Hey you two, stop talkin' like I can't hear you," Dick said trying to sound angry. "And I'm doin' alright. I'm goin' to be around for a lot longer to harass everyone."

"You better, you old marine," Jordan laughed. As Jordan walked away, he couldn't help thinking how bad he thought Dick looked.

Jordan mingled the room until he gathered up William and Kyle. He was leading them to his private office in the rear part of the house, when Bishop Conway stopped him with a call, "Excuse me, Jordan, may I speak with you a moment?"

Jordan quickly turned to William and Kyle and ordered, "You two wait right here. I'll be right back." Turning back towards the Bishop, Jordan walked over to him. "Sure, Your Excellence, what can I do for you?"

"First you can stop with the excellence stuff. Bishop will work fine."

Jordan smiled and shrugged, "Yes, Bishop, what can I do for you?"

"I just wanted to thank you for this privilege you've given me; the privilege of conductin' your marriage to that wonderful woman. I know flyin' me and Rob down here on a private jet was expensive."

"There's no thanks are necessary, Bishop. It was our privilege to have you do it. I know it meant the world to Kat. And I don't care about the expense. You and Rob are very important to Kat and there's nothin' more important to me than Kat."

Bishop Conway lowered his head shaking it. "Fact is, Jordan, that's what I wanted to hear. That's why I stopped you to talk. I wanted to be sure that you know what a wonderful woman you've gotten. But you answered all my questions with what you just said. So, I'll let you get back to your friends."

Bishop Conway turned and started back to the others but Jordan called after him, "Bishop," Bishop Conway stopped and looked back smiling. "I'm really glad that Kat has someone like you lookin' after her. And I know Rob personally. So rest assured that I'll keep my vowels to Kat. I'll never mistreat her, and I'll honor her for the rest of our natural lives, and if God will permit, even after. Oh, and by the way, Bishop, you and Rob are goin' to have company on your trip back to D.C. tomorrow. I'll be joinin' you as far as Dallas. I have to get back to school." Bishop Conway simply waved and turned and walked back to join the others at the food table.

Jordan hurried back and picked up William and Kyle where he had left them. "Come on guys followed me I want to have a short chat in my office."

As they hurried along through the maze of the large house, William asked, "Why do you always want to have talks?"

Jordan didn't answer, he just lead them to his private office. The office was huge. It had an oversized desk with a large cushioned office chair behind it. There were bookshelves all along one of the side walls. The bookshelves were mostly empty. Around the desk were four nice cushioned client chairs. The walls were bare of any pictures, certificates, or other documents. The office actually looked like a work in progress. To William and Kyle's surprise Jimmy Orland was sitting comfortably in one of the client chairs with his feet propped up on the desk. As they entered, Jimmy didn't bother to stand up; he only nodded and gave them a short wave.

Jordan hurried around the desk and sat down in the office chair. He signaled William and Kyle to take a seat, which they did. "Okay, to start with I guess we all know each other so there's no need for introductions."

"I guess we should after three weddings," Jimmy said laughing.

"I hope this isn't like our last meetin'. I mean for more advice," Kyle moaned.

"Nope, no more advice needed," Jordan answered as he rocked back in his plush office chair, "but you may have noticed that I did take your advice from our previous meeting. I'm in the Marine Reserves and I turned down the consortium seeking my oil and gas holdings."

Kyle and William smiled at each other. "And how did all that work out?" William asked.

"It worked out better than you might think. When I told the consortium that I wouldn't sell all my holdings, they just kind of broke up back into their original entities. One of those entities was a major natural gas company located in Dallas. Once the consortium was completely dissolved, they came back to me and offered me twenty-five million for just the rights to all of my natural gas leases. They didn't want anything to do with my oil holdings. All of which worked out just like I wanted it to. And all thanks to you two guys."

"Well, did you make the deal and take the twenty-five million?" Kyle asked.

"Of course I did."

"So, what's this meetin' all about?" William asked in a puzzled voice.

"I guess the first thing I need to know," Jordan asked leaning forward, "is if you guys intend on stayin' in the army?"

There was a short silence as both men thought about the question. Finally, William said, "Could I ask the purpose of that question?"

"Yeah, you can. But I've got my reasons and I'd just like to know before I continue."

William sat forward in his chair and said in a steady voice, "Just speakin' for myself, of course, I'm not sure. I still got about five years of commitment left to Uncle Sam. That's quite a ways to go yet and I've no idea how I'm goin' to feel at that time. I guess it depends on how my career goes."

Jordan listen intently and then looked to Kyle, "And you, Kyle?"

Kyle looked somewhat nervous and answered slowly, "The truth is I've been given a new assignment. I haven't told anyone about it yet; not even Kel. I'm still workin' out a few issues before I tell Kel."

"What is it?" William asked.

"I've been ordered to become the liaisons officer between the army and Bell Helicopter in Fort Worth. My job will be to advise and help design new updates to the AH-1 Cobra. I was picked because I had combat experience, even though I never flew a Cobra in combat, and because of my Aeronautical Degree. Anyway, it's a real sweet assignment. It's a possible fast track for promotion and I'll be lot closer to home and Kel."

Jordan again rocked back in his chair. He tapped his fingers on the arms of the chair and said in a flat tone, "So, I can gather from all this that you both'll be in the army for the foreseeable future."

Kyle and William both nodded and leaned back in their chairs. At this point, Jimmy took his feet off the desk and stood up. He looked over to Jordan and said with a smile, "I guess my services will not be required."

"I guess not," Jordan said, "but thanks for bein' available, Jimmy. And thanks for all your help."

"I'm always here for you, Jordan. Just yell for me." With that, he waved at Kyle and William and left the room.

Kyle looked worried and asked, "What was that all about?"

"Jimmy's been helpin' me with another one of your pieces of advice. He helped me decide where to diversify. With the new infusion of money, I can now invest in some other things other than oil and gas. Jimmy wants me to first buy about five million in gold as a hedge against the economy. Then, he advises me to invest in healthcare and strip malls."

"But what's that got to do with us?" William asked.

"Well, I was goin' to ask the two of you to work for my new Diversification Division. I'm goin' to need good help because I'm goin' to be in school for the next nearly four years. Then, I've got to pass the BAR. But I guess you're goin' to be tied up for at least several more years."

"What could we do?" Kyle asked in a disbelieving tone.

Jordan shrugged his shoulders. "You're both university educated guys. I'm sure you could do whatever was needed."

Kyle and William looked at each other in frustration. "God, Jordy," Kyle stammered, "I'm really sorry if we let you down. But...."

Jordan held up his hand to stop Kyle. "Not to worry," he said. "I was pretty sure before I started this that it wouldn't work out at this time, but maybe later." Jordan walked around the desk. "Come on you guys let's get back to the reception or I'll be in trouble with Kat. She's been good about delaying our honeymoon until Christmas break so I won't miss any school. So, I don't want to give her anymore issues to worry about."

William and Kyle got to their feet and everyone started for the door but Kyle stopped them. "Guys," he started, "the girls are always makin' a Pac. You know things they swear on. I'd like for us to make a Pac, because after today, we're all goin' to be so busy with our personal affairs that we won't get to see or talk to each other as much as we'd like, even though we're all in Texas somewhere, except for Bill who'll be who knows where. I love you guys. You're my relatives, friends, and my brothers in war. I want us to make a Pac to never get separated for too long a time. That we'll always be there for each other no matter what. Can we make that Pac?"

Kyle had spoken passionately and the others responded. "Here's my hand on it," William said holding his hand out palm down.

"And mine," Jordan responded by placing his hand on top of William's.

"And here's mine," Kyle said with a huge grin, "we now have a bondin' Pac."

PART SEVEN

The Summer of 1987
The Reunion

CHAPTER FIFTY-ONE

The Next Six Years

Over the next six years following the marriage of Jordan and Kathleen, things went just about as Kyle had predicted. All of the couples were extremely busy with their own personal pursuits. Only Kathleen and Kellie saw each other occasionally, and that was only at Jordan's condo in Dallas when Kathleen came to Dallas to be with Jordan, and Kellie could get free from her medical schooling. Even though Kellie and Veronica's homes in Coalville were only about five miles apart, Kellie was nearly always in Dallas and Veronica, when not working on the renovations at the farm, was with William where ever he was stationed; mostly at Fort Campbell in Kentucky. The men saw each other only on rare occasions.

Veronica and William lived a life of here and there. Veronica would be on the farm for a month and then join William at Fort Campbell for a month, where they would live in a small house on base. Things never worked out for them to get the honeymoon that William had promised. The main reason for that was that Veronica would be the first member of The Tart Trio to become pregnant. Her pregnancy would limit her trips to Fort Campbell and would eventually end the trips altogether in her seventh month. At the same time, being unable to keep up her obligations to the Army Nurse Corps Reserves, she resigned her commission and was discharged with the rank of captain. She would deliver a healthy seven pound, eight ounce son on December 2, 1971 at Baylor Hospital in Dallas. They would name him Billy George Barnett in honor of both of their fathers.

William had been at the hospital at the birth of his son. With him were his mother and Veronica's parents as well as Michael Connors. Kellie had cut classes to be at the birth and, fortunately, Kathleen would be at the Dallas condo and was able to be there also.

Veronica and the baby spent most of their time on the farm where William would visit as often as possible. But then William was promoted to major and given command of a Quick Strike Battalion, which meant his battalion was on ready alert nearly all the time. It also meant that if anything happened that required military intervention, his battalion would be one of first ones to go into action. As bad as Veronica wanted to be with William, she refused to make the baby travel until he was one year old. After that, she and the baby moved back to Fort Campbell and stayed with William until she became pregnant for the second time. She stayed with William at Fort Campbell until her sixth month and then she insisted on going back to the farm. She wanted her baby born at home in Texas, which it was. She delivered her second child on January 12, 1974. It was another boy that they named Michael Lee Barnett, in honor of Veronica's long time benefactor.

The remainder of those six years was hard on Veronica and William. With him being mostly tied down at Fort Campbell, and her being at home with two children, it was a struggle to be together, but they fought through many lonely times apart. However, their love never faltered.

Kathleen and Jordan had a relatively hard next six years. Jordan worked hard at getting his law degree, which he accomplished in May of 1974. He then went on to pass the BAR in 1975. While Jordan was accomplishing all of that, Kathleen was commuting between Marfa and the Dallas condo. At some point during all the commuting, Kathleen accomplished what she said she wanted to do; make babies. She became the second member of The Tart Trio to become pregnant. She delivered an eight pound, three ounce son on August 24, 1973 at the Marfa Medical Center. They would name him Robert James Costillo in honor of Kathleen's father. Present at the birth of her son was only her mother, her husband, and Gerald Kellen and his wife Millie. The other members of The Tart Trio were too heavily involved with motherhood, pregnancy, or education to be able to make the long trip out to Marfa.

Kathleen's commuting came to an end as she stayed home to be with her baby. And, as with Veronica, she reluctantly resigned her commission in the Army Nurse Corps Reserves with the rank of captain. After his graduation and while he studied for the BAR, Jordan stayed at home. He sold his Dallas condo for a nice profit. It was during this time that Kathleen became pregnant again. She delivered her second child, a girl, on September 3, 1976 again at the Marfa Medical Center. They name her Mary Rosa Costillo in honor of Kathleen's mother and Jordan's mother.

In early 1976, Jordan would make his first major investment outside of the oil industry. He invested in the building of a medical clinic in Coalville, Texas. He named the clinic The Collie Medical Clinic because he insisted that Doctor Kellie Collie be the administrator and head doctor of the clinic. He worked closely with Kellie in the design and building of the clinic and he made sure that it had the best and latest equipment and technology.

The next six years for Kellie and Kyle were rewarding in many ways. First, Kellie graduated from medical school in May of 1973. Then, during her internship at Presbyterian Hospital in Dallas, she became the last of The Tart Trio to become pregnant. On April 9, 1974 at Presbyterian Hospital, she delivered a six pound, four ounce baby girl they named, Carol Sue Collie in honor of Kellie's mother and Kyle's mother. Present at the birth was her husband Kyle, who brought nearly the entire Collie family with him, her father, who had flown down from Minnesota, Veronica, who was still nursing a new born, and Kathleen, who was at the Dallas condo.

Kellie would then balance motherhood with finishing her residency at Presbyterian Hospital and in June of 1975 she would finally get the MD behind her name as Kyle had promised her dad. Then in March of 1976, she would start work with Jordan to build the Collie Medical Clinic just two blocks from her home in Coalville.

Kyle stayed in the military and was liaisons officer at Bell Helicopter until June of 1975, when he was promoted to lieutenant coronal and assigned as Aide-De-Camp to now Major General Nathan Blackwell. The promotion was good for Kyle's career but it was hard on his family life because the assignment was in Washington D.C. This made being together with Kellie extremely hard. She was busy with a new child and at the same time getting her MD certificate, so she couldn't fly to D.C. very often and Kyle couldn't get free from his job as much as he would have liked. But like Veronica and William, they worked through it and their love never faltered.

CHAPTER FIFTY-TWO

The Summer of 1987: The Reunion

It was June 24th of 1987 as Jordan sat in his big office chair looking across at his three children, who each sat in a client chair watching their father. The office that was once mostly bare when he had last met with Kyle and William now had bookshelves that were full of law books, literary classics, and picture albums of his family. There was almost not an empty space on the office walls, as they were covered with degrees, certificates, documents, and pictures of his family and friends. Along one wall was a complete row of file cabinets that held all his law work and his investments. On his desk was one of the new Personal Computers that had just come out. He was fascinated by it and had hired a personal coach to teach him how to use it.

Jordan had gathered his children together while their mother was out of the house. Kathleen had gone to a late meeting at the VFW Hall to discuss the progress of the effort to get a memorial in Washington D.C. honoring the women who served in Vietnam. She believed in the effort with all her heart and had given it a lot of her time to help.

The children sat quietly waiting for their father to speak. They were seated in the order of their age, which they seemed to do automatically. How they came to do that was a mystery to Jordan since he had never asked that of them. On the far right sat soon to be fifteen year old Robert James, who they called Rob. Born on August 24, 1973, he looked much like his father but with less Hispanic features. His eyes were a hazel-green and his hair, though black, had a lighter shade. They were set a handsome face with a strong jaw and a small, straight nose. His body was lean but muscular due to the hard work he did in the oil fields each summer. Just because they were wealthy, Jordan didn't pamper his children. They all had chores and they all worked at specific jobs during the summer months when not in school.

In the middle sat ten year old Mary Rosa. Born on September 3, 1976, she was almost the spitting image of her mother, with the exception that her hair, which was red, wasn't the flaming red of her mother. Her eyes were a dark green and set in a face that had the structure and beauty of her mother. Her skin didn't have the whiteness of her mother but was rather a shade darker and she had no freckles. Her body was thin at her young age but showed the promise of beautiful development. Mary was very smart and very mature for her age. Although Jordan loved all his children dearly, Mary was secretly his favorite.

Sitting in the last chair was eight year old Richard Orland, who they called Dick. Born on October 22, 1978, Dick was thought to be some kind of throwback to another time, because he didn't favor his father or his mother. From somewhere he got sandy blonde hair, dark brown eyes, and light skin. His face didn't look like anyone in his family. He was tall for his age and was thin enough to be called skinny. His Aunt Cheryl swore he looked exactly her husband Dick Jordan when he was a young boy. Dick was the serious type and rarely smiled. Jordan often joked that Dick must be the product of Kathleen and an unknown boyfriend. Dick, even at his young age, didn't see the humor in the joke.

Jordan moved the PC to the side of his desk and leaned forward. "Okay kids does everyone know what they're supposed to do?" He asked in a serious tone.

Since Rob was the oldest, he spoke up of the group, "Yes, Sir, I'm sure we do," he said with a puzzled look. "But why're we doin' this now? Wouldn't it be better to surprise Mom on her birthday or somethin' like that?"

Jordan put his hands together and scanned his children. "That's a good question, Rob," he replied. "But your mom might be expectin' somethin' on a special day. You see on a day that is not significant at all, she'll surely be completely surprised. Do you get it?"

Rob smiled and nodded to his siblings, "Yes Sir, I get it. And that's a good idea."

"Now," Jordan started, "just to make sure we have it all straight each of you tell me your jobs. We'll start with you Dick."

Dick nodded and said with his customary seriousness, "I'm to watch for Mom to come up the walkway. As soon I see her, I'm to come and get you as fast as I can."

"That's good, Dick," Jordan nodded. "Okay, Mary now it's your turn."

Mary sat up straight in her chair and smiling said, "When I see Dick goin' to get you, I'm to have the caterers start puttin' the food on the tables in the back livin' room and to be sure all the drinks are in place."

"Very good, Mary," Jordan said smiling at his favorite. "Rob, what about you?"

Rob nodded and said quickly, "When Mary goes into the back livin' room, then I'm to go to the guest livin' area and get all the people to come to the back livin' room and have them stand around the fireplace."

"And are the pictures in place, Rob?"

"Yes, Sir, they're hung on each side of the fireplace and are covered by the black cloth you gave me."

Jordan stood up and laughing said, "That's great, kids. I couldn't have done this without you. So let's all go get in our places and give your mom the happiest surprise of her life. She said she'd be back by eighteen hundred hours, so I'm expectin' her anytime now."

"Dad," Mary said in a frustrated tone, "can't you just say six o'clock?"

"Oh, sure I can; six o'clock. Now, let's everybody get goin'."

Kathleen pulled into her parking space in front of the first large three car garage. She checked her watch and saw that she was almost a half hour late. She had promised to be back by eighteen hundred hours but now it was almost nineteen hundred hours. "Oh, well," she thought, "there's nothin' goin' on today so nobody should mine. Anyway, her meetin' was a good one today. They were gettin' closer to bein' able to have the memorial." She climbed out of her new 1986 Jeep Wrangler and gathered up her documentation she was using for the memorial effort. She loved her Wrangler because it reminded her a little of the jeeps in Vietnam. Jordan, on the other hand, wanted a luxury car like the Lincoln.

Unknown to Kathleen, Dick had spied her pull up into her parking space and he reasoned, "Why wait until she's on the walkway. Go now." So he immediately took off for his dad's office. Mary saw him as he ran by from her position in the foyer and jumped to her feet and headed for the back living room. When Rob saw Mary enter the back living room, he immediately ran for the guest living area to round up the people. Things were now in motion for Kathleen's surprise.

Kathleen had just come in the gate that guarded the walkway. She balanced her documents in her hands and kicked the gate closed with her foot. When she turned to start up the walkway, she was surprised to see Jordan approaching her. She continued to walk and when they reached each other he unceremoniously reached over and took her documents from her. "I'll take these for now," he said. "You just follow me."

She started to fight him but decided against it. "What's goin' on?" She asked.

As they went in the front door and entered the foyer, he placed her documents on a small table next to the coat closet. "Jordy, what're you doin'?" She demanded.

"I have a surprise for you," he said calmly as he took a sleeping mask out of his pocket.

"What kind of a surprise?"

"The kind you're goin' to like. Just let me put this mask over your eyes and I'll guide you to the surprise."

"Jordy, I'm not sure I like this." As he slipped the mask over her head and covered her eyes, she laughed softly and asked, "Is this one of your kinky games? The kids are here you know."

"No," he said, "I'm savin' that for another time." Once he was sure she couldn't see, he took her hand and started guiding her through the house.

"I know this house inside out," she said as she allowed herself to be guided along, "I know we're headed towards the back livin' room."

"My goodness," he said mockingly, "you are a smarty pants."

As they entered the back living room, Jordan quickly looked around to see that everything was in place before he removed her mask. The food was spread out on a large table and the bar area had the drinks ready. The people stood by the fireplace; one group on the right side and the other group on the left side. The two super large pictures, which were at least five feet by three feet each, were hanging on either side of the fireplace and were shrouded by black cloth. Jordan smiled to himself and thought, "Great job, kids."

"Okay, are you ready?" He asked as he took hold of the mask.

"I think so."

"Then, here goes," as he spoke he pulled the mask from her eyes and off over her head.

At first, she was too stunned to speak. There standing before her eyes was her dearest friends and their families. On the right side of the fireplace stood Veronica and William and in front of them stood their two children. On the left side of the fireplace stood Kellie and Kyle and in front of them stood their two children. There was a long pause and then Kathleen let out a loud scream that Jordan was sure could be heard for miles. The scream seemed to be a signal and all three women charged each other and the traditional Tart Trio hugging, kissing, and slapping on the back began. It would go on for over five minutes. And as it went on, the men drifted together and shook hands and hugged.

When Jordan thought it was time, he held up his hands and shouted for everyone's attention. "Okay group," he yelled, "before we get any deeper into this I think each family should introduce their families and give us short update on their status. I know we've been in touch somewhat and we may know some of what you tell us, but I think a complete overview is in order anyway. And I think we should start with Kellie and Kyle."

Kyle pointed to Kellie and said, "You take it, sweetheart."

Kellie was drying her eyes with the palms of her hands but managed to say, "Okay. Okay. Let me see where to start. Oh, yes for heaven's sake our kids." She reached out and pulled both children over in front of her. Then pointing to the girl and said, "This is our oldest, Carol Sue. As most of you will remember, she was born on April 9, 1974; making her thirteen years old now." Carol Sue was an exact copy of her mother. She had the same long beautiful jet black hair and the same clear light blue eyes that could turn cloudy when she was angry. She had her mother's beautiful face and was already taking on the same well-formed body. "And this," Kellie continued pointing to the boy, "is our youngest, Benjamin Daryl, we call him Bennie. He was born on June 10, 1978 and he just this month turn nine years old." Bennie was a mixture of Kellie and Kyle. He had Kyle's bright blonde hair and deep blue eyes, but he had Kellie's well-structured face. Bennie was obviously going to be tall because even though he was five year younger than Carol, he as almost as tall as her. His body was lean but firm. "And I'm proud to say that they're both on the honor roll at school." She paused and looked around as if in confusion but gathered herself and said, "Now as far as our status, I'll turn that over to the man of the house."

Kyle took center stage and gave a mock bow. "Well," he started, "there's not a lot to tell. The main thing I guess is the great accomplishments of my wife. She managed to get her MD certification and she's a full time doctor now at her own clinic in Coalville; The Collie Medical Clinic. And, as most of you know, much of that we owe to our dear friend and investor, Jordan Costillo and Costillo Enterprises. I'm happy to say that we're havin' great success with the clinic and that Costillo Enterprises is gettin' a good return on their dollar. Another good thing about the clinic is that our dear friend Veronica Barnett has been our head nurse and RN for the last six years. As for me, I put my twenty in and I retired from the army in 1984 as a full bird coronal. I tried just hangin' around the house for a while but I was drivin' Kel and kids crazy so I took the job of Administrator of the clinic, which freed Kel up to be the head doctor and not have to mess with admin. I've been doin' the job for the last two years so I guess I haven't mess it up too much." Then he paused and took a deep breath, bowed his head and said softly, "I guess the only real downers we've had is that my Grandma Mary died in 1972 and in 1979 we lost my Uncle Dick Jordan. We loved both of them. And may they rest in peace in God's Heaven." He stopped and stood up straight and announced, "And I guess that's it for the Collie clan."

Jordan step forward and again held up his hands. "Thank you, Collie clan," he said with a wide grin. Then pointing at Veronica and William he continued, "Now, it's your turn Barnett clan."

William pointed at Veronica and said, "I guess we'll follow the same format as the Collies, so you can start us out, Ronnie."

Veronica took center stage and gave quick salute. She gently positioned her two children in front of her. Then pointing to the taller boy, she started, "This is Billy George, who I'm sure most of you remember as you were there at his birth on December 2, 1971. This December he'll be sixteen years old. He plays football and his coaches tell us they want him to stay through his senior year. Problem is that we've already secured an appointment for him to West Point. And, like his father, we hope to send him to the Texas Military Institute for his senior year. But we still haven't decided for sure, so we intend to discuss it in depth with Billy later on." There was no doubt that Billy was William's son. He had all of William's features from his sandy blonde hair and deep brown eyes to his handsome face that still had light freckles on it. He was a bit huskier than William was at his age because of the football training. As he stood there, he worn the same infectious smile that William could display. "Now, this," she said pointing to the smaller boy, "is our youngest son, Michael Lee. He was born on January 12, 1974. He turned thirteen years old this year. We're very proud to say that he's an honor student and is a member of the National Honor Society." Michael mostly favored his mother. He had her bright blonde hair and facial features, but he didn't have her green eyes; he had his father's deep brown eyes. Michael wasn't husky like his brother, but rather had a thin frame. His smile and face radiated intelligence. She stopped talking and looked around smiling. "Now," she continued, "I guess I'll follow the format and turn the status over to my dear husband."

Veronica took the children and stepped back and William bashfully took center stage. He wrung his hands together and looked out at everyone. "Okay," he started, "I'm much like Kyle in that my lovely wife has been the real accomplisher in our family over these last seventeen years. She used the money that Jordan so kindly gave us to first take care of her parents, then she renovated the farm house to the point that it doesn't look like a farm house today, but, instead like a large estate. It's beautiful and comfortable. And she did all this while takin' care of two rambunctious boys and travelin' all over creation to be with me. Then, six years ago, she joined The Collie Medical Clinic and started workin' with her sister in arms, Doctor Kellie Collie. As for me, like Kyle, I put in my twenty years and then retired from the army a full bird coronal just this last May." He quickly pointed to Kyle and teased, "You see I caught up to you in rank."

"That's only because you're a West Point man," Kyle shot back.

Everyone had a short laugh and then William continued, "I'm stayin' round the farm and helpin' my mom with the fertilizer store in town. We have an offer from a large store in Athens to buy our little store. But Mom is reluctant to sell because she feels an obligation to the Collie family, because it was from Kyle's Grandpa James that she bought the store. She's talkin' with Kyle's dad, Daryl, now and we should know her answer within a week or so. On the sad side, we lost Ronnie's dad in 1985. Although we helped him get his finance squared away, he was just too worn down. Ronnie's mom is now livin' with us. Because of Ronnie's renovations, we have plenty of room. My step brothers have both moved out and gone to good lives of their own. One's in Seattle workin' for Microsoft and the other one is servin' in the Coast Guard. Mom is sixty-five now but insists she wants to take one more trip to England and she wants me and Ronnie to go with her. I'm tryin' to put the trip together but I worry about her health and stamina for such a trip." He paused and spread his arms out wide and said to finish up, "And I guess, that should get everyone caught up."

William stepped back and joined his family as Jordan returned to center stage. "Well, it looks like it's our turn," he said looking at Kathleen. "But before we get to that, I want to thank all of you guys for makin' the long trip our here for this reunion. It means an awful lot to me and Kat both."

Jordan was about to continue when Kyle stepped forward and held up his hand to stop him. "Before you go on, Jordy, can you give me a couple of extra minutes."

Jordan shrugged and said matter-of-factly, "Of course, Kyle. Go ahead."

Kyle reached into his pocket and pulled out his wallet. He removed two pieces of paper and handed them to Jordan.

"What's this?" Jordan asked puzzled.

"It's a couple of checks," Kyle said simply. "It's from me and Bill both. After we got your request and the money to pay for all our expenses to come to this reunion, Bill and I talked with our wives and we all agreed."

"Agreed on what?" Jordan asked holding the checks before him. "These are the checks I sent you guys to pay for your trip here."

"We agreed," Kyle continued, "that no amount of money could keep us away from this reunion. It wasn't required for you to send us money, Jordy. We would've come no matter what. Seventeen years ago in your new office, you, Bill, and I made a Pac. It was a bondin' Pac. Part of that Pac was that we would try and see each other as much as possible. I don't think we've done such a good job on that part. And it's not yours and Kat's fault; it's mine and Bills. We know you're wealthy, Jordy, and spendin' money like this doesn't bother you at all. But this particular thing does bother us. This reunion is on all of us. It has to be on all of us, Jordy, or we're not very good friends and we're not very good war brothers. Are we?"

Jordan smiled and slowly torn the two checks into small pieces and sprinkled them on the floor. "You and Bill are exactly right about this bein' on all of us. And I should've known. If Kat would've been involved, she would've known. I guess sometimes I forget that my money doesn't hold all the answers. That's what bein' exposed to so much money will do to you. When we were in 'Nam, I used to always say you guys acted differently around me because you knew I was rich. I said you didn't mean to but you did. That's what I said. Now here I am doin' pretty much the same thing. Except for me, it's actin' different because I have money. I don't mean to but I do. I can only ask that you forgive me. But don't you ever, ever think you're not good friends and good war brothers, because you are. I swear that you are. Our brotherhood is still tightly bound."

After he was finished speaking, except for the children, there wasn't a dry eye in the place. Jordan took a deep breath and laughed, "Now can the Costillo clan get on with their report?"

"You have the stage, Sir," William said making a portly bow.

Jordan returned the bow and then turned to Kathleen, and while still in his bow, said, "Please take center stage, Dear."

Kathleen came forward herding her three children before her. She reached what was being called 'center stage' and position herself with her children lined up in front of her. "Okay, I guess I'll follow the same format as guys did," she said smiling. "Then I'll turn it over to Jordy." She spent the next fifteen minutes introducing her children very carefully and elaborated on each of them. When she finished, she guided the children back and she pointed to Jordan and said, "Now it's your turn Mister Costillo."

Jordan took center stage again. His face looked worried because he was struggling with exactly what to say. He made several attempts to start but stopped each time. Everyone was looking at him trying to suppress their laughter. Jordan never admitted to being a good speaker. "Okay, I can see all of you tryin' not to laugh," he said sternly. "So, here goes. Like you two guys, after puttin' in my twenty I retired from the marines in 1983 with the rank of major. While Kat was strugglin' with the new house, her mom, and havin' babies, I was busy gettin' my law degree and startin' the new division of Costillo Enterprises which I call, rightly enough, the Diversification Division. Using the advice of Jimmy Orland, I invested in healthcare and strip malls. The first of those investments was, of course, The Collie Medical Clinic, which turned out so well that I now have two other medical clinics; one in Dallas and one in Midland. And when I can, I get Kat to help me hire some of the nurses she worked with in 'Nam to work in 'em. I love hirin' vets. I have four new strip malls; one in Abilene, one in Midland, and two here in Marfa. All of these investments are turnin' a very good profit. My only problem is help. Jimmy retired from Mobil Oil in 1970 but continued to help me. But after I got my law degree, he pulled more and more away, wantin' me to take it all over. As it stands now, he'll still advise me if I ask him but he no longer looks after my money and my holdings. He and Judy are busy runnin' all over world and havin' great adventures now that their kids are grow and gone. As I speak to you today, I need some help runnin' Costillo Enterprises. Oh, I've got accounts watchin' over things and makin' sure I'm not losin' money and that my taxes are taken care of, but I got no one to help me with my investments and research of future investments. You two guys need to think about that. But this is a fun time, so I won't speak of it again. Though, in short, things have gone well for me and Kat. I guess our biggest downer was the loss of my treasured half-brother, Dick Jordan. It was he who helped me get what I wanted in the marines and he and Aunt Cheryl stood by me from the first day they found out that I was his half-brother and that we had the same father. Retired Marine Brigadier General Dick Jordan was one of the best of the best." He paused for a short moment to regain his composer and then finished with, "I guess that's about it from me."

There was a long silence when everyone just milled around a bit and didn't speak. Finally, Billy walked over to where Jordan was standing and looked up at him with a blank look on his face and asked, "Mr. Costillo is it okay to eat now?"

That broke the ice. "Oh, my God," Kathleen shouted. "Of course we can. I hope the food is still hot."

Mary walked calmly up to her mom and said matter-of-factly, "Not to worry, Mom. The food was my job. I saw to it that the caterers brought warmin' devices to keep the food ready to eat at all times."

Before Kathleen could reply, Jordan ran over scooped his daughter up into his arms. "That's my girl," he shouted with pride and planted a big kiss on her forehead. As he sat Mary back down, he yelled for everyone to hear, "Okay, everybody let's go dig into some chow. I promise it's the best Tex-Mex and Barbeque you've ever eaten."

Over the next hour, everyone ate until they were uncomfortably full. The adults had migrated to the bar area where they were enjoying after dinner drinks. Jordan had asked Rob to take all the children to the game room where they could entertain themselves with a variety of games and TV. Now, as they stood around bar quietly talking, Kathleen interrupted with, "Why don't we all freshen our drinks and go sit at the dinin' room table?"

Everyone nodded and proceeded to get their drinks freshened up and then followed Kathleen to a large dining table, which was in a large dining room just adjacent to the living area where they had been eating. After they were all settled at the table, Jordan asked, "I hope Rob got all of you fixed up okay in the guess rooms? Is everythin' comfortable?"

Kellie leaned back in her chair and sipped on her drink. "Everything is just fine, Jordy. It just couldn't be any better." Then, turning to Kathleen she smiled and said, "You know, Kat, this is just like the wish you made at our New Year's Eve party in 1968 at that little hooch near China Beach. Remember? You said you wanted to have a big house on the beach were we all could have our own room, and it would have a big living area for us to party in. Well, look around. You've got all that except for the beach."

"You're right Kel, I do. And I want to share it with you guys anytime."

"Be careful, Kat," William said with a soft laugh, "you might get what you want."

"You know," Veronica said seriously, "we got lots of room at the farm. I say that five years from tonight, that would be 1992, that we have another reunion at our farm. What do you guys think about that?"

Kellie looked at Kyle who nodded yes. "You can count on us," she said.

"We'll be there," Kathleen replied excitedly, as she looked at Jordan. He only smiled back at her and tipped his drink to her.

"Even though my wife didn't consult me on this," William said in mock irritation, "but I think it's an outstandin' idea."

"Ronnie, do you need me to help organize?" Kathleen asked.

"No, Ma'am. This is on me. I'll send out a reminder each year at this time just to make sure everyone still remembers and is still on board."

"So, it's a done deal," William said holding his glass up. "Everybody drink to it."

Everybody held their glasses up and clicked them together. After which, they all took a deep drink. At this point, Jordan stood up. He looked down a Kathleen and said mysteriously, "There's still one part of my surprise that's not complete. I've kind of been waitin' until the end of the evenin' before I sprung it."

"There's more?" Kathleen asked. "How could there be more?"

"There is," Jordan replied simply. "Come on everybody, let's all go back into the livin' room." Once Jordan had gotten everyone back in the living room, he arranged them in the order he wanted. He stood them in a line side-by-side about ten feet in front of the fireplace. He had Kyle and Kellie on the far left, he had William and Veronica in the middle, and he and Kathleen were on the far right. He stepped out of line and asked Kathleen, "Kat, do you see anythin' different about the fireplace?"

She bent forward to examine the fireplace. After a few moments she straightened back up and said, "Yes, I do. I see two large rectangle type things, one on each side of the fireplace and both are covered with black cloths."

"I'm surprised you missed them before," Jordan commented as he walked over to the rectangle thing on the right and took hold of the black cloth.

"Sorry," she said, "I was busy seein' my friends and all the other stuff."

Suddenly, Jordan pulled the cloth down and then quickly jumped back in line. There on the wall was a huge blow up of the picture taken of all six of them on that New Year's Day in 1969 at the 95th EVAC Hospital near Da Nang, South Vietnam. They stood in the exact same order as they now stood. Kathleen buried her face in her hands and began to cry uncontrollably. The others clapped and hooted loudly.

"Holy shit, Jordy," Kyle yelled out. "How did you get that blown up that much and still have such good quality?"

Jordan smiled a wicked smile, "I know this photo place in Dallas that can work miracles."

"Jordy, is there any chance we could get one of these?" Veronica asked, as she slowly stepped forward to get a better look.

"Yeah, Jordy, can we all get one of these?" Kyle asked.

"As a matter of fact, both of them should be at your houses by the time you get home tomorrow," Jordan replied proudly.

"Oh, my God," Kathleen shouted finally getting control of her crying. "You said both of them. What's the other one?"

Moving quickly, Jordan stepped over and pulled the cloth down on the second rectangle thing. Looking up, the group saw a huge blow up of The Tart Trio that was taken on the same day and at the same place. The girls had their arms around each other's neck and they were laughing. Kathleen was in the middle, Kellie was on her left, and Veronica was on her right.

Kathleen stepped out of line and went to Jordan. She put her arms around his waist and buried her face into his chest. "Thank you, Jordy," she said through the tears. She spoke softly so only Jordan could hear her. "You're the best husband in the world. God, I love you."

Jordan kissed her on top of her head and then gently pulled away from her. "Well, that's all the surprises," he said. "I know you guys have to be up earlier to get to Midland and your flight to Dallas, so I guess we can all go gather up our kids and made it to our rooms."

As the group started to shake hands and give goodnight hugs, Kathleen held up her hand and said with emotion, "I have one last request if I could?"

"Of course you can, Kat," Kellie replied, "what would your request be?"

"It's a little strange and out of the ordinary."

"I'd say we're all a little strange and a bit out of the ordinary," Veronica laughed.

"Yeah, go ahead, Kat, shoot," Kyle said. "Anyway, it still early even for old farts like us."

"Okay, here it is," Kathleen started. "I'd like for of each of us, one at a time, to stand before the picture of all of us and salute it in honor of someone you think was special in Vietnam. It should be someone that meant a lot to you or made a difference for you. And you have to say who it is and why you're honorin' them. And you have to say it out loud so we all can hear it. To kick it off, I'll go first."

Everyone looked at each other. "Gees Kat, do we have a minute to think about it?" William asked.

"No, that wouldn't make it true. It has to be what comes to your mind first. Come on, I'll go first."

"Yeah, but you probably know who you're goin' to honor," William challenged.

"Yes, I do, but come on guys."

"Go ahead, Kat, and I'll go second," Veronica said.

Kathleen stepped up close to the picture and came to attention. She snapped a smart salute and held it while she said, "I honor Major Marjorie Morningstar. She was my first head nurse. She taught me so much it's hard to tell it all, but mostly she taught me how to do my job, how to deal with people, and, at the end, she became a damn good friend." Upon completing her honor, she snapped her hand down and then stood back.

Veronica was next to step up. She snapped her salute and said, "I honor all the nurses I served with at the ten-six-six. We called them by their nick names like Max, Marty, Sandy, and May. They were the most selfless, courageous, and dedicate people I've very known. It was an honor for me to serve with them." She then dropped her salute and stepped back.

Kellie now stepped up. She snapped her salute and said, "I honor Lt. Coronal Nobel Vickers. He was my first CO at the ten-six-six. He taught me about honor and dignity. But most of all he taught me how to command and be a head nurse." Kellie then dropped her salute and stepped back.

Jordan was next up. He snapped a sharp marine salute and said, "I honor 1ˢᵗ Lieutenant Berry Clyde. Although gravely wounded, he removed his bandages and covered my back during the battle of The Alamo in the Jungle. He died while coverin' for me." Jordan dropped his salute and stepped back.

Kyle stepped forward next. He snapped a sharp salute and said, "I honor the two crews that served with me during Vietnam. My first crew helped me win the Bronze Star at the Battle of Hue and my second crew went down with me at the Battle of Hamburger Hill." He dropped his salute and stepped back.

And last to step forward was William. He snapped a sharp airborne salute and said, "I honor Medic Corporal Bobby Miles from Alpha Company, 3ʳᵈ Battalion of the 187th Regiment of the 101ˢᵗ Airborne Division. A farm boy from Missouri who dressed my wounds on the top of Hamburger Hill after chargin' up that hill with nothin' more than his medical kit and a great deal of courage." He then dropped his salute and stepped back.

For several long minutes everyone stood silently looking up at the two pictures, until Kathleen finally step forward and turned and looked at her friends. "Thank you," she said, "for doin' this for me. It meant a lot to me for many reasons that I won't go into. I'll just say that it helped me conclude in my mind what I'd already concluded in my heart. I know you all know that I'm avidly involved in the movement to get a memorial established in Washington D.C. to commemorate the service of women durin' Vietnam. It's called 'The Vietnam Women's Memorial Project'. What I asked you to do tonight simply helped me put my mind in alignment with my heart. Thank you again."

Veronica hurried over to her dear friend and grabbed her shoulders. "If you need any help and if I can do anythin', you just call on me, Kat. I'll be there for you."

"Ditto for me," Kellie chimed in.

"I think all of us guys will step up to bat for you, Kat," William said as he walked up behind his wife.

"Count me in," Kyle said.

"And you know you can count on me," Jordan said as he put his arm around Kathleen's neck as if to choke her.

"I should have a recordin' of this," Kathleen laughed softly. "Because you all may be gettin' a call from me, and I'll remind you of this night."

"I don't think you'll have to remind us of this night, Kat," Kyle said with emotion. "I think we'll remember this night until we meet again five years from now on Bill and Ronnie's farm. And I would hope that the honor salute will become a fix event at each and every reunion we have."

"I'll drink to that," William said heading for bar.

Veronica hurried and jumped in front of him. "Oh no, that's all the drinkin' for tonight," she lectured. "Oh-six-hundred hours will come early in the mornin'. We've got to round up our kids and get everyone in the sack. Can someone tell me where this game room is?"

"Just follow me and Kel," Kyle said waving her to follow. "We found it when we first got here. Since we got here before you two, Rob took us there to help occupy Carol and Bennie."

"Right behind you," Ronnie said as she pulled William along behind her. "We'll see everyone bright and early."

Jordan and Kathleen watched as their friends disappeared across the room and down the connecting hallway. Soon it was silent and Jordan and Kathleen looked all around the room. "When did the caterers clean up and leave?" Kathleen asked puzzled.

"I don't know," Jordan replied laughing, "maybe Mary can tell us. Anyway the rest of this stuff we can take care of tomorrow."

Kathleen walked up close to Jordan and leaned against him. She toyed with the buttons on his shirt. "I was wonderin', Jordy, that after we got the kids all squared away in bed, if you'd carry me to our bedroom and make love to me?"

As Jordan scooped her up into his arms and started carrying her across the room, he said firmly, "Don't worry about the kids, they know their way around this place."

EPILOGUE

On Veteran's Day, November 11, 1993 the efforts of so many Vietnam Veterans, men as well as women, came to fruition, as the **Vietnam Women's Memorial** was dedicated in Washington D.C. on the National Mall before over 25,000 people.

It stands a short distance south of the Vietnam War Memorial, or as it is called 'The Wall'. Among the names on The Wall, are those of eight nurses who died in Vietnam.

In the immortal words of Winston Churchill; 'Never in the field of human conflict was so much owed by so many to so few'.

AFTERWORD

The children had now been secluded in the game room for approximately three hours. They were, as it could be said, *gamed out*. During all this time they had become very acquainted with each other. There were a few personality clashes but all-in-all they got along quite well. Billy, being the oldest, took charge of the games. But it was Mary who slowly got them started relating to each other.

Mary was about to make a request of them all, when Veronica and Kellie came into the room. "Okay, kids," Veronica ordered, "let's go. We've all gotta hit the sack."

"Same for us," Kellie said clapping her hands.

The children began to break up but suddenly Mary yelled out, "Mrs. Barnett, Doctor Collie, could we have just ten more minutes alone?"

The other children looked at her in surprise. What could she possibly want that they couldn't've done over the last three hours?

Veronica and Kellie looked at each. They both look tired and a little put out, but Kellie nodded okay to Veronica. "Okay," Veronica said in a serious tone, "but only ten minutes and I expect you to be in your rooms. I'm goin' to check so don't let me down."

"Yes, Ma'am, ten minutes and no more," Mary replied smiling.

After Veronica and Kellie had left the room, the other children gathered around Mary. "Okay, what's this all about?" Billy demanded.

Mary looked into their wondering faces and said, "Make a circle."

"Aw come on, Mary, what's goin' on here?" Billy demanded again.

Billy seemed to be the only one irritated, because no one else made any arguments.

"Just make a circle and see," Mary pleaded.

Everyone made a circle except Billy, who stood back. "Oh, come on Billy," Carol said tiredly, "let's see what she wants."

Reluctantly, Billy joined in the circle. "Now," he said, "is everyone satisfied and can we get on with this, whatever it is."

"Our parents are always makin' Pacs," Mary started.

"What's a Pac?" Bennie interrupted.

"A Pac is like a pledge to do somethin'," Rob answered.

"Yeah, it means you promise each other to do somethin'," Dick interjected.

"It's more than just a promise," Mary said in almost a whisper, "it's more like you're swearin' to do somethin' and if you don't keep it somethin' bad will happen to you."

Billy let out a long sigh and said, "Okay, now we all know what a Pac is. So, what happens next?"

"I think," Mary said excitedly, "that we should all make a Pac."

"What kind of Pac?" Michael asked.

"I think we need to hurry this up," Dick said, "our ten minutes is runnin' out."

With Dick's warning, Mary decided to speed things up. "I think," she continued, "that we should make a Pac to all meet again right here at our house in exactly ten years from now."

Everyone looked at each other. There was puzzlement at first but then grins began to form on their faces; everyone's face except Billy's. "How're we goin' to do that?" He asked. "How're we goin' to keep track of everyone? It's impossible."

"My mom and dad say nothings impossible if you just don't quit," Carol said firmly. "I'm in, Mary, and I'll help you keep track. You and me, we can make it work."

Mary held her right hand into the middle of the circle with her palm down. "Here's my hand on the Pac."

Quickly, Carol placed her hand on Mary's, "Pac," she said.

"Pac," Rob was next to put his hand in the circle.

"Pac," Dick was next.

"Pac," Bennie followed suit.

"Pac," Michael was next.

Now there was only Billy who hadn't put his hand in the circle. "Come on, Billy," Rob pleaded, "this could lead to somethin' important, even great."

Slowly, Billy placed his hand in the circle and then smiling said, "Pac."

So, on a June night in 1987 in the small town of Marfa, Texas, the children of the children of the Greatest Generation made a Pac to all get together again in exactly ten years. Doing the math, that would be in 1997. Can such a young group ever hope to accomplish such a Pac? Well, that's another story.

www.ingramcontent.com/pod-product-compliance
Lightning Source LLC
Chambersburg PA
CBHW020915140626

46545CB00015B/55